AF248653

DON'T BLAME
THE TREATIES

DON'T BLAME THE TREATIES

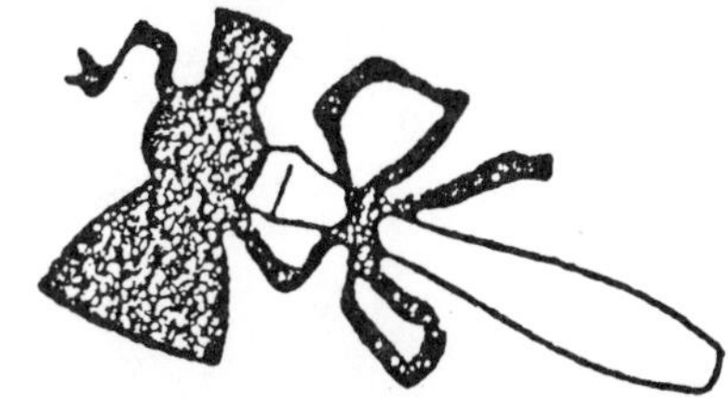

Native American Rights
and the
Michigan Indian Treaties

by Philip McM. Pittman
with George M. Covington

A&M

Altwerger and Mandel Publishing Company, Inc.
West Bloomfield, Michigan

Altwerger and Mandel Publishing Co., Inc.
6346 Orchard lake Road, Suite 201
West Bloomfield, Michigan 48322

Printed in the United States of America
ISBN 1-878005-59-6 (paper)
ISBN 1-878005-11-1 (cloth)

Designed by Mary Primeau

Maps by Joan B. Seller

Edited by Thomas B. Seller

THIS BOOK IS FOR MARGARET,
MY MERMAID

Also by Philip McM. Pittman

The Les Cheneaux Chronicles: Anatomy of a Community
Ripples from the Breezes: A Les Cheneaux Anthology
The Portrayal of Life Stages in English Literature, 1500-1800
        (with Jeanie Watson)

CONTENTS

PREFACE

Three extraordinary Michigan legal opinions created the "treaty waters" of the northern Great Lakes. They span the 1970s, and so are of exceptional interest to all who would understand the tumultuous shift in the legal interpretation of "rights" to fish in northern Great Lakes waters that has led to the misunderstanding and confrontation between Indians and non-Indians that characterized the 1980s and promise to define the 1990s. That's right. The judges created the treaty waters and invented the tribal rights that have accrued within them. The treaties themselves have very little to do with the issue and in this book we would like to absolve the eighteenth- and nineteenth-century documents of the blame popularly laid upon them. So, with deference to Ted Williams, don't blame the treaties.

Judge Noel P. Fox's opinion in *United States v. State of Michigan* is reported in 471 Federal Supplement 192 (1979). Justice John Swainson's opinion in *People v. Jondreau* is found in the Michigan Reporter (384 Mich. 539). Justice G. Mennen Williams's opinion in *People v. LeBlanc* is in the North Western Reporter (248 N.W. 2nd 199). Though it will require a trip to a legal library, I hope that the interested reader will seek them out and discover that once he cuts through the headnotes and cross-references to other cases there is nothing terribly mystifying about them. They are important, if historically misguided, and interesting in their own right.

They are sloppy in that they too easily provide a distorted version of history, the sort of history that is nurtured in the adversarial climate of the courtroom. The courtroom is an arena for confrontation in which each party is expected to be partisan and the judge is expected to choose from among the partisan positions presented before him. The interpretation of history that emerges from such an environment is thus more than usually subject to identifiable bias—slant—and may easily become

specious because it is slanted, because it is written to a purpose other than presenting historical matter as a thing unto itself. The same, of course, may be true of non-
legal historical texts.

It all began innocently enough and the early judicial history is summarized by
Justice Swainson in the Jondreau case. As early as the 1830s Chief Justice Marshall's
Supreme Court established liberal guidelines to govern the construction (interpretation) of federal treaties with the North American Indians; under these treaties the
federal government assumed full responsibility as trustee for the well-being of its
wards under treaty, the Indians. This benevolent relationship under law prevailed in
theory throughout the nineteenth and into the early twentieth century. No matter
how well or ill it may have worked itself out in practice, the principles stood.

During the twentieth century, however, very much in accordance, it would appear,
with the theories of integration and amalgamation expressed in the nineteenth-century Michigan Indian treaties, the Indians came to be regarded as citizens of the
United States—with all the ordinary rights, privileges, prerogatives, and responsibilities that are part of citizenship. But recently, more liberal courts, notably of the
1970s, returned to the earlier emphases by reassigning special status to tribal communities as separate sovereign nations with special rights to self-determination even
within the geographic and political boundaries of the United States—rights guaranteed, it is said, by last century's treaties. These are the "rights" that dominated the
courtrooms in the 1970s and 1980s.

Judge Swainson, writing for the Michigan State Supreme Court in *People v.
Jondreau,* approaches a liberal decision cautiously and moderately (not to mention,
relatively speaking, briefly). He keeps his eye firmly on the judicial history of the
matter, on the cases in precedent, and on the documents that led most directly to his
court's decision. Nevertheless, his opinion handed down, the tribes suddenly had
hunting and fishing prerogatives that were not previously recognized.

Within months, to test the case it must be assumed, Abe LeBlanc set his unlicensed and supposedly illegal gill nets in Pendills Bay and thus initiated *People v.
LeBlanc.* Justice G. Mennen Williams wrote the majority opinion of the state Supreme
Court in this matter in 1976. The nineteenth-century United States Supreme Court
had called for applying historical method in the approach to litigation growing out
of federal treaty law. Accordingly, the Williams Court, in an early instance in
Michigan, considered carefully the principal treaties themselves (as well as related
documents, such as the minutes of the negotiations), and came to a decision that
reaffirmed that of the Swainson Court. The Williams Court is to be commended for
considering straightforwardly these important historical documents. Many will find,
however, the dissenting opinions of Justices Lindemer, Coleman, and Ryan as compelling and persuasive as the majority opinion.

Well before the LeBlanc case was concluded, however, in 1973 the federal government filed in Federal District Court on behalf of itself and the Bay Mills Indian
Community, and thus *United States v. Michigan* came before Judge Noel P. Fox.

Judge Fox documents his obligation to apply historical method and enthusiastically approaches his responsibility—at some length, one can fairly observe. His opinion affirms and then extends the liberal opinions handed down in the earlier cases. Unfortunately, the judge ranges himself, and permitted the federal government's expert witnesses to range, far beyond the documents that are central to the matter (even beyond the history that correctly pertains to it); in so doing he almost loses touch with the actual historical background and the important documents that emerge from it. He produces an extensive document that will survive as a significant contribution to laws still in formation and not yet tested in the courts.

It will also stand as a perfect example of the imperfect application of historical method. Unchecked by the legislative branch and immune to the pleas of the ordinary citizen, the courts have generated a proliferation of legal precedents that are unfair and unjust in that they violate the same rights and interests of the ordinary citizen—civil, proprietary, and constitutional—the courts are supposed to protect and nurture. The judges have created in fact a most favorite minority composed of separate but sovereign foreign nationals living within our geographic and political borders—and at our expense.

The justices who wrote the opinions are now dead. Their work, however, lives on to affect the work of a new generation of judges and untold generations of citizens who must live under the law created by their cases. And the cases do go on, stubbornly ambiguous as to which points of law are finally settled because the Michigan treaty rights issue has not found its way to the United States Supreme Court nor has the federal legislative branch seen fit to review the matter. *United States v. Michigan* now proceeds under the supervision of Federal District Judge Richard A. Enslen in Kalamazoo and Francis McGovern of the University of Alabama Law School, called in as special master to mediate the ongoing litigation between the defendant State of Michigan and the several plaintiff tribal groups.

This litigation led to the entry of a court-generated consent order in March of 1985, which is supposed to be the device for resolving continuing differences between the state and the tribes and which establishes an executive council as the forum for discussion and resolution. It is sad to report that the various parties, the state (Michigan Department of Natural Resources, representing the interests of the citizens of the state), the tribes, and the federal government (Department of the Interior, Bureau of Indian Affairs) have been able to resolve very little of any consequence and the United States citizens of the northern Great Lakes, whose lives and livelihoods are daily affected by the ongoing negotiations, have been excluded from the process. But that will be the subject of another book.

ACKNOWLEDGMENTS

The ongoing contemporary controversy over treaty "rights" in the northern Great Lakes, especially as they apply to the allocation or conservation or both of the fishery resource, forms the backdrop for this book. My previous work with the history of the northern lakes early on led me to an interest in and then a fascination with the ordinances and treaties that fashioned the Northwest Territory and then the five states destined to be formed within it. These documents, as the judges have emphasized, come together as the primordial law—some even preceding the United States Constitution and dignified by having been reaffirmed by its framers—informing and governing life in this vital national region. They tell the important story of one of the earliest phases of our national evolution as well as providing the background for the legal skirmishing that defines the current controversy.

I began work with the documents not knowing what I would find in them. Like many others who lived in or cared about the district of the northern lakes I was deeply disturbed by the publicity surrounding Judge Fox's decision in *United States v. Michigan* (1979), but had no immediate means of getting beyond the publicity and into the matter itself; that would have to come later. Besides, at the time I was caught up in researching *The Les Cheneaux Chronicles: Anatomy of a Community* (1984), to the exclusion of other projects. But at that time I first looked at the succession of Michigan Indian treaties and, sensing that what I saw there was different from what seemed to be filtering down from the courts, determined that I should look far more carefully at the whole body of documents that inform this important aspect of our history and our law.

Countless friends and associates of every degree have helped and encouraged me at every turn—more, I am afraid, than I will be able to remember well. Many have already been acknowledged elsewhere, so much is my study of history an ongoing project. These few stand out in memory as deserving special thanks for their help in pulling this book together.

Following informal conversations about the progress of my early work, Chuck and Bernice Weiss concurred with me about the importance of the treaties as historical documents and, on their return to Washington, D.C., visited friends at the Library of Congress and there photocopied for me the first of the treaties I worked with.

Not long thereafter George M. Covington, Esq., kindly took what became a sustained interest in my evolving project and made available to me the resources of his Chicago law firm, Gardner, Carton & Douglas, whose kind and gracious staff provided further photocopies of ordinances and treaties.

Fred H. Keidan, Esq., of Troy, Michigan, together with our friend Bill Lewis (also a Troy attorney) reviewed my work as it progressed, joined Covington's effort to keep me from arguing points of law with lawyers and judges, and located copies of documents as the later need for them became apparent.

In an exercise in pure serendipity Janet A. Carrington found on her mother's bookshelves in Indianapolis a copy of Jedediah Morse's important though obscure *Report,* which she concluded should spend time with me, at just the right time.

Dr. Gene Peterson, retired director of the Mackinac Island State Park Commission, has been generous in lending his encouragement, time, and valuable historical advice as this book has progressed.

U.S. Rep. Bob Davis and Gov. James Blanchard have both offered discreet encouragement, each requesting an early draft of my manuscript for staff review.

Wes Maurer and Dave Murray of the *St. Ignace News* have been kind in their encouragement and in allocating space to me on those occasions I have wanted to be known in print.

The evolution of this project would have been very different indeed but for the offices of my friend and consultant, Mark Clymer, whose extensive files, scanner, and computer expertise got me through some very rough spots. I also owe special thanks to our friend Gary Reid and all the participants in the Les Cheneaux Community Action Committee, whose hard work and good faith have sustained us all.

Oliver Birge has been a good friend and adviser on all subjects since my work began almost ten years ago. He has drawn the maps and contributed the art that has graced my books.

Verna Lawrence, of Sault Ste. Marie, Michigan, has been a good friend and adviser on several practical matters.

Bob Mandel and the staff at A&M Publishing have been uniformly helpful and encouraging, believing in my work from a time when it all seemed a pipe dream and then seeing it through final editing and production.

Tom Seller, of Harrison, Michigan, worked with me to edit the manuscript in preparation for publication. He is thoroughly professional and has been extremely helpful in reshaping and refining the final product. He is also a wonderfully cheerful and encouraging voice on the phone.

Denise Brink Didion believed in me and found Bob Mandel.

Margaret, of course, has helped me in every way. My special thanks to her and, once again, to my family, who are able to put up with me (or perhaps without me) when I am abstracted by research.

I have read portions of the text of this book as papers for the Les Cheneaux Historical Association, The Historical Society of Michigan, the Les Cheneaux Sportsmans Club, and the Indian River Kiwanis. I thank them for their interest in my subject.

A partisan treatment of the treaty rights issue, based on the courtroom history, has recently appeared in Robert Doherty's *Disputed Waters: Native Americans and the Great Lakes Fishery* (Lexington: The University Press of Kentucky, 1990). I should point out that I neither belong to nor associate with any group party to the treaty rights debate, nor have I sought or received financial or other help from any advocacy group or granting agency—nor do I pretend to policy recommendations in the name of either justice or injustice, preferring to leave these matters to the reader who may be inclined to them.

INTRODUCTION

Twentieth-century politicians, judges, lawyers, and members of the fourth estate—influenced, we may safely assume, by the same politicians, judges, and lawyers—have long put forth a litany of woe the intent of which has been to protect, preserve, and uphold the presumed rights of native Americans. The good conscience, fine intention, and liberal goodwill of all the named parties has been and remains unquestioned. It has resulted in the most generous and unrestricted social welfare system ever designed in the Western world to benefit a small, though not insignificant, minority. It has also elevated that minority to a most favored status that should be the envy of other significant minorities—though its system of entitlements is tainted by paternalism, social apartheid, financial unaccountability, and socialist economics and politics wholly self-guarded within the separate sovereign nation designation of the American Indian community. The trick, and it has been worked on all of us, is that our "native" Americans, in any reasonable sense of the term, are no more either native or American than any other of the visitors who have become established on the American continents since the early sixteenth century, perhaps much earlier if we can accept the Scandinavian claims.

Homo sapiens, simply, is not native to the Americas. The ancestors of our current native Americans crossed some kind of bridge across the Bering Strait from Asia, and there is some evidence that in migrating they devastated—with their own new diseases, we may presume, as well as with their new generation of hunting and warring tools—the descendants of a previous migration that had made the same crossing. Then came the various Europeans with yet newer and more devastating diseases and far advanced tools for the hunt and for warfare—for civilization as we have conventionally come to understand it—and an excessive appetite for some of the natural products of these new continents. This is the international background for the question of the possession of North American soil and the rights that in both international and national law derive from possession, as opposed to the advantages and privileges that derive from occupation or tenancy and are often designated usufructuary.

The first significant and permanent European presence on the North American continent was at the French outposts on the St. Lawrence, first at Quebec (about 1603, counting from Champlain's first voyage) and then upstream at Montreal slightly later. But the French never posed the threat of an expanded presence on the land; in size, the Laurentian colonies and consequently their need for land were modest and emigration was carefully controlled to keep it that way—which got them into considerable trouble when they came to blows with the British over their North American holdings. Though the French, starting with Champlain and his company, wanted to explore the continental interior with an eye to finding the other end of it and so accessing a supposed oriental trade, they did not intend to expand their Laurentian base by encouraging settlement to the west.

Indeed, the rules specifically forbade it. The French colonies were tightly held feudal corporations whose business it was to coax peltries out of the northern interior and down to the St. Lawrence to help a bankrupt throne. The northern tribes, especially those of the Algonquian language group, were especially adept at gathering the furs because it was what the individual tribesmen did all winter anyway. The migratory nature of their life fit perfectly with the economic scheme according to which the French wanted to do business, they loved the trade because it brought them the advanced tools that both improved their lot in the woods and extended their harvest so that they could benefit further from the trade, and so the two cultures complemented each other in an instance of practical symbiosis. Never mind that the ugliness of brandy and guns finally entered in. The Frenchman and the Indian shared and, beyond the relatively small areas approved by royal charter for ribbon farms and feudal estates, the organization and ownership of the land was never an issue—except for the fortified trading posts that evolved in the interior later in the game as a means to further encourage and protect the trade.

Not until after the Plains of Abraham (1759) and the first Treaty of Paris in 1763, which gave the whole show over to the British. The English colonies along the Atlantic seaboard had evolved according to a different set of rules. As opposed to the closed feudal society and royally chartered, closely held trading corporation that was the French model, the British colonies were open to emigration, settlement, and development from the very beginning. The rule at the Home Office was benign neglect and the rule in the New World was freedom to act, acquire, and develop. The Britisher who wanted to take his chances in North America could generally make his passage. A natural result of the policy of noninterference was a burgeoning population along the East Coast that had managed its own affairs for five generations, including such arrangements for living space as had to be made with the Indian tribes, and was now looking for space in which to expand.

Like the French ones, in origin the British colonies were founded on the authority of royal charters, several of which (those to which Massachusetts, Connecticut, and Virginia trace their origins, for instance) included a convenient coast-to-coast feature. These land claims later became important items in the agenda of negotiating the governance of the Northwest Territory and ratifying the Constitution when Maryland refused to ratify unless the states with such claims gave them up and accepted western borders east of the Ohio River. Never mind that no one yet knew where the other coast might be or that, at first, almost no one wanted to go out beyond the mountains and into the unknown land of the nasties anyway. Nevertheless, both international law as it was understood at the time (the time, that is, of the Jacobin charters) and national law as it was while forming itself recognized the validity of the claims, the ability of the states information to assert or nullify them, and the rights and responsibilities attached to them, which in the Northwest were transferred to the fledgling Unites States government. As a matter of international law, even preexisting national law, thus, the principle of ownership and the rights and responsibilities that derive from it traces itself to claims made by discovery, colonization by royal charter, and international treaties conventionally signed, at the time, in Europe.

As the British colonies developed, so did their economies. Necessarily rural and agrarian economies gave way to the rise of towns and then cities boasting economic diversity: manufacture, trade, service industries, and rapidly expanding markets. The North American British naturally sought out trading partnerships with their European counterparts, and the Europeans, especially the British, proved as eager. The growth of trade did in the Home Office policy of benign neglect and encouraged Parliament to impose some sort of government on the colonials. After their victory on the Plains of Abraham, the British found themselves on the road to empire; they also found that managing an empire is an expensive business to which the various elements of the empire to be managed must contribute to pay the bills. That suggested the need for taxes, which were at no time less popular than they were to the previously untaxed British citizens of North America. It also called loud for protection of the stake the British had won in the fur trade, especially the fur trade that siphoned out of the Old Northwest and from the upper Great Lakes.

At the same time, the coastal colonial population, now both economically advanced and demographically crowded, was seriously looking for land for settlement and opportunity for investment. The land to the north and west of the Ohio River offered both; it promised territory in which to settle and the chance to speculate in land acquisition as well as access to the fur trade. But the London government was determined to regulate the fur trade and use the profits to service its own financial needs, much to the detriment of the coastal colonials. To this end Parliament, in October, issued what is known as the Proclamation of 1763. The proclamation provided in part: (1) that a line be established along the crest of the Appalachian Mountains beyond which settlers were forbidden to go and that (2) trade and other relations with the Indians were to be carried on through superintendents responsible to the Crown rather than by agents of the colonies. In a single document, then, the colonials, still loyal and constitutionally equal freeborn subjects of the Crown, were denied rights guaranteed by royal charter and implicitly reaffirmed in the Parisian treaty of 1763 in favor of their counterpart subjects back home; they faced unfair governmental restrictions where none had been before. And they were furious that their charter rights as British subjects were illegally preempted. These rights derived from the disposition of the land and dominated the mood in the colonies that led to the American Revolution.

In our centuries we think of the land we inhabit in terms of ownership absolute—by quitclaim, purchase contract, government patent, insured title, or whatever. These devices of ownership presuppose land that is formally organized: surveyed, recorded, platted, and offered for transfer in a market that can be appraised as being driven by variable but definable factors. That is almost a modern invention and tends to cloud our view of occupancy and ownership or both in societies older than ours. Sixteenth-, seventeenth-, and eighteenth-century international law, however, devolves from a different social and political climate, a climate that the American and French revolutions radically changed. This law, which remains relevant to the social and political historian as surely as it does to the legal one, derives from the medieval/feudal principle of suzerainty: a monarch (answerable, perhaps, only to the Holy Roman Emperor and to God) is the only true master of the land that is his domain. His domain is whatever he can acquire and hold, and his peers, the nobles, and their retainers hold their lands at the sufferance of the monarch. This is a remnant of the feudal system as it passed into and through the Renaissance and age of discovery. Ownership as we understand it is not even an issue; authority or control—mastery —is the only issue.

Felix J. Cohen in his *Handbook of Federal Indian Law* traces this aspect of international law to the Spanish courts of the sixteenth and early seventeenth centuries and their deliberations over the responsibilities of the discoverer/conquerors to the Indian inhabitants of Central America, Mexico, and southwestern North America. The Spaniards concluded that the new suzerains had the same responsibilities to the inhabitants of territories gained by discovery or conquest as a medieval overlord might have to the inhabitants of his fiefdom. Again, there is no question as to who is the suzerain, who is what we would understand as the "owner" of the territory.

The only question involves the responsibilities of the suzerain, and these early courts determined that the responsibility of the new masters was to deal with the inhabitants fairly and kindly insofar as possible. This, Cohen points out, is the basis in international law for the patterns played out first by the French, then the English, then the Americans on the North American continent. Nowhere is the ownership of land as we understand it, and thus the possibility of acquiring it by purchase, even introduced. Neither did the Indians in North America introduce it, in part because the concept of ownership of land was foreign to them. Certainly the migratory northern tribesmen moved across the land and were confined according to their customs (mostly the warlike ones) to loosely defined territories; certainly they harvested what the land gave up to them; in some cases they even planted limited crops, usually in natural clearings during the spring migration, to be left untended and harvested on the return migration in the fall. But seldom in any sense greater than this did the northern tribes settle on a piece of the land, tame it, and make it their own. In no realistic sense was their land marketable.

Eminent domain as it applied to European colonial development in North America derives from ancient suzerainty and was an issue every bit as important as the levying of taxes leading into the Revolutionary War. Philosophically, the question arose as to who were to be the practical suzerains of what was still British territory in North America: the Crown and Parliament (who were not getting high marks among the colonials) or the colonials themselves armed with a central government as yet unformed and probably unconceived. Having cast off the yoke of the Crown and Parliament and with it the barrier line down the Appalachians together with the threat of unwanted taxes, our new nation turned its attention to its most pressing problems: forming a government and organizing a geographically and politically defined country. Shortly after war's end, even as the Constitutional Convention met at Philadelphia, the Congress of the Confederation convened in New York to conduct the affairs of the nation on an interim basis. Until a constitutionally based government could be formed, all practical governmental affairs fell to the Congress of the Confederation.

The Congress of the Confederation quickly focused on the west, the Old Northwest, that is, the territory north and west of the Ohio River to the Mississippi and the Canadian border from which the states of Ohio, Indiana, Illinois, Michigan, and Wisconsin were destined to be carved (even though the headwaters of the Mississippi had not yet been found and much of the watery part of the border was to remain long unsettled). The Treaty of Paris in 1783, which formally concluded the Revolutionary War, established the suzerainty of the fledgling United States, in effect reaffirming the old royal charters and affirming eminent domain, which came to be called "manifest destiny." The new territorial suzerains would now exercise the authority they could claim as theirs deriving from the elderly principles of international law as deliberated by the Spaniards, whether they wanted to be in bed with the Spaniards or not.

The series of ordinances proposed to the Congress of the Confederation to deal with the Northwest Territory began with one written by Thomas Jefferson in 1784 that suggested a very general and imperfect scheme of political organization for the territory. Though adopted by Congress as drafted, it was never enacted and was superseded by the far more comprehensive and coherent Ordinance of 1787. The Ordinance of 1785 established the broad policies that would govern the organization of the land itself. In it we see affirmed public ownership of the lands entrusted to a central federal government as yet unformed, benefitting the citizenry and inhabitants alike (that is, both the Indian population and remnant foreign nationals, French and British), together with a series of compromises designed to govern the transfer of public ownership (that is, federal, the suzerain in fact) to private ownership.

A war-ravaged and desperate national treasury without sources of income other than the sale of the land itself accepted the New England system of survey and marketing, by which lands to be transferred were to be presurveyed at the cost of the government. It was a chancy gamble. The ordinance also provided that legal title to large tracts of land could be cleared only by agents of the federal government by treaty with the Indians extinguishing their claims and that the Indians were to be treated fairly according to the dictates of an evolving unencumbered land market. The Ordinance of 1785 in these respects became the blueprint for American expansion into the Northwest as well as a document marking the transition from suzerainty to private ownership in a free economy. It is well to remember that the Old Northwest was the "west" to which Horace Greeley later invited the young men of his generations. It was early on regarded as the land of true opportunity for the industrious and the eager.

As the Ordinance of 1785 addressed organizing and transferring the land, the Ordinance of 1787 was the first to provide government for the land so organized (Jefferson's suggestions in 1784 notwithstanding); because it addressed itself exclusively to the Old Northwest, it is known as the Northwest Ordinance. It reaffirmed the principles written into the Ordinance of 1785, guaranteed most of the common rights and privileges promised under law in the east, and repealed the Ordinance of 1784. It also promised that survey and organization would proceed only after Indian title was extinguished and that the "utmost good faith shall always be observed towards the Indians; their lands and property shall never be taken from them without their consent; and in their property, rights and liberty they never shall be invaded or disturbed unless in just and lawful wars authorized by Congress; but laws founded on justice and humanity shall, from time to time, be made, for preventing wrongs being done to them, and for preserving peace and friendship with them."

The ordinance, which defines itself as a "compact," a most solemn term in eighteenth-century law signifying a contract between a government and its people (the example of which in 1828 Webster gave as the Constitution), "forever to remain unalterable, unless by common consent," clearly gives the Indians status deriving from both property and lands. At the same time, it reserves the right of "primary disposal of the soil by the United States in Congress assembled" and introduces the language of "extinguishing" Indian title, while failing to clarify what Indian title may be. The previous discussion of ancient international law, about which there seems to have been little doubt at the time of the several Parisian treaties, clarifies the matter. The as yet unformed United States government in the Northwest Ordinance is pledged to perform its benevolent responsibilities to the Indians according to the principles laid down by the Spaniards, including the recognition of certain property rights. At the same time, the document assigns to the federal government the rights and prerequisites of the suzerain in the "primary disposal of the soil." Thus, though allowing that Indian title and claims can be justly ended, "extinguished," at no time does the ordinance oblige the United States to purchase the land by any exchange agreement, which, with no known value system among the tribes, not to mention a depleted national treasury, would have been impossible in any event.

In the same year in which the Northwest Ordinance was issued by the Congress of the Confederation, the Constitutional Convention in Philadelphia reported out, our first constitutionally founded government was formed, the Congress of the Confederation was adjourned, and our country began its jerky way into its future. Among the primary items of business for the new Congress of the United States was the reenactment and reaffirmation of the ordinances of 1785 and 1787. The first documents in law for the governance of the Northwest Territory and the states to be formed therefrom were firmly in place, "forever [to] remain unalterable, unless by common consent."

Immediately after the Revolution, even as policy for managing the Northwest Territory was being formulated, owing to intense pressure from would-be settlers in the east, the United States negotiated treaties with the Indians at Fort Stanwix (1784) and Fort McIntosh (1785), which cleared a large area in what is now the state of Ohio north of the Ohio River Valley. Though these treaties were later repudiated by the tribes, and the stream of settlers into the Ohio Valley they let loose was the primary reason for the Ohio and Indiana Indian wars that led Anthony Wayne to Fallen Timbers, even before the ordinances were issued these documents show the United States operating in good faith according to what would become the spirit of the ordinances. In other words, they extinguished tribal claims and opened the territory by negotiated treaty before encouraging settlement. They carried forward the process, based on ancient international law and implicit in the two Parisian treaties of peace. Anticipating the spirit of the ordinances, the states, in forming themselves into a separate sovereign nation and accepting in that the responsibilities of the suzerain, also recognized the separate sovereignty of the Indian nations. The United States, that is, encouraged the tribes to retain a separate national identity while at the same time exercising their legal suzerain powers, derived from international law as it was understood at the time, as the new lords over the land.

Nevertheless, the treaties at Stanwix and McIntosh were not successful. Several of the important northern tribes claimed that they had not been properly represented—or not been represented at all—and so were unjustly deprived of ancestral lands. This resentment led to bloody uprisings in Ohio and Indiana and the disastrous Ohio campaigns of Generals Harmar and St. Clair. Indeed, until Gen. Anthony Wayne marched north out of Cincinnati in October of 1793, the tribes held the upper hand and the Ohio Valley residents lived in terror. The documents were not executed by representatives of the constitutional United States government; the Constitution was as yet unwritten, the government only temporary. Given the failure of the treaties, it was unlikely that the youthful constitutional government would insist on reaffirming them.

General Wayne marched his army into a truly nasty situation and conducted himself brilliantly. At Fallen Timbers, in August of 1794, he completely broke the back of the Indian resistance, leaving the allied tribes soundly thrashed and vanquished nations; more than that, they were beaten as the mercenary operatives of another nation (the British, still occupying Detroit, encouraged and supplied them, continuing a war already long over). It is no wonder that the British would soon agree to vacate their northern posts; remarkably, the United States neither undertook nor asked for immediate and firm punitive action, nor simply claimed what had now been won twice and thereby end it. Nor did Wayne stage, resupply, and continue his campaign thereby clearing the north. That he did not and was not ordered to do so is one of the remarkable paradoxes of American history; in Wayne the United States had the opportunity to clear militarily most of the Northwest.

In that it did not, as a matter of choice, but chose to stick by and reaffirm the ordinances and principles already in place, Wayne's negotiations at Greenville would set the pattern of nation building in the Northwest. Instead, the government chose to honor the covenants and contracts it had set forth in the Northwest Ordinance, thereby affirming for all residents of the Northwest, including the Indian ones, in practice what it had promised in principle. Even this early, a war lost to the United States could prove a profitable venture. Having won the war, Wayne called all the tribes of the Northwest to a solemn conclave at Greenville in the following year, and there, on August 3, 1795, consummated the Treaty of Greenville.

Just as the Indians had repudiated the earlier treaties at Stanwix and McIntosh, so now both parties by agreement voided all treaties previously made between themselves since the creation of a United States government by consent of the three other governments sitting at the Paris peace talks in 1783. The point of it is crystal clear. The Greenville treaty was to be the new beginning, the model from which all further treaties extinguishing Indian claims and so securing the lands of the Northwest for sale and settlement would be constructed. This treaty was to set the pattern by which the United States would commence its inevitable westward expansion. In this respect, and because it honored and reaffirmed the principles set forth in the ordinances of 1785 and 1787, Greenville is not only the first but, therefore, the most important of the treaties of cession that would open the lands of the Northwest and thereby finance the new government for the benefit of all its people, including the aboriginals, who were promised from this point of beginning all such benefits as might be within the power of the government to bestow and nothing less. The treaty is unprecedented in its liberal treatment of a twice-vanquished belligerent people.

Importantly, the Greenville Treaty, like the Michigan treaties that derive from it, is not a purchase; it is a land cession with considerations on the other side in annuities, allowances, goods, and the opening of trade—an unprecedented social welfare system and entitlement program set up by an essentially unfinanced government betting on its capacity to somehow pay for the organization and sale of the land ceded. The distinction is made clear in Article V, in which certain lands are relinquished to the tribes with the stipulation that if in the future the tribes wish to sell these lands they may do so only to the United States government. That government thus retains its suzerain authority while promising to accept its suzerain responsibility as trustee for the vanquished nations.

The federal treaties with the Indians governing the territory that would become the state of Michigan follow meticulously the pattern of understanding of title and claims derived from ancient international law and most recently manifested in the ordinances and then the Greenville Treaty. From Governor Hull's treaty at Detroit (1807) to Governor Cass's treaty at Saginaw (1819) to Henry R. Schoolcraft's treaty at Washington (1836)—the major treaties of cession accounting for the state's terriroty—the intent was always the same: to extinguish by cession Indian claims to territory not actually inhabited by the tribes in return for the pledge of the United States to assume a trust relationship like that assumed by the medieval suzerain in favor of the aboriginal peoples at least until such time as they could be properly accommodated within the new civilization and so provide for themselves. This was the case until the second generation of treaties, such as that at Detroit in 1855, which intended to assure that all federal responsibilities had been fulfilled so that the aboriginal citizen was or had the opportunity to be on equal ground with the ordinary citizen.

In 1820 the Reverend Jedidiah Morse, father of Samuel F. B. Morse and a conservative and enthusiastic clergyman-would-be-missionary, was commissioned by President James Monroe's secretary of war, John C. Calhoun (whose department housed the Indian Department at the time), to travel through Indian country and report on the state of the aboriginals. The *Report* (1822) is an extremely important and little known document that includes a wealth of contemporary information. It was clearly generated by President Monroe's determination, amid the treaty-making years, to review Indian policy and law with an eye to the inevitability of further expansion into the west. In it we find citations from prominent attorneys of the day, as well as the opinion then of the United States Supreme Court, on the subject of Indian title, together with the legal citations. John Quincy Adams, for instance (just before becoming the sixth president of the United States), argued before the Supreme Court that Indian title "is mere occupancy for the purpose of hunting. It is not like our tenures; they have no idea of a title to the soil itself. It is overrun by them, rather than inhabited. It is not a true and legal possession.... It is a right not to be *transferred*, but *extinguished*. It is a right regulated by treaties, not by deeds of conveyance. It depends upon the law of nations, not upon municipal right." Similarly, the Supreme Court in its decision on *Fletcher v. Peck* (the same case Adams was arguing) wrote: "The majority of the Court is of opinion, that the nature of Indian title, which is certainly to be respected by all courts, *until it be legitimately extinguished,* is not such as to be absolutely repugnant to seisin in fee on the part of the State" (italics mine).

Further, Morse cites the deliberations of the commissioners at the Treaty of Ghent (1814). The American commissioners wrote: "The recognition of a boundary [by international agreement] gives up to the nation in whose behalf it was made, all the Indian tribes and countries within that boundary. It was on this principle that the undersigned have confidently relied on the Treaty of 1783, which fixed and recognizes the boundaries of the United States, without making any reservation respecting the Indian tribes." The commissioners, thus, like John Quincy Adams and the Supreme Court at a slightly later date, recur to the international law of nations as superseding and making possible national and municipal law. That law assigns to the tribes the privileges and advantages of occupancy on the land, not rights, which can derive only from the ownership of it.

The course of the interpretation of American history by modern courts and other public figures is clear; they would take our history and make it what they want it to have been to suit their own purposes. It is well for historians to consider, as best they can, what it was objectively.

CHAPTER ONE

THE TRIBES OF
THE NORTHERN LAKES

Referring to that time in the only dimly remembered past before the tribes of the northern lakes came into contact with the European white man, John Osogwin, a full-blooded Chippewa Indian and designated chief at Hessel, Michigan, said to Oliver A. Birge, his white friend also of Hessel: "It's a good thing you guys came along; we were so busy knockin' each other off in our own wars that we would have done ourselves in."[1] Osogwin's observation may not stand as a conclusion that justly wraps up the story of the complex interrelationship between the northern tribes and the Europeans (then Americans, though the Indians, in the early years especially, had some difficulty distinguishing among the nations of the pale-skinned intruders). It certainly suggests, however, a version of truth quite different from the more popular Rousseauian one popularized by the romantic novelists in the school of James Fenimore Cooper of the innocent and noble savage cruelly ousted from his paradisiacal home by a scheming and treacherous enemy.

The Mackinac historian Eugene T. Peterson has observed that the

romantic notion is advanced by some writers that the prehistoric Indian was basically a conservator who, in contrast to the European, wisely understood the relationship between unnecessary killing and use. There is no great evidence to support this. His attitude toward wildlife was simple and fundamental. Nature had put the animals in his environment, and he killed them as necessary to survive. Long-range concepts of preservation or even restraint in killing were unknown to him. But because he had only crude stone-age weapons, he was never a threat to the supply of fish and game.[2]

Before his prolonged contact with the white European, that is to say, the Indian American was in balance with his environment, a chief predator at the top of a food

chain that he could not, because of his small numbers and inefficient means of pre-
dation, seriously threaten. Nor had he any means of understanding nature's balance—beyond the unpleasant fact that if game gave out in one part of his territory
he had to move on to another part—or any need or wish to do so.

The pelted animals had always been in the woods, the trout had always been at
Michilimackinac, the whitefish had always been at Bowating; they would, therefore, always be so. Population dynamics was a much later discovery. The prehistoric Indian American did only, and exclusively, what he had to do to survive. He
made no moral judgments about the natural world in which he lived, and had neither scatology nor any means of oathing or swearing (any form of "dirt" was as natural for him as leaves or rocks or pine cones; someone else would have to discover
that for him also, and introduce it in a foreign language). His first law was survival.
Survival is necessarily amoral, sometimes grim. That is not to say unmoral or immoral.
It does have its rules.

Peterson continues his inquiry into the history of hunting in Michigan by observ-
ing that the arrival of Etienne Brulé in the vast Canadian interior, probably in the
fall of 1610, proved both a historic and a symbolic moment. In it, for the first time
in North America's vast northern interior, some Stone Age inhabitant of the continent came face-to-face with a representative of an advanced civilization living far
across an ocean he barely remembered, and "prehistory ended and the historic age
began. For better or worse, life would never be the same. Before long the Indian
would be holding a flintlock musket, and [his] squaw would do her cooking in a
copper pot."[3]

This new technology, coupled with the Indian's only natural Stone Age mental-
ity, forever upset the natural balance in the New World. It is not reasonable under
the best of circumstances to expect that any species of predator could quickly adapt
his mental set to an entirely new and more efficient means of getting prey—especially when its natural dress provided market access to yet more of the new technology in the form of guns and metal traps and improved hatchets and knives. It
was probably considerably later in the seventeenth century before the Dutch in what
is now upstate New York first traded guns to the Iroquois, but Brulé's contact set
the scene. Ted Williams quotes contemporary historian Calvin Martin: "The record
seems emphatic on this issue: the post-contact Indian wasted game with gusto." He
used the new technology primarily to extend his long-established habit of exploit-
ing game wherever possible and in whatever numbers it could be taken, slaughter-
ing wantonly bison, elk, caribou, and all the creatures that made up the fur trade.
Williams goes on to quote Samuel Hearne, chief factor at Fort Prince of Wales near
Hudson Bay, who kept a journal in the 1770s in which he recorded the Chippewa
extermination of caribou and musk-ox, "eating a few tongues and leaving the car-
casses to rot." Hearne wrote of these northern Indians: "Indeed, they were so accustomed to kill everything that came within their reach, that few of them could pass
by a small bird's nest, without slaying the young ones, or destroying the eggs."[4]

Williams also quotes a nineteenth-century ethnologist, Alanson B. Skinner, who reported on the Saulteur Chippewa: "One of [their] most redeeming qualities is their exceedingly poor marksmanship, for they seek to slay every living animal they see, whether it can be of any use to them or not." The point is an eloquent one. The pre-contact Indian functioned as a *natural* predator: contact with European technology made him *unnatural*. "Natural predators are opportunistic, taking whatever they can get whenever they can get it. . . . They alternate between famine and feast. If they can procure sufficient tongues, they will eat tongues only. Their environment is too harsh and too demanding for them to indulge themselves with the luxury of putting everything to its best use. Conservation of anything other than themselves is irrelevant to natural predators because there are never enough of them to make a difference."[5] The new technology, however, coupled with a universal ignorance of what we now call population dynamics, badly unbalanced the equation. No one, red or white, had any clear concept of the consequences of killing game faster than it could possibly reproduce; no one could even understand that such a thing might be possible. What evolved in this unhealthy situation, beyond the Indians' increased capacity to kill one another as well as the game on which they depended, was market hunting, perhaps the only fully logical outgrowth of this sudden intermixing of cultures.

We do not think there are any set good guys or bad guys in this scenario, for good and bad imply the need for explicit moral distinctions that simply do not apply. Cultures have been coming into conflict and displacing one another since long before any history was ever recorded and this is not necessarily a good thing or a bad thing—only, probably, an inevitable thing given animal and then human nature and population dynamics. It is simply an example of Hegel's historical dialectic: when a technologically superior culture comes into conflict with a technologically inferior one, the superior culture is likely to prevail in the resulting synthesis. Though possibly cruel, as when it happens through the device of war, the process is as natural and as void of moral implications as is the predator-prey relationship. The one survives by using and then assimilating the other. The record of it is the broad scope of human history. To be sure, there were, just as inevitably, good individuals and bad individuals on each side of the equation. But for the most part the conflict between the Indian Americans and the European Americans represents the perfectly natural antithesis of cultures in different stages of social evolution. The project, still, is to achieve an effective synthesis based on an honest search for historical truth.

The truth tries at all times to be objective and for the Indian American probably lies somewhere between the extremes of the Rousseauian noble savage and the strictly savage. Clearly, however, the romantic Fenimore Cooper image of the Indian as innocent prey to an ungenerous and unprincipled white-skinned predator has captured the popular imagination. That self-conscious and generally liberal reading of one of the important chapters of North American history simply falls so far short of objective truth that it is a scholarly embarrassment. Insofar as it has infected the reasoning powers of our lawmakers and judges, it affects the lives of the many who must live with and within its practical application—not to mention the entire citizenry that must pay for it. It becomes a distortion of history, indeed a rewriting of history with a clear political and philosophical bias, much like the purging of historical texts we know the Soviets have indulged. And it carries exactly the same weight of policy and then of law. Thus bad history translates to bad policy and bad law, bad because it is grounded in historical distortion, even if it is terribly well-intended and in fact *the* law. The greatest danger is that, in the reverse of the process as it works itself through, what is the law—documented in cases and published for the record—becomes, more or less officially, *the* history. *That* our free society should not tolerate and *that* is the principal motivation for this book.

In it we do not propose to argue the law on any case-by-case, precedent-by-precedent basis with our judiciary or the lawyers who argued before the courts. Though some consideration of legal opinion is inevitable in a project such as this (in which the legally trained consultant will retain provenance), as a practical matter to be placed before the public our main concern is the understanding of history that informed—or should have informed—the justices who heard the arguments and wrote their opinions and the attorneys who made the arguments. Our "case" is a rebuttal based on the same principle of historical method, mandated by the United States Supreme Court in construing Indian treaties and employed by the justices in the cases presented,[6] that rightly belongs to all of us who would use it; the documents we present are published as historical documents. The judges' opinions are deeply grounded in the treaties with the Indians of the Great Lakes area and with Britain as well as in the principles set forth in the Northwest Ordinance as issued by the Congress of the Confederation (New York, 1787) and reaffirmed by the constitutionally armed Congress of the United States in 1789. We here make available the documents themselves, on which the arguments and opinions are based, so that the reader who will can trace the continuity of the evolution of the law as it now stands and affects so many. Because the law evolved out of consideration of the historical matter, it seems fair to present the package of important primary documents whole.

Elsewhere I have written:

By the time Britain conceded the impracticability of sustaining a winning effort in a war [the American Revolutionary one] waged against her own subjects a whole ocean away. . . the back of the North American Indian was clearly to the wall. His life was in every way a savage one, made all the more so by his growing dependence upon the European and the goods in trade he provided—most especially the guns and ammunition and knives and hatchets and other items of worked metal that made both life and warfare in the woods both easier and more exciting. As a corollary to his Spartan and generally nomadic existence, his populations remained relatively stable and small; like a wolfpack dependent upon what its territory can provide and entirely vulnerable to famine, periods of killing weather, and all of the other little surprises that nature builds into her scheme of balance, the Indian [of the Great Lakes area] managed not to overpopulate.[7]

It seems clear enough, now, that it is probably substantially inarguable that his ancestors crossed over the Bering land or ice bridge in waves and gradually swept over the American continents, establishing widely differing cultures as he explored the different environmental possibilities the two continents offered. Little, it seems, can be said sociologically or historically of these original immigrants or of their reasons for emigration. There is some evidence that the Asiatic intruders conquered and displaced some non-mongoloids already here, but the evidence seems sparse.[8] About all that can be said of them with certainty, if for no other reason than their emigration, is that they were apparently nomadic hunter-gatherers after the usual Stone Age model sufficiently advanced socially that they were prepared to adapt to various environments and evolve within those environments. It is attractive, and probably safe, to assume that some notion of agriculture and the social stability that it implies came out of Asia with them, which then blossomed in its own evolution, particularly in the warmer areas in the south and southwest. It is also clear that these earliest known travelers in our continents had passed through and adapted to an environment made exceedingly harsh because of ice-age temperatures and so were entirely prepared to evolve in the context of the northern forests—and even above the tree line.

How exactly the patterns of migration in North America worked cannot be known with any certainty. About all we can assume is that some bands of the mongoloids-to-become-Indian Americans, probably following the warmer waters of the ice-age equivalent of the Japanese Current, made their way south along the Pacific coast eventually reaching Central and South America. Others, perhaps those more adept at hunting the large fur-bearing herbivores and so sustaining themselves, somehow and somewhere contrived to cross the coastal mountains, migrating east, finally, as far as the Atlantic coast. The accidents of migration led common Asiatic stock into the different environments that in turn encouraged different sorts of social and economic organization. The warmer climates, for instance, both temperate and tropical, lent themselves to the development of agriculture beyond the more primitive practice of gathering what naturally grew in any given area. Natural bounty, after all, is for the most part highly seasonal; agriculture, even in its most primitive sense, extends the season. It also keeps its peoples tied to the gathering area in which they live and the plots they plant and cultivate. Also, and very importantly, it promotes a form of social organization that amounts to a stable community. What is grown and gathered efficiently becomes a medium of exchange at the moment it is gathered or grown beyond the level of simple subsistence. A community of people living in one place tends to become specialized and in the promotion of specialization the community becomes interdependent. This, together with other sorts of population dynamics and the pressures they bring to bear, leads first to villages and then to what we would designate towns and cities—a social organization based on permanence, agrarian in its essence, but also encouraging the development of other special skills, services, and products for the community good.

The stock that was destined to become the northern tribes, specifically the tribes of the Great Lakes and Michigan, both geographically and ethnologically, took a different route. In immigration, life, first (as always), was at water's edge. There were found the blubbery mammals that could be taken with ease by the Stone Age hunter. They provided food, warm clothing, shelter, and, in their bones and teeth and sinews, the raw materials for the tools to continue the hunt. To water's edge also came the steelhead in the spring and the salmon in the fall, together with the furry omnivores that preyed on them in their seasonal profusion. Hooks and spears of bone or simple nets or snares of bone, sinew, and hide were all that were necessary to the primitive hunter; such was the profusion of his prey and so few were his numbers that he could kill all he wished to kill—and the climatic conditions permitted easy storage over a long period.

The same implements were all he needed to harvest the large herbivores: caribou, then elk, musk-ox, moose, and deer (all of whom, not having had much contact with man, had little fear of him). And so, we may suppose, certain of the northern hunting tribes followed their herds of land-dwelling cattle-on-the-hoof into and through the mountains and onto the plains of the continental interior. Here they found their next natural herds, stupidly unafraid, now of buffalo and the other animals of the plains. Through all of this the hunting-gathering process was quite easy, requiring little more than the cunning to stalk a large and herded animal in the open that had as yet no fear of his most formidable predator. And so the process must have perpetuated itself, one species giving way to the next as the American Asians made their nomadic way across the continent, following herd after herd, the continent obligingly providing food on the hoof for them as they passed from watershed to watershed, to the wooded region of the western Great Lakes with its abundance of white tailed deer, then moose and caribou, to the Niagaran escarpment and beyond, down the Ottawa and St. Lawrence rivers to the shores of the Atlantic.

Throughout this progress the life-style of the northern hunter-gatherer changed little. It did not have to. The predator had but to follow his prey and he could easily enough provide for himself. He learned to stampede the hoofed animals of the plains over escarpments and to mire them in the deep snow of winter, to hunt for deer and elk at night using torches (shining), and to run the same animals into the water where they could be easily corralled and dispatched by clubbing and drowning. He learned to snare and trap the smaller fur-bearing animals and became adept in this technique long before the Europeans came on the scene with leg-hold traps and guns, which only made the gathering process easier. He learned to use a deadfall on bear in the summer and to kill them in the slumber of winter hibernation. He learned that deer, weakened by winter, could be easily run down by a man on snowshoes when disabled by crusty or deep snow.[9] He even learned to celebrate the early spring, and to vary his diet by making maple sugar. As long as game abounded in the woods the northern Indian was well provided for, and the pursuit of game mandated a continuation of the nomadic life. The warm months lent themselves to other pursuits, including coming together in sometimes large groups in specific and traditional places for fishing. Survival during the cold months, however, called for dispersal.

For all his emerging skill in the Stone Age technology of the hunt, the woodland Indian was still a primitive predator—gatherer subject to the same population constraints that bedevil all predators. No small area can support a large population of them because they will quickly reduce the forage that sustains them. Thus permanent villages and towns and the social and cultural stability they imply could never be prominent in the life of the northern Indian. Early in the postcontact period there is evidence of stockaded structures among the Iroquois in upper New York State, the Hurons when they were located in southern Ontario, and the Winnebagoes in the western Great Lakes. But these amount to oddments. The Iroquois were more or less perpetually at war with whatever Algonquian tribe might be reachable (or whatever Frenchman or Englishman) and their structures, perhaps even patterned after what they saw at Montreal and Quebec, were thrown up defensively, having little to do with the other aspects of woodland life that amounted to survival as opposed to dominance at war.[10] The Hurons of Ontario were more docile than the other woodland tribes (the reason they early were chosen by Champlain to host Brulé in his visits to the interior and then became the darlings of the Jesuits), considerably more given to agricultural pursuits, and so more interested in permanent places of settlement—until, because of their permanence, which made them a stationary target, in the 1640s they were savaged by the Iroquois almost to extinction. The Jesuits had to abandon their friends by 1650, leaving the last remnant of the nation on the Christian Islands at the far southeastern end of Georgian Bay.[11] The surviving elements of the Huron nation thereafter migrated to the western end of Lake Superior, next to what is now Ashland, Wisconsin, out of the range of the Iroquois. The Winnebagoes originally were the rice gatherers of Wisconsin and so, more than the other woodland tribes, were tied down by their own agricultural interests; they were also able to defend their interests, as when they routed the Iroquois in 1653, sending the remnant invaders back to Bowating where at Point Iroquois the Saulteur Chippewas ended the terrible uprising of that period.

The precontact woodland Indian of the Great Lakes, thus, for the most part led a life of perpetual migration. He had already crossed an entire continent led on by the game that sustained him. That game also, as the staple of his diet, dictated his annual movements. Like any other predator, the Indian did not waste more energy pursuing his prey than would be returned to him by a capture. Nor did he, nor *could* he, overpopulate an area. To do so meant starvation. During the warm months the forests and waters provided nicely for the hunter-gatherer, who could reap his bounty with ease. Game of all sorts moves freely and less timidly as all natural things green and grow and batten against the frigid difficulty that ends the annual cycle;

the waters, free of ice and warming, bring the various fish, each according to its own cycle, into the shallows to feed and to spawn. The warm months offer up a season of plenty in the woods, a season during which primitive man could assume survival without special effort and turn his mind to other matters. During the warm months the woodland Indian could afford to congregate and socialize, usually at traditional places that offered special advantages in what they provided. During the warm months the brave could indulge his urge to travel sure of finding his food along the way, including that form of travel he called the warpath, knowing that the young and old and female of his community could forage successfully for themselves. During the warm months, in short, the precontact woodland Indian community was pretty much at ease.

The cold months were a different matter. During the northern winter the predator-prey relationship was always in its most difficult and delicate phase. It is not hard to understand that a large seasonal concentration of predators in any area would have a rapid and devastating effect on the numbers of prey animals using that same area, even if the predators were primarily engaged in taking something other than the prey animals, fish, for example, or rice. Further, during the cold months for a variety of reasons—all of which have to do with survival—the animals that do not provide for themselves (unlike squirrels, for instance, and beaver) tend to spread out. Forage becomes scarce for all of them and as it does so they range and thin out; the predator species must follow. The Indian was no exception to this rule. Except for the dogs he commonly kept by him (which were eaten, usually, with great ceremony and only on occasion; yellow-dog stew was highly regarded as a delicacy) he had no domestic livestock. If he was to eat and so survive he had to disperse with the animals, traveling often to extremely remote hunting grounds where predatory pressure was low and he could expect to capture a meal. Virtually every form of animal that could be taken was of some use, nutritionally or otherwise. In this respect the winter hunt was also important. The coats of the fur-bearing animals come into their prime during the cold months, denser, richer, and so warmer than they are during the summer. As these, at first, became clothing (before, that is, they became peltries in the trade), it was of practical value to take them during the cold season.

The mode of dispersal was usually by family. A single hunter could afford to have by him no more mouths than he could reasonably expect to feed, but he was obliged to take with him his squaw (or squaws, as the case commonly enough was), children, and such other close family members as he figured he could look after. The old and infirm who could not find patronage were expected to stay quietly behind—or disappear quietly into the woodland solitude. Winter was an extremely delicate matter for, as Peterson observes, "in this world the game and fish were not always plentiful, and starvation was not unknown. Cycles of abundance were followed by unexplained shortages. Severe winter storms sometimes drove the usually plentiful deer into remote parts of the forest that were inaccessible even to natives on snowshoes. [The English trader Alexander] Henry saw a cave where an Indian who could find no other food had killed and eaten a member of his family."[12] In truth, this form of cannibalism (as opposed to the more ritual and wartime forms, which were also practiced), regarded every bit as amoral as an arctic explorer eating his dogs to stay alive, though not exactly a way of life, was a common enough measure of the precariousness of the survival of the Great Lakes Indian. If a brave and his squaw and their child went off to the winter hunt and only the brave and the squaw, or even only the brave, returned, it was just not a matter to be questioned. The survival of the race depended on the brave; he could make, after all, another family.[13] So, as it evolved into a way of life, the natural life cycle of the precontact woodland Indian of the Great Lakes area was one of almost perpetual movement. He followed his prey east and then, once established in the eastern woodlands, again adapted his life as a predator to most efficiently take advantage of it. He was in harmony with his environment only to the degree that a lone wolf is in harmony with it; for the most part he was pitted against it. Only by prevailing in this constant struggle could he hope to survive.

Other factors also contributed significantly to his nomadic and predatory life. By the time the French established a continuing presence on the banks of the St. Lawrence at what would become Quebec (Champlain visited first in 1603 and returned with provisions and personnel with which to found a colony in 1608[14]), the Indians of the continental interior were already busy in their already traditional internecine wars of extermination. The Indians Champlain first met were representatives of the Huron, Algonquin, and Montagnais nations. All were loosely allied nations of the Algonquian language group, all lived to the north and mostly to the west of the great river, and all were summer visitors to the area of Quebec—and all brought furs, though it is unclear how they knew to bring furs to the Europeans or how they knew the Europeans would be there to receive them.

Champlain quickly learned about the Indian wars, experienced them firsthand during his foray into upper New York state in 1609, and then figured out how to use them to his best advantage. What he learned was that the Iroquois nations, claiming as their territory virtually everything to the south of the St. Lawrence and Lake Ontario, had formed a confederation to protect their territory and make perpetual war on the Algonquian nations (and the French one) to the north. The Iroquois were so formidable as to have closed off the open-water route through Lakes Ontario and Erie and forced the interior tribes to use the Ottawa River route on their journeys to the St. Lawrence. They also regularly sent war parties north of the St Lawrence, were a constant threat to the Hurons in what is now southern Ontario, and had already sent the Chippewas and Ottawas packing from their traditional eastern grounds into the northern Great Lakes. They would virtually exterminate the Hurons and send war parties up the lakes as far as Green Bay later, though there they would be destined to be stopped.

So again the tribes of the northern lakes, notably the Ottawa and the Chippewa, had been on the move. Indian historian George L. Cornell points out that as early as A.D. 1001 Norse fishermen visited the shores of eastern North America on wood-gathering expeditions sent out from their coastal fishing villages in Iceland. This early, he concludes, the tribes that would become dominant in the northern lakes were in contact with European visitors on the eastern Canadian coast. The contact featured, Cornell suggests (and tribal tradition affirms), their first experience with European diseases against which they had no immunity: smallpox, diphtheria, scarlet fever, measles, and tuberculosis. He does not mention the venereal diseases or foreign forms of influenza. The effect, Cornell concludes and Indian tradition confirms, was devastating; the tribes suffered mortality rates as high as 70-80 percent, a figure comparable to that generated by the European colonials in the seventeenth century.[15] An immediate result was that at least some surviving elements of the tribes, to escape the pestilence, began the westward migration that would bring them back to the Great Lakes. Others seem to have remained in the east, finally joining the other Algonquian nations in their continuing wars with the dominant Iroquois confederacy.

Because the participants were unlettered, it is probably not possible to assign anything like accurate dates to these wars, not, at least, until the French established their presence on the St. Lawrence about the turn of the seventeenth century and began keeping records. But it is probable that the last elements of the Ottawa and Chippewa made their way west, fleeing their numerically superior Iroquoian enemy, not terribly long before the French arrived. This accounts for the continuing violent hatred between the northern and western branches of the Algonquians and the Iroquois confederacy that defined their wars through the seventeenth century, and the continuing commerce and commingling between the lakeland Algonquians and those who remained in the east.

So the remnant Ottawa and Chippewa, like the Hurons about the same time, sent west by the Iroquois, made their way via Canada and the northern lakes as far as what would become Wisconsin and Minnesota, there to encounter the equally warlike Sioux, Foxes, and Dakotas. As their historian, William W. Warren, describes them, the northern tribes were now perpetually warring, intending to exterminate.[16] Once again, because of the pattern of subsistence that had evolved as their way of life and because of the vagaries of their version of human nature, the tribes were in constant flux, living without permanence even if they had wanted it—and there is really little evidence they did. War is waged by two parties, not one, and the Chippewayan wars with the plains tribes were as surely aggressive as the Iroquoian ones with the Algonquian tribes. But the last migration, in flight from the Iroquois and not that far previous to the turn-of-the-seventeenth century contact with the French on the St. Lawrence, is the accident, and it is strictly an Indian accident, that brought the main bodies of the Ottawas (from their home on the Ottawa River, the river of "trade" from which they derived their tribal name) and Chippewas to what would become northern Michigan as its "native" occupants and suzerains. At no point did they pretend to own it or to want to own it; their own population dynamics pinned them in on it because they could not again go east and could go no further west. Their only claim to ownership was by accident, not design; they passed through the area twice, once headed east and then again headed west, and ended up stuck on it with no other place to go.

CHAPTER TWO

CONTACT
WITH THE FRENCH

The French presence on the St. Lawrence represented yet another pressure to encourage the already migratory life of what were becoming established as the dominant tribes of the northern lakes. As early as 1603 Champlain, in his first voyage to New France with Francois Pontgravé, made the fur-trading connection with the Indians of the North American continental interior at exactly that time when fur in the form of fine felts for hats was becoming the style in Europe. Even at that early date, it would appear, the Great Lakes tribes were represented by the visiting Hurons, and through them the first European trade goods made their way into the western interior. Traps and knives and hatchets and metal kettles and yard goods for clothing, at first, all contrived to make the savage life easier and more efficient so that the tribes could bring yet more furs down to the St. Lawrence. The Frenchman ventured westward, at first, only on trips of espionage (such as Brulé's life among the Hurons, and also the early adventures of Nicolet, Marsolet, Hertel, Marguerie, Nicholas Vignau, and others) and exploration (such as Champlain's trips west in 1609, 1613, and 1615 and Nicolet's in 1634).[1] His object, which became Champlain's policy, while all the time trying to punch through this stubborn North American continent on the way to the Orient, was to encourage the flow of peltries from the interior *down* to the St. Lawrence, avoiding therefore the danger and expense of trying to convey trade goods, men, and supplies into the unknown interior. If they wanted the European trade goods the Great Lakes Indians had to risk the dangers of the long trip downstream. Once again, this was neither "good" policy nor "bad" policy on any map of moral guidelines; it was sensible and prudent policy. And the Indians wanted the trade goods very much indeed.

So now the pattern of annual migration of the Great Lakes Indians refined itself

with a new twist and the winter hunt took on a new significance. Almost immediately French trading policy had a profound effect on the life of the Great Lakes tribes,
not so much by changing it as by giving it a new focus. The migratory nature of the
northern Indian's life, the only style of life, really, suitable to his complete dependence on the hunt as his distinctive mode of subsistence, and his consequent imper-
manence on the lands he moved across, was long established before any sort of
European contact. He was naturally nomadic as a matter of dietary choice; the forests
and waters provided virtually everything he needed to survive as long as he did not
overpopulate and so overharvest, which he could not. No predator can. Starvation
is nature's check and balance and her laws in this department are unforgiving. Nor
does this have anything to do with prudent management of game or any other
resource; it has everything to do with survival according to the inflexible rules of
an arbitrary though natural balance. The rules are the same as for the wolf pack; if
the pack grows too large or just kills too much within the bounds of its territory, its
numbers must be reduced. Individuals must leave or die. To this end the she-wolf,
apparently through some dietary trigger mechanism, can arrest her pregnancy in a
famine. Much the same was so with the northern woodland Indian. The natural
world in which he lived kept him in balance with his environment. There could be
no thought about it, no need to manage anything; if he overharvested he had to move
on to more productive territory or endure until natural attrition or some other occurrence restored the balance. The limitations of his technology, his incessant inter-
tribal wars, and the vastness of his territory all worked to keep him in balance. Even
if he overharvested an area, or if some other natural catastrophe took the game from
him, owing to his small numbers he could generally find some alternative means to
survival within the life-style that had become uniquely his. The permanent residence
of the Europeans, however, both along the St. Lawrence and on the East Coast, dramatically changed that natural balance.

Initially, at least, the Laurentian French were the preferred neighbors from most
points of view. As French policy formed and then solidified under Champlain and
his successors, Quebec and then Montreal were only outposts put in place first for
exploration and then for the development of the fur trade. They were early on intended to be as self-sustaining as possible, but the French, though they claimed the continent by right of exploration, were never truly colonial. That is to say they carefully
controlled emigration only to those who were necessary to sustain the communities
and did not until late in the game allow what we would call colonialism. They
explored, developed the fur trade at the Laurentian trading centers, and kept their
habitants at home, never expanding westward in any program of extensive land
acquisition and so colonial expansion. These policies would leave them dramatically outnumbered and done in by the time the British took them to task on the Plains
of Abraham.

The French adventure in Canada amounted to the development of a well-regu-
lated, efficient feudal corporate enterprise the whole purpose of which was profit

through the fur trade to help save a bankrupt Bourbon throne. Insofar as they came to trade at the Laurentian centers, the Indians shared in a feudal vassalage on the land of a continent used for mutual benefit: the propagation and harvest of furs, which, as it turned out, returned to them the very European trade goods that made both their "old" and their "new" lives easier. No one sought to own the territory they occupied in the vast interior; no one wanted to change their lives. The French only wanted the only product perceived as being of value and growing naturally within the continent. The Indians were already good at harvesting it and bringing it in; that was already part and parcel of the natural cycle of their lives.[2] And the French, for sound and practical demographic and political reasons, made their new North American friends among the northern Algonquian tribes, who were willing and able to bring in peltries; it was to their advantage to join the Algonquian alliance against the Iroquois, keeping the five (or six, depending on who counted and when) nations at bay to the south of the St. Lawrence and the Niagara, and the Ottawa River route to and from the rich fur-bearing lands of the far north open.

The British were a different story. Their Atlantic coastal colonies were open for emigration and development in the usual colonial sense. Britain's land mass is small, her population large; her people needed a place to go and a means to sustain themselves. The only model for development was the agricultural one, which gave land a value by the acre and led naturally to the development of interdependent rural and urban communities along still recognizable lines: the various forms of specialization providing goods and services, which, within a market system of exchange, make possible the agrarian social and economic organizational model. This called for acquisition of land for individual settlement, survey, passage of title, and expansionism. The British colonies on the Atlantic coast were self-sustaining from the beginning, permanent in their agricultural base, and programmed for growth, both by natural propagation and by receiving more and more immigrants. There were no government-controlled licenses to control trade, which also meant no government subsidies to develop it; the coastal British were on their own to build economies and local political structures. The French feudal settlements were in every way closed and tightly controlled outposts of a Parisian national corporation; the British colonies were open and free to develop according to their own evolving rules. The two could not have been more different and the difference could not be better exemplified than it was in the British victory on the Plains of Abraham. The French feudal policy, in every way medieval in its conception, lost a continent; the British colonial one, in every way "modern" and nonrestrictive, won it.

The French proved good friends indeed to the Algonquian tribes of the northern interior. Their continuing presence suggested the establishment of an unlimited market for a seemingly infinite commodity. All the Indian had to do in order to participate in this market was what he was already doing: hunting and trapping according to the normal cycle of his life. His life did not really change, except that the winter hunt intensified and shifted in its values, and the summer migration had a new destination, the trading centers on the St. Lawrence. And the Frenchman treated the Indian as the Indian would be treated—a favored child of the woods, to be coddled, gifted, cared for, aided and abetted (as in his wars with the Iroquois). When the French sent an *interpreteur* out (Brulé, for instance) on a mission of what we would call espionage, he lived as an equal among the tribals, sharing and even interbreeding. Thus the French were invited into the wilderness as guests and, like good guests, on journeys to explore they did not overstay their invitation or make unwelcome claims upon the territories they visited. The Jesuits who toiled among the savages were generally viewed as friendly and helpful; though eager to play at the game of conversions, they did not play their hand too hard. Their presence had practical and diplomatic values far beyond the more apparent religious ones.

The French trade with the Algonquian tribes, including those living in the northern Lakes, thus evolved naturally along lines already drawn. Because of previous migrations and the unfriendly Iroquois to the south, the Ottawa River route to the interior was well known and generally safe. The same Iroquois blocked contact with the coastal Europeans, which was not terribly desirable anyway; there was as yet no economy there that could foster a substantial corporation to invest in or manufacture the trading goods with which to open a significant market. In the early phases, at least, until the Hudson's Bay Company intruded via James Bay later in the seventeenth century, the only natural flow of furs was to the St. Lawrence, and the Indians of the interior were exceedingly eager to participate in that trade. They had good reason for participation.

Peterson has noted that the hunting arsenal of the precontact woodland Indian was extremely crude—Stone Age in fact. "Mostly he used spears and bows and arrows with points laboriously chipped out of flint and affixed with leather thongs….When the hunters discovered copper outcroppings on Isle Royale in Lake Superior, they soon fashioned arrow and spear points out of that metal. Although both stone and copper [points] were made in various sizes and shapes, over 10,000 years of hunting brought no significant change in these basic hunting weapons."[3] The pattern of life into which the woodland Indian fell as a natural extension of his function as a hunter-gatherer, together with his relatively small numbers (W.B. Hinsdale estimates that at no time was there an Indian population of what is now the state of Michigan greater than fifteen to twenty thousand[4]), called for significant advances in his weaponry no more than it did for the separate invention of the wheel. He had no draft animal, which would have encumbered him. The water was his primary highway, the Indian file trail his secondary one; what he had was enough to provide for himself and so he had little incentive for technological refinement or improvement.

Contact with the Europeans, however, changed all that, turning, as Ted Williams has pointed out, a natural predator into an unnatural one hunting, quite suddenly, for a market. European technology combined with woodland resourcefulness made this new function possible—and tribal life in the woods as an efficient harvester of the North American continent's first cash crop considerably more comfortable. It could never occur to him that it might be possible to run out of beaver and other furs for the trade, any more than that he could run out of whitefish at Bowating or trout at Michilimackinac. Thus the Indians of the north happily set about exterminating the very source of their new livelihood—to the good fortune of the French, then of the English, and then of John Jacob Astor. Thus, too, as the furry populations were depleted, the Indians required ever expanding territory just to sustain themselves in their developing relationship with the white man. This requirement taken together with colonial Americans' inevitable march westward, mandated a difficult confrontation.

The migratory life of the precontact Great Lakes Indians followed a pattern of seasonal dependence. In the winter he spread out, depending on what his hunting and trapping skills could bring him. In the early spring he repaired to his sugar bush, depending on the sap flowing there to provide him with maple sugar. During the warm months he could afford to congregate in especially productive gathering areas where game might be assumed to be plentiful or where there was a special harvest to be reaped. Fish were such a special harvest. Fishing was by no means a strictly seasonal pursuit for the Great Lakes Indians, but it certainly had its important seasonal aspects.

The dominant food species of the northern lakes early on, as more recently (until the ravages of the sea lamprey in the mid-twentieth century), were the whitefish and the lake trout and the Indians had both specialized means and natural seasons for taking both. Both species are temperature sensitive and the northern Great Lakes are stratified, meaning that their waters turn over spring and fall and organize into thermal layers at all times. One effect of this is that the fish recede into the deeper strata of the lakes during the cold months, finding there comfortable temperatures and compatible forage and there becoming largely inaccessible and less active. During the spring, however, when the water turns over and other life cycles awaken for the year and before the shallower water begins to warm, both species return to more accessible depths, the trout feeding around rocky reefs and shoals, the whitefish often congregating near the surface and even in shallower bays to feed on aquatic insect life. Through the summer in the northern lakes both species can be fished with nets set from small boats close to shore. Both species again mass in shallow water to spawn in the fall.[5]

Though the northern Indians undoubtedly congregated in many special locations for the annual harvest of fish, the Saulteur Chippewa held both Michilimackinac (the whole area of the Mackinac Straits, not just the island) and Bowating (both sides of the St. Marys narrows at the rapids) as especially important locations for their yearly gathering. At Michilimackinac the harvest was primarily lake trout; at Bowating the Chippewa were adept at taking whitefish with long-handled hand held hoop nets from their canoes as the fish ascended the rapids during their fall spawning run. From Bowating they undoubtedly fished Whitefish Bay with gill nets all through the summer for both species. The plentiful supply of fish at both locations made possible large encampments in both places. To these places of summer encampment the winter furs came in the spring and from them the canoe trains set out on their annual journeys to the St. Lawrence for trade.

Thus by not long after contact with the French a modified pattern of migration was set that did not again change substantially until the supply of Great Lakes fur gave out in the nineteenth century. The white man, first European and then American, changed his tactics and his trading locations from time to time—the British taking the trade into the lakes themselves in the shadows of their forts, the Americans finally going themselves into the woods with smaller trading outposts. But as early as the period of the French occupation of the lakes in the late seventeenth and early eighteenth centuries it became the summer job of the Indian to seek him out, camping by him through the trading session. That quickly he became almost entirely dependent on the intruder who provided the technology in trade goods that in turn allowed the Indian to maintain his harvest of peltries to get yet more of the goods in trade. This modified pattern of dependence did not bode well for the lakeland tribes.

The German historian—philosopher Georg Wilhelm Friedrich Hegel, who began his career about the turn of the nineteenth century and in contemplation of the immensely important sociological events both here and in France, postulated that history presents itself as a logical sequence of resolved confrontations in which an established order (which he called *thesis,* or that which is already given—an *ancien régime* in France, and Indian-European balance here) will. inevitably be challenged by a new order (which he called *antithesis*—successful revolutionaries, both here and in France), and through the process achieve a new accommodation (*synthesis*— which did not work out very well in France, but which became the United States here). Nowhere is the Hegelian dialectic better exemplified than in the American movement into the Northwest. In this country it has been most popularly called "manifest destiny." Nobody planned it; both the British and their colonials tried manfully to control it. It does not require, does not imply, or admit any moral judgment or ethical credo.

As a culture, the North American Indian of the interior lakes was both inferior and deteriorating. Somewhere in his dim past there had been traditions of: metalworking, mound building, primitive agriculture (corn, pumpkins, squash, peas, and beans, planted indiscriminately in the late spring, left untended through the warm months, and harvested in the fall on the return to the winter hunt), town building (such as the stockaded towns of the Hurons, Iroquois, and Winnebagos), and other evidences of cultural stability. By the time the European arrived in the lakes, however, most of this was but a foggy memory, except for a remnant knowledge of the planting of maize and a vague clinging to holy places (the island at Michilimackinac) and gathering places (both Bowating and Michilimackinac). With the sudden introduction of the gun into the trade by the English and the Dutch in mid-seventeenth century, the Indians became especially intent on exterminating one another—and whomever else might be on the other side. The Hurons were almost completely annihilated by the Iroquois, and the other northern tribes settled into a life of perpetual migration, avoiding one another, seeking fishing grounds in summer and hunting grounds in winter, and, always, jockeying about for a favorable trading position with the European friends on whom they became increasingly dependent for the trade goods that eased their wilderness lives and undermined their powers of invention. Culturally, the eastern North American Indian was regressive, sliding downhill of his own accord and with unintentional (though undeniable) European help.

The French had called the Indians *sauvages,* connoting uncultivated and uncivilized men of the woods; when the British were through with them they were more likely savages in the usual sense of the word. One of the great testimonials to European moral, ethical, social, and political conviction is that no great army was ever sent to sweep the Northwest, subdue, conquer, and so own it. The technologically and culturally superior coastal Europeans could at most any time have made such a move, and all the odds favored it. But the British tradition, at least officially and when dealing with ownership, called for fair play; the colonials had been born British and they chose to carry the tradition on.[6]

The French were the first and probably the best European friends the Great Lakes Indians ever had. During the French administration of the lakes (1608, roughly, until 1759), the Indians rapidly became all but entirely dependent on the Europeans for the trade goods they could not manufacture themselves. Their very subsistence came to require especially the metal implements (finally guns, powder, and balls as well as the other items that improved rather than changed their arsenal and their lives) that the French provided and they modified the pattern of their life to sustain access to this new market. The trading presence of the French, it is fair and accurate to say, allowed the Indian to participate in his first true economy, even if he understood it none too well. Before contact he had gathered during the warm months at places that became traditional as providing special bounty; soon after contact he also congregated at the white man's outposts, first along the St. Lawrence, slightly later at such interior outposts as Michilimackinac, Detroit, St. Joseph, and Green Bay, there to reap a different kind of harvest. To develop a backwoods diplomacy and so encourage the trade, and above and beyond the trade itself, the French gave gifts, including brandy, and maintained a festive carnival atmosphere throughout the trading season. The summertime encampments at the fortified locations became formidable, soon rivaling the natural encampments at such locations as Bowating and occurring for a parallel reason: now the Indian was harvesting what the white man would give him to encourage him in his winter hunt and bring him back to trade again during the next season. It is not hard to imagine how and why the Indian accepted the Frenchman as his friend: he was benign and paternal and encouraged the Indian's way of life, improving it without intruding on it; he had gifts to give that were highly valued by the primitives; and he accepted as having value beyond the comprehension of the aboriginal mind the one commodity the Indians could offer .

CHAPTER THREE

THE
BRITISH ADMINISTRATION

The British administration was a much different matter and created almost immediate problems. The French had had about 150 years in which to figure out and finally mismanage the affairs of what was destined to become the Northwest Territory; the English would have but 36. Through the first three of these, from the French surrender at Montreal (1760) until the first Treaty of Paris (1763) formally ended the French and Indian War, the French continued to exert their long-standing claims and great powers of suasion among all the residents of the area. And through the last 13 of which, after the second Treaty of Paris (1783) formally concluded the American revolutionary matter and until the orders to evacuate the Great Lakes outposts were finally issued in June of 1796, the fledgling United States technically had control.[1] The British, thus, operated under a much streamlined agenda—only, really, the 20 years between the two Parisian treaties—in which they engineered a whole new set of mistakes to accomplish their loss of the continental interior.

The Indians of the Great Lakes were utterly baffled by the French surrender at Montreal and could not comprehend its effect on them. They had, after all, 150 years of experience with their French friends, an extended friendship that had kept them safe from their Iroquois enemies and prosperous in the economy of the fur trade. They had had limited contact with the British of the Hudson's Bay Company, who came south occasionally from posts at James Bay, but generally, especially after the establishment of the French fortified posts in the lakes, they vastly preferred both French goods and the French attitude, which was paternalistic after the feudal model, friendly, and familiar. The two cultures were already interbred in almost every way (thus accounting, for one thing, for some immunity among the surviving Indians against the European diseases that had ravaged them in the past), which amounted to a successful partnership.

The British were different. Though they came into the woods they kept to themselves and conducted their affairs strictly as business; the market dictated their prices, not a benevolent national corporation, which often had the effect of driving their prices up. The Indians could not understand this phenomenon, or why a gun with a long barrel (the long rifle in the trade; guns were at one point traded for a stack of furs equal to their length) should be more costly than a gun with a shorter one. It was incomprehensible that the great French Father should enter into an agreement far across an ocean that would cause his agents to surrender the interior to the agents of some unknown British Father. The Indians, unable to comprehend disputes between Europeans and their invisible chiefs and the effect of these disputes on their own destinies, were still allied with the French, whose sudden disappearance from beautifully fortified and fully garrisoned positions could only be considered eccentric. Surely the French Father was only sleeping and, perhaps with some tribal help, would soon reawaken and again assert himself.

The French and Indian War, ended suddenly at Quebec and Montreal and, though the matter was not formalized until the 1763 Parisian treaty, Britain that fast found herself suzerain over an immense transatlantic property—roughly the entire eastern half of North America. In the year of France's surrender at Montreal, England also crowned a new king. The first two Georges, who reigned from 1714 to 1760, had been distinctly German-Hanoverian, inept, uninterested, and boring. The principal legacy of their administrations was the further evolution and firming up of the parliamentary compromise and the system of ministers by which Britain proved that she could find a way to govern herself despite an indifferent and unenlightened monarchy. They left most matters, specifically the job of overseeing the New World colonies and finally revamping the military and so engineering an unquestionable victory over here, to Prime Minister Sir William Pitt and his Parliament. But on the death of George II his twenty-two-year-old grandson ascended the throne as George III (who would reign until 1820) and once again Britain had a British-born and English-speaking monarch. He also liked the job to which he came by accident of birth and therefore took an interest in it, though he honored the Hanoverian tradition of ineptness, finally descending to what was widely perceived as mental incompetence, and therefore a regency, after the turn of the nineteenth century. In his person the throne would claim at least coequal powers with Parliament and the ministers, which he remarkably achieved—for a man without benefit of a perceptible drop of British blood in his veins and without the backing of the peerage. He determined to become much more of a king than his immediate forebears had been, perceived himself as head of a royal house with claims to empire around the world, and set about managing these vast assets—if not very well.

Since the day when the hapless King John capitulated to his barons at Runnymede in 1215 by assenting to the articles of the Magna Charta, the English peers had held their monarch in check by successfully asserting a split balance of power. The balance was rarely equal, depending on the relative personal force of the monarch and the peers, but the ascendant parliamentary and ministerial systems as they fully and finally evolved under the neglect of the first two Georges insisted on such a balance, established it as precedent, and made it work. Never again would a British monarch reign absolute. The third George was therefore denied much power at home. But in the dominion of the Crown Colonies, a previously untended field, he saw the opportunity to assert himself for the good of both crown and country and thereby strengthen his administration by getting a return on investment. A good possession, after all, including a colonial one, must contribute to the general welfare and thereby pay for itself; insofar as it may require management, it must pay for that management and still show a profit for its managers.

This much was and remains sound business practice, which, as it turns out, can sometimes get even a well intended monarch into trouble. For such management creates expenses that call for taxation, and the North American coastal colonials, many of whom were freeborn and unencumbered British subjects who had managed their own affairs quite nicely for upward of five generations, did not like the idea. This prospect inclined many of the conservative peers at home to sympathy with the colonials that might not otherwise have evolved. They did not object to exploitation in the colonies in the interests of private enterprise (in which they, after all, might very well choose to participate), but they firmly objected to the Crown strengthening itself by that exploitation to become further independent of the peers.[2]

The problem was that, though the Crown at its own expense had whipped the French and brought them to their knees at Quebec and Montreal (and then Paris), it had taken on thereby the huge administrative responsibility implied in managing the Northwest. On this side of the Atlantic the terms, as proposed by the crown, were unacceptable. From the coastal point of view (the only point of view in British North America at the time), out there were: an imponderable and traditionally foreign (that is to say, French) hostile Indian problem, a whole series of fortified posts that had to be garrisoned, maintained, and paid for, and a fur trade, representing the only profitable economy in the territory, that was coveted by the Crown and destined to send its profits to London to the exclusion of the coastal colonials, who also still had only limited means of participating in it. On the other side was the spectre of management and the costs implied in it. The whole situation added up to the clear threat of taxation to cover costs they at no time asked to be incurred and the coastal British did not like it at all.

The Crown now had two new sets of subjects, French ones living at the Laurentian centers and at places in the interior such as Detroit, Michilimackinac, La Baye, and St. Joseph, and Indian ones spread throughout the territory but congregating for the trading season at the accustomed centers. The preliminary job of the agents of the crown in the Great Lakes was a diplomatic one, to realign the Indians with the British and to assure the French *habitants* that their new monarch would deal with them fairly. And in its earliest phases the project went quite well. The official attitude of Britain toward her new subjects, French and Indian alike, was as liberal as the times could possibly allow—as much a laissez-faire compromise as was conceivable. The immediate purpose of it was to buy time so that the British could figure out their new managerial responsibilities and begin the transition into a new administration.

To the New World Frenchman, England extended her long-standing policy of colonial noninterference, allowing them to retain of their possessions lands, homes, goods, and chattels (tangible and intangible)—at their own pleasure, rather than that of the Crown, and permitting the very important point of at least limited religious freedom (of worship, if not of the practice of Bourbon Roman Catholic international politics). The hope was that, after the model of the British Atlantic coastal colonies, a nonrestricted socioeconomic organization left to a status quo could best pay for itself in the long run. This approach also cut short-term administrative costs. But there were still costs attached to the plan and the coastal colonials remained not at all pleased at the prospect of paying them. Thus the French *habitants* at Detroit witnessed the ceremony of surrender with seeming indifference and the new British personnel passed a pleasant winter there (1760-61), well furnished for all their needs by the French population and enjoying the robust vivaciousness of the European community.[3] Indeed, the French at first were well enough pleased by the change in administration.

The British relationship with their new Indian subjects, however, was from the very beginning an uneasy one. As early as that first winter at Detroit, Capt. Donald Campbell was presented with rumors of an impending attack on his fort, and he himself reported that the Indians were becoming more and more restless and demanding. When, in the spring, the first English traders made their way in, they did not bring the trade goods the Indians expected and their prices were unexpectedly high. About this time also a rumor raced abroad that the Seneca Iroquois, alarmed at the prospect of the British presence, now, both to the immediate north and the immediate south of them (it is well to remember the British policy of colonial development on the coast), were plotting to unite the western tribes in an attack on the now British positions in the interior. All of this in mind, and reflecting a less liberal British policy as laid down by General Amherst, Campbell, and the other commanders at the interior posts, locked up his rum and forbade its sale to the natives. Once their position was secure, or so it seems, at the first hint of unrest among the Indians a liberal English policy became a conservative one, in marked contrast with the brandy-flushed enthusiasm of the gift-giving French that had prevailed for so long. In the conduct of his trading partnership, the Indian's relationship with his European sovereign was about to change dramatically. Campbell sat tight at Detroit, waiting for substantial reinforcements before he would garrison the remaining forts in the north and thus secure the lakes.[4]

The expected reinforcements arrived at Detroit in September of 1761 in the form of a large expedition in the command of Maj. Henry Gladwin and including Sir William Johnson and George Croghan; owing to his extensive experience among the Mohawks in what would become upper New York state, Johnson was to act as

Indian agent for the Northwest—the first white man to come into the Northwest in this position, his appointment established the model the Americans would later follow—and he and Croghan were to organize and orchestrate a grand council conceived to pacify the Indians. Gladwin's responsibility was to take command at Detroit and oversee the occupation of the remaining forts in the lakes. The council was held on September 9 and seems to have been a grand success, each side pledging cooperation with the other for the good of both, with two demurrers.

First, there were no gifts for the Indians; Johnson had been specifically instructed by General Amherst that the policy of giving gifts, to which the Indians had become accustomed (as a version of their own traditional diplomacy) both throughout the French occupation and during the recent war, on both sides, was to cease. He reasoned that, with the French now happily out of the way, such up-front concessions to encourage friendships and so secure alliances were no longer necessary. The Indians were now to be managed sensibly and in a proper businesslike manner; they were to be given only what they traded for, just like the agents of any other foreign nation or any other subjects. They were no longer to be coddled like children; they were to be treated as responsible adults, trading partners, gentlemen, and coequal subjects. This was intended as a fine gesture. The Indians could not understand it and considered it a terrible affront to their sense of diplomacy. Second, it should have been a matter of great concern that the Ottawa chief, Pontiac, played no recorded role in the negotiations.[5] Both the policy change and the ominous absence or silence of Pontiac would have extremely important and immediate consequences.

Across the sea, a fledgling but ambitious British monarch contemplated his transatlantic possessions to determine just how they could best pay their own way and contribute to the Hanoverian power base. The French were beaten but not yet completely out of the game. Though whipped at Quebec and Montreal and so at least for the moment out of power in North America, they were still at war with Britain in Europe—called the Seven Years' War, it would cost the French an empire and gain one for the British—and so could possibly win back a staggering amount here by winning there. And the Indians, especially those of the northwestern interior who still remembered their generations of friendship with the French, began to perceive that their treatment at the hands of the English was going to be different from what they had grown to expect from Europeans.

The French—*interpreteurs, coureurs, de bois, voyageurs,* and *habitants* alike—treated as the Indians coequals; they shared food, shelter, hardships, the trade—and squaws, with whom they interbred. From the viewpoint of the French feudal hierarchy, the men of the North American woods, both native and European, were but licensees, functionaries to be indulged like children as long as they performed to the benefit of the economic system into which they fed. They were to be protected, patronized, and left alone to pursue their own ways; gifts were freely exchanged. The French did not intrude, by establishing colonies in the interior and encouraging them to grow; they *shared*. Furthermore, the Indians did not understand land ownership, so feudal vassalage, by which they were workers coequal with the European woodsmen feeding the pleasure of a benevolent Father across the sea who in return sent trade goods that improved their lives, was appealing. It implied no irritating responsibilities to counterbalance the benefits of the trade. Thus French policy from the viewpoint of the Indians was not only comfortable, it was *natural.* What was unnatural and confusing was that the French Father should turn tail and bestow these lands, which he could not "own" in the first place in order to make such a bequest, upon the English Father, who similarly could no more possess all of this (as he could a hatchet or a gun or a woman) than the other fellow.[6] And neither of them ever showed up to look or act much like an owner anyway.

But the British, after their seventeenth-century civil war, armed with mercantilism, constitutional rights, civil liberties, and parliamentary balanced common law—based on the laws of *ownership* exclusive of the pleasure of the throne—acted very much like owners: of the land, of the trade, and of the native. The Indians no longer had any perceptible rights, conceived as prerogatives; they had the responsibilities of coequalization. In fact they had no perceptible choices. They must now take what the English had for them or do without. If they transgressed, they would be punished according to the dictates of English law; if they trespassed, even where they had always been welcome before—even on the land to which they were born—they must be treated as trespassers. These fundamental differences between French and British attitudes and their resultant policies came quickly to the Indians' attention. They were now expected to behave themselves in civilized fashion or be punished for breach of etiquette. It was all a bit much and a bit sudden.

Thus in 1762, though the French had surrendered to the English in North America and the English had occupied all their outposts in the interior and taken over the fur trade by running the Frenchmen out, still England could not declare victory because the war continued in Europe. Though France had withdrawn her military personnel and given over her strategic points of control, she still entertained at least a glimmer of hope that she might get it all back by prevailing in the European conflict. In the meantime, the Indians were confused, alarmed, and not very happy with the attitudes and evolving policies of their new British overlords.

A part of this was the English habit and policy of colonization (so self-evidently successful along the Atlantic coast) at the expense of Indian sovereignty. Where the French had practiced cohabitation and restricted colonial development to the St. Lawrence, where they controlled immigration and so restricted their population (which amounted to a major problem for them when faced with a swarm of angry British colonials with a population of more than one million), there were already alarming reports of settlers penetrating western Pennsylvania, Kentucky, and Tennessee,[7] though official policy forbade settlement west of the Alleghenies (perhaps as much out of fear of as out of deference to the Indians). The English had cunningly used their alliance with the Iroquois when it was necessary to compete with the French, but now England viewed such alliances as no longer necessary and barely tolerated the Indians, driving them away from their homes and managing them like livestock to be husbanded.

And yet the Indian was dependent on the white European for his imported goods in trade, which by now included almost all the items on which he pegged his very survival: guns, powder, ammunition, traps, knives, and hatchets. With the French out of the way, the English now enjoyed a very real trading monopoly (though in a market different from that created and controlled by the French), which they approached as good fortune and the proper spoils of war, to be managed prudently and to maximum benefit as a practical asset. In the process, perhaps ironically, the Englishman treated the Indian according to his own proper though rigid set of rules as an equal: what was bought or fairly won (even land) was owned; an agreement once struck became a legally enforceable contract; law mediated dealings among gentlemen, and the Indian was expected to behave as a gentleman as surely as was the Englishman. The Indian could not understand all this and it is no wonder that the remnant French, whom the English permitted to stay on (yet another example of good British manners), sought to take advantage of the resultant confusion in the only way left open to them: the Great French Father, it was said, was only sleeping, allowing the British Father a momentary place in the sun. Perhaps his Indian children could help him regain his holdings and so restore the old balance which had proved so comfortable for the Indians.[8]

This is the background of "Pontiac's Conspiracy" (1763–64), the worst, or possibly the very best, Indian uprising in the history of the Northwest. Before it was over, dulled by the news of the Parisian peace accords later in 1763 and of resultant French impotence in the interior, all British installations in the territory except Forts Niagara, Pitt, and Detroit would fall, and Detroit barely labored on, cut off and besieged for 153 days, the longest siege in the history of American Indian warfare.[9] Apparently during the summer of 1762 there had been a solemn and secret council of war at the Ottawa village on the banks of the Detroit River that was attended by representatives of the Hurons, Potawatomies, and Saulteur Chippewas. The Chippewas brought with them two Frenchmen disguised as Indians and the talk was all of a massive and coordinated attack on the British forts in the interior. This was Pontiac's answer to the council called by Sir William Johnson and George Croghan the previous September. It was a planning session, but an important one; from it were dispatched runners to the tribes in the south camped in the Ohio and Wabash River valleys, hoping to enlist their support. Wampum belts calling for war passed back and forth among the tribes and thus the conspiracy was hatched. This was the *actual* welcome the Indians had for the British in the Great Lakes.

It is not necessary here to retell the stories of the capture or siege of the Michigan forts. At St. Joseph and Michilimackinac the Indians performed brilliantly and the forts fell instantly; at Detroit Maj. Henry Gladwin performed well, holding his installation until relief arrived in August of 1764. Alexander Henry left behind a fine first-person account of the attack and massacre at Michilimackinac, and Silas Farmer preserves good accounts of the fall of the southern forts. Both are graphic in recounting the Indians' atrocities in the name of war.[10] Even though Detroit never fell, Pontiac accomplished pretty much what he had set out to accomplish; the British were penned in and powerless, able to sustain themselves only because they had two lightly armed supply ships at their disposal and thus a means of receiving provisions routed through Fort Niagara. The failure in 1763 was all French and that failure crippled Pontiac's cause. For the French were beaten in Europe and capitulated in Paris in that year; never again did they have serious pretenses in North America. Word of the Parisian treaty reached Detroit in October of 1763 from the French commander on the Mississippi; he could offer no help. With this news, considering that the garrison at Detroit remained supplied, though he remained in control and was not personally brought to terms of peace until 1765, Pontiac's uprising was over. The French capitulation at Paris meant no less to the Indians than the loss of all their choices; they had become totally dependent on European goods in trade for both their welfare and their wars and now their French ally and trading partner was surely gone. If they were going to get what they needed to survive, they would have to get it from the British.

Though they were no longer very much at war, running low on ammunition and other supplies (of which, in the current situation, they had no source of supply), and many had scattered for their winter hunt as preference to siege and starvation, the Indians at Detroit had not been brought to peace; Detroit was still at risk and the other Great Lakes forts were still in hostile hands. Thus Gen. Thomas Gage, British commander in North America, determined to carry the war to the Indians and end it once and for all with a proper treaty of peace. He organized two armies, one to proceed via Fort Pitt to the Ohio River Valley and thence northward to the lakes; the other, under Col. John Bradstreet, was ordered to travel via Lakes Ontario and Erie direct to Detroit and thence against the tribes who still held the northern and western forts. Bradstreet's force comprised more than twelve hundred regulars, together with as many as four hundred Indians of various persuasions—the first to acknowledge and accept the new British supremacy—in loose escort. Bradstreet reached Detroit on August 26, 1764, bringing food, supplies, and clothing to a grand celebration; a garrison and its surrounding community that had been confined and threatened for some fifteen months was finally relieved. Even more important, Bradstreet's army was the largest and most impressive military force yet seen in the Northwest; he did not meet significant resistance (it may well be that not a shot was fired), but in him the British said loud and clear that they meant business.

The French failure cut the Indians off from any possible alternative source of supply with which to press their insurrection—or just sustain themselves in the woods to reenter the trade with a new partner. The British would now occupy and hold the positions on the lakes they considered important for managing their vast new asset and by now had a modest fleet of ships in place, virtually impregnable to the Indian canoe, with which to supply them. The display of raw power represented in Bradstreet's arrival at Detroit could not have been better contrived; the Indians were so overwhelmed that they never again seriously resisted British dominion. The tribes near Detroit, joined by delegations from the farther north and west, immediately sued for peace. The peace was concluded at a council held on September 7, on the day after which Bradstreet, now commanding the lakes from Detroit, sent a force of three hundred north commanded by Capt. William Howard with orders to reoccupy Fort Michilimackinac, which occurred without awkward incident. The British never reestablished garrisons at either Sault Ste. Marie or Fort St. Joseph; Fort Michilimackinac was now undisputed mistress of the upper Lakes.

It is nowhere clear that the British wanted the ownership of or responsibility for the vast interior territory of the Great Lakes. It was perfectly typical of the mid-1700's that France and England were more or less perpetually at war. Though an uneasy peace between the neighboring powers prevailed from 1713 until 1744, it held because of a curious combination of circumstances all of which would come together to underscore the fundamental differences that would have the two soon at war again, first in a sort of preliminary sparring match, then again in deadly earnest. Perhaps because she was laboring through the uncommon circumstance of back-to-back absentee and incompetent monarchs (the first two Hanoverian Georges), England was both progressive and prosperous. She was Protestant and mercantilistic; her citizens enjoyed chartered rights as opposed to rights derived from the throne; she had achieved the parliamentary compromise and evolved the ministerial system; though the one occasionally intruded on the other, church and state were generally and fastidiously separate. She had severed her ties with the feudal past and stumbled her way toward a future based on individual ownership and freedoms based on individual rights. France, though for the moment prosperous enough, was politically, socially, and economically regressive. That is to say, she was still both Bourbon and Roman Catholic—essentially and importantly feudal. Citizens' rights, of ownership as well as behavioral freedom, derived from the throne; church and state were hopelessly intertwined and their joint power was unchecked. She was still wrapped up in her medieval past. Her institutions, political, social, and economic, would self destruct in the Revolution with which the century wound itself down. The contrast between the two international neighbors in policy and principle could not have been more clear; it reflected in their North American affairs and strongly suggested yet another clash. They just did not like each other very much for some very silly and very human reasons.

The warm-up session was called King George's War in North America and the War of the Austrian Succession (1744–48) in Europe. This was principally a war of alliance, France with Prussia and England with Austria, and not one of great importance except that it pitted France and England once again against each other and thus preluded the next and vastly more important conflict—certainly from the North American point of view. Though England and France remained more or less officially at peace until 1756, hostilities broke out here in 1754. In Europe the French and Indian War was called the Seven Years' War; when it was over (not until the Parisian peace accords of 1763), by winning overwhelming victories both here and on the other side of the Atlantic, England suddenly attained empire while France lost it; she retreated in shambles, her overseas possessions stripped from her and her institutions crumbling, as though to prepare for her own revolution and Napoléon's last futile attempt to achieve empire and restore her to her former prestige.

Though the last and vastly important chapters of the story of this conflict were written at Paris, other factors than European ones had long been drawing the French and English closer to contest in North America. As long as the French stuck close to the St. Lawrence and the English remained on the coastal side of the eastern mountains—and they all minded their own business—there was neither need for nor probability of conflict. But, as early as 1609, just two years after the founding of the Jamestown colony, James I granted to the London Company a charter for Virginia including "all that Space and Circuit of Land, lying from the Sea Coast of the Precinct aforesaid, up into the Land, throughout from Sea to Sea, West and Northwest."[11] This description and land claim is certainly vague, probably intentionally so (for no one at the time had the foggiest notion of where the western sea might be, or even what was behind the mountains, other than the Iroquois), and of no importance in its century. As a practical matter few coastal colonists ventured far to the west of their seaside interests, discouraged by general policy from intruding on the Indian interior, as well as by the mountains and the Indians themselves. King James dissolved the London Company in 1624 and assumed the land claim for the Crown. No one seems to have paid much attention to this, or to the fact that subsequent charters granted to Connecticut and Massachusetts also included the convenient coast-to-coast feature. The English claim to the continent was by right of colonization, a preliminary attempt at organizing the new land, and the English king neglected to consult with the French and Spanish ones when he drew up his New World charters. Through the seventeenth and early eighteenth centuries such claims had little political and almost no practical value; no one wanted to go out there anyway—and the vastness of the continent was only beginning to be perceived, without a hint of an idea as to what anyone would want with it all. In the meantime the French quite early claimed the interior of the continent by right of discovery and exploration from their Laurentian bases, and at the Pageant of the Sault (1671) claimed "everything west of the Great Lakes and south along the Ohio and Mississippi River valleys all the way to the Gulf of Mexico. It was inevitable that one day someone would notice that the claimed interests of the two nations were in conflict."[12]

It all took a while to develop, but in the mid-eighteenth century this is exactly what happened. The British coastal colonials, now prosperous, increasingly adventurous, exceedingly numerous, and armed with their colonial charters, began to look inland, especially at the verdant Ohio River Valley with its rich soils, pleasant climate, and easy access to the Mississippi and the Mexican Gulf. Their mood was ripe for speculation. Already investors were looking west for profit in lands, and traders were ready to try to gain access to the riches of the interior fur trade, now approaching via interior routes from their coastal base rather than from the difficult perspective of Hudson Bay. By 1744–45 the traders had penetrated as far as the southern lakes, and the Pennsylvania Irishman George Croghan was operating trading posts in the upper Ohio River Valley from which he sent trading expeditions to the west. He also constructed a palisaded fort at the Miami village of Pickawillany (near what is now Piqua, Ohio) and lured the chieftains of several tribes of the Ohio Valley to the site of Logstown, Pennsylvania, where they signed a treaty aligning themselves with Britain rather than France. At about the same time a group of Virginians, calling themselves the Ohio Company and encouraged by their governor and the claims of the Virginia colonial charter, obtained a huge land grant along the Ohio River.

This all was not contrived to please the French, who well remembered their claims to the same territory and, as impracticable as military occupation, supply, and defense might be from their Laurentian bases, were not yet prepared to give over their claims by right of discovery and exploration. They countered in two ways. First, in 1749 they sent a military expedition down the Ohio, not to lay siege to Fort Pickawillany (which would have been almost impossible without a supply train coming all the way from the St. Lawrence), but to place lead plates proclaiming the river as French territory, thus introducing a physical presence and palpable claim. Second, they decided to shore up their position in the north by fortifying Sault Ste. Marie, which position had been largely neglected since the Pageant of the Sault and where they now intended to block any British approach from the north. To this end, following the precedents already set along the St. Lawrence and at Detroit, Governor la Jonquière of New France granted a seigneury—a landed estate bordering on the St. Marys River—to Louis le Gardeur de Repentigny, who there erected a stockade and installed Jean-Baptiste Cadotte and his Indian wife as tenants. Of far greater importance, however, was the arrival in New France in 1752 of a new, able, and strong governor, the Marquis Duquesne, who broke the recent succession of dull-witted, impotent, and largely incompetent administrators in that office. His mission was to strengthen New France against the threat of English infiltration.

Duquesne quickly perceived the disadvantage: though his strategically located garrisons on the Lakes commanded the main water routes and assured his control there, he lacked both developed outposts in the area to the south of them that was to be contested and trained personnel and supply routes with which to secure it. He therefore tore a page from Champlain's commonplace book of tried and successful policy and went to work shoring up the old Indian alliances in the hope of getting someone else to do some fighting for him while he recruited, trained, and organized. He thus in 1752 dispatched the successful half-breed trader Charles Langlade to Detroit with orders to recruit Indians there (principally Ottawa) and attack Croghan's fort at Pickawillany. The campaign was a success; the fort was destroyed and the local Miami chief, who had led the Indians over to the British side, was killed, boiled, and eaten by the Ottawa. The Indians were impressed and many of the southern tribes, including the defected Miamis and Hurons, returned to their old French allegiance. In the earliest years of the French presence in North America Champlain had learned the important diplomatic lesson of how to encourage the Indians and so keep them properly at war with one another; in siding with the Algonquians in their ancestral hatred of the Iroquois he sustained his trading alliance with his near neighbors and insured the flow of furs down the Ottawa River route. Now again the French sought tactical Indian help to commence the flanking engagement by which they would assert their claim to the Ohio Valley and so an interior route down the Mississippi. The waters were the highways and the highways were the means to trade. The diplomacy involved in manipulating the Indians would not be lost on the British. The Indian would prove an all too willing pawn in Europeans' wars.

The successful razing of Croghan's fort gave the French a momentary advantage on the Ohio frontier and in the next year Duquesne followed up and made clear his strategy of establishing a strong military presence in the area to the south of the Great Lakes. He was headed for the important junction of the Allegheny and the Monongahela rivers, which forms the Ohio (at what is now Pittsburgh), from which point he reasoned he could command the entire Ohio River route to the Mississippi and rebuff any invasion from the coastal colonies or from the south and west. He moved up the lakes and constructed his access outpost, which he called Fort Presque Isle, near the present site of Erie, Pennsylvania; just to the south and west, guarding the southern end of the portage to French Creek, he built Fort Le Boeuf; south of that, on French Creek at a point from which he had a clear float to the Allegheny, he built Fort Venango (near the present village of Venango, Pennsylvania). These preliminary installations secured a supply route from the lakes into the river system of the disputed territory by which the French could hope to sustain a military effort within the territory itself. Down this supply route in 1754 Duquesne sent a force of about five hundred with orders to build the fort at the junction of the Allegheny and the Monongahela.

The French regarded Duquesne's maneuver as a brilliant defense of their territory claimed by right of exploration and were determined to hold the advantage it gained for them. The English regarded the building of the new French forts on the western frontier as an act of intolerable hostility—an intrusion on their chartered territory—that called for a decisive counter. Gov. Robert Dinwiddie of Virginia, championing his colony's charter claims to the Ohio Valley, thus sent out a young surveyor, George Washington, on a European style diplomatic (and, undoubtedly, espionage) mission; he was to meet with the French, remind them of Virginia's claim, see firsthand what they were about, and ask them to withdraw peacefully. The French received Washington cordially enough, but declined his invitation to withdraw. Washington reported to Governor Dinwiddie, Dinwiddie decided that Virginia should try her hand at fort building also—and the brief race for the Ohio was on. Washington was sent back to the frontier with a company of Virginia militia and orders to establish himself at the junction of the Allegheny and the Monongahela and was there surprised by a large flotilla of French canoes (the force of five hundred sent to build what they called Fort Duquesne). In short, Washington was beaten to the river junction by a vastly superior force, put up a temporary entrenchment to the north and east of the French location, which he called Fort Necessity, and was there soon and soundly thrashed. He capitulated and was permitted to withdraw with the stipulation that Virginia was to abandon her plans for the Ohio Valley. Duquesne had now achieved a considerable advantage on the western frontier.[13]

Unfortunately for the French—and their Indian allies—larger issues and broader tactics than the control of the Ohio River Valley would decide the North American portion of the Seven Years' War. At first, Duquesne's rush to the western frontier looked like a brilliant coup, and so it might have been if that were destined to be the major theater of action in a simple war of territorial dispute. But that was not to be the case. Once war was declared in Europe (1756) Britain was bent on crushing France and her institutions in Europe and in North America and that would leave the dispute over the Ohio River territory with which the war in North America began as a distinctly secondary issue and a diversion from the main order of business. This main order of business would do in the old alliance of the French and the Indians and leave the Indians, who could not understand it, wholly dependent on a new and more businesslike sovereign, who was not even sure he wanted the responsibility of them.

A sustained infantry engagement on the western frontier would have been exceedingly difficult for both sides; even though the French had a fortified supply route in place and the British had no military problem in accessing the area, both sides faced the perplexing problem of moving the men, machines, and materials of war over long and difficult miles—in the one case largely by canoe and portage and in the other by crossing the eastern mountains. A war fought in western Pennsylvania, then, or even extending to the French positions in the northern Great Lakes, though possible was by no means probable. The improbability of it is evident in Gen. Edward Braddock's single campaign into the west, where he was ignominiously defeated (and killed) by an inferior French force.[14] Thus for a few years (1754-57) the war went poorly for the British, or so it seemed. The French military in North America, organized and led by the cunning Marquis de Montcalm, performed very well indeed.

But in 1757 the tide began to turn. A new ministry came to power in London, headed by the vigorous and intelligent William Pitt, who perceived both the value of the North American colonies and the vulnerability of the French, even with their fortified claim to the Ohio Valley and their solid positions throughout the lakes. By now England and her allies were at war with France and her allies on the European continent; Pitt thus sent substantial subsidies to his new ally, Frederick the Great of Prussia, with which to finance a sustained campaign the essential ingredient of which was to keep the French armies, attentions, and finances fully occupied in Europe.

Pitt reasoned that with the help of the Prussians he could hold the European French at bay, whip the North American French, and then turn his full attention to the European theater of war and there prevail. At the same time, recognizing the global value of it and also the tremendous stakes for which he was playing around the world, Pitt injected massive new strength into the Royal Navy in the form of new ships, new capital, and new personnel. He rid his military of a generation of incompetent officers (the likes of Braddock and the "pompous windbag" Earl of Loudon, who had so disgraced the service in North America), who had risen in the ranks through purchased commissions, seniority, and social connections, and put in their place sparkling, well-trained commanders of a new military generation: Col. Jeffrey Amherst, Gen. James Wolfe, and Gen. John Forbes. In short order these men won North America.

They came in with proper backing and a plan that would work. In 1758 the reinvigorated Royal Navy blockaded the mouth of the Laurentian Gulf and captured the French access fort there at Louisburg on Cape Breton Island. At about the same time another British force moved up the St. Lawrence, bypassing Quebec and Montreal, and laid siege to and won Fort Frontenac at the east end of Lake Ontario by the head of the St. Lawrence. France was thus tied up in Europe and her Laurentian colonies had their supply lines cut both to and from the Great Lakes and to and from Europe. In the same year General Forbes led an overland expedition that captured Fort Duquesne, which he rechristened Fort Pitt, after the ascendant prime minister. In 1759 forces led by Lord Amherst captured Forts Crown Point and Ticonderoga (in proximity, in the district of southern Lake Champlain), and also Fort Niagara. The back of New France was broken. She was cut off from Europe and her interior posts; her strings of forts south of the St. Lawrence and the Lakes were cut; she had been dramatically outmaneuvered and was drastically outnumbered—more than fifteen to one, by population count in North America. Little was left but the fall of Quebec to General Wolfe (September 17, 1759) after the most celebrated battle of the war, on the Plains of Abraham, in which both Wolfe and Montcalm lost their lives.

The French were still not without hope. The British held Quebec but were iced in, starving, and later under siege by the Chevalier de Lévis, Montcalm's successor. The French held on at Montreal and Detroit, sapped but ready to make a stand. But ice goes out in the spring and when it did so in the St. Lawrence in the spring of 1760 the British fleet, with men, munitions, and supplies, sailed in. The remnant English force had held out against Lévis, the Indian allies had dispersed, and the French had no choice but to retreat to Montreal, where three English armies converged in September. On the eighth day of that month, Lévis and his men laid down their arms and the Marquis de Vaudreuil, the last governor of New France, surrendered all French possessions in North America except New Orleans to the English.[15]

What had begun in 1754 as a squabble over some Ohio Valley territory escalated by 1756 into a contest for global empire, which the British achieved (reluctantly, one should remember) in Paris in 1763. British strategy through the latter years of the Seven Years' War was to trounce the French, to be sure; to what end remains more obscure, though it almost certainly had more to do with the war in Europe, where the French were a threat at home, than the one in North America. On this side of the Atlantic the ministers surely saw value in their colonies, now developing in their seventh generation or more into trading partners, and also perceived the colonists as coequal British citizens whose further development was being threatened as surely as were their charter rights. They did not wish to alienate their own citizens, nor did they want the American British to raise an army and so move toward independence when there was already a perfectly good professional military. Clearly, it was expedient to enter and win the contest in North America.

The difficulty was that the tactics of the winning strategy would have to involve, as the spoils of war according to the rules of engagement as they were then understood, the immense territory of the entire eastern half of North America. And it was not territory that they wanted, except groups of speculators like those in the Ohio Company; there was much private interest in the furs that could be brought out of it, but the vast land itself as yet had no value for settlement or other development. It was too far removed from the coast to contribute to the national trading venture and loaded with problems (such as Indians) and potential administrative costs (such as garrisons and forts to be maintained to secure the territory, protect settlers who might go out there, and encourage the fur trade). Someone would have to pay the costs of this administration. The coastal colonials didn't want to, any more than they wanted the cost of raising and maintaining an army when there was already one, and neither did the citizens at home. More terriroty than what was wanted for agriculture and developing trade along the coast was simply superfluous and exceedingly expensive according to the British system of managing things—and aboriginal peoples. Thus it is no surprise to find that during the negotiations preliminary to the Paris Treaty of 1763 a lively debate sprang up in Parliament as to whether England should demand of France her North American possessions or her West Indian islands, Guadeloupe and Martinique—producers of sugar. All of eastern North America was thus valued about the same as two modest tropical islands.[16]

The decision to take North America was in deference to the citizen-colonists already established along the Atlantic Coast; the next problem was what to do with it and how to manage it. Pontiac's uprising came on the heels of the Paris Treaty, which was signed in February, though it took until July for the news of it to reach Detroit, and called for immediate policy-making decisions. The English were already at work forming some general Indian policy, aware of the need they had encountered for dealing with the savages during the recent war. As early as 1758, to secure the help of several of the Iroquois nations, at the Treaty of Easton the English had pledged to reserve the region west of the Alleghenies for the tribes. The news of the 1763 uprising reminded the British of their promises and of the immense tactical difficulties they faced trying to manage the interior. Detroit and Michilimackinac were examples: in each a military minority was the only vestige of authority, vastly outnumbered by an indifferent (at best) French population and many unhappy and unfriendly Indians. The English desperately needed time to get into better position to secure and control the new territory. That is why Gladwin's efforts at Detroit earned him a hero's welcome at home and why General Gage sent the two large armies west. He could not afford again to indulge the vulnerability he discovered at his western outposts.

The man entrusted to formulate policy for the preliminary governance of British North America was the Earl of Shelburne, president of the Board of Trade (which suggests something of the value the ministers placed on the American colonies), industrious member of Parliament, and protégé of Gen. James Wolfe (who had perished at Quebec in 1759). In June he proposed the policy that was adopted and announced in October and thereafter known as the Proclamation of 1763. Before this date, despite the provisions of the Treaty of Easton (1758), attitudes, fears, and largely unofficial mandates pro tem governed British Indian policy in the colonies. It just did not make much sense for anyone to worry about what was going on on the other side of the eastern mountains or to make any fuss about going there in any fashion that would upset the Indians anyway. Just like the early French *interpreteurs,* and then the Jesuits and then the early military personnel, Croghan could set up his trading posts, and even a fort, at his own risk and without upsetting anyone (except the French). The proclamation was thus the first official implementation of British policy vis-à-vis the Indians (and also the French population) to be enacted in the Northwest. Word of it undoubtedly reached Detroit with Colonel Bradstreet and Sir William Johnson in 1764 and its provisions represent the first British attempt to bring law and civil organization to the newest citizens of the empire. The proclamation provided:

(1) The Colony of Quebec was created from the Atlantic Ocean up the St. Lawrence to the Ottawa River. A governor and a council were to be appointed by the king, and an elected assembly was promised in the future. English law was to be introduced, and English courts were to be established. The question of religion was ignored. (2) To protect the Indians from the intrusion of settlers, a line was drawn across the crest of the Appalachian Mountains beyond which, for the present, settlers were forbidden to go. (3) Trade and other relations with the Indians were to be carried on through superintendents responsible to the Crown rather than by agents of the colonies.[17]

The proclamation ended up as the constitution of Quebec until 1774 and accounts for the continuation of military rule in the Northwest, for no alternative was provided. Save for the provisions intending to protect the Indians, all the interior to the west of the new Colony of Quebec was left a no-man's-and temporarily without law, civil organization, or recognized authority other than the military one and the Indian superintendents. The idea seems clear that the British intended to develop their new posts in the interior solely under military supervision at least until the

populations increased and stabilized to the point at which other forms of government might become practicable—or necessary. Shelburne's program was extremely well intended as an interim measure for both the Indian and the European occupants
of the interior; by it he would preserve the status quo (often a good idea while possible changes are contemplated), protect the Indians from any immediate incursion
of settlers from the east (such as the ill-fated Ohio Company represented—and not
to mention protecting prospective settlers from the wrath of the Indians), and provide for an evolving system of law and government, even self-government, for the
colonies already in place along the St. Lawrence, all according to the fairest and
most proper British scheme of things.

The But the English understood imperfectly the new subjects they so proposed to
govern. The Indian cared little to be treated fairly according to the dictates of a market he could little understand; he wanted the patronage that only a benevolent feudal monarch bearing gifts could give. The same was true of both the French Canadians
and, for different reasons, the English colonists on the Atlantic seaboard. The French
Canadians liked things as they had been; they were secure and happy in being looked
after by the feudal coalition of church and state, mistrusted an unfamiliar legal system, and feared the proclamation's ominous silence on their religion as presaging
either religious suppression or a perhaps equally unwelcome tolerance: they wanted no Huguenots to threaten the purity of bloodline in Canada. They did not like
the idea of allegiance to a foreign crown, especially one that willingly shared its
power with an unfamiliar representative Parliament, and had no desire for an elected assembly, even if that might be a "fair" and "proper" idea. They were used to
having government done for (or even to) them. To the English colonists along the
Atlantic, the proclamation was anathema because it restricted western settlement;
there were by now prominent land speculators who, under the original colonial charters, were anxious to profit from investment in lands to the west. This they were
denied, as they saw it, for the sole benefit of a handful of quarrelsome Indians; their
charter rights as British subjects were being illegally preempted. The several thousand inhabitants of the west were simply ignored by the proclamation. The extension of unchecked military authority was perfectly palatable to the garrisoned military
personnel, the French *habitants,* and, for that matter, the Indians. But the English
traders, artisans, and other ancillaries who began arriving at the western outposts
wanted civil law; as surely as the coastal colonials felt denied their charter rights as
born citizens, so those of the interior felt disfranchised from the due process that
was similarly a birthright. Thus the best-intended preliminary program of government pleased almost none of those whom it proposed to govern.

The trick is that Shelburne conceived his program as a temporary one, whose
principal intent was to appease the hostile Indians and buy the time necessary to get
in place for managing them effectively.[18] This implied the need for an expanding
military presence in the west to promote and protect development near the outposts.
Shelburne viewed the west as a prime area due for expansion and colonization, and

his proclamation gave the first step for its development. At least in his person the British "appear to have contemplated a gradual and orderly acquisition of Indian lands through purchase by imperial agents."[19] This aspect of his plan for the west, however, seems to have been activated only in 1781, when Maj. Patrick Sinclair negotiated a deed and purchased Mackinac Island from the Indians before moving his fort there from the southern mainland.

But the fortunes of politics being what they are, though his program was happily accepted, Shelburne was removed from office in favor of Lord Hillsborough even before the proclamation was announced. Hillsborough was influenced by Sir William Johnson (first Indian agent to the Northwest, as noted above), and Johnson adopted a protectionist attitude toward the Indians—and viewed Shelburne's temporary policy as the means to such protection as well as to developing the fur trade according to his own devices. His idea followed the old French model; he would protect the Indians and preserve the vast interior for them, confining the trade to the posts and to licensed traders and so forcing the Indians to come in with their peltries. This policy created a storm of protest along the St. Lawrence, where the merchants feared that unregulated remnant French and Spanish traders could command a substantial portion of the trade if the British were confined to the posts. Capt. William Howard, at Michilimackinac, issued several permits to trade outside his post, for which he was criticized by both his superiors and those who did not get the permits.[20]

The worst problem with the Proclamation of 1763, which affected virtually everyone on this side of the Atlantic, was political instability in London. By 1767 Shelburne was back in office formulating a plan for three new colonies: one near Detroit, one in the Illinois country, and one along the Ohio River. His intention to acquire land and develop it in an orderly fashion could not have been more clear. But before he could take his plan to court he was again replaced by Hillsborough: "Hillsborough's plan was neither to follow a determined policy of imperial control nor to put the responsibility squarely on the colonies. The Indian agents were retained, but with reduced authority. The colonies were to pay the salaries of the lesser officials at the posts and were to supply presents for the Indians, a wholly impractical idea. No new colonies were to be authorized. The plan utterly failed to give the colonies any stake in the West, yet, for reasons of economy, it made imperial control ineffective."[21]

Still the Northwest was in limbo. The land, though squarely won (by the standards of the time) by right of military victory and international treaty, though already included in the charters of three colonies, remained closed to development; the coastal colonists were beginning to feel the pinch of having to pay for the administration of what they could not use or even have access to, which realized their worst fears from the beginning. The Indians had no advocate among their new masters and thus no help in adjusting to dramatically changed circumstances in their lives.

Thus indecision at home led from one mistake to another. What had been conceived as interim policy prevailed in the long run and offended nearly everyone directly affected by it, and one must suspect that Hillsborough's bungled compro-

mise was at least partly intended to check the growing power of George III in that
the Indian agents, originally agents of the Crown, already enjoyed reduced and confused status, which did nothing to stabilize or placate the Indians. The Quebec
Canadians were disaffected and frustrated, the colonials on the Atlantic were restless and angry at what they considered the nullification of their chartered rights, the
Indians were left to fend for themselves in a market they could not understand, and
the European residents of the interior had neither law nor rights nor liberties, save
at the pleasure of a military command they did not much care for.

The French and Indian War represented the first substantial commitment of energy and money to the English colonial claims in North America; before, the British
colonials on this continent had been left to their own devices. Under a policy of
benign neglect they had prospered and come to enjoy the prospect of self-determination. The French possession, similarly, had been left pretty much to itself and its
peculiar brand of political and economic management. But the war changed all that.
It had been expensive: the English national debt had more than doubled, and then
the cost of mustering armies to put down the Indian uprisings and maintaining garrisons to administrate and insure stability added substantially to the national commitment. The British had not been certain that they wanted what they then won and
now the prize was costing dearly. Somehow, from most any practical point of view,
the investment had to start defraying its own costs—if not indeed paying for itself.

The issues had little to do with the Atlantic coastal colonials, where politically,
militarily, and economically matters were both stable and in hand. The overbearing
issue was the Northwest and the colony of Quebec, where the Indians were unruly,
the French population disgruntled, the English population crying out for orderly
civil process, and the military presence therefore essential. Colonial taxation was
seen as necessary to pay for all this; the unfortunate corollary was that the taxable
population lived in the organized colonies along the coast.

The British faced an extremely delicate situation: (1) economic sanity demanded that their transatlantic possession become quickly productive beyond the returns
possible from a fur trade not owned by the government (the proceeds of which went,
according to the British system, into private hands and thus gave only modest returns
from licenses and a tax base); (2) the great Indian territory of the interior was at best
an untested asset; (3) the taxable population of North America had virtually nothing to do with the costs of either the war or its aftermath in the Northwest and, as
published policy after the Proclamation of 1763, was specifically excluded from the
territory whose expenses it was going to be asked to pay; and (4) the French population throughout the continent was dissatisfied with British civil process and uneasy
over the mute issue of religious toleration. This was not the aftermath of the usual
European war, where boundaries could be redrawn and loyalties resettled according to civilized principles deriving from the rules of engagement and conquest. The
mere presence of the French feudals, who had only a slight sense of ownership,
common law, and consequent due process, and the Indian aborigines, who did not

understand it at all, was presenting an expensive problem indeed. Trying to balance it all would be difficult, if not desperate, and the British bungled it badly.

Concern over the French population was evidenced early. Not long after the 1763 Paris peace, rumors filtered from the west—from both the Illinois country (Fort Vincennes on the Wabash, together with Cahokia and Kaskaskia on the Mississippi) and the Great Lakes (Detroit and Michilimackinac were loaded with French loyalists)—of disorder, disloyalty, and discontent among the French citizenry. They did not want the British version of civil government and outnumbered the British population who did. As a result nothing was done to wind down the military regime.

General Gage considered and wrote an order (1n 1772) to deport the French from Vincennes, just as the British had earlier moved the French Acadians from Nova Scotia to Louisiana.[22] It is likely that this was to have been the first stage of a more general policy of removal. For it was Gage's idea and Hillsborough's policy to leave the Indians alone in their territory and encourage them to bring their peltries into the British forts, where the traders were located and the trade could be easily supervised—all of which, in concert with a policy restricting colonial development in the west, could be nicely managed under military rule. A report of the Lord Commissioners for Trade and Plantations at the time reads in part: "It does appear to us that the extension of the fur trade depends entirely upon the Indians being undisturbed in possession of their hunting ground, and that all colonizating [sic] does in its nature, and must in its consequences, operate to the prejudice of that branch of commerce. . . . Let the savages enjoy their deserts in quiet. Were they driven from their forests their peltry-trade would decrease."[23] But again political fortunes in London changed; Hillsborough was out of office, the Earl of Dartmouth was in, and the policy of deportation was abandoned in favor of a more conciliatory posture.

England's diplomatic and administrative problems were deeply rooted in economic ones; ownership, she discovered, requires regular maintenance and intelligent management, which imply annual costs. Enthusiasm at home for the costly, unruly, and Indian-ridden transatlantic territorywas never high, so any taxation to support it there would have been politically unwise, if possible at all. Parliament thus began casting about for a formula to govern colonial taxation that might prove both fair and tolerable to a colonial population that was neither used to nor disposed toward any taxation. Many different schemes were attempted, almost all quickly repealed. Strong opposition was inevitable and immediate from the British citizenry on this side of the Atlantic, and Parliament also encountered unanticipated difficulties: there was much sympathy among the counterpart subjects at home (who viewed any selective taxation as a dangerous and possibly capricious precedent); further, the mechanics of administering and enforcing an unwanted tax an ocean away proved all but imponderable. The British garrisons in the west meant little to the coastals except expense and trouble; the practical effects of them were to exclude the coastals from territory they considered theirs by charter right and to guard a licensed fur trade (from which they were similarly excluded), the profits from which went directly into the wallets of the London merchants. The last of the taxes to be repealed was the one on tea, which had occasioned the well-known celebration in Boston Harbor in December of 1773.

For all practical purposes the attempts at selective colonial taxation had failed, and Britain would have to find other ways to finance her administration of the Northwest. She next turned to achieving a political compromise designed to make her transatlantic subjects governable—and so possibly taxable in the future. In 1774 Parliament passed a series of four acts all designed to reduce the political power of the colonials so that English government could be set in place and, specifically, so that the port of Boston could be closed after the disrespect shown there. They were called (here) the Intolerable Acts precisely because their intent was repression, especially of the colonial assemblies, in favor of some home rule as yet imperfectly formulated. It was the beginning of a short-lived attempt to nationalize the colonies. Of even greater importance, however, in the same year Parliament passed a fifth act, called the Quebec Act, which was intended to appease the Canadian French, bring them into political alliance, and make them governable by giving them the government they wanted.

Briefly, the Quebec Act provided: "(1) that all the Indian country extending to the Ohio and the Mississippi rivers be annexed to the province of Quebec, and that a lieutenant-governor be stationed at each important post; (2) that English criminal law be continued in force, but that French civil law be re established, thus permitting the maintenance of the feudal system; (3) that an appointed legislative council be provided for Quebec instead of an elected assembly; and (4) that the Roman Catholic religion be protected."[24] The Canadian French, along with the other French inhabitants of the western interior, were delighted. Their political territory was vastly enlarged, they were given back both a legal and a political process that they could understand and be comfortable with, and, finally, their religion was secure. But in pleasing the North American French (a historically peculiar concession), the British implemented the only one of their acts to be addressed in the American Declaration of Independence.

From one limited point of view the Quebec Act was successful in that it kept the Canadian French loyal to the British when the American Revolution broke out. They were happy with its provisions and guarantees, especially that of religious toleration and protection; when the Continental Congress invited them to join the Revolution, they were suspicious of the political model of the English colonial-elected assemblies and feared the possibility of religious intolerance by the Puritan New Englanders. From a broader point of view, however, the act fired the worst fears of the English colonials. The Proclamation of 1763 had already extinguished in principle what they considered their charter rights in the west; the Quebec Act completed the disfranchisement in fact by annexing that whole territory to Quebec. The whole Northwest, substantial portions of which were claimed in the charters of three colonies, was arbitrarily taken by the same government that had granted the charters and given to the vanquished enemy. This seemed both unfair and unprecedented. Further, and nearly as important, in omitting an elected assembly for Quebec the English colonials saw a violation of the acceptable parliamentary process that was also their birthright as British subjects and a probable model of the form of government the English would try to force on them. In these regards the Quebec Act was firmly associated in the minds of the New Englanders with the other coercive acts of 1774 that they called "intolerable."

The resentment created by the combination of acts in 1774 was strong enough to drive the Virginians into league with the New Englanders and this most important element made the revolutionary success possible. What had been conceived by Shelburne in 1763 as an interim policy to lead into orderly administration, acquisition, and colonization in the Northwest ended up written as an indelible and bungled principle whose net effect was the thoughtless and unnecessary alienation of the coastal colonists whose interests were such that it should have protected and benefited them.

Perhaps the most interesting phase of the revolutionary war was fought out of Fort Detroit, with Fort Michilimackinac standing staunch as a back-up position removed from the action only by the accident of geography. She was considered tactically important, made ready, and even moved, but never engaged. The war just never quite came north. With the outbreak of hostilities England became more than casually interested in her western holdings; about the only immediate return on her investment there came through the fur trade, which the war occasionally hampered but never quite stopped,[25] but now entered the matter of pride. No upstart colonials in such a recently acquired land that had already cost so much should be permitted to unhorse John Bull; the colonies must be brought to their knees so that they might repay what they had already cost. Even a casual look at a map of North America tells the tale of the British tactic. The English were inextricably committed but found themselves in a position parallel to that of the French in 1759: either they had to trust an untested French Canadian ally—so recently an enemy—or rely on supply lines that had to cross an entire ocean. From a strategic point of view their situation was grave, perhaps desperate. They were badly outnumbered and, with the probability of a continental military force supplied by France (who could surely be counted on to side with the rebels as a means of getting back at England and so perhaps getting her foot back in the door of North America), first defending the coast and then sweeping into the west, possibly outpositioned.

Thus they tore yet one more page from Champlain's daybook and the French record of North American conquest. It was necessary to develop alliances already in place, to use personnel already available, and create a large and discomfiting diversion in the backyard while Britain's regular army and vastly superior navy went to work on the coast. In short, it was necessary to use the Indian in a protracted and carefully orchestrated (insofar as that might be possible) guerrilla operation in the rear. Yet once more the Indian was to play pawn to the European; yet once more he was to find himself on the losing side. Since 1763 the British policy toward the Indian had been one of protection, appeasement, and conciliation; on the American side one of the hottest issues was the right to settle in the west. Though still not entirely happy at being thrust into a new European trading market, and though he still preferred the memory of his old French friend, it was as inevitable that the Indian would come in on the British side of this conflict as it was that the French would cast their lot with the colonials.

The center of command for this guerrilla operation was Detroit, and the principal commander there was Lt. Gov. Henry Hamilton.[26] Hamilton arrived at his post from Montreal in November of 1775 and almost immediately found himself in the uncomfortable circumstances that would earn him the name "hair-buyer." Well before the outbreak of the Revolution and in violation of the Proclamation of 1763, certain Virginians, George Rogers Clark prominent among them, had infiltrated Kentucky and settled there. The Britisher had to consider this a clear violation of the law of the land he was sworn to uphold; the Indians considered it a flagrant violation of their ancestral territory. They therefore demanded of Hamilton arms, ammunition, and supplies for expeditions against the Kentucky settlers as well as bounties for the scalps they proposed to bring back.[27]

This was no longer a trading situation; it was one in which, whether they understood it or not, the Indians were entering into a military contract as mercenaries. Silas Farmer explains:

> The chief duties of the lieutenant-governor. . .consisted in distributing goods to the Indians, in order to induce them to make war on the "rebels," in fitting out the warriors and encouraging them to keep on the "war path." Nowhere was this work so diligently carried on as Detroit. Of all the posts west of Montreal and New York, at the time of the Revolution, this was the most important. It was not only a leading army center, but also the chief naval depot of the West.... It is almost impossible to realize the extent of English operations in this region during the progress of the war, and it is certain that no one location in the East was the field of so many and such varied manifestations of the strife as were exhibited here. The prominent feature in every scene during that period was scores of hundreds of painted savages, with uplifted tomahawks, scalping knives in their belts, and fusils, lead, and flints at hand. All the materials for war were supplied by their "white father," and all were to be used against the American rebels. Everything that could be done to attach the Indians to the service of the King was done in unstinted manner. They were coaxed with rum, feasted with oxen roasted whole, alarmed by threats of the destruction of their hunting ground, and supplied with everything that an Indian could desire."[28]

The Indians took their opportunity and had their way; in so doing they cemented a bond with the British that, like Pontiac and his troops in 1763, would keep them fighting long after the Parisian treaty of 1783 had ended hostilities. Once again the Indian had become someone else's willing backwoods guerrilla infantry.

The Revolution was neither won nor lost in the west, but it was certainly fought there and the grisly pattern of Britain's use of her newfound Indian ally was forged at Detroit. The effect of the Detroit-inspired Indian raids to the south was felt almost immediately, for George Rogers Clark seems quickly to have understood the source of the attacks on the Kentucky settlements. During the winter of 1777-78 he traveled to Virginia, conferred with Gov. Patrick Henry, and proposed raising an army to carry the war into the west. His plan was to attack the British-held posts in the Illinois country (Vincennes, Kaskaskia, and Cahokia) and, ultimately, attempt to capture Detroit— thereby sealing off supplies to the troublesome Indians and so quieting their depredations. By this time an alliance between the colonials and the French was assured, and Clark hoped that news of it would help him gain the backing of the remnant French habitants at these old French positions. Governor Henry acceded to the plan and offered some assistance, as well as the blessing of the eastern authorities.

By August of 1778 Clark had occupied the three positions in the Illinois country and was well in control there. Too, he won the respect of the Indians (now that they were very much troops engaged in war), who had come to admire the fighting abilities of his "Big Knives" and who, after all, liked his presents about as well as those given by the British. The Indians could see little practical difference between European British and North American ones anyway; they clearly came from the same culture and had the same royal "Father." It was just that the ones living along the Atlantic Coast now wanted to live in the Ohio River Valley as well, which was not a comfortable thought. Perhaps the two bunches of them would shoot at each other enough— with Indian help on his own side of the territory—that they would all go away, leaving the tribes to occupy their territory, bring in their peltries, and return the interior to the pervious norm.

When word of Clark's successes reached Detroit, Hamilton was alarmed, for it meant that the enemy, no matter what his strength might be (and it was not much), was strategically in position beneath him and thus his own position could become vulnerable to attack from that quarter by land. He determined to counter this threat and so gathered a force of Indians, militia, and regulars to strike a blow in reprisal, with which he left Detroit in October heading for Fort Sackville at Vincennes. Clark was spread too thin; Fort Sackville was lightly manned but not garrisoned, and Hamilton had an easy capture in mid December. The *habitants* renewed their allegiance to King George. Hamilton thought he was secure at least for the season, reasoning that the Americans would be unwilling to undertake an expedition of attack in midwinter. This, however, is exactly what Clark did, banking on the element of surprise that Hamilton so obligingly handed him. He descended the Mississippi and ascended the Ohio and the Wabash. The British were completely unaware of the attack until Clark's troops opened fire. The *habitants* were swayed right back and gave the Americans food and ammunition that they had squirreled away; the Kentucky riflemen were devastating, and Hamilton was forced to surrender on February 25, 1779.[29]

Clark's victory at Vincennes together with his general success in the Illinois country threatened the balance of power in the Northwest. He now held secure positions in which he could be reinforced and supplied from the east or the south and had demonstrated the fickleness of Indian and *habitant* alike. At least in the west, it began to look like the revolutionaries had a fighting chance—and both the Indian and the remnant Frenchman might want to come out on the winning side. Col. Arent Schuyler de Peyster, British commander and lieutenant governor at Michilimackinac, had left the north with a force of Indians and was making his way south along the western shore of Lake Michigan under orders from Detroit to join with Hamilton in his campaign against Clark when, near what is now Milwaukee, he received word of Hamilton's surrender. The Indians refused to go farther. About the same time, reports began dribbling in about Indian defections elsewhere; Clark's agents had been at least marginally successful among the Ottawas, Chippewas, Potawatomies, and Wyandots. Capt. Richard Lernoult, temporarily in command, witnessed some such declarations at a council held at Detroit in June of 1779 and answered them by strengthening his defenses and building what was later called Fort Lernoult behind the town. Clark's presence to the south was now a bona fide threat, especially in the light of the wavering Indian allegiance. Though the expected attack never came, Britain's ramparts on the lakes, and so her hold on the Northwest, could no longer be considered secure. And Governor Hamilton was in the hands of the enemy.

In 1779 Maj. Patrick Sinclair finally arrived at Michilimackinac to claim the lieutenant governor's position to which Gov. Guy Carleton had appointed him in 1774, and de Peyster was transferred to take military command at Detroit. The British, though now threatened from the south, still had unchallenged control of the old Ottawa River route to the northern Lakes and it was time to take further measures there. Should the threat from the south intensify, should a massive attack on Detroit take place, they could shift their command center in the interior to Michilimackinac, use the Ottawa River or Lake Simcoe routes or both into Georgian Bay for supplies and reinforcements, and direct all operations in the west from that location. In fact, Michilimackinac was a tactical headquarters for an unsuccessful assault expedition the British sent out against Cahokia and Spanish-held St. Louis in 1780. (Spain had joined in the North American fun in the previous year, if not on the side of the revolutionaries, decidedly against the British—and hoping for a larger stake in the territory in the war's aftermath.) To better accommodate this new tactical importance and to shore up against the possibility of a sweep up the lakes by Clark's troops in Illinois, Sinclair, in 1779, transferred his garrison from the mainland on the south side of the Straits to what we now call Mackinac Island and began to build a new and far more substantial fortification. Now the ramparts would be of stone, impervious to flaming arrow and ship-borne cannonball alike. Sinclair sent a ship to Detroit for cannon in the summer of 1780 and negotiated a deed for the island in the next year—for five thousand pounds, which can only be considered a handsome figure for wilderness at the time.[30] This negotiation, the first of its kind in the Northwest, sets a curious precedent for subsequent clearing of title to land in the territory. It is doubtful that they needed to, or were required to according to the understood rules of international relations at the time, but the British treated the Indians, already costly in their mercenary position, as a coequal foreign nation whose possession should be purchased in an orderly fashion. We can only construe the price, and the fact that the deed was negotiated at all, as fair, lacking any market. By the summer of 1781 the old Fort Michilimackinac on the south side of the Straits had been abandoned, disassembled—its usable timbers removed for use on the island—its remains burned, and the British were entrenched in their new and superior facility, ready to carry on.

CHAPTER FOUR

ARTICLES OF PEACE
PARIS (1783)

Unfortunately, the home office was not ready to carry on. In just a few months the British troops at Yorktown laid down their arms in capitulation, the government fell in London, and the new Parliament voted against prosecuting further wars in and about North America. The French had been successful in their naval campaign against the English in the West Indies (as well as in transporting Washington's troops to the siege of Yorktown), and in March of the following year peace negotiations opened in Paris. The peace was not confirmed and proclaimed by treaty until January of 1783, and sporadic hostilities involving the Indian mercenaries continued in the Northwest long after that. But the splendid new Fort Michilimackinac was essentially a cenotaph—an empty monument to tactics that would never be used in a war that was destined to be fought no further.

As the war had begun in economic controversy, so it ended on a note of economic despair, at least in Britain. And nowhere were the economics of the Revolution more clearly displayed than in the Northwest. Governing and administering North America proved extremely costly; the coastal colonials were ungovernable because of their already independent ways and both the Canadian French of Quebec and the inhabitants of the interior, native and European, were undependable. Further, the Indian mercenaries became exorbitantly expensive though absolutely essential allies, on top of the expense of maintaining and provisioning garrisons and entire settlements—Detroit, for instance.

At the beginning of it the Indians were willing to be protected and then cajoled into taking the British side of an argument they could hardly be expected to understand, beyond the fact that the colonial side represented settlers in Indian territory and consequent pressure on traditional hunting grounds. "They soon learned [however] how much depended on their action, and from asking a gift or accepting a favor, they demanded everything as their right. The expenses of the Indian Department grew so large that letter after letter came from General Haldimand [successor in wartime to Governor Carleton] complaining of the 'enormous' and 'amazing' expense of the goods for the Indians."[1] Now the Indians had discovered the proper uses of monopoly for themselves. Silas Farmer prints an almost incredible "Estimate of Merchandise Wanted for Indian Presents at Detroit from 21st of August, 1782, to 20th of August, 1783" prepared by de Peyster as commandant and estimates that "during the war several millions of dollars worth of goods for the Indians were distributed at Detroit"[2]—indeed an "enormous" and "amazing" calculation given the monetary values of the times and the modesty of actual Indian requirements. The British were beaten on the battlefields only in the east; they still held the west (and continued to command the lakes until 1796), but could hardly afford it. This was a clear case of good money after bad and, finally, financial good sense dictated that they try to recoup their losses elsewhere.

The American victory at Yorktown was mostly a symbolic affair; there was no simple military victory that ended the Revolution, set territorial lines, and determined spoils for the winner. After Yorktown matters just came to a standstill over here, while the negotiators hammered out the Articles of Peace at Paris. Instead, as had happened before and would happen again, the British chose to fight no longer because they lacked the will, the finances, and the national solidarity to pursue the matter. It is well to remember that a significant sector of the British population viewed the American colonists as English subjects whose constitutional rights were being tread on capriciously and who therefore had a grievance. The Americans had some exceedingly well-placed friends in England who wanted to restore good relations for trade as well as balancing out other international relationships. One of history's wonderful ironies is that at the end of the American revolutionary war Britain gave over a large population who were her subjects by birth and retained sovereignty over a smaller number of North American French nationals—who just happened to be a bit less fastidious about who governed them or how as long as the form of government was more or less familiar and their anti-Anglican religion was protected. But all of these were coastal concerns; the main economic problem that had brought on the war, the management of the Northwest, remained unsolved if it had even been addressed.

When the American negotiating team packed off for Paris in 1782 (Benjamin Franklin, John Adams, John Jay, and Henry Laurens most prominent among them), matters in the North American interior were far from settled. George Rogers Clark and his army were in place in the Illinois country and he had scored some surprising wins against a vastly superior military machine; but he was undermanned, undersupplied, probably (with the completion of the new Fort Michilimackinac) outpositioned at least in the long pull, and his hold on the west can be considered only tenuous at best. The British, in the meantime, still controlled the lakes and their traffic; substantial garrisons remained at Detroit, Michilimackinac, Niagara, and other northerly positions to the east. Thus, had England retained what she held at war's end, virtually all of what would become Michigan together with substantial portions of what are now Wisconsin and Minnesota, as far as the headwaters of the Mississippi, would have ended up British-Canadian. That this did not happen had little to do with Clark's victories in Illinois or the measured American military successes in the east; it devolved from the usual convolutions of European politics at the time.

Both France and Spain had joined the revolutionary fun over here, France on the side of the revolutionaries (through whom she might hope to regain a claim of some sort), Spain mostly for the sport of fighting against the British (all the old antipathies still alive) and to protect her claims in the far west; the British had to regard both as belligerents and concede that each had a stake in the settlement. Spain sustained her claim in the far west and so sought to extend her territories; in 1763 France had lost her entire North American claim and, having put herself on the line for the Americans, now wanted back into the game. Insofar as Britain was to be required to recognize American independence, there were now four players at the table; the United States was for the first time to be recognized as a national power negotiating on its own merits. Militarily in North America, Clark's installations at Cahokia and Kaskaskia held the Spanish at St. Louis in check and, together with Vincennes, at least technically counterbalanced the British control of the lakes while the French and the coastal colonials successfully held out against the British in the east. The negotiations to end the American Revolution thus involved the international European balance of power as much if not more than it did territory in North America; England was negotiating her stake in the New World against three adversary nations and had to make some sharp decisions to reach an acceptable compromise.

Both politically and diplomatically England was greatly disadvantaged in Europe. The sudden prospect of empire had spread her financial commitments and responsibilities around the world, but the first returns from this vast and ambitious enterprise had yet to come in (the tea in Boston, for instance, together with its tax, had been there in part to help bail out a financially ailing British East India Company); at the same time, as the Empire was expanding due to her vast territorial gains and the profits anticipated therefrom, Britain was viewed with growing suspicion and alarm by her neighbors in the European community, especially France and Spain, who did not have a tradition of liking her anyway. Both remained Roman Catholic and so essentially feudal in political organization as opposed to England's Protestantism and "modernist" parliamentary compromise. It was not likely, therefore, that in the negotiations over the disposition of North America the British could expect to gain much comfort from their European adversaries—who had joined in the war because they disapproved of Britain in the first place.

What the British did have going for them was the Articles of Peace negotiated at Paris in 1763, a multinational agreement establishing the eastern half of North

America as theirs. This was destined to be the high trump card. Britain had no reason for conceding much of anything to the French or the Spanish anyway; what she did need was another alliance with which to poise herself against further trouble from her Roman Catholic adversaries and answer those at home who nurtured trading interests and friendships in North America. This was her ace in the hole. England could unilaterally cede whatever she wanted, within reason, to the Americans and use the process to establish friendly relations and finally alliance with the nation she would thereby create. She could also thereby hope to position herself as parental watchdog over the forming government virtually everyone expected to fail—and so be able to step in again as might well be expedient. In the current circumstances it was to the advantage of the English to give away; the only questions were exactly what, to whom, and to what purpose. Historian Thomas A. Bailey explains:

> In the first place, Prime Minister [in the new government] Shelburne had long been kindly disposed toward the colonials. He was eager to close the bloody chasm and avert future friction, particularly over the inevitable westward expansion of the American republic. He likewise desired to establish profitable commercial relationships, to wean the United States away from French post-war influence, and perhaps to lure the Americans into a loose tie with the British Empire. . . . Finally, the attractive English terms must be considered in light of the European conflagration. At the time when Jay opened separate negotiations, Britain was in desperate straits. Here was a golden opportunity to improve her position by seducing America from the ranks of the enemy.[3]

Very simply, then, the British preferred to see the United States get all territory to be ceded rather than see Spain (or, God knows, France) get any of it. Our negotiators in Paris were in a far better position than the military history of the American Revolution could ever indicate.

Benjamin Franklin's first proposal was that the British cede everything they held, Canada and Nova Scotia south to Florida, to the United States, and apparently Britain was willing at least to listen to this of proposal. But, even as it was being considered, news came in that the French and Spanish assault on British-held Gibraltar had been repelled, and with this the British stiffened; they would stand by their Canadian subjects, who had stood by them through the North American hostilities. The principal question remaining, thus, was how much of the territory south of Canada the United States would receive. Out of loyalty to our wartime ally, the Continental Congress had instructed the commission to negotiate jointly with the French. On arrival, however, Jay discovered that the French had already sent an emissary to confer unilaterally with British officials in London. Assuming this to be an egregious breach of diplomatic protocol, he persuaded his fellow commissioners that they too should enter into separate negotiations. This was the tactic that carried the day.

The British clearly wanted nothing to do with the French, flatly rejected a proposal made by Spain, and ceded their interests in North America south of Canada to the United States. The final question was that of a border. The United States offered two choices: either the forty—fifth parallel from its junction with the St. Lawrence westward to the Mississippi (which crosses Michigan's Lower Peninsula just south of Gaylord and north of Traverse City); or, a line to be surveyed and completed at an unspecified later date from the junction of the forty-fifth parallel with the St. Lawrence, up the remaining reach of that river, through Lakes Ontario, Erie, Huron, and Superior and their connecting waters. The first choice would have had the effect of creating a closed border across the St. Lawrence about where Cornwall, Ontario, is, which would have cut the British and the Canadians off from the Great Lakes.

The British still had their garrisons in place on the lakes and were still the dominant partner in the northern fur trade; American capital, in part because it was restricted by policy and in part because it was not yet sufficiently developed, had not yet challenged the transatlantic investors—nor was our government yet prepared to challenge the British fortifications. To maintain access to their northern garrisons (still the only vestige of authority and administrative organization in the north) and also to preserve their position in the trade, though it left open the question of an established border, the British took the second choice and in so doing gave to the United States most of Michigan's northland together with much of what is now Wisconsin and most of what is now Minnesota—roughly the upper half of what thus became the Northwest Territory. As important, this Parisian treaty lent the full force of international law to an ongoing principle that would be reaffirmed in the Northwest Ordinance (1787) and again in the Treaty of Ghent (1814): the great interior waterway of the St. Lawrence drainage was eased for common use and established as the first international commercial highway in the interior of North America, to be shared by all and no more to be owned than the oceans. Because the promise to share worked, and because there was no reason as yet to rush the survey of unknown islands and shorelines, though it stood in principle from 1783, the line was not run until a joint United States-British commission undertook the task between 1822 and 1827.[4] The treaty specifically gave Lake Superior's Isle Royale to the United States, but left the fate of other islands (many little known because they were only vaguely mapped) along the boundary to be determined at an unspecified later date.

The essentially political and largely European resolution to the revolutionary war had little practical effect on life at the Great Lakes outposts. According to the terms of the new Parisian treaty, the British had agreed to withdraw all garrisons from territories ceded to the United States, but they had no reason to leave either Detroit or Michilimackinac and, hence, were little inclined to do so. In the first place, no one with any authority ever showed up to claim the fortifications. As the British had agreed in principle to give them up, so the Americans in principle wanted to have them; in fact, just about everyone was too busy with other matters to worry much about the western posts for the moment. The English stayed on under the pretense that the Americans had not fulfilled their part of the treaty to the letter; it can be as persuasively argued that the British, in continuing their occupation of the Lakes and in other particulars, as surely failed to live up to their part of it. Neither argument holds much water.

It seems that "winning" the Revolution solved none of the problems that had caused it, from taxation to support the cost of government and administration to land policy, Indian policy, or settling the west and protecting the frontier; now the Americans would have to come to grips with these weighty matters themselves. Once again the land and its occupants had come under new masters who once again would have to work out the devices for managing it. This kept the new administrators sufficiently occupied that they may well have been at first pleased to have the British occupying the west. British garrisons, after all, added up to British responsibility and thus British expense, which was not far from what the Americans had wanted in the first place; and British personnel, as long as the treaty held valid and the British wanted to be friendly (as they had said in Paris), could hold the forts and protect the frontier at least as well as Americans. Too, the British still had their stake in the fur trade to protect (while the Americans necessarily had to be preoccupied with more fundamental matters than base commercial ones) and so very much wanted to keep the waterways that they had preserved for themselves open and secure for the benefit of British subjects in Montreal and Quebec—as well as the London merchants. Furthermore, the Articles of Confederation that bound the infant states were widely perceived in Europe as entirely too weak to hold in the long term; it might therefore be wise to remain in position to pick up the pieces should the whole experiment fall apart. For all these reasons, then, the British stayed on in the lakes, pretty much with American consent—or at least without a serious American challenge—until the Americans finally and firmly asked them to leave in 1796. Until that date Michilimackinac was governed under simple martial law and Detroit, because there was little the Americans could provide there anyway, was governed and administered as an extension of British Canada.

None of this, however, is meant to suggest that the British were behaving themselves well. American attempts to claim the recently won western forts were, for the most part, diplomatic and distinctly lacked muscle. The British refusal to hand the positions over was an attempt to buy time, to see if the American confederation would hold together. While doing so, they did all they could to undermine it. Their device, once again, was the Indian, and Detroit—so conveniently attached, for the moment, to British Canada—was the center of the operation. After the Revolution and subsequent treaties with the Indians at Fort Stanwix (1784) and Fort McIntosh (1785), by which the United States government acquired a tract of land to the north and west of the upper Ohio River, eastern settlers commenced pouring into the west, especially the Ohio River Valley. This upset the northern Indians as yet another and greater intrusion on their grounds (no matter who signed the treaties or what the treaties provided for whom), and the British happily took advantage of it.[5] Once again they sent the Indian down the warpath, encouraging him, equipping him, passing intelligence to him, and in every way managing him as a guerrilla army whose job it was to pester and annoy and intimidate the Americans as they came west to claim in fact their newly won territory. The tactic worked; insofar as the Americans might send an army into the west, they would have to confront only the hostile savages, not the British puppeteers and their forts along the Lakes. Only after a new and firmer treaty with Britain negotiated by John Jay (1794-95) and the brilliant Indian campaign in the western Ohio and Indiana country of Gen. Anthony Wayne (1793-95) together with the failure of the French fur market and Britain's renewed declaration of war against France (both of which in the wake of the collapse into the chaos of the Reign of Terror [1793-94] of the French Revolution), did the British concede that their positions at Detroit and Michilimackinac were sufficiently weak that they were obliged to abandon them. The order to evacuate was dated June 2, 1796.[6] Only then was the Northwest truly in American hands.

CHAPTER FIVE

THE NORTHWEST ORDINANCE

The processes according to which the American invasion of the Northwest commenced were complex, time-consuming, and arduous. From very early on the colonials were intensely aware of the problems they faced and determined to face them squarely; they had the numbers, the technology, and the superior civilization—and they accepted eminent domain as fact. That the superior culture (with its also superior numbers) was going to intrude on the inferior one and in so doing change it was an inevitable demographic fact; the central problem was to control the process to avert the possibility (perhaps even, alternatively, the need for) extended wars of territorial conquest or extermination.

In buying Mackinac Island, a result of another demographic factor brought about by an evolving wartime situation, the British had set a precedent; for there is no question that by military superiority and the mandates of wartime necessity they could simply have taken the island and held it as their own. There is also no question that according to the terms of an international peace accord (Paris, 1763) the island was already recognized as theirs—won fair and square from France, whose claim to it had been similarly valid, according to the standards of the times, by rights of discovery and exploration. But they also needed to appease the Indians during the revolutionary years and so chose instead to accept the responsibility implied in eminent domain and attempt to determine and compensate justly.

In so doing they raised for the first time the incredibly difficult problem of establishing a market for territory in the Northwest: pointedly, how does one party go about computing a fair value for a commodity held by a second party who will not claim ownership of it, who values it only as it is a means to the natural production of other commodities to be used in a barter exchange, and who has no conception of or need for (according to the tenets of his culture) a system of monetary exchange—until such is thrust on him after the fact? This problem would bedevil the Americans throughout the years of domestic treaty making, largely during the nineteenth century (1784-1859). Indeed, this is the overriding story in the Old Northwest from the close of the American Revolution to the opening of hostilities in the Civil War: the attempt to achieve peaceful and fair extinction of Indian title and so make possible survey, organization, private ownership, and thereby settlement of the land.

By the time of the revolutionary war five states had claims to territory in the Northwest: Massachusetts, Connecticut, and Virginia had claims originating in their colonial charters; Pennsylvania and New York exercised claims deriving from treaties they had independently negotiated with the Iroquois. But when the war broke out, all thirteen colonies found themselves fighting for the interior; the various claims, therefore, had to be resolved in principle to hold the confederation together. Maryland, which had no such claims, forced the issue in 1778 by refusing to ratify the Articles of Confederation until the landed states ceded their claims to the central government; because all the states were fighting for the territory, the Marylanders argued, a device should be found by which all could share in it equally. Other circumstances strengthened Maryland's position. The war at the moment was not going terribly well for the colonials, and it became clear that a strong union was going to be necessary to succeed in the struggle for independence; too, the Indian problem in the interior was severe enough that it was unlikely that the individual states would have the resources to deal with it at all effectively. A brilliant compromise was suggested: that the Northwest, if the states' claims to it were ceded, would be eventually "formed into separate republican states, which [should] become members of the federal union, and have the same rights and sovereignty, freedom, and independence as the other states."[1] Thus New York gave up her claims in 1780 and in the same year Pennsylvania agreed to a western boundary with access to Lake Erie; in the next year Virginia ceded most of her claims and this was enough to persuade Maryland to ratify the articles. Massachusetts and Connecticut were more reluctant, but gave their claims over in 1785 and 1786 respectively. The general pattern of the development of the Northwest was thus set and the states of Ohio, Indiana, Illinois, Michigan, and Wisconsin were destined to be carved out of it.

The principle thus established, Congress had next to deal with the practicalities of acquiring and then transferring the land from the public to private ownership and then providing government and law. The primary responsibility of the federal government regarding the land was to obtain clear title to it, which meant extinguishing Indian claims. Just as the British found in acquiring Mackinac Island for their new fort, the international and often multinational treaties habitually written at Paris failed to impress the American native; he could not understand how France could give the land on which he lived to England who could then give it to the United States (which thereby became a brand new fact of life on everyone's agenda) when he had not given it to anyone—nor did he "own" it to dispose of it—in the first place, nor was he party to the European negotiations that determined this dubious "ownership." That he was going to have to share the land with the white man was inevitable; what he might want for it was unclear; what its value might be was completely unknown.

The succession of agreements reached in Paris, as subsequent events unfolded in North America and the organization of the land evolved, determined not who owned the land but who would have the right to acquire it; the means to acquiring it were pretty well left to the discretion of the nation in charge at any given moment. The British had established a precedent of fair exchange (as promoted by Lord Shelburne) and the Americans carried it forward; as opposed to simply taking the land by military conquest (following the usual European model), we chose to regard the Indians as a coequal foreign nation with rights to fair compensation (whatever that might be, and whatever form it might take) and also rights to cohabitation, participation, and private ownership in the long run. Because ongoing war with its own set of expenses was the other option, we had to arrange to extinguish general Indian claims to the land, then describe, survey, and map it so that it could be sold (and thus generate the money to cover the whole venture), then get it back into the hands of individual Indians so that they could become equal partners in it. This process the federal government, as opposed to the individual states, would have to orchestrate through the series of intranational treaties begun at Fort Stanwix (1784) and Fort McIntosh (1785). Only then could the orderly distribution and administration of the land proceed.

The first ordinance proposing to deal with the disposition of the lands in the Northwest was drafted and adopted by Congress in 1784 following recommendations by Thomas Jefferson. He suggested that the territory be carved into ten states and proposed a tentative plan for imposing a general political organization on the territory. Though passed, the ordinance never went into effect as it was superseded by the more coherent and comprehensive Ordinance of 1787.[2] The final paragraph, however, of this the first of the ordinances designed to give order to the territory west of the mountains and north of the Ohio River is extremely important as defining what the earliest federal government thought it was doing in publishing the ordinances—what the ordinances, as documents of law, were thought to be:

> That the preceding articles shall be formed into a *charter of compact;* shall be duly executed by the President of the United States in Congress assembled, under his hand, and the seal of the United States; shall be promulgated; and shall stand as *fundamental constitutions* between the original thirteen states, and each of the several states now newly described, *unalterable* from and after the sale of any part of the territory of such state, pursuant to this resolve, *but by the joint consent of the United States in Congress assembled, and of the particular state within which such alteration is proposed to be made* (italics mine).

The language is Jefferson's and is carefully reechoed in the Northwest Ordinance (1787). An ordinance created a "compact," the most solemn agreement known in eighteenth century law and politics. Because it was not promulgated and so put into effect, the Ordinance of 1784 could be, as it was, repealed. The document leaves behind, however, a fine definition of what an ordinance, as a document in law duly proclaimed and so promulgated, was—as well as how one could be modified. Modifying is exemplified in the northward march of the borders of Indiana and Illinois; and its bungling in the squabble over Michigan's southern boundary. Noah Webster would later (1828) define compact by giving the Constitution as his example (see note 6 for chapter 5, page 194).

Of far greater practical importance was the Ordinance of 1785, which established the broad policies that would govern organizing the land itself. The problem was how to transfer public ownership to private ownership—and ultimately from federal to state ownership for certain remnant, publicly held lands—and congressional debate seems to have been lively. Many, contemplating a war-ravaged treasury and the consequent pressing need for administrative funds, favored what was called the "southern system," whereby the purchaser would obtain a warrant for the tract he wanted and then bear the cost of survey himself. Such a system would have the advantage of generating badly needed money relatively rapidly and doing so without the necessity of cumbersome expenses to the federal government up front; it would have the disadvantages of piecemeal survey work, buyers not knowing in advance exactly what they were proposing to buy, and, consequently, inevitable property line disputes. Others favored what was known as the "New England system," by which the government by law, as the suzerain of the land secured by treaty, would bear the cost of survey before sale as a part of its investment. This system would have the advantage of giving both vendor and purchaser warrantable knowledge of the commodity in exchange balanced against the disadvantage of the pre-contract expense of survey. The cost of the survey could be factored into the purchase price, but the process would slow down the flow of money into a treasury desperately in need of it.

Despite of the feature of up-front expense, the wisdom of presurveying prevailed and was written into the Ordinance of 1785 as the law of the land. Other issues were even more clearly economic and included: whether the land should be sold in large tracts to wealthy speculators and land companies who would in turn resell it for profit or whether it should be sold only restrictively and directly to those who proposed to settle on it, and whether the land should be promoted for sale quickly and on easy terms to encourage settlement or be regarded as a national treasure to be managed conservatively as an investment that could yield far greater returns. The ordinance evolved as a compromise of these issues. It provided: (1) that large territories could be secured only by agents of the federal government by treaty with the Indians; (2) that the Indians were to be treated fairly according to the dictates of an evolving unencumbered land market; (3) that the lands so acquired were to be surveyed into townships six miles square, each containing thirty-six sections one mile square; (4) that it was to be sold at first by the section at public auction (to establish the market and allow the speculator and the settler alike an equal crack at it) at a minimum of one dollar per acre; (5) that alternate townships could be sold intact (to satisfy the speculators and so guard a free market); and (6) that section sixteen of each township was to be reserved from government auction, later to be turned over to local units of government to benefit schools.[3] Though the Ordinance of 1785 was modified from time to time to meet changing circumstances, in general it became the blueprint for American expansion into the Northwest. It became federal policy to hand over land title to the states as each was formed and admitted to the Union, and the reservation of section sixteen thus became the first ever form of government aid to education—a provision not incorporated into the Constitution itself.

As the Ordinance of 1785 addressed the problem of organizing and transferring the land, the Ordinance of 1787 was the first attempt to provide government for the land so organized (Jefferson's suggestions in 1784 notwithstanding) and, because it addressed itself exclusively to the Old Northwest, it is known as the Northwest Ordinance. It was pushed through the Congress of the Confederation to try to serve the interests of two groups of eastern land speculators, the Ohio Company and the Scioto Company, both out of Boston, each of which proposed to acquire a huge tract of land in what is now southern Ohio.[4] These speculators, acting in concert, demanded provision for government in the region where their tracts were to be. The 1784 ordinance was ready to hand, but as a major defect it prescribed no plan for the orderly evolution of new states in the west. Jefferson's document was fixed and arbitrary and therefore impractical; it was based upon what he thought ought to be, without considering what might be. Government is neither practical nor necessary until there is a population that wants governing, and it is pretty hard to tell in advance just how, when, and where that is going to happen. The speculators were pushing into virgin territory that carried no guarantees as to geographic-political boundaries, connection with the federal government (save the managerial-administrative one with which the project began), or systems of law and civil rights. To address these problems, the Northwest Ordinance "provided for the division of the Old Northwest into not less than three nor more than five states and set forth the [tentative] boundaries of these future states; second, it stipulated three stages of development through which these divisions would pass as they progressed toward statehood [and guaranteed the right to statehood eventually]; and third, it contained a statement of rights guaranteed to the people who settled in the region."[5] The government officials of the Northwest Territory were, at first, to be appointed by Congress: a governor, a secretary, and a court consisting of three judges who had jurisdiction in all matters of law. As soon, however, as the territory attained a population of five thousand free, adult males, self-government was to commence; now the voters of the territory could elect a house of representatives, which in its turn could nominate ten men from which Congress was to select five as a territorial legislative council. Thenceforth the laws of the territory were to be made by the legislative council, the house of representatives, and the governor, the consent of all three being required on any issue. Too, as any tentatively designated state should arrive at a population of sixty thousand, the right to apply for statehood was guaranteed. The house of representatives and the legislative council had also the right to choose by joint ballot a delegate to the Congress of the United States. The delegate was to represent in the east the interests of his territory and participate in governmental process there, but he was to have no vote, only an initial right and responsibility to lobby. The Northwest Ordinance also reaffirmed certain principles written into the Ordinance of 1785, guaranteed most of the common rights and privileges promised under law in the east, and repealed the Ordinance of 1784. The text of the Northwest Ordinance begins on page 160.

The ordinance builds on the British Proclamation of 1763 in protecting the French populations within the territory (at Kaskaskia, Cahokia, and Vincennes), who had aligned themselves with Virginia's claim, with respect both to their religion and to their laws and customs "relative to the descent and conveyance of property" (Paragraph 2). It also provides for taxation (Article IV) and the encouragement of education (Article III). It is important that the ordinance defines its own force as law (Paragraph 14) according to the accepted legal terminology of the day as a contract, like the Constitution,[6] between the original states and the people and states of the territory as yet unformed, which was to "forever remain unalterable, unless by common consent." The Treaty of Paris (1783) established shared waterways in North America, a principle parallel with if not derived from the international marine law that confines nations within their watery boundaries. It is extremely important that, in Article IV, the ordinance reaffirms the same principle with respect to the navigable waters of both the St. Lawrence and the Mississippi watersheds, which, it asserts, "shall be *common highways,* and *forever free,* as well to the Inhabitants of the said territory as to the Citizens of the United States" (italics mine). The contractual aspect of the ordinance was regarded as important enough that, on completion of the Constitution in 1789, the new Congress of the United States in its first session officially reenacted it as the law of the land (see Judge Fox, *United States v. Michigan).*

The waters, thus, of the Great Lakes and the great rivers were set aside and eased for common use—not to be owned, divided, taxed, or controlled by any party in any way conceivable to the framers of the Northwest Ordinance, and this principle was written into the articles of a legal contract between the federal government and the citizens of the Northwest living in states as yet unformed and binding into perpetuity, "unalterable, unless by common consent." From July 13, 1787, then, (if not, indeed from the proclamation of the Parisian treaty in 1783) these waters were designated indivisible nonterritory, which could be ceded or even considered in later treaties of cession and extinction of Indian claim to title (clearly anticipated and provided for in Article III, as was the probability of "just and lawful wars [with the Indians] authorized by Congress") no more than they could be owned or controlled or divided by any party owning land adjacent to or within them. Land and unconnected and therefore unnavigable water only was to be salable and acquirable and thus subject to the usual rights of land ownership—riparian, littoral, or usufructuary.

The business of federal government at this time, including the framing of the Ordinance of 1787, was conducted by the Congress of the Confederation sitting in New York City. The adequacy of this Congress as a legislative body is attested in its ability to minister to the problems of the Northwest Territory and provide for its future. Such liberal features as freedom of religion (an acknowledgment of the French *habitants*) and trial by jury were notably missing from the original Constitution of the United States—to be added later in the amendments—and the prohibition of slavery (Article VI) was more than seventy years before its time, perhaps a feature introduced to protect the Indians from the Virginians as surely as, in permitting the return of fugitive slaves escaped into the territory, the same article acknowledges property rights as they had evolved in the original thirteen states. Too, the framers of the Constitution (at the same time) did not consider education a responsibility of government.[7]

Still, the weakness of the fledgling federal government under the Articles of Confederation was amply demonstrated in its inability to deal with other and fundamental problems: taxation (provided for in the Northwest Ordinance, not at the Constitutional Convention, and much needed to support the cost of government and the cost of surveys in the Northwest alike), the Indian problem (acknowledged in the Northwest Ordinance, not in the Constitution), and the failure to maintain a standing army after war's end and thus deal with the continuing British military presence in the ceded territory of the Great Lakes (closely related problems the British were happy to take advantage of).

The British were right in perceiving the United States under the Articles of Confederation as too weak to hold together. With a sadly hampered authority to tax (though taxation was provided for in the Northwest Ordinance), the Congress of the Confederation simply lacked the money to conduct the surveys, negotiate effectively with other governments, or muster an army with which to deal with the Indians or the British, and this encouraged Gov. General Haldimand in Canada to cling to what he continued to hold—and manipulate the Indians, his faithful native mercenaries. Once again the central problem was an economic one. In the meantime, however, the Constitutional Convention remained in session in Philadelphia, and its work (completed in 1789) would be one of the decisive factors tipping the balance of the newly created and, then, constitutionally founded United States of America.

In the same year in which the Constitutional Convention completed its nation-founding work, and clearly influenced by the revolutionary affair on this side of the Atlantic, the people of the Parisian Commune stormed the Bastille to secure for their National Guard the arms and munitions stored there and *that* revolution was on in earnest. The combined costs of participation in the American Revolution and one of the most silly and prodigal regimes in French history (under the dull-witted and

ill-educated Louis XVI and his pretentious consort, Marie Antoinette) had bankrupt-
ed the throne and collapsed the French economy. France's high-risk investment in
the recent North American conflict had gained her nothing at the Paris peace talks;
she would now dethrone and execute her monarch—thus disrupting the Bourbon
dynasty that had ruled her for hundreds of years—and enter into the chaos of the
Napoleonic wars that would keep her at war with most of civilized Europe (including, pointedly, England) until 1815. These matters would keep almost everyone on
the other side of the Atlantic busy during that extremely important period and, thus,
give the fledgling but constitutionally founded United States an opportunity to form,
organize, grow, and test itself.

On this side of the ocean the state of affairs was similarly chaotic. To the dismay
of, especially, the northern Indians, settlers poured into the Ohio Valley, great portions of which had been ceded by Indians who claimed it as theirs to cede at Fort
McIntosh in 1785. The northern tribes felt they had an ancestral stake in it and had
not been properly consulted in the cession. In the meantime, civil government came
to the Northwest Territory; it gained its first substantial American settlement and
first capital when Gov. Arthur St. Clair, together with a territorial secretary and three
judges, arrived at Marietta (at the junction of the Muskingum and Ohio rivers) in
July of 1788 just a year after the Congress of the Confederation issued the Northwest
Ordinance.[8] The growth of the American community along the Ohio was sudden
and exceedingly alarming to the Indians, who became more and more an open threat.

Because Congress could not supply troops, militiamen assembled in the Northwest
under George Rogers Clark and Benjamin Logan to undertake protecting the
Americans trying to establish themselves on the recently ceded land. Clark's force
mutinied before they even sighted an Indian; Logan's troops destroyed some Indian
villages and supplies but failed to engage the savages. Yet the American presence
was painfully felt, and now both the Algonquian and the Iroquois nations repudiated the treaties of cession they had signed at Fort Stanwix (1784) and Fort McIntosh
(1785). The Fort McIntosh treaty was signed by representatives of the Chippewa,
Ottawa, Delaware, and Wyandot nations, but both treaties were disputed by other
groups of Indians in Ohio, Indiana, Illinois, and Michigan who had not been consulted; it is not clear what claim, other than the vague ancestral one, they had that
might supersede the claim of the signatory tribes.[9]

The British were not blameless in all this; Governor-General Haldimand, especially through his operatives at Detroit, encouraged the Indians to form a strong confederation like the earlier five- or six-nation Iroquois one so that they could show a
unified and organized front. He also continued the British policy of gift giving to
the Indians that had been reinstated during the revolutionary war and so effectively continued the Indian mercenary portion of that war. But the Indians utterly failed
to cooperate with one another and so seriously weakened themselves; nevertheless,
by the fall of 1789 a new and full-scale Indian war had broken out, centered in the
valley of the Ohio.

The situation along the Ohio was not good, and was destined to get much worse. First, in the fall of 1790, an American force was mustered at Cincinnati and sent north commanded by Gen. Josiah Harmar with orders to confront and discipline the Indians. But this ragtag and untrained army moved so slowly that it could never catch any Indians to confront; its efforts ended when a lumbering detachment was ambushed and massacred—183 men lost. In late summer of the following year a much larger force of about three thousand marched north, again from Cincinnati, commanded by Governor St. Clair himself. This army reached the Maumee River without serious incident and there camped, without posting adequate sentries. During the night they were surrounded and at dawn furiously attacked and soundly thrashed—630 dead, 283 wounded.[10] St. Clair and his men slipped away and made their way back to the south, but the Americans were again humiliated. These nonprofessional armies were clearly not up to the task assigned them. Though still not well organized, in two years of campaigning the Indians had scored consecutive and decisive victories. This only fed their appetites; the lesson learned was that the Indians could prevail in their wars against the Americans—who, as it turned out, were not yet so well organized themselves.

In the still British north Haldimand was delighted and all too happy to provide the materials of war. The Americans, still without a professional standing army and disadvantaged in their troubles with the Indians of the Northwest, were still in no position to invite the occupation forces out of Detroit and Michilimackinac; the British could continue to sit tight in the lakes and watch the Indians keep the Americans thoroughly occupied, while they contemplated the course of their North American internal policy and the international affairs that would dictate their next move. The Indians continued to operate as successful mercenaries in a war that was only technically over on this continent. The Revolution in France was by now becoming of great concern (England would declare war with France in February 1793, the month after King Louis lost his head), as was the fact that the Americans had hammered out a constitution and so formed a coherent government that just might succeed. Nevertheless, the North American British still had time—and they used it well.

By 1792, then, the Indian problem in the Northwest was of national concern with a high priority; if the evolution of the nation was going to proceed, the matter would have to be resolved. Investors and settlers alike were clamoring for tracts along the Ohio River, land that had already been for sale and that all thought was secured by treaty; yet, after the unilateral denunciation of the Ohio treaties by the Indians, the only settlements where safety was assured were those at Marietta and Cincinnati—where the numbers of settlers were sufficient that they could defend themselves. The new government desperately needed the money represented in the sale of this land and the Indians posed a serious threat to this market; the government's principal source of revenue, and so its future, hung in the balance. The British also realized this and it informed their strategy of sitting tight and profiting from the situation by manipulating the Indians.

CHAPTER SIX

THE TREATY OF GREENVILLE (1795)

Throughout his life, President George Washington had been deeply interested in and committed to developing the Northwest, which he viewed as a national destiny and as the means to financing the national evolution. He concluded that the financial crisis devolving from the Indian threat called for decisive action. In 1792 he called in Gen. Anthony Wayne, called "Mad Anthony" because of his brilliant and courageous, if sometimes apparently reckless, career during the Revolution; he offered him the command in the Northwest with orders to bring the Indians into line with their treaty commitments and, if necessary, to engineer a new one. Wayne accepted the command and ordered an army to be assembled for him at Pittsburgh, to which he traveled in the same year with plans to move on to Cincinnati where his campaign would commence.

Wayne's army was little different in numbers or composition from those mustered by Harmar and St. Clair, but Wayne was a different sort of commander; he knew the importance of military precision, martial skill gained at the expense of intense training, and of resultant absolute discipline. Both Harmar and St. Clair, in Wayne's view, had blundered into the field with ill trained and unprepared troops, had got themselves into tactically disadvantageous positions, and had therefore been needlessly defeated at immense cost—a good part of which was the lesson to the Indians that they could prevail. What may appear to be cunning and dash, even recklessness, can also be a result of tactical skill and careful preparation. Wayne proposed to enter the field with the deck carefully stacked in his favor. The story of his advance from Pittsburgh to Cincinnati is the story of a general whipping his army into shape—courts-martial, lashings, daily drill, and regular exercises in everything from marksmanship to hand-to-hand combat. Much to the frustration of those waiting in the east,

Wayne patiently drilled his men for over a year until he knew without question that they were ready. Any risks he would run would be carefully calculated.

Wayne's campaign, if more time-consuming than his political bosses would have wanted (though he was also waiting out a final effort at a negotiated peace, which was thwarted by the British),[1] was thoroughly organized and meticulously planned. As his army advanced, it built a series of forts so that there was always a defensible position to which to retreat if necessary, to which supplies could be delivered after the army had secured the route, and from which operations could be planned—all at a safe distance from the settlements along the Ohio, which could therefore proceed with their development.

He advanced northward from Cincinnati in October of 1793, halting at the site of what is now Greenville, Ohio, where he built Fort Greenville as a base camp and winter headquarters for the whole operation. There he drilled and trained some more in the cold weather and, perhaps more important, trimmed his army to fighting weight. Supposedly friendly Indians, women, and other assorted camp followers had been permitted to travel with the armies of Harmar and St. Clair. Wayne would make few concessions to humor his troops, and Fort Greenville was the stepping-off place for all this unnecessary baggage; the army that finally advanced northward from this position was a finely tuned and thoroughly professional force to which Wayne could trust his life and his nation's destiny. They moved on to the site of St. Clair's defeat, where they built Fort Recovery, and there suffered their first engagement with the savages. A large force of Indians, perhaps two thousand, had gathered around the plucky war chief Little Turtle and, remembering St. Clair's defeat, determined to turn the same place into Wayne's disaster. But they badly underestimated their foe, lacked the tactical skills and technical materials necessary to besiege a fortified position, suffered severe casualties, and so retreated in disarray. General Wayne's mobile machine of war was proving its tactical and practical value; his was the most efficient and skillful army yet seen in the Northwest—infinitely superior to those of Harmar and St. Clair, far greater than the professional ones sent out by General Gage. Little Turtle and his allied chieftains were thoroughly alarmed, and so were the British. Every bit as important as the preliminary military victory, at Fort Recovery Wayne gathered the first hard intelligence as to exactly what the present British involvement was:

> In his report on this engagement, Wayne wrote that he had virtual proof that there were a considerable number of Britishers and Detroit militiamen mixed with the savages in the attack on Fort Recovery. There is unmistakable evidence that the British supplied the natives with provisions and ammunition. The old French fort on the Maumee, near the present Perrysburg, Ohio, was occupied by a British force and named Fort Miamis. This was such an open violation of the peace that it was made the subject of a strong protest, communicated through John Jay, who at the time was in England attempting to negotiate a treaty between Great Britain and the United States.[2]

This intelligence aided materially in the negotiation of Jay's Treaty (November 1794), which resulted in removing the British from the posts on the lakes (1796) to positions on the Canadian side of the as yet only vaguely defined border. Wayne waited at Fort Recovery for supplies and reinforcements and then, in July of 1794, advanced to the junction of the Auglaize and Maumee rivers and there built Fort Defiance (at what is now Defiance, Ohio). Wayne's presence and evident command of the situation sufficiently concerned Little Turtle that he now advised the confederated chiefs to make peace, but his pleas caught few ears. Thus, on August 20, 1794, Wayne's army engaged the Indians about twelve miles south of what is now Toledo, Ohio; a tornado had passed through the area and gave that engagement its name: the Battle of Fallen Timbers. His victory was complete there, his losses minimal; the back of the Indian resistance was broken. He moved on to the west to the present site of Fort Wayne, Indiana (near the head of the Maumee River drainage, and thus a head of Indian navigation on the route south), and there built the installation named after him; from there he repaired to Fort Greenville, having secured the Ohio River Valley and its settlers with his northern posts.

At Fallen Timbers once again the Indians had been betrayed, and far more surely so than they had been by the French at Detroit, though for similar reasons, which, again, they could little understand (being negotiated at London by John Jay, this time, instead of Paris). The battle had been fought just a stone's throw from old Fort Miamis, from which the British contributed guerrilla infiltrators (we would call them advisers), arms, and munitions. But, because of the technical peace of 1783 and Jay's negotiations in London, the garrison failed to come to the Indians' aid, and this surely contributed to Wayne's victory. The British would arm, supply, and advise their guerrilla mercenaries—as well as illegally occupying the old fort—but not enter the engagement directly; that would have been too much in any gentleman's eyes. Just as the failure of the French to sweep the lakes had left the Indians no choice but to deal with the English, so the British failure to give overt assistance at Fallen Timbers would leave the Indians no choice but to deal with the Americans—who were, now, both numerically and technologically superior, and needed the interior lands to expand their new nation.

The Indians were not only vanquished, they were beaten as the belligerent mercenary operatives of another nation continuing a war already over. It is no wonder that the British would soon agree to vacate their northern posts; it is remarkable that the United States neither undertook nor asked for immediate and firm punitive action—nor did it simply claim what it had now won twice and thereby end it. Because it did not choose to but instead chose to stick by and reaffirm the ordinances already in place, Wayne's negotiations at Greenville would set the pattern of nation building in the Northwest. Though Wayne's brilliant campaign handed the young government a golden opportunity to take a far easier route, the government chose to honor the covenants and contracts it had set forth in the Northwest Ordinance, thereby affirming for all residents of the Northwest in practice what it had promised in principle. Even this early, a war lost to the United States could prove a profitable venture.

Wayne declared that a solemn conclave would be held at Greenville the following summer and dispatched runners to all the tribes of the Northwest to summon their chiefs to attend so that the negotiations would be known to and understood by all the Indians. The Treaty of Greenville was consummated on August 3, 1795, ratified by the president and the Senate, and proclaimed in December of the same year. The text of the Greenville treaty begins on page 164.

Just as the Indians had repudiated the earlier treaties at Stanwix and McIntosh, so now (in Article X) both parties by agreement voided all treaties made between themselves since the creation of the United States government by the consent of the three other governments sitting at the Paris peace talks in 1783. The point of it is crystal clear. Greenville was to be the new beginning, the model from which all further treaties extinguishing Indian title and so securing the lands of the Northwest for sale and settlement would be constructed. This treaty set the pattern by which the United States would commence its inevitable westward expansion. In this respect, and because it honored and reaffirmed the principles set forth in the ordinances of 1785 and 1787, Greenville is undoubtedly not only the first but, therefore, the most important of the treaties of cession that would clear title to the lands of the Northwest and thereby finance the new government to benefit all its people—including the aboriginals, who were promised from this beginning all such benefits within the power of the government to bestow and nothing less. The treaty is unprecedented in its liberal treatment of a twice vanquished belligerent people.

Under the terms of the treaty, the Indians ceded to the United States most of what is now Ohio (except a small strip along Lake Erie), a modest piece of what is now Indiana, and several sites in what is now Michigan, including: a strip six miles wide running up the Detroit River from the River Raisin to Lake St. Clair, all of Mackinac Island, the parts of the mainland on either side of the Straits at Michilimackinac that the Indians had explicitly or implicitly given the French or the English to use, and a six-mile strip on Point St. Ignace extending three miles inland.[3] One feature of the Greenville Treaty, then, was to establish United States ownership of the territory surrounding and including the still British installations on the lakes and the approaches to them on the American side of the still unsurveyed border. Even though the British were still in place in their lakeside forts, our case for evicting them (having won the positions once and now secured them by separate cession) was growing stronger as our government gained in credibility. The "particular tracts of land" delineated for cession in Article III, each one small enough in itself, are so stipulated as to make possible an extensive military network in the territory. Not only was further Indian trouble possible (which other articles also anticipate—Article IX, for instance), but the British remained a threat in the north, which the events of 1812 proved. It is notable that this was the second cession of Ohio and the second acquisition of Mackinac Island; transfer of title in Detroit, dating to the French feudal land grants there, is even more ambiguous.

The Chippewas in the north made "an extra and voluntary gift" of Bois Blanc

Island, apparently to atone for their part in the insurrection. The treaty provides for survey of ceded lands as might become necessary and proper, protects the Indians with the promise of timely notice thereof, and adds to and further defines (Article III) the navigable waters feature of the Northwest Ordinance. The principal waters of the Great Lakes and Mississippi drainages are not considered in the treaty precisely because they were already defined and eased in the Northwest Ordinance. The treaty is explicit (Article V) in relinquishing to the Indians lands outside the agreed-upon borders of the cession and protecting the tribals there from American intrusion until they might want to sell those lands, only if the Indians acknowledge *only* the United States as sovereign—a provision aimed directly at the tribal relationship with the British, though not successfully. The treaty is also specific (Article VII) in permitting the Indians to hunt, and that *only,* on lands ceded to the United States, and in opening a controlled and protected and mutually beneficial trade by license with them (Article VIII).

So the Greenville treaty established as United States policy the British precedent of negotiating for peace and acquiring land only by cession and thus legal extinction of Indian claim. Some of the dollar amounts (Article IV) may seem small from a present perspective (as does the price of one of Henry Ford's contraptions), but one must consider several factors: (1) this, like the later treaties, represents a cession, not a purchase, in return for which the United States promised goods and services in the form of annuities to help the vanquished tribes into a new future; (2) almost all the land so acquired had no market value (certainly so in what would become Michigan) unless there was access to it by navigable water; (3) the Indian in the Northwest had no cash economy and so valued only goods in trade, which in themselves carried low market value by today's standards; (4) until the land could be surveyed and transferred by sale to private ownership, there was precious little in the treasury with which to purchase it; (5) because the Indians of the Northwest understood only barter and could not conceive of the value of a possession they normally failed even to acknowledge, it was nearly impossible to establish a market with them; (6) the Indians had no experience with the white man's sale contract and thus happily demanded to sell over and over again certain self-evidently attractive parcels (Mackinac Island, Detroit); and (7) through the "civilizing" process, as we imposed land ownership on them, brought them into our economy, and so created a value for land by the parcel, we were going to have to take care of the Indians with annuities for which the land itself would have to provide the capital. It is altogether remarkable that the process was even attempted; a result of it, as early as 1795, was the first and largest social welfare system the United States government ever attempted. But these entitlements were also supposed to end; the end was supposed to be equality, land ownership, citizenship, and economic participation for the aboriginal.

All of this, especially the detail that there was little or nothing in the national treasury, suggests that the initial investment should properly have been kept low; the annual payments, until the land was fully organized, surveyed, and returned to individuals by the parcel having an established market value (in Michigan, not until after the Detroit Treaty of 1855), would be far more important as a welfare system. The whole business was like a blind man's guessing game; the wonder of it is that it was attempted at all. The Greenville treaty was in principle a land contract calling for a down payment of goods to be valued at $20,000 and an annual allowance "forever" of goods to be valued at $9,500 (Article IV). This was much less costly than the British bribery at Detroit during the Revolution (though a big obligation for an unfinanced government), but the British, through the fur trade and from a tax base at home, had much more to bribe with; they also had a continent at stake and all the future return on investment that that implied. We, on the other hand, had won the continent, kicked the competition off the field of play, and were now trying to make economic sense out of the whole affair—including finding a way to provide for our native citizens without capital save that represented in the land itself.

In the meantime, with a constitution now written, a government formed, a president in office, and a solution to the Indian problem in the Northwest well in progress, the United States sent John Jay back to London to negotiate another treaty with the British in 1794, the two objects of which were to end commercial discrimination and so normalize trade and to persuade them to evacuate Detroit and Michilimackinac. What would have been impossible five years previous now looked promising. Politically, against great odds, the United States had scored a success in forming itself and strengthening its federal government; what Wayne achieved in the Northwest in securing the Ohio River Valley no less than provided the financial base that would make it possible for government to continue. Too, Jay had the news of the British indiscretions at Fort Recovery and would soon be armed with the detail of American ownership, by cession and extinction of Indian claim to title all secured by treaty, of both Detroit and Michilimackinac.

In Europe the British were necessarily preoccupied with the French, whose revolution had turned into a war of international aggression and who began scoring an alarming series of successes in late 1793. The British were prepared to make some concessions to the United States to keep us at arm's length from our old bedfellows, the French, and out of the league of "Armed Neutrals"—who could easily jump in on either side but would certainly prefer the winning one. Jay's mission, however, was undermined by Alexander Hamilton, President Washington's pro-British secretary of the treasury, who informed the British minister at Philadelphia that under no circumstances would the Americans join the Armed Neutrals. The trade aspects of Jay's Treaty, therefore, were weak enough that the proposal almost escaped ratification; the British simply refused to open their ports to American traders on a free and equal basis. But Wayne's success in the Northwest, together with the American acquisition of Detroit and Michilimackinac, was enough to persuade them to evacuate the Great Lakes forts—if their Canadian subjects would be permitted to continue their trade on an equal basis, even on American soil, with the Americans who would undoubtedly take up the licenses and enter the trade. On these terms, little gained but the fortified positions on the lakes and our relations with the British still strained, the treaty was signed in November of 1794 and ratified by a narrow margin after heavy debate in June of 1795. The British were to give over Detroit and Michilimackinac on June 1, 1796, though the Americans failed to show up to claim their prizes until later.

But not much changed in the upper Northwest beyond the color of the uniforms worn by the garrisons. In the far north the British relocated their garrison on St. Joseph Island, some thirty-five miles to the northeast of Michilimackinac near the mouth of the St. Marys River, though without the expense of permanence they had indulged in their move to the island at the Straits of Michilimackinac. In the south they moved barely ten miles to the south and slightly east to the present site of Amherstburg, Ontario, and there built Fort Malden.

The Americans still had little venture capital and the British therefore still owned the fur trade—and sought to protect it by staying reasonably in place. For this reason they had chosen the vague international boundary through the lakes in the first place, sacrificing territory to maintain access. It is also unquestionable that, even as the United States formed itself and emerged as a coherent government with a land-based agricultural economy, the British used the fur trade as a tool to continue instigating among the Indians—mercenaries still, and again in a losing cause. The old war was still not quite over, nor would it be until British dominance was toppled once and for all at the conclusion of the War of 1812 in the Treaty of Ghent.

In the meantime, Ohio petitioned for statehood in 1802 (granted in 1803) and what would become Michigan was temporarily attached to the new Indiana Territory (1803-5), which infuriated the residents of Detroit; but it was not yet valued for settlement and development, and was therefore mostly an administrative burden. It was an uphill battle by petition to get separate territorial status for Michigan in 1805. Her population was still negligible, but now the work of governmental administration could be done at Detroit (incorporated as what would be Michigan's first town in 1802). In the year Michigan became a territory of the first grade, Gen. William Hull arrived in Detroit as her first governor. Just before his arrival, fire ravaged the town.

CHAPTER SEVEN

THE TREATY
OF DETROIT (1807)

Hull's early career at Detroit was checkered at best, but with him came the first nonmilitary government of what would become the state of Michigan. Perhaps Hull's finest achievement as governor of the Territory of Michigan was the treaty he concluded with the Ottawa, Chippewa, Wyandot, and Potawotami Indians at Brownstown (on the river south of Detroit) on November 17, 1807.[1] In 1806 and 1807 Hull heard rumors of plans for an uprising, instigated and supplied out of the British-Canadian Fort Malden just to his south, and so called up the militia to strengthen the defenses at Detroit and to prepare for an attack. Hearing this, and fearing a reversion to yet another Indian war in the Northwest, President Jefferson decided it would be wise to treat with the Indians again in the hope of securing enough territory in southern and eastern Michigan to protect Detroit and thus permit some development from there.

To this end he appointed Governor Hull a United States commissioner with full federal authority to negotiate a treaty of cession.[2] Hull called together a council of all the tribes who had any discernible interest in the area; they met at Brownstown and there successfully negotiated the cession of roughly the southeastern quarter of Michigan's Lower Peninsula (as far north as White Rock, just to the south of Harbor Beach on the Thumb) according to the pattern established at Greenville of a down payment of goods and annual considerations into the future. This was the first major cession in what would become the state of Michigan. The territory ceded included the strip up the western Lake Erie shore and the Detroit River, then the only land in Michigan perceived to have any practical value, which had already been ceded to the Americans three times—at Paris (1783), Fort McIntosh, and Greenville—not to mention the international legal process by which the French claimed it from the

Indian proprietors and then passed it on to the British. The text of the treaty begins on page 169.

There is no evidence that Hull had any difficulty negotiating the treaty or that the Indians were in any way displeased with the consummation of it. There is evidence that Hull's presentation was carefully planned, that previous treaties were reviewed, and that the Indians understood to everyone's satisfaction what they had done in the past and what they were now doing: divesting themselves of any claim to land that they had used as their own by cession and quitclaim (Article I). It is likewise crystal clear in the language of the treaty that the cession was of land only, "comprehended within the following described lines and boundaries." The boundary lines on the east side of the cession ran through the waters of the Miami and Au Glaize rivers, Lake Erie, the Detroit River, Lake St. Clair, the St. Clair River, and Lake Huron. But the waters were only the vehicles carrying the lines (which were indefinite anyway, for the international boundary was not yet run and the geography was imperfectly known); the waters themselves, defined in the Northwest Ordinance as "common highways," "forever free," were at no time a consideration.

The method of payment, as at Greenville, called for the immediate delivery of goods and services (blacksmithing and agricultural help) together with annuities "forever" (Article II). Article V stipulated the Indians' *"privilege"* to hunt and fish *"on the lands ceded"* (italics mine) until they should pass into private or state ownership only. Clearly the treaty stipulates these privileges as temporary easements on the land just as the Greenville Treaty stipulated the Americans' right of safe passage for survey.

It is important that the stipulation granting the hunting and fishing *privilege* on the ceded lands was given specifically by the United States during its tenure as owners of the land *only;* it was certainly not a "right" reserved by the tribes because it was not specifically ceded. Just as the Greenville treaty reserved within Indian territory small parcels for American military use, so the Treaty of Detroit reserved to the Indians certain parcels of land for their use. As with the hunting and fishing privileges, it is clear who is reserving what for whom: the government of the United States promises to preserve and protect tribal communities already in place within the cession—even while conceding a limited privilege of subsistence on public lands, but only as long as they were to remain public. Once again, navigable waters were excluded from the whole question of ownership and so from the usual rights devolving therefrom, as was mandated in the Northwest Ordinance.

For the most part the Indians were coming to enjoy their still increasing dependence on the white man (no matter what his political preference or national origin might be), to understand that he would honor his end of an agreement, and to accept the fact that each cession they granted made their life a bit easier as the annual payments grew. Nevertheless, the rumors of war that Hull had picked up were altogether substantial, and it can well be argued that the Indians' strategy at Brownstown was to get what they could from the Americans even while plotting with the British to overthrow them. On the American side, thus, the treaty is one that intends to cover both peace and alliance (both the preamble and Article VII), as was the Greenville treaty; the rumblings of war from the north made it necessary to secure the territory to the south to protect the potentially vulnerable frontier of the Ohio River Valley. On the Indian (and thus British) side, this aspect of the treaty was most blatantly breached in events leading into the next war—only five years away.

It is almost impossible to appraise the matter accurately, but the strong public sentiment in the west was that once again British-Canadian subjects, who were still prowling the Michigan woods and shores promoting the fur trade—all according to Jay's Treaty—were once again manipulating the Indians toward hostility against the United States. It is almost certainly true that the regular gift giving continued from the British posts, for it is sure that the Americans were not significantly represented in the fur trade and were not passing out arms and ammunition to the tribes. This sentiment in itself, regardless of how true it was, was one of the main forces that moved the United States toward war with Britain in 1812. Indeed, in the west the conviction planted itself and grew that the only way to ease the Indian menace was to drive the British out of Canada. On the other side, also in the west, it is undeniable that the Indians were becoming increasingly alarmed as they watched their land claims dwindle and the settlers flow in, especially down the Ohio Valley, but inevitably elsewhere as well. Federal policy was clear: the Indian nations were to be dealt with fairly as a coequal foreign government with justifiable claims to territory desirable to the United States; we would exercise our claims by permitting settlement only after the consummation of legally binding treaties of cession agreed to by parties with proper authority.[3]

It is clear, also, that implementing federal policy was not uniformly clean. Settlers did not always abide by the rules and often enough chose to stray where they had no business to "squat" lands that were not yet available for market—to which Indian title had not yet even been extinguished. Worse yet, certain unscrupulous government commissioners, unchecked by proper federal regulation or simply ignoring the limitations of their commissions, became so aggressive and insensitive that they would treat with the most inconsequential and irresponsible delegations of Indians under almost any pretext to aquire lands. The predictable result was a series of land acquisitions in the name of the United States (few of which were ever enforced) that were close to fraudulent and highly unethical.

Perhaps the most notable of these was William Henry Harrison, governor of Indiana Territory. Harrison seems to have assumed that he had a federal mandate to acquire propertyby whatever loosely legal means possible and therefore was determined to pursue a policy of his own, by which he would deal with any combination of "chiefs" he could find or induce to come together under whatever circumstances. He thus commonly treated with renegade splinter groups out for personal profit without regard for their nation or the combination of nations.[4]

Following this procedure, lands could be ceded and a spurious documentation assembled without the knowledge or consent of either the tribal councils that should have been legally responsible or the federal government in whose name the business was being conducted. All of this was both frightening and confusing to the Indians, especially the part where an appointee of the United States government could do business without authority with Indians who similarly lacked authority.

It was intensified by a sudden eastward migration of the powerful Sioux nation into Wisconsin, where they sought entry into the fur trade on the lakes and thereby blocked off that attractive quarter. The Indians in Michigan were badly squeezed: Ohio was ceded and established as a state beneath them, the Sioux were in place to the west, and the British held and administered what is now Ontario, to the east and north. The Indians' concern over the situation in which they found themselves was counterbalanced by growing American enthusiasm for investment in the land, settlement, and development—coupled with at least occasional administrative indiscretion. It was not policy on either side, as witness the ease and striking success of Hull's negotiations at Brownstown; it was, however, unfortunate fact. The situation in the Northwest was not good.

In Tecumseh, a chieftain among the Shawnee, for the first time since the days of Pontiac the Indians had an able leader perhaps the match for any white man on the frontier. Born in Ohio and so familiar with the American incursion there and the subsequent loss of tribal lands, Tecumseh conceived a deep hatred for the white man, especially the American white man, and his ways. He was a skilled orator and wide-ranging traveler who together with his brother preached successfully on a single theme: if the Indians would purge themselves of their terrible dependence on the white man and revert to a pure and primitive mode of life, they could drive the whites from their land and live as it had been ordained for them, at peace. Tecumseh's brother was a one-eyed mystic called the Prophet, who enormously influenced the savage types by performing an eclipse and its removal (June 6, 1806)—the imminence of which he had learned from a British trader.[5] These brothers proved a formidable combination, not just among the Shawnees but among all the nations.

As early as 1806, while the Prophet was learning how to perform his miracle, Tecumseh was focusing on organizing an Indian confederation to resist the Americans. He succeeded in uniting the northern Algonquian nations, but failed to involve the Iroquois to the east, and later traveled south trying to enlist the Indians of that region to his cause. In 1811 he left his brother in charge at the Shawnee settlement that was the base camp of the resistance operation—called Prophetstown, at the junction of Tippecanoe Creek and the Wabash River, near what is now Lafayette, Indiana— with instructions under no circumstances to commence hostilities. Governor Harrison, meanwhile, alarmed by Tecumseh's successful confederation, assembled an army near the Indian encampment. Against the orders of his absent brother, the Prophet, assuring his savage friends that the whites would be made helpless by his magic, ordered an attack on the morning of November 7. There followed a pitched battle during which both sides sustained heavy losses (about two hundred dead and wounded each), though Harrison's army outnumbered the Indians by about three hundred. As the Indians evacuated their position, Harrison burned their camp, declared victory, and withdrew. He then wrote a report to the secretary of war in which he asserted that the Indians had sustained the worst defeat in the history of their involvement with the whites. Such is the silly stuff of legend; twenty-nine years later Harrison rode into the presidency as the hero of Tippecanoe—for performing only adequately with a superior force.

Of far greater importance than the battle or its inconclusive outcome, was documented evidence in his report that his men had found the Indians equipped with guns and ammunition much of which was still in the original British wrappings. The Indian-guerrilla portion of the Revolutionary War was still on. This proved to be the hard intelligence that carved in marble the western belief in the danger of continuing British involvement with the Indians and gained support for that belief in the east.

Nowhere was the conviction of British involvement with the Indians stronger than in and around Detroit. Though they had surrendered Detroit to the Americans in 1796 and moved across the river to Fort Malden, the British seem persistently to have nurtured the belief that somehow the fortunes of war or international events (or the failure of government in the United States without a substantial professional military) would again give them control of the Northwest. British officers from Malden continued to assert authority on American soil, happily tracking down and reclaiming their deserters in Detroit and impressing crew and supplies from any victim ship that happened along the high seas.[6] In July of 1810 Governor Hull wrote to the secretary of war complaining that many Indians from the south and west continued to visit the British post at Amherstburg (Fort Malden) and were there supplied, more than usual, with arms, ammunition, and provisions—cleary violating the treaties governing the territory. In September of 1811, Governor Harrison also wrote to the secretary of war:

> All of the Indians of the Wabash have been, or are now, on a visit to the British agent at Malden; my informant has never known more than a fourth as many goods given to the Indians as they are now distributing. He examined the share of one man (not a chief) and found that he had received an elegant rifle, ninety-five pounds of powder, fifty pounds of lead, three blankets, three pieces of strouds, ten shirts, and several other articles. He says every Indian is furnished with a gun (either a rifle or a fusil), and an abundance of ammunition. A trader of this country was lately in the King's store at Malden, and was told that the quantity of goods for the Indian department, which had been sent out this year, exceeded that of common years by 20,000 pounds sterling. It is impossible to ascribe this profusion to any other motive than that of instigating the Indians to take up the tomahawk; it cannot be to secure their trade, for all their peltries collected on the Wabash [in] one year, if sold in the London markets, would not pay the freight of the goods which have been given to the Indians." [7]

Whether Harrison's information out of Malden was accurate or not, the concern he expresses was enough to take him to Tippecanoe. The persistence and enormity of the British gifting to the Indians fully suggests that the United States harbored a substantial, well armed, and hostile infantry in the Northwest—completely supplied and encouraged to make trouble by another none too friendly foreign neighbor. At least in that quarter, the situation was ripe for war. Harrison's encounter with the Indians at Tippecanoe proved to be a preliminary skirmish.

Other forces were also stretching American dissatisfaction with the British toward a declaration of war. During the several years before 1812, the allied effort in Europe against the French and Napoléon—long since crowned emperor and having turned revolutionary ideological fervor into a war of conquest and empire waged against the entire Western world—had gone badly. England's share in it was costly in every way and, because of the terrible consequences implicit in Napoléon's possible success, her commitment had to be absolute. Because of the cost of the European campaign her economy was suffering, and because of the sheer magnitude of the war she was in constant and desperate need of military personnel, especially naval personnel, for the superiority of the Royal Navy gave her unquestioned mastery of the seas and this was her most important and necessary tactical contribution to the allied effort.

The British naval tactic was to blockade the ports controlled by France and the nations friendly to her and to embargo her own ports to block trade with neutral nations that would not join the alliance. The first was an attempt to starve France out; the second was an attempt to impose economic sanctions against nonaligned nations to force them into the alliance. Further, because they had the maritime muscle and were fighting a war of national survival, the British happily enough interrupted commerce on the high seas, recruited seamen, and attached supplies by impressment; the survival of the nation justified almost any conduct in any area beyond national boundaries. Too, the British still considered the United States a sort of bastard child that needed discipline to gain acknowledgment and thus be permitted to grow and develop—not to mention the fact that we were also nonaligned and therefore potentially hostile. The pragmatic British would do what they could to keep us busy with our own problems (like the Indians and the organization of the Northwest) to keep us unarmed in the international theater and out of league with France, our old ally. The apparently immense cost of supplying the Indians for their campaigns was, after all, still much less than the cost of war. We suffered from every phase of this nearly hostile posture.

As nonaligned and unarmed neutrals in a European war, our trade was cut off by blockade or embargo from virtually all European ports. If British military officials did not in fact arm the American Indians, they surely sanctioned the process and turned their backs while their traders did—all, once again, to use the Indian to stir up trouble on the western frontier to annoy the Americans into compliance or just keep us busy and so out of trouble. And, as that bastard child in want of discipline, our ships were as subject as those of any other nation to challenge, search, seizure, and the impressment of seamen. The matter was made even more complex by the fact that the Napoleonic challenge grew out of a revolutionary movement championing liberty, equality, and fraternity, which sounded like the principles over which we had just fought a successful revolutionary war. Napoléon levied his own set of trading sanctions for the same reasons. Our neutrality was thus earnest, firm, and a matter of uncomfortable circumstance, in return for which we were punished by both sides and so caught in the middle of someone else's war.

In 1807 President Jefferson answered Europe by shepherding through Congress the Embargo Act, which prohibited American commercial ships from sailing to any foreign port. The intent was to punish both Britain and France for interfering with our trade; the immediate effect, however, was to punish the American economy even more by further removing our merchants from their foreign markets. President James Madison followed suit by urging his Congress to pass yet more laws intended to punish both Britain and France; but more and more it was the American people who were most severely punished. Many would have preferred a shooting war to this devastating economic one—and the behavior of the British-armed Indians in the Northwest gave some urgency to this preference.[8] British trading and gifting, on the one hand, was intense; on the other, Tecumseh and the Prophet were rallying the tribes and achieving some organization and military order. Both the Ohio River Valley and the posts in the northern lakes might be vulnerable to a joint effort on by the British and the Indians.

Then, in 1810, because of the plight of its own people, Congress passed an act reopening trade with both France and England, promising that if either nation would withdraw its trading restrictions we would refuse to trade with the other. Napoléon, militarily successful but economically distressed, snapped at the bait. President Madison proclaimed nonintercourse with England, and the United States found itself in the familiar (if by now ironic) position of trading with France and so sanctioning implicitly an emperor aggressively seeking empire and aligned against the European allies who would stop him and in the process preserve their own national destinies. Never in our history have we accepted a stranger bedfellow. All of this failed to amuse the British; it is strangely fortunate that they were so occupied with Napoléon that they regarded, and continued to do so until 1815, events in America as a mildly interesting sideshow.

In the meantime, a new Congress had convened during the winter of 1811-12 and its mood was to stop tinkering with a trading war and get on with the real thing. By June of 1812 the "War Hawks" had succeeded in pressing through a resolution of war with England. In Europe, Napoléon had begun his foredoomed invasion of Russia; this gave Britain some breathing space and freed a portion of her military, especially her navy, whose blockade of the French ports was in place and unchallengeable even if maintained by fewer ships, for service in North America. This would have devastating effects on this side of the Atlantic. In short, never was the United States less prepared for a major war, especially an early nineteenth-century one with England.

Any war with Britain destined to be fought in North America would have to be fought along a highly vulnerable United States-Canadian border where, especially in the Northwest, it was an absolute certainty that the dispossessed and therefore cranky Indian nations would take up the British side of the issue. Geography and demographics being what they were, the American defensive effort would have to focus on the East Coast just to protect our seat of government and principal centers of population; though this effort evolved as a tactical necessity, the British would inevitably want to put on all the pressure they could from the west—making full use of their Indian mercenary allies. From Canada they would want to gain control of the Great Lakes to use the position there as a base for infiltrating the area to the south of Lake Erie and so the Ohio Valley. Thus a land-based war would be carried to the American rear guard while the vastly superior Royal Navy hammered away at and blockaded the East Coast and other armies prepared to invade from Montreal and Quebec. If they could succeed in this, or even significant portions of it, they could set in place a long-term tactic of containment and slow siege from all sides.

Just as in Europe, the navy was to be a crucial factor; it was to close down American ports and establish such land bases as might be possible in the east while Canadian and Indian armies moved in from the west. In 1812 the Royal Navy included more than a thousand vessels, by far the greatest naval force in the world; to oppose it, the United States Navy comprised some sixteen frigates and a ragtag collection of brigs and sloops. The regular army of the United States sported about seven thousand officers and men, mostly dispersed as garrisons at distant frontier posts; the officers corps was mostly aging remnants from the Revolution and the postrevolutionary Indian campaigns.[9]

In addition, inland transportation and so communication was slow and difficult, partisan politics divided the nation (the New England Federalists were so firmly opposed to the war that the governors of Connecticut and Massachusetts refused to call up their militia when the president ordered them to do so), and disorganization was the general order of the day in both the east and the Northwest. The war was, in short, plucky but stupid. It was just a stroke of good luck that the British were still occupied with Napoléon so that the principal enemy army and its command were overseas and busy. In Washington, the attention of the leadership was necessarily on the defense of the Atlantic coast and on several mostly irrational schemes for invading and conquering Canada. Predictably enough, 1812 was not a good year for the United States. By the end of it Mackinac had fallen, Detroit had fallen (thus giving the British tactical mastery of the northern lakes), and the Royal Navy on the East Coast had wasted our pathetic fleet of men-of-war (only the *Constitution* and a few smaller ships even remained in commission) and set its blockade. It looked as if our brashness had caught up with us.

Fort Mackinac was the first to fall. After the surrender of Fort Michilimackinac in 1796, the British had repaired to St. Joseph Island near the mouth of the St. Marys River and there put up Fort St. Joseph; as with Fort Malden to the south, they just moved a bit off and built a counteremplacement to balance the one given over to the Americans. In 1812 Capt. Charles Roberts was in command. This northern installation was intended to maintain the continuity of the British fur trade and for this reason, as well as the whole set of international political ones, the same policy of gifting to the Indians, of such intense concern in Detroit and Indiana, was the order of the day. The Indians throughout the region were fully armed and loyal to the British. Owing to their activities among the tribes and the understandable American resentment of them, the British outposts were better prepared by rumor for war than were the American ones. The overt arming of the Indians, after all, was calculated to invite war; at the same time, it was not yet clear that the East Coast Americans valued their Great Lakes possessions enough to garrison them for war or make any concerted effort to preserve them. All garrisons in the interior were modest, and accordingly Roberts had by him only a small force of regulars, perhaps fifty or less; but to prepare for hostilities he had called in forces from Wisconsin, raised by British loyalists Robert Dickson and John Askin, Jr., enlisted the help of John Johnston at the Sault, organized a force of voyageurs, and, importantly, rallied over three hundred friendly Indians to round out his force—a considerable, though mostly non-professional, army under the circumstances. On June 26, 1812, Sir Isaac Brock, governor and military commander of Upper Canada, wrote to Roberts announcing a state of war and ordering an immediate attack on Fort Mackinac. It is also possible that Roberts received advance word of his impending orders from a loyalist agent of John Jacob Astor's, who had been sent to St. Joseph to safeguard trading goods stockpiled there.[10] Nevertheless, the orders were no surprise and knowledge of hostilities reached Roberts long before it did Lt. Porter Hanks, commander of the American garrison at Mackinac; he was fully prepared and had a plan of attack.

But Hanks was not insensitive to the rumors of impending war and on July 16 he dispatched Michael Dousman, a civilian fur trader with friends at St. Joseph Island, whom he thought would arouse no suspicion, to sniff out those rumors. On the same day Roberts and his main force set out from the St. Marys with a large flotilla of canoes and other small boats escorting the brig *Caledonia,* intending a dawn surprise attack on the American fort. Dousman ran directly into Roberts's main force, was taken prisoner, and then released to return to Mackinac to warn loyalist civilians to take cover. In this conflict, as American fur company functionaries also found, a civilian with friends on both sides could play both sides. Roberts waited for the cover of night, then approached and came ashore at the place still called British Landing. He scaled the hill behind the fort (replete with a six-pound artillery piece), and from that commanding position at the fort's unprotected rear greeted the American garrison at dawn. Lieutenant Hanks commanded "fifty-seven men fit for active duty" and was not only surprised, but seriously outmanned.[11] He had no choice but to surrender on the spot.

British conduct with and among the Indians at Fort Malden, together with the strengthening of their garrison, increasing their supply of provisions, and erecting batteries, was clearly a cause for alarm in Detroit. In October of 1811 the situation there was considered so dangerous that Governor Hull himself traveled to Washington seeking assistance; just as was the case farther to the north, the Detroit garrison was modest and the county militia both small, as a part of a still small population, and ill trained—not to mention the persistent problem of mixed loyalties in the area. The westerners well understood both the vulnerability and the tactical importance of Detroit, even if it was just a fledgling frontier town that happened to be growing up around a fort. In Hull's absence a citizens committee called out the militia for a drill and parade in May of 1812. Daily exercise and discipline were ordered and so began Detroit's preparations for war.

In the meantime, Governor Hull had succeeded in his mission to the east; he was granted one regiment of regulars and three regiments of militia, to be raised in Ohio. Because of his excellent record during the Revolution, from which he retired as general, he was asked to command. At first he refused because, taking his lessons from both the French and the British experience, he doubted Detroit could be held unless Lake Erie were secure against an invasionary force from Lower Canada, and as yet there was no promise of that; the British had a small fleet of armed vessels on the lake and the Americans did not. Ultimately, however, he accepted and in the spring of 1812 set out from Washington to assume his command at Dayton, Ohio, vested with the rank of brigadier general.[12] The Ohio militia regiments were commanded by Cols. Lewis Cass, James Findlay, and Duncan MacArthur and in late May this army of about twelve hundred, plus several hundred more rank and file, marched north with General Hull carrying orders to secure and hold Detroit against the possibility of hostilities with Britain.

On June 30, Hull's army reached the site of the old British Fort Miamis near the mouth of the Maumee River and there secured a small schooner, the *Cuyahoga*, to carry supplies while the army made a forced march to Detroit. Though Hull had received a dispatch from the secretary of war several days earlier, and though it was dated June 18 (the day on which war had been declared), it spoke only of the probability of war, not the fact of it. Hull was thus unaware that hostilities had commenced. Without Hull's knowledge, and probably against his orders, all his personal and military papers were placed on board the *Cuyahoga*. The ship's master, also ignorant of the declaration of war, chose the easier channel northward on the east side of Bois Blanc Island, came under the guns of Fort Malden, and was captured on July 2. The British thus had detailed knowledge of Hull's army, right down to the month-end muster rolls. On the same day Hull received a second dispatch from the war department, also dated June 18, that informed him of the state of war. Hull and his army reached Detroit on July 5 to find Reuben Atwater, secretary and acting governor, at the head of the standing militia and the small garrison of regulars. This brought the whole force to about eighteen hundred.

On July 12, Hull invaded Canada, crossing the Detroit River just to the south of Belle Isle and there establishing his temporary base of operations. He intended to attack Fort Malden, over which for the moment he enjoyed the advantage of numbers, but he vacillated. He very likely overestimated the strength of the British garrison there; he was concerned that the guns of the three warships stationed at Amherstburg could have been used effectively against him, and he waited while gun carriages could be prepared for his artillery. Meantime, toward the end of July Hull received the grave news of the fall of Fort Mackinac, which implied that hordes of British and Indians would soon be swooping down the lakes to join with the garrison at Malden in an attack on Detroit.

The hordes of British were indeed coming, not from the north but from the east, and Hull's hesitation lost for him what might have been the best opportunity he would have to take the British installation. Sir Isaac Brock was making his way westward with a substantial army to reinforce Fort Malden and engineer the capture of Detroit. Gen. Henry Dearborn, American commander on the Niagara frontier, had been ordered to engage Brock's army, at least in a diversionary skirmish designed to slow his progress, while Hull did his work in Detroit and at Fort Malden— which the war department assumed could be taken before Brock could get there. Hull's hesitation scrapped this strategy. Also, Dearborn had disregarded his orders and declined the opportunity to engage Brock at all, except socially to sign a separate armistice agreement with him in which Hull's army and the other American forces in the Northwest were not included. This opened and further secured Lake Erie for Brock and the British, hastening his progress to Fort Malden, and so emphasizing Detroit's vulnerability. Hull was now open to attack from the north and the east, and his watery supply route from the south was in enemy hands. His only source of supply was the military road he had so recently traveled running north from Ohio. Not for long.

During this indecisiveness a detachment under Colonel Cass skirmished successfully with a detachment of British at the Canard River, just north of Amherstburg, but this was ordered only as a containment tactic to keep the British in place. Shortly after, more grave news came in: Tecumseh and his Indian army had successfully blocked the Ohio supply line near Brownstown. Hull tried three times to send detachments to join forces with Capt. Henry Brush, whose supply train was blocked, and three times failed. Mackinac, and so control in the north, had fallen to the British and Indian consortium there, the Indians controlled the supply line from Ohio, and Brock's army had broken through at Niagara, gained control of the access to Lake Erie, and was advancing toward Malden. It was likely that Detroit would fall.

There was still plenty of fight left in his Ohio colonels, who questioned Hull's capacity to lead, but his quandary was a specific and tactical one. If Tecumseh's army could so easily disrupt and so control the Ohio supply line, if General Dearborn could issue his own separate peace and in so doing give the British control of Lake Erie and an open line of commerce and supply from Montreal and Quebec, if an insubstantial wilderness garrison at St. Joseph Island with the help of some Indians and some amateurs could take Fort Mackinac at a stroke and without firing a shot and so reassert British dominance in the north, if Detroit, in short, could be so quickly and easily cut off from *every* direction, how many lives was a protracted military engagement worth just to prolong the miserable existence of an abandoned and so apparently expendable American outpost? General Hull retreated across the river to Detroit.

The British to this point had performed brilliantly, earning maximum return on minimum money spent and in the process setting their long-range tactic in place; with the fall of Detroit they would be poised to gather all their Indian allies and sweep south into Ohio. The initial American response in a stupidly declared American war had been, predictably, stupid. In effect the battle for Detroit was already over. Hull would not permit his gunners to fire on the British as they erected batteries on the shore opposite the American fort, though he did indulge in a day's worth of bombardment across the river—in which two British gunboats also participated. On the night after this engagement, however, British regulars and their Indian allies established a beachhead before the fort, the supply line from the south was still broken (despite the best efforts of Cols. Cass and MacArthur), the British had the immense tactical advantage of provision and reinforcement through Lake Erie, and the threat remained of a British and Indian offensive from the north. The northern offensive would be a certainty if Detroit held out because the British would want to gather their forces in the area on their way to Ohio anyway. As had Porter Hanks at Mackinac, Hull threw in the towel to avoid the needless waste of human lives. Detroit was once again under the Union Jack. Brush and his supply train never did reach Detroit and retreated to the south. Col. Henry Proctor, previously commander at Fort Malden, was left in command at Detroit as well.

In 1812 the United States had attempted two other invasions of Canada, one from Niagara and one from Lake Champlain; both were easily repulsed.[13] Our luck was better, once again, in Europe. By year's end Napoléon was deep in his ignominious retreat from Russia, that part of his army not frozen on the verge of starvation and his campaign a disaster. This permitted England and her European allies to regroup and reinforce, while watching the great Bonaparte in the throes of defeating himself—with a little help from Russia, some rotten weather, and the eastern armies. This was the truly great moment and the center of attention, for only in Napoléon's ultimate defeat could the French threat be put down for good, and only in that could England breathe easy. The war with the French was a war of national survival; the war in America was mostly an amusement, and the upstarts were well in hand anyway.

Governor Harrison of Indiana Territory succeeded Hull as commander of the American army in the Northwest, and he quickly set about raising another army in Ohio with which he proposed to gain back what had been lost at Detroit or, at the very least, block the expected incursion to the south by the British and the Indians. Tecumseh still controlled the supply trail to Detroit north of the Ohio border, and the British hold on Lake Erie permitted rapid movement of men and supplies from the east to their Great Lakes positions. This was not a good tactical situation and the Americans had to do something to challenge it before the British could put it to practical use. In January of 1813, Harrison sent north to the Maumee River a large detachment, about one thousand strong, of Kentucky militiamen to put up a fort near the present city of Toledo. The fort would check and protect the supply route, challenge Tecumseh's Indian army, serve as a storehouse for necessary supplies and equipment, and become the base of operations for the army with which Harrison hoped to recapture Detroit. Gen. James Winchester was in command, Col. William Lewis his subordinate. Almost immediately Winchester received an appeal from the people of Frenchtown (near what is now Monroe, at the mouth of the River Raisin) for protection against the threat of Indian attack.

Winchester responded by sending about seven hundred of his force under Colonel Lewis to skirt the ice along the Lake Erie shore and give assistance. Lewis crossed the also frozen River Raisin under heavy enemy fire and successfully drove a mixed force of about six hundred British and Indians out of the settlement, from which they retreated first to the woods and then back to Fort Malden. Fearing reprisal by a much larger force supplied from the fort, he sent for reinforcements. Winchester arrived on January 20 with his remaining three hundred troops; the soldiers camped in a nearby open field while Winchester made himself comfortable in the home of a prominent local citizen.

On the morning of January 22 the men awoke to find themselves surrounded and under heavy attack; by the time Winchester could get to his panicked men it was too late and he was captured. Colonel Proctor, still in command at both Malden and Detroit, demanded that Winchester surrender, arguing that if he did not the British would not be able to restrain their Indian allies from an out-and-out massacre. Winchester acceded. Proctor, fearing attack, it is said, by General Harrison, returned with prisoners and walking wounded to Fort Malden, leaving behind the more seriously wounded to be cared for by the residents of Frenchtown and two army surgeons. In the morning, about two hundred drink-crazed Indians stormed the settlement, sought out the wounded, murdered and scalped them without hindrance, burned the houses in which they were being cared for, and threw those who tried to escape into the conflagrations. This Indian atrocity was found not terribly amusing by the Americans, especially those from Kentucky, and it marked the high point of British success in the Northwest during this year. It also created a rallying point, "Remember the River Raisin," from which grew a renewed American determination to make sense of the so far badly bungled war on the western front.

During the late winter and early spring of 1813, however, Harrison got his fort built on the Maumee and christened it Fort Meigs, after Return J. Meigs, governor of Ohio. Confident after his success at Frenchtown, Proctor led a mixed force of

British and allied Indians against the new American installation on April 23, knowing that if he were successful he would be in place, with a new fort built at enemy expense for a base, to invade Ohio. But the Americans held their position through a siege that lasted until May 9, as they did through a second attempt by Tecumseh and his Indian army in July. Trying to save face after these failures, Proctor next determined to attack an American installation near what is now Lower Sandusky, Ohio, where the youthful Maj. George Croghan commanded. Again he failed, sustaining significant losses against Croghan's insignificant ones; the small garrison held against a far greater besieging force. Croghan became a hero overnight and for the third time a British and Indian attempt to invade the south shore of Lake Erie and thus gain access to Ohio failed. The war at and for the south shore of Lake Erie was at a delicate standoff, the American positions precarious but stiffly tenacious—and able to be supplied and reinforced and developed from the south. But the British still controlled the lake itself, and this left them free to supply and develop their positions to the north of it.

A general sort of apathy toward North American affairs in London, where Napoléon was still the number one item, likely saved the day for us; it would be just too costly to flood Canada and Detroit with the professional troops, munitions, and supplies necessary to assure a successful invasion of Ohio. Furthermore, there was no reason to doubt the security of the British positions at Mackinac, Detroit, and Amherstburg—or the success of the blockade of the East Coast ports—so this impetuous little war was still well enough in hand, even with a standoff on the south Lake Erie shore, that it could be dealt with later.

Curiously enough, even as they were preparing to try him for treason, the best brains in Washington finally determined that General Hull was correct in his conviction that Detroit and the upper Lakes, as well as the area to the south of them, remained vulnerable as long as the British retained control of Lake Erie. If, on the other hand, the United States could gain control of the lake, we could block British shipping on it and so put the squeeze on their activities in Upper Canada—including shipping arms and munitions for the soldiers and their Indian allies, which would surely slow the invasion of Ohio, if not stop it altogether, and secure the Ohio Valley citizens—while holding and strengthening our northerly supply line from Ohio. Hull had pressed for a naval fleet to be built on Lake Erie when he was commander in the Northwest, and the job had been begun at yards constructed for the purpose at Presque Isle (now Erie, Pennsylvania, a shallow and therefore fully protected natural harbor with a barrier bar into which the British men-of-war could not sail). But the work had progressed slowly until the arrival there, in March of 1813, of Lt. Oliver Hazard Perry.

Perry stepped up the pace of construction and by late spring had the skeleton of the first United States naval fleet on the Great Lakes assembled and ready for commissioning—two brigs and three schooners, the armament for all transported overland from Philadelphia and Pittsburgh. Now he had to man his fleet, get it across

the same shallow bar that kept the British fleet out of Presque Isle harbor, and somehow finesse the British fleet itself. Commanded by Com. Robert H. Barclay and
attached to Amherstburg, and knowing of the American construction project, the
British fleet had developed the mildly unpleasant habit of patrolling outside Presque
Isle harbor. On July 31, however, Barclay was obliged to return to Amherstburg
with his fleet to replenish his supplies and regroup; now it was Perry's turn. He
removed all armor from his ships, floated a sunken flat-bottomed scow along each
side of them, ran timbers through the gunports above the scows, pumped the scows,
lifted the ships, and thus floated the little fleet over the barrier bar and out onto the
lake. Armaments, supplies, and provisions were then barged out, his men joined
their ships, and Perry set sail for Sandusky Bay. There he rendezvoused with officers and men sent by General Harrison, including about one hundred Kentucky riflemen—none too happy about the River Raisin incident—and then was ready. Four
other American-owned boats joined this impromptu navy and gave Perry the numer-
ical edge over Barclay, nine boats to six. The sixth of Barclay's craft, the *Detroit*,
kept him in port and therefore contributed to Perry's escape from Presque Isle; it
was nearing completion at the British shipyard at Amherstburg and, not knowing
what he would face or when, but suspecting an American surprise, Barclay waited
for its commissioning. Perry also had the advantage in the number of guns assigned
to his command; but Barclay had the advantage in long-range equipment and in the
training of his officers and seamen—not to mention his own training, which gave
him the worldwide prestige of the British Royal Navy.

The Americans had accomplished what might have seemed impossible. The
British, with only the modest fleet of gunboats at Amherstburg, had complete control of Lake Erie and its ports after General Dearborn's capitulation at Niagara. Their
superior armies with their Indian allies commanded the positions at the various narrows from the St. Lawrence to the north and west, and the Americans had nothing
anywhere on the Lakes with which to challenge the Royal Navy. Our only hope,
therefore, lay in the almost impossible task of creating a navy of our own, virtually under the British guns, which could be equipped only via overland routes from
the East Coast. It was a brash attempt; and it worked.

The story of the Battle of Lake Erie has been well and variously told.[14] Because
of Barclay's hesitation while waiting for the *Detroit*, Perry was able to get both
manned and positioned. He chose as his headquarters Put-in-Bay, in a cluster of
small islands to the north of Sandusky Harbor and convenient, therefore, to
Amherstburg and the Ohio coast. There, because he could under no circumstances
afford to engage the British fleet while moored under the guns of Fort Malden, he
waited; the engagement had to occur, because as long as the British remained penned
in at Amherstburg the rest of the lake was useless to them and wide open to further
exercises in Yankee ingenuity, which had just become formidable. Unless they
engaged and won, then, the whole point of their western campaign was lost and the
Ohio Valley remained secure while the Americans improved, supplied, and

reinforced their northern Ohio positions. For the first time in this war, the Americans' position was brilliant; we had accomplished what the British thought we could not and were in place to engage them in a decisive sea battle that was now inevitable with most of the advantages on our side

Lack of money and enthusiastic support from London had permitted a disastrous turnabout. If the Americans could pull out a win in a single naval engagement, for which (against all odds) they were now fully prepared and manned, they could completely counter the British offensive in the west and make the British positions at Amherstburg, Detroit, and Mackinac meaningless—as vulnerable to a prowling American navy, blockade, and slow starvation as had been Detroit when General Hull arrived with his command. The British came out, as they had to, on September 10. Perry engaged them and won decisively: "We have met the enemy and they are ours, two ships, two brigs, one schooner, and one sloop." As surely as Hull knew that Detroit was lost when General Dearborn let General Brock through at Niagara, so now the British knew that they were doomed at both Detroit and Fort Malden— and Mackinac, from any military and strategic point of view, was for the first time reduced to the stature of just another wilderness outpost in the north without much point or function except as a center of trade.

Meanwhile, General Harrison had mustered an army some seven thousand strong with which he was ready to move on Malden and Detroit; all he needed was for Perry to clear the lake, which Perry conveniently did. At Malden, Proctor read the same scenario and on September 24, even as Harrison was moving his troops to the Canadian side preparing to carry the land battle to the British, he evacuated Fort Malden. Two days later he pulled out of Detroit, after burning the public buildings. Intending to retreat to Toronto, then called York, he proceeded eastward along the south shore of Lake St. Clair toward the Thames River, with Harrison's army now in hot pursuit. Tecumseh and his Indian army, disliking Proctor's retreat, stood and fought but were easily pushed aside by Harrison's vastly superior force. Proctor, forced now to engage, chose a position on the north side of the Thames, so as to inflict on Harrison's army the inconvenience of having to cross the river under fire.

A hard charge by a regiment of mounted Kentucky riflemen, still remembering the River Raisin, was all that was needed; while Proctor escaped to the east, the remains of his army surrendered to Harrison. The Indians fought on, but when Tecumseh fell they scattered. Lacking provisions for an immediate full-scale invasion of Canada, Harrison withdrew to Detroit, and the Kentuckians, who had contributed so much manpower and shooting skill, returned home. Fort Detroit was rechristened Fort Shelby, after the governor of Kentucky who had come to Harrison's aid. Harrison and Perry were now national heroes and Detroit and the lower Lakes were back in American hands. The immediate threat of a British invasion in the west was broken. In October the two departed for the Niagara frontier leaving Col. Lewis Cass in command at Detroit; shortly thereafter President Madison named him territorial governor, a position he retained for eighteen years.

The fall of Detroit and Amherstburg created serious problems for the British garrison at Mackinac; the closing of the Detroit River blocked their supply line from the south and winter canoe trips along the old Ottawa River route were at no time very popular. Capt. Richard Bullock (having replaced the ailing and aging Capt. Charles Roberts) was now in command and his garrison was small: only about forty British regulars together with about seventy-five veterans and nonprofessionals.[15] The British policy of gifting to and so arming their savage friends persisted there, a large band of Indians had appeared from the west during the summer of 1813 and exhausted supplies, and during the fall only a single ship, belonging to the North West Company, made it through from the south, having barely escaped capture by the Americans in the St. Clair River. Harrison had planned to send an expedition to take the northern fort in the fall, but the cold weather came too fast and the plan was postponed.

This delay bought the British some time, and their strategists assigned Fort Mackinac a high priority as their only remaining position in the northern lakes and so the key to any possible reentry there. From York (Toronto) via the Lake Simcoe route, they began moving provisions—dried foodstuffs, flour, biscuits, salt pork, salt, rum, and armaments—to Nottawasaga Bay at the southeastern extremity of Georgian Bay, from where they could be moved in the spring to Mackinac. In the spring Col. Robert McDouall, commanding a regiment of one hundred men, was sent to the same embarkation point; the provisions and reinforcements reached Mackinac in May of 1814. In the meantime, Bullock had his garrison build an outwork behind his principal fort, which he called Fort George, in order to guard against the same sort of surprise Captain Roberts had engineered in 1812. Thus, in the summer of 1814 the British position at Fort Mackinac was much stronger than it had been the previous fall, though it fell far short of the wartime garrisons built up at Malden and Detroit.

By the end of 1813, then, American successes in the Northwest had turned the tide of war in our favor, at least there. In the east the picture was less bright. The British blockade of the coast remained in place, they captured Fort Niagara in December, and in Europe the annihilation of Napoléon's armies after the disastrous Russian campaign assured his defeat. Germany and Sweden rose against him, his armies were beaten back, and at Fontainbleu, in 1814, he abdicated and was exiled to Elba. He was brought back for the final engagement at Waterloo in the following year and there soundly thrashed by the allied British, Belgians, and Prussians. When this bit of European nastiness was over, the British were expected to turn their attention to their problems in North America. In 1814 they sacked and burned our national capital, terrorized the eastern seaboard, and New England, which had been opposed to the war from the onset, threatened to disrupt the Union. In the Northwest, though Lake Erie and Detroit were lost, the British repulsed a not very clever attack on Mackinac and retook their fort at Prairie du Chien (in Wisconsin); thus they solidified their hold on the far north and continued their threat from that distant quarter.

The American brilliance on and near Lake Erie was thus a spotty and isolated showing at best.

In June news reached Colonel McDouall at Mackinac that an American expedition out of Missouri had captured the British fort at Prairie du Chien, the center of the fur trade in what is now Wisconsin, trying to block a possible British incursion into Illinois and Missouri via the Mississippi—which would have been an extension of the strategy that had taken them to the south shore of Lake Erie. But the Americans foolishly thought that a garrison of sixty men could hold the position. Against them McDouall sent two hundred mixed British regulars and Indian allies, which force doubled in size as it passed through Green Bay, up the Fox River, and down the Wisconsin, picking up Indians as it progressed. The American defenders surrendered to this superior army after a three-day engagement. Whether they could ever do anything with it or not, the British hold on the north proved tenacious.

The American attempt to take Fort Mackinac was similarly abortive. An expedition left Detroit in early July; Capt. Arthur Sinclair was the naval commander, Col. George Croghan—hero of Fort Stevenson, near Lower Sandusky, in the previous year—and Maj. Andrew Hunter Holmes were in charge of infantry. The fleet included several ships that had participated in the Battle of Lake Erie and also the *Caledonia,* which had been used by Captain Roberts to transport his men from St. Joseph Island to Mackinac in 1812 and thus won the unique distinction of participating in both British and American expeditions against Mackinac:

> The operation was bungled and mismanaged from the beginning. Sinclair and Croghan had orders to destroy on their way north the British installations supposedly built at Matchadash Bay to supply Fort Mackinac, but after the ships arrived in Lake Huron it turned out that no one knew how to get there! Instead of moving against Mackinac Island the ships entered the St. Mary's [sic] River. The fort on St. Joseph's [sic] Island that the British had abandoned was burned. A party under Holmes then proceeded to the Soo, where it seized a ship belonging to the North West Company and goods that were the property of the trader John Johnston.[16]

When the expedition finally got to where it was supposed to get to do what it was supposed to do, it became clear that no one had given much thought as to how to get it done. They even made the alarming discovery that the deck guns on the ships could not be elevated enough to score a hit on the fortress on the heights. The party finally came ashore at British Landing, apparently remembering the surprise the British had engineered from that location, where the Indian allies ambushed them and Major Holmes lost his life before they could retreat to the boats. Sinclair and Croghan left two of the smaller ships behind to challenge any supply ships that might show up and proceeded to Nottawasaga Bay (just to the north and east of which they would find Matchadash Bay) trying to knock out the British supply station there. They leveled a blockhouse and captured a schooner laden with supplies destined for Mackinac; that was the success of the expedition. The two ships left near Mackinac, the *Scorpion* and the *Tigress,* were promptly taken by the British as they patrolled near Drummond Island.[17]

The British were elated; they still controlled the upper lakes, the Lake Simcoe supply route was still open, and again they had ships to carry provisions for the winter—and goods so that their Indian mercenary friends could carry on. They had withstood a feeble American challenge and held the beachhead for the season, preparing for the all-out assault that would undoubtedly be ordered in the next year.

CHAPTER EIGHT

THE TREATY
OF GHENT (1814)

The all-out assault the British expected was not quite ordered by the Americans in the next year. Napoléon's abdication in April of 1814 loosened the British military obligation in Europe and permitted the shipping of thousands of veterans of the Napoleonic wars for service in Canada. By September a substantial army was gathered in the east commanded by Gen. George Prevost and prepared to invade the United States via Lake Champlain, intending to cut off the still disaffected New England states and carry the offensive to the belligerent central and southern ones, thereby perhaps capitalizing on New England's threat to break the Union. A British supply fleet preceded the army down the lake, was engaged by Com. Thomas MacDonough and an American fleet, and defeated decisively. At the same time an American army commanded by Gen. Alexander Macomb turned back General Prevost's force, which, faced with the loss of the supply ships, retreated to Canada. Concurrently, the British landed a force in Chesapeake Bay, which captured and sacked Washington; they moved up the bay to Baltimore, but Fort McHenry held (the occasion that inspired our national anthem).

A third army was carried by ship to the mouth of the Mississippi, where Gen. Andrew Jackson commanded and, in January of 1815 (after war's end but before word of it could reach there), brilliantly beat off a frontal attack.[1] In the fall of 1814, thus, the British, though still in command in the north, had been repulsed in the east and brought to a stop in the Chesapeake (the Battle of New Orleans was still to be fought). The war was still far from a dead issue, but it was about to become an exceedingly expensive one. Further, the Duke of Wellington, a national hero of recognized military brilliance after the Napoleonic wars, refused an offer to command in Canada.

Heavily burdened by debt after the European conflagration and recognizing the necessity for an extended commitment to achieve even the possibility of an uncertain victory over an essentially ungovernable people, the British instead of pursuing the matter sued for peace on the basis of *status quo ante bellum.* Preliminary negotiations were already under way at Ghent, Belgium, where a treaty was signed on Christmas Eve, 1814. Once again Britain's economic distress and a dose of Yankee good luck provided a North American peace—without victory, but on favorable terms. The text of the Treaty of Ghent begins on page 171.

There is really nothing remarkable about the Treaty of Ghent. It is simply an agreement to cease hostilities, determine and fix still ambiguous borders, and return other matters, insofar as it was practicable, to *status quo ante bellum.* As such it recurs to and reaffirms the principles of the 1783 Paris treaty—notably the commissioners to survey and determine the still unsurveyed Canadian-United States border, including the portion of it that runs through the Great Lakes. It is notable that it focuses specifically on land, including islands, many in the Great Lakes region still imperfectly known because they were unsurveyed and uncharted. It is important, once again, that the international waters of the interior are treated only as the vehicle carrying the boundary line; ownership, control, or further subdivision of them just do not enter in. The principle inferred in the 1783 treaty and clearly enunciated in the Northwest Ordinance would appear to be a given: the waters are understood to be shared, common highways, no more to be owned than the air. Only lands within the waters, islands both known and as yet unknown, are referred to the authority of the commissioners.

The ninth article alone takes up the Indian problem. Its main intention, clearly, is to bring the Indians into the state of peaceful relations Britain and the United States were engineering for themselves. Beyond the mutually pledged assurances that both Britain and the United States would war no more with the Indians (provided that the Indians would do the same), its language is vague enough in binding the United States to restore to the tribes "all the possessions, rights, and privileges, which they may have enjoyed or been entitled to" in 1811—the year fixed as determining the antebellum status quo. The year 1811 found Tecumseh fomenting among the tribes in general, the Prophet attacking Governor Harrison at Tippecanoe, the militia in arms at Detroit, and Governor Hull traveling to Washington to raise an army with which to defend his territory. It featured the Indians already fully armed—by the British from all their outposts, as Harrison proved at Tippecanoe and Hull knew all too well at Detroit—and functioning as belligerent mercenaries for the British. It featured aggressive preparations for war on the British and Indian side and hurried defensive measures on the American one. It was just not a very good year for status quo.

What rights and privileges the Indians might properly claim in that year, all things considered, is a question that remains stubbornly ambiguous at best. The main effect of the Indian provisions in the Ghent treaty, thus, was to reaffirm the principles of

Indian occupancy and proprietorship, title as enunciated in the Northwest Ordinance. The Indians never themselves sued for peace as the war wound down, though they had certainly acted like enemies; they could thus be considered still at war. The United States still had armies in the field and the Indians were now without a source of supply; with the British out of the field, once again it would have been logical and not difficult to conclude the Indian war properly and thus end the whole question of title. That we acceded to the Indian provisions and did not carry the war to its final military conclusion is in every way remarkable.

Word of the peace seems to have reached Detroit in March of 1815, for on the twenty-ninth of that month a "Pacification Dinner" was celebrated and attended by former enemies from both sides of the river. No one, however, seems to have thought to send word to Colonel McDouall at Mackinac until May 15, when he received a long-delayed dispatch informing him that he would have to surrender his forts and move his garrison and until which date, therefore, a state of war continued in the north. The communication delay did not add up to much, for McDouall was essentially holding the fort while waiting for further orders, fully expecting provisions and reinforcements with which to prepare for a major campaign to the south. The British continued their standing policy of gifting to the Indians (under the pretense of encouraging the trade) and provoking them against the Americans while protecting their exclusive trading arrangements. The British Indian agent Robert Dickson persisted requisitioning for his charges, insisting that the British had to honor their obligations with the prospect of future hostilities in mind. After another bad winter (and not knowing what might lie ahead for his military personnel) McDouall and his officers corps wanted to reserve the provisions for the garrison. Friction between the Indian department and the military grew so bad that McDouall finally had Dickson arrested and held—later released without trial or investigation.

McDouall was amazed at the order to surrender his post; even his farewell remarks to the Indians were contrived to foment trouble for the Americans with the vague promise of future hostilities and fine gifts from the Great English Father for continuing alliance.[2] His greatest practical fear was that the Indians, disillusioned by the British surrender, would turn to military alliance with the Americans and take their trade with them. Nevertheless, he dutifully handed Fort Mackinac over to the Americans in July. The Americans rechristened Fort George as Fort Holms, after the young officer who lost his life in the foolish American assault in 1814. McDouall chose the site for the third British fortification in northern Lake Huron on what soon came to be called Drummond Island, after Sir Gordon Drummond, who succeeded General Brock as commander of British forces in Canada. McDouall referred to the island by name in a letter dated September 24, 1815.[3]

When the British departed Mackinac to occupy their new post on Drummond Island in 1815, the squabbling between British and American factions was far from over.[4] British civilians, after all, were exactly as happy about being ruled by upstart Americans as the Americans had been about British rule. Too, legislation passed in

Washington in 1816, and undoubtedly influenced by John Jacob Astor, now forbade trade with Indians living on American soil, or even service within that trade, to all but American citizens—save that special licenses could be granted by the president or his designates.[5] This sent a clear signal to the north that Astor was about to be turned loose to the disadvantage of the British trading companies and the British trading theater, which the British had worked so hard to preserve and for which they had sacrificed so much in territory in Paris in 1783. The only certainties were surrender of the Great Lakes positions and the *status quo ante bellum* peace that reopened the fur trade—now on an altered basis favoring the Americans. The British were desperate to protect their interests in the lakes, including their share of a restructured trading operation, but the cessation of hostilities and the Treaty of Ghent left the Americans free to legislate, and legislate they did, closing trade to foreign nationals on American soil and opening it to Astor. Once again the Indians faced an unfamiliar situation they could not comprehend.

What they faced was American capitalism operating in a marketplace now closed to their British friends, and the British tried every trick they knew to keep their Indian alliances while they developed their own marketplace at Drummond Island. British citizens who stayed on at Mackinac Island complained through Colonel McDouall at Drummond, intending to annoy and embarrass the American command; McDouall, for his part, continued to incite the Indians and both sides jockeyed for position while the international trading issue was being sorted out. Though it is not possible in the understandable confusion to sort out all details in fact, the American perception of British activities then is summed up in a letter written to McDouall by William Puthuff, a resident of Mackinac Island, which reads in part:

> It has been repeatedly observed to me by the Indians that you[r] council[s] with them on Drummond Island in the name of your Government have forbidden them to trade with the Americans, have ordered them to bring their corn to their British Father or, if prevented by stress of weather, to leave it with the British traders only on the Island of Michilimackinac, or bury it until Spring. That you have sent your order to an Indian Trading at La Arbre Croch for Michael Dousman, forbidding him to trade for or deliver his corn to an American. That you have a few days since held a council at which barrels of Rum were opened to them, minute guns were fired, and, when they were informed that the Tomahawk would again be raised early in the Spring, the Red Wampum and tobacco mixed with Vermillion [were] distributed. That they were advised to be on the alert as it was the intention of the Americans to invite them to this island with a view to Massacre them. That you would again appear in the night with your Big Guns upon the Island of Michilimackinac and that the Americans would not dare oppose you. These and many other reports of like character have been repeatedly made to me, which I hope may be discovered not to have originated in fact.[6]

All the while the British were preparing to shift their trading center to Drummond—if they could get trading goods in, maintain their Indian alliances, and compete effectively. They thus wanted to disrupt Indian trade with the Americans while they built and developed their new installation.

The termination of hostilities, however, made the British strategy among the Indians more complex. The new governor of Canada, Sir John Coape Sherbrooke, ordered McDouall at Drummond to make every effort to keep the Indians at peace and directed the British minister, Charles Bagot, to inform American Secretary of State James Monroe of the orders. In this the British sought at least to look good in the aftermath of the Treaty of Ghent while new international trading policies were being settled; it would not be wise to enrage the Americans or risk being cut off from the Lakes—and the United States now had the muscle to do it. By inserting the Indian provisions into Article IX of the treaty, the British gave themselves some leverage to continue meddling. While officially promoting peace among Indians and whites they could continue to argue, certainly among the Indians, that not every-thing was exactly as it was in 1811 and that the Americans were therefore in viola-tion. Settlers, for instance, continued their relentless western migration; an American army could be perceived as a threat; because the Indians had not yet capitulated and sought peace on their own, war could again break out and blow the whole thing. Pointedly, the whole pattern of the trade was shifting as American interests for the first time entered aggressively into it and, on Michigan soil, the British were barred from it.

Through all of this, because they had made no separate peace agreement (and there was precious little incentive for the United States to seek such a settlement on its side, all things considered), the Indians had no more to protect them than an uneasy understanding with the Americans written into a clause in an agreement the United States had signed with Great Britain at an unknown place an ocean away. On their side, the Indians could understand only that an unexpected peace with unan-ticipated terms and involving their wellbeing had been entered into without their advice or consent. They hardly knew who, if anyone, to trust. They preferred British trade goods and British trading policy (which, together with the magnanimous gift-ing, was both familiar and comfortable—in that it offered some hope of redress from the Americans), but, in entering a separate peace for no discernible reason, the British had betrayed them. They regarded American trade goods as inferior and expensive and they did not much like the Americans anyway because of their habits of pur-chasing (which was acceptable) and subsequently settling the land (which was not).

In the meantime, even before and during the war, John Jacob Astor and his agents moved aggressively into the trade. Even as the war was building, Astor formed the South West Company in partnership with some British-Canadian investors. Astor had the capital, and the partnership guaranteed he could do business on Mackinac Island no matter which side "won" the war. The terms of the Ghent treaty were favorable to the American partner and, with the 1816 legislation barring foreigners from the trade on United States soil, because they could not do business at the com-pany headquarters, the British-Canadians had no choice but to sell out to Astor.[7]

Thus the South West Company was absorbed into the American Fur Company, which was reorganized on the heels of the 1816 legislation. Its Northern Division was headquartered at Mackinac Island and placed in the charge of Ramsay Crooks and Robert Stuart, who remained in charge on the island for eighteen years. The company eagerly set out to eliminate its competitors, usually by buying them out. Astor had positioned himself and timed his move brilliantly; there was virtually no one in the field who could hope to compete with him. The foreigners were put out of business in Michigan by law, and Astor had the capital to purchase their assets.

Gov. Lewis Cass at this time had been appointed presidential agent with responsibility to control trade in the territory, including prohibiting foreigners from engaging in it except by special license. Astor formed an alliance with Cass and thus could work with him to develop his effective monopoly. The seemingly unusual favors Cass passed his way are mostly explained by Astor's eastern connections; even the War Department sent instructions west that Cass should do everything in his power within the law to facilitate the operations of the American Fur Company.[8]

Astor's influence did much to promote the new American dominance in the trade in which he profited nicely. Fur was regarded as Michigan's only significant natural resource and though fur trading contributed substantially to founding his financial empire, Astor was plowing his profits back into the United States treasury by buying huge tracts of public land for development. In a time without taxes (and within memory of the hated British ones), this was the most efficient use the government could make of the territory it controlled but did not yet own. It encouraged entrepreneurs such as Astor to invest on two levels, first in the natural resource and then in the land, and turned the government into a publicly controlled banking house-holding company for acquiring the lands that produced the resource and then to resell them to finance and then perpetuate a properly financed government. The government could then provide for its citizens—including the Indians from whom it had acquired the land and to whom it would eventually give it back. It could do so by holding in trust the agreed upon reservations and by conferring title to individually owned parcels that in themselves became a means of sustenance and an asset that could be subdivided, traded, or sold. Just like the white citizens, except that the Indians, having already ceded the land to the United States, could choose their parcels first and receive protected title for free. This is what was called the "civilizing" process. It was thus vastly to the government's advantage (and so it became its policy) to protect the trade for Astor, thereby promoting and acceding to a capitalist economy, developing its resources as they came to have value, and, with minimal cost to a never comfortable treasury, paying for its future.

Though Astor maintained a facility at Detroit (and happily enough expanded westward, via St. Louis, as that territory was opened and became the source most plentiful), Mackinac Island remained the center of his operations in the northern Lakes and so the heart of his lakeland empire. In the fall his army of traders would sortie to their predetermined posts for the winter, their boats laden with goods for trade in the wilderness. It was finally the wily American entrepreneur with his trading monopoly earned by investment and the hard work implied in developing a business who established a policy of carrying the trade to the Indians and thereby securing all of it. In the spring the peltries would be gathered and loaded on "Montreal barges," each capable of carrying as much as eight tons in good weather, and floated with the aid of oars or sail or both to Mackinac for the summer trading season.

The organization of the company was such that now the Indians were the gatherer-laborers, the individual traders were the supervisors and suppliers, and the company was the wholesaler to the retail markets in the east whence came the capital to recommence the whole cycle. At the height of the season during the heyday of the American Fur Company, as many as three thousand Indians could be found camped along the beach at Mackinac Island during the warm season; the company employed as many trappers, traders, and boatmen and more than four hundred clerks at the island headquarters. This state of affairs lasted until the supply of northern furs failed owing to the incredibly aggressive harvest of them; in 1834, Astor sold the American Fur Company, the Northern Division going to Ramsay Crooks, who continued doing business on Mackinac at a reduced scale, and together with some other interests, under the same company name.

Demand for pelts was dropping because of a developing interest in silk in the hat industry. St. Louis was by then the emerging center of trade owing to its access to the far west and the untapped harvest in furs available there; Michigan's first great natural resource had been trapped down to only modest efficiency in its harvest. The Indian trappers had become so skillful and relentless that they did themselves in. Further, treaty making and land acquisition in Michigan was by then sufficiently under way that survey was proceeding north; settlers were expected to follow and the natural restocking of the resource seemed unlikely. It was time for different ventures and development.

The British attempt to develop at Drummond a post that would rival the thriving trading colony at Mackinac Island failed. Though they kept them open, the Americans controlled the Lakes and Mackinac—still mistress of the north, though of limited tactical or practical value as long as the peace held. Even more to the point, Astor and his fur-gathering organization was just too big and too aggressive. The international boundary through the St. Marys River area, and so the final permanent British position in the north, would remain at issue until 1828; the problems of financing and developing a new trading center to rival Mackinac were just too great. Too, without a burgeoning trade to protect, once the peace provided for the Great Lakes under the Treaty of Ghent proved lasting, the military importance of Fort Collier (so originally called, together with its location, Collier's Harbor; later it was called Fort Drummond) became negligible. Thus as the American community, military and civilian together with the American Fur Company, thrived, the command at Drummond passed from the historically important Lieutenant Colonel McDouall to a far less well-known major and finally to a lieutenant commanding only about one-half of a company. It was strictly a man-and-maintain post and even this small command was destined to be transferred to St. Joseph Island after the Ashburton Treaty was ratified in 1828.

Even after hostilities ended and the Lakes were opened to commerce and travel, the flow of settlers into Michigan was slow. There were several reasons for this: (1) until the Erie Canal was completed in 1825, overland travel from the population centers in the east to the Lakes and around Niagara was extremely difficult, as was the long trek through Ohio up from that river valley; too, there were as yet no passenger boats on the Lakes. (2) as Ramsay Crooks had found when he came west prospecting for John Jacob Astor, financing at Detroit was nearly impossible while in the east venture capital was tight and interest rates thus high; prospects for settlement in Michigan Territory, then (as opposed to the prosperous and secure states of Ohio and Indiana), were not good; and (3), probably most damning, was Michigan's reputation. In 1814, for instance, Duncan MacArthur wrote from his station at Detroit to William Woodbridge, who was considering an offer to become territorial secretary: "I have no hesitation to say that it would be to the advantage of Government to remove every inhabitant of the Territory, pay for the improvements, and reduce them to ashes, leaving nothing but the Garrison posts. From my observation, the Territory appears to be not worth defending, and merely a den for Indians and traitors. The banks of the Detroit River are handsome, but nine-tenths of the land in the Territory is unfit for cultivation."[9]

Further, after the war Congress had passed legislation providing for some two million acres of national land to be distributed among its veterans and turned the matter over to Edward Tiffin in the office of the surveyor general of the United States; he was to sort through the various possibilities to determine which lands should be so distributed. He reported of Michigan that "in his opinion not more than one acre in a hundred or perhaps a thousand, would admit of cultivation. Congress, as a result, designated land in Illinois and Missouri for the veterans."[10] With this publicity in the east it is hardly a great wonder that settlers were not knocking down Michigan's doors. The interior of the territory, which was still little known to the white man, was thought to be mostly malarial swamp and unarable sand and rock. Even the Detroit area was rumored to be unhealthy.

The matter was made even more complex because, except around Detroit and Mackinac, it was impossible to obtain title to lands in Michigan until 1818, when the government opened a land office in Detroit. Government surveyors had commenced work in 1815, but not for three years had they completed enough work to make the land office practicable. That the survey work in Michigan was slow was due to two prominent factors. First, owing to everything mentioned above taken together with the lingering fear of the Indian population and their British friends (the war, after all, was a recent and pertinent fact in everyone's lives, especially in Michigan, and the Indians had not been formally brought to peace), demand for Michigan lands was low. Second, following government policy as established in the

Ordinance of 1785, the land could not be privately purchased until it was surveyed, and the surveys were not to begin until the lands to be surveyed had been fairly and legally acquired by cession and extinction of claim to title from their Indian proprietors. Until 1817 in Michigan this included only the Detroit-Lake Erie strip, Mackinac Island and the Point St. Ignace strip, and the substantial piece of the southeastern Lower Peninsula for which Governor Hull had successfully negotiated in 1807. This land, because there was no demand for it, had little or no value beyond what the federal government had originally put into it, so there was no rush to invest in the survey work, which could come in good time as demand called for it.

CHAPTER NINE

THE TREATY
OF SAGINAW (1819)

So far, except as a political and demographic vision in the future, Michigan was a distinct pig in a poke, a costly white elephant inconveniently removed from the general path of westward migration until water transport was introduced on the Lakes at a later date. Michigan lands were unwanted by settlers who failed even to show up to look them over, no longer important even from a military point of view, plagued by Indians about whose intentions everyone was uncertain (and who, according to the mandates of federal policy, still controlled most of them), and as yet not even populated sufficiently to move into the second stage of territorial development. It is fortunate that in Gov. Lewis Cass the territory had a man of vision and strength to speak for it and forward its cause; else the likes of Tiffin and MacArthur could easily have had their way. Cass suspected that Michigan Territory would prove to have value and committed himself to finding and defining it. The process would take about twenty years, through eighteen of which he served as governor and chief promoter.

The first step necessary for Michigan's further development, whether the current land market would support it or not, was to acquire land and extinguish Indian title so that organization, including survey and so possible sale, might proceed. To this end Governor Cass was appointed United States commissioner for securing, by cession and thus extinction of Indian claim to title, further lands in the Michigan Territory. The incentive for this otherwise perhaps unlikely move seems to have been a consortium of easterners who had visited the Saginaw Valley (north of the lands ceded to Governor Hull in 1807), saw potential there, and became interested in participating in its development.[1] These were perhaps the first serious customers for outlying land in the Territory. In any event, Cass first went to work at Fort Meigs (built by General Harrison by the Maumee River rapids during the War of 1812), where in September of 1817 he negotiated the cession of a small tract along the Ohio border just to the west of Governor Hull's acquisition; this has been usually called the Treaty of the Foot of the Rapids.[2] Next, pursuing his larger mission as dictated at Washington, he called the chiefs of the northern tribes, Ottawa and Chippewa, to council with him in September of 1819 at the junction of the rivers that flow together in the Saginaw Valley. There on September 24 he concluded the Treaty of Saginaw, by and in which he secured for the United States government that portion of Michigan's Lower Peninsula included within a line drawn from the mouth of the Thunder Bay River (at what is now Alpena), up the same to its headwaters, south and west to a point not far from what is now Kalamazoo, and from there east to the western border described in Hull's treaty in 1807.[3] About one-half of the Lower Peninsula had thus by this date been ceded to the United States. The text of the Treaty of Saginaw begins on page 176.

The language of the treaty could not be more clear. It is a cession of *land comprehended within lines and boundaries,* some still not even defined (the international border with Canada), none of it surveyed. The navigable waters of the Lakes and their connections are not considered; we can only assume that the Northwest Ordinance, following the Treaty of Paris (1783), had defined them with the force of law as eased for common use and therefore not open for consideration. The treaty reservations on both sides are explicit; it follows the Greenville Treaty (and specifically refers to it, in Article 5) in allowing the Indians to hunt, and that only, on the ceded land while it continues the property of the United States, and that only, and adds to this right the right to make maple sugar on the same terms—with the usufructuary stipulation that they commit "no unnecessary waste upon the trees." On the other side, the United States reserved the right to build roads across land reserved by and for the Indians. There is a cash consideration, the promise to pay for improvements on ceded parcels of land, and, importantly, help with the "civilizing" process: blacksmithing (to repair traps, guns, and, hopefully, agricultural implements), farming utensils, cattle, and other agricultural assistance and advice. It is not possible to determine if a democratic majority of the tribal members welcomed the terms of the Treaty of Saginaw; it is proper to observe, however, that no fewer than 114 designated tribal leaders placed their mark on a contract with the United States government, duly witnessed and binding to both parties.

The cash values involved in this treaty can too easily seem absurdly low: $3,000 down (which appeared in cash and on the table, presaging the stipulations in Article 4), plus $1,000 per year "for ever," plus the other considerations in Article 8 depending on the continuing goodwill and discretion of the president of the United States. This is a consternating and possibly ambiguous stipulation and one wonders that the Indians would have acceded to it at all, especially given the low cash value of the treaty itself. It is important to recognize, however, that the Indians of Michigan had not yet sued for peace and could, still so close to war's end, be hostile.

The Saginaw Treaty is not a treaty of peace; it is purely and simply a treaty of land cession and contract between two none too friendly nations. It is also significant that the United States treasury, hit hard by the recent war and with obligations to acquire land elsewhere, was not then well endowed for acquiring Michigan lands, so alternatives to cash on the table had to be found. The first alternative was vested in the land itself; in the background there remained the eastern speculators, willing to pay for it and thereby establish a market value for it. Thus it is significant that the treaty reserves for the benefit of the Chippewas some 111,640 acres, 101,400 acres to be held as general reservations and 10,240 acres as reservations for prominent persons and their families—more land up front reserved in trust for the tribals than in any other Michigan treaty. The land itself, thus, with the promise of a general survey and improvements (roads, for instance) soon to follow, held the hope of the future. The other alternatives amounted to help—principally blacksmithing, mechanical, and agricultural—in the civilizing process that should further increase the value of the land so reserved.

This was not a new feature of the treaties, it having been incorporated in both the Greenville Treaty (1795) and the one at Detroit (1807), but in the absence of cash value at Saginaw it takes on a new perspective. From now on cash values would have to be kept low and the emphasis would have to be placed on the promise of annuities and other considerations. The cash was just not available and the land had to be acquired, whether it was much wanted or not, to provide organization and government. Too, the land in Michigan as opposed to, for instance, the Ohio Valley (with its inland waterway to the Mississippi and easy access from the east), which had been perceived since colonial times as having value, was worthless until future, unknown circumstances could create a value for it. Further, even considering the age-old fur market, only the white man could create that value; only to him in his life-style could the land provide, beyond sustenance, anything that in fact might be valued.

The Indian, by now long disassociated from his traditional life-style and evolved into a successful parasite on the white economy, still had no economy of his own beyond barter—and he was running out of things with which to barter. The American government was thus faced with a curious moral obligation in its dealings with the natives. Though our carefully enunciated national policy was to treat with them as coequal foreign nations (such as France or England or Spain), they were different because they had no understanding of ownership as we understand it and therefore no economic system with or within which we could work. Nor did they deal well with the European contract; the land was held and used strictly in common and provided bounty to be similarly used in common for mutual benefit. A stack of furs could be shared to acquire a gun, which in turn could be used to procure another stack of furs, which could again be used to get something else. Ownership had little to do with it. There was no bank to put it in, no account (except the perpetual one of debt to the traders) from which to deal it out. From an Englishman, in the worst of times, one could win Mackinac Island fair and square (or worse come to very worst, buy it) and that would end it until one party reneged on the contract that sealed the deal—after which there was recourse to arbitration by law. From an Indian, one had to buy Detroit four times and he still failed to understand that he could not sell it again. It thus became necessary to "civilize" the Indians; the alternative to it was going to drive the best brains in Washington over the edge.

The Saginaw Treaty thus followed the Greenville and Detroit treaties in offering assistance in the civilizing process aimed, finally, at the gift of citizenship and full participation, in theory the finest gift the white man could confer on the aboriginal. Because fair market value for the land was nearly impossible to determine, and because the Indians had no use for cash anyway (save to give it immediately back to the white man to procure whatever whimsical thing they wanted at the moment—or to pay off debts incurred in anticipation of treaty money coming in),[4] this treaty affirmed the principle of recompensing the Indians other than with cash or goods with cash value. The intent was protective. Cash could be immediately spent and goods could be given away or traded, leaving nothing; agricultural skills and the means of participating in a productive economy with improved land would be lasting benefits. This would be the way into the future, the theory that would govern subsequent Indian treaties in Michigan.

This begins to unravel the ambiguous and otherwise seemingly self-serving language Cass wrote into the treaty. Cass's instructions as treaty commissioner had come to him from Secretary of War John C. Calhoun, and one of the specified objects of his negotiations was removal, with the option to stay on within reservations to be provided and held in trust by the United States for the tribes. The Indians were offered the option of land in the far west comparable to what they were giving up (and still swarming with furs, so that they could follow their accustomed livelihood in their move) and removing to it. The Michigan Indians, however, were not interested in the removal option, so Cass dropped the issue and reinforced Article 2, which stipulates the reservations. The language of removal, even as an option, does not appear in the treaty. The Indians themselves, therefore, refused this first-offered valuable consideration—land either to use or to be regarded as an investment. If we consider land an entity implying substantial value in the long run, and if we remember that land was the federal government's first means of financing itself to look after its citizens, we should then realize that in retaining its claim to the western lands the government also retained the cash value that those lands would ultimately represent; it could therefore and thereby afford only to promise other valuable considerations to the Michigan Indians in the future, though neither party could at the time know what these might be.

Thus the American intention was not only to secure the land but also, and at the same time, to teach the Indians the use and value of it within a working economic system and so accommodate them within that system. This led to far more than the development of the reservation system, which is outside our scheme of economic organization (and leaves the Indians to live as they please on land communally held by tribal councils); it led ultimately to the practice adopted in the 1855 treaty at Detroit, *after* the surveys in Michigan were completed, of giving the land back by the section to the Indians individually—for their ownership and use or resale or both.

Cass, together with Solomon Sibley, again treated with the Ottawas, Chippewas, and Potawatomies at Chicago in 1821. On August 29 they concluded a document by which the tribes ceded most of the remaining land in Michigan's southwest corner south of the Grand River, except for a small triangle in the extreme southwest (which the Potawatomies ceded in the Treaty of Carey Mission in 1828). This completed Cass's mission as a United States commissioner. Except for the Detroit-Lake Erie strip and the southeastern corner negotiated by Governor Hull, largely through Cass's efforts the United States now had secured title to roughly two-thirds of Michigan's Lower Peninsula, enough to proceed with survey and development with an eye to attracting settlers. Other factors would help in this department.

The period from 1819 to 1822 was extremely important in the development of relations between the United States federal government and the Indian tribes living in the Northwest Territory; here the pattern for treaty making in all the western territories toward which the East Coast population was surging was destined to be forged. The problem was a widely recognized one, perhaps then the paramount one. James Monroe was the fifth president of the United States (1817-25) and John C. Calhoun was his only secretary of war—who had responsibility for the Indian Department according to the administrative blueprint of the period. The domestic portion of the peace after the War of 1812 was tenuous at best; the Indians of the Northwest, for instance, still preferred their friendship with the British on the other side of an agreed-upon but not yet determined international border and were prepared to take their partisanship into any incident that might present itself. These were disquieting times on the western frontier—and the Northwest Territory was the first western frontier (so defined in the Northwest Ordinance), the frontier on which policy along subsequent western frontiers would be molded.

The previous "solutions" to the Indian problem, along the Ohio River Valley, for instance, and in Indiana, though just and fair in intention, had been necessarily heavy-handed—which is to say military, as handled by Generals Wayne and Harrison. Negotiations in Michigan, and in areas to the west for which Michigan would set the pattern, were to be different. Having survived the American Revolution and the War of 1812, the United States had achieved internationally recognized control of geographic territory and political organization; unfortunately the Indians occupied the area into which this control and organization were headed. The United States government had to come to some formal understanding of the aboriginal culture it was going to displace by simple recognition of the old legal principle of eminent domain. The truly remarkable thing is how far the still fledgling federal government, reeling from the costs of the War of 1812 and essentially without money, attempted a fair and peaceful resolution of the problem, one important facet of which was an understandable ignorance along the East Coast of the culture and customs of the frontier Indians.

How far, the easterners wondered, could Indian culture be integrated and accommodated as an alternative to encompassing, suffocating, and so exterminating it? The Indians of the Northwest were already a vanquished people brought to terms by the Treaty of Greenville and provided for but not represented in the Treaty of Ghent; the problem was how to deal humanely with peoples who otherwise could have status only as belligerants, prisoners of war, or displaced aliens living on lands they had occupied for generations but in no legal sense recognized at the time owned.

Jedidiah Morse, of New Haven, Connecticut, was a conservative and orthodox Congregational clergyman and doctor of divinity long interested in missionary work among the western Indians and already affiliated with several British missionary societies. He was also the father of Samuel F. B. Morse, the artist who invented the telegraph. In February of 1820 he was in Washington and received from Secretary Calhoun a presidential commission; under the terms of the commission, commencing as early as practicable in the spring, he was to travel, first, among the northern tribes and then among the southern ones and return with as complete a written report as possible for the war secretary on virtually every aspect of Indian life and activity. The commission was so conceived as to send a political nonpartisan, even a man who might be expected to take the Indians' side, into politically volatile territory to gather objective knowledge of the tribes. The assumption was that those who already knew the Indians most intimately, the frontiersmen and the likes of Cass and Harrison, possibly could not maintain a strict objectivity because of their long dealings with the tribes through the years of war on the frontier.

Morse's *Report,*[5] published in 1822 with a compendious appendix of relevant documents, is a remarkable work from which can be traced the beginnings of the serious study of North American Indian ethnology and history that would flower not long after in the lifelong work of Henry Rowe Schoolcraft. As was customary then in such a book as Morse's *Report,* he documented his observations by publishing with them in his appendix the documents on which he based his observations and conclusions. Thus, when he refers to a speech he made to the assembled chiefs of the Six Nations of the Iroquois at Buffalo in June, he publishes as Appendix A the speech itself. So too, when he writes an opinion that addresses a legal matter, he publishes the legal opinions on which he bases his own. And he addresses some important legal matters—among them, prominently, the ownership of the land and the rights that derive from it. In our century judges, though calling uniformly for the application of historical method, have been fond of rights that attach to or derive from the ownership of land—riparian, littoral, and usufructuary—all of which, because they derive from ownership, they consider as *transferable,* for they uniformly argue that the tribes retained all rights not specifically ceded or otherwise transferred.

The twentieth-century Supreme Court, however, in case after case has insisted on the application of the historical method in construing the nineteenth-century treaties. In the nineteenth-century the question of Indian ownership was considered, at best, ambiguous; the only clear relationship between the tribes and the land was that of occupancy. The tribesman was considered a tenant by sufferance only, on land that was either not owned at all or owned by someone else according to the law of nations. He was assigned no rights by the legal theorists and practitioners of the day, including the United States Supreme Court, which could derive only from ownership; he had only the privileges of an occupant, which had to be legally extinguished by treaty of cession—as distinguished from deed of conveyance, seizin in fee. It is interesting, therefore, to consider the deliberations of the courts contemporary with and preceding the treaties where the distinctions between rights deriving from ownership and the privileges of occupancy are so clear. It is also, thus, important to understand what extinguishment by cession means and that the Supreme Court recognized even the privileges of occupancy *only until* legally extinguished by treaty cession. That is exactly what happened. On Indian title, Jedidiah Morse writes: "The relation which the Indians sustain to the government of the United States, is peculiar in its nature. Their independence, their rights, their title to the soil which they occupy, are all *imperfect* in their kind" (p. 67). Morse points out that in almost all respects the tribesmen enjoyed, and were assigned by the United States government, the independence and self-government that can be attached only to a sovereignty that was never challenged. Yet, he argues, that sovereignty was a social and political entity, and was permitted and encouraged to exist, within the larger suzerainty of the United States in forming itself according to the proclamation of the international treaties at Paris (1783) and Ghent (1814). The basis for this relationship, and here Morse argues the prevailing legal understandings of his time, is found in ancient international law that at once clarifies and makes complex the notion of ownership of the land. The Indian peoples, thus, enjoyed their independence as though they were the owners as well as the proprietors of the land:

> Yet the *jurisdiction* of the whole country which they inhabit, according to the established law of nations, appertains to the government of the United States; and the right of disposing of the *soil,* attaches to the power that holds the jurisdiction. Indians, therefore, have no other property in the *soil* of their respective territories, than that of mere *occupancy.* This is a common, undivided, property in each tribe. When a tribe, by Treaty, sell their territory, they sell only what they possess, which is, the right to *occupy* their territory, from which they agree to remove. The *complete* title to their lands, rests in the government of the United States. (P. 67)

In his appendix Morse includes several contemporary jurists' opinions on Indian titles, first an eminent though anonymous attorney, then the lengthy and highly rhetorical opinion of John Quincy Adams, both of which inform his own observations (pp.

279-83). He then presents the summary of John Quincy Adams's plea on the matter before the Supreme Court in *Fletcher v. Peck,* in which pleading he prevailed:

> What is the Indian Title? It is mere occupancy for the purpose of hunting. It is not like our tenures; they have no idea of a title to the soil itself. It is overrun by them, rather than inhabited. It is not a true and legal possession. *Vattel b.*1. 81 p. 37. and 209. b. 2. p. 96. *Montequieu b.*18. c. 12. *Smith's Wealth of Nations. b. 5. c.* 1. It is a right not to be *transferred,* but *extinguished.* It is a right regulated by treaties, not by deeds of conveyance. It depends upon the law of nations, not upon municipal right. *Fletcher v. Peck, Crach.* Vol. 6. p. 121. (p. 283)

He also extracts from the Supreme Court decision in the same matter:

> The majority of the Court is of the opinion, that the nature of the Indian Title, which is certainly to be respected by all courts, until it be legitimately extinguished, is not such as to be absolute repugnant to seisin in fee on the part of the State. (Ibid. 143) See also the opinions on this subject, of the Commissioners at the Treaty of Ghent.—Amer. State Papers—1812 to 1815. Vol. 9. p. 389 to 425.

> "The recognition of a boundary," say the American Commissioners, "gives up to the nation in whose behalf it was made, all the Indian tribes and countries within that boundary. It was on this principle that the undersigned have confidently relied on the Treaty of 1783, which fixed and recognizes the boundaries of the United States, without making any reservation respecting the Indian tribes." (Ibid. p. 424)

The Supreme Court thus recognized some form of legitimate Indian claim to title—and left the matter ambiguous—but only until it is extinguished by treaty. The Court boldly affirms, however, the old principle that the right to the disposition of the soil, and therefore complete title, rests wholly in the government of the United States.

To protect the anticipated settlers as they came in and to guard the frontier against the possibility of further Indian troubles (there was still no treaty of peace in Michigan), the United States began some modest fort building: Fort Gratiot (1816), near the present city of Port Huron and named for its first commander; Fort Saginaw (1822); Fort Brady (1822), at Sault Ste. Marie and named for its first commander; and Fort Howard, at the present site of Green Bay, Wisconsin. In 1818 steam navigation was introduced to the Lakes when a steamship of 330 tons burden, the *Walk-in-the-Water,* was launched at Black Rock (now Buffalo); other steamers followed and more sailing vessels, as well. With the opening of the Erie Canal (1825), an improved route and method of travel between Michigan and the east, together with a much promotional work there, made the territory more attractive—as did the increasing knowledge of the land gained from the survey work. Governor Cass was at the very center of all this activity, not only acquiring and promoting, but going out himself to explore his territory and so coming to know it firsthand.

CHAPTER TEN

TREATY AT
THE SAULT (1820)

In 1816 Indiana had been admitted to the Union as the nineteenth state, and in 1818 Illinois was organized and admitted as the twenty-first. Three states had, therefore, been carved out of the Old Northwest. The pattern of their emergence underscores the path of westward migration as it followed the central river valleys, in which developed the first substantial midwestern population centers. Development along the Great Lakes would come a little later. At the time of the formation and admission of Indiana, Congress attached all that remained of the Northwest Territory—all of what is now Wisconsin and a good chunk of Minnesota—to Michigan Territory. This added an immense acreage to Governor Cass's responsibility. Michigan sported a terrible reputation at the financial centers in the east, and she now had appended to her a vast tract most of which was known only to trappers, traders, and Indians.

Cass thus determined that it was essential to gain knowledge of the area to the north in order to make intelligent recommendations as to what to do with it. He wanted an assessment of the natural resources in order to promote them to settlers and investors and, as United States Indian commissioner, he wanted to meet with the northern tribes (still influenced by the British at Drummond Island), caution them to keep the peace, and so pave the way for the further treaties that would undoubtedly follow—once the United States could determine what to do with the land. Cass first secured permission and backing from Secretary Calhoun for an expedition to the shores of Lake Superior and west, if possible, to the source of the Mississippi; from there he would go south to the Wisconsin River and back into the Lakes via the Fox, and from there south along the western shore of Lake Michigan and across the southern counties of the Lower Peninsula back to Detroit—thus circumscribing his entire territory save for what is now the extreme southerly part of Wisconsin.

Cass's party included forty-two men, Indians and voyageurs as guides and boatmen, ten soldiers and an officer for protection, two interpreters, a geographer and his two assistants, a geologist, a physician, a reporter, and his private secretary. The geographer was Capt. David B. Douglas, and Henry Rowe Schoolcraft was the geologist—heading north to an unexpected career. The expedition left Detroit in three large canoes on May 25, 1820, and two weeks later landed at Mackinac, where Cass added twenty-three soldiers to his military complement. The first object of the expedition was to confront the Salteur Chippewas (thus the military escort) and shake their allegiance to the British—so far was that issue from being settled. The Americans intended to build a fort at the Sault (Fort Brady, 1822) to check the continuing British activity at Drummond and guard the entrance to Lake Superior. The way for this intention had to be paved by asserting the American claim to the strip of land on the American side of the Sault narrows, which the Indians had ceded specifically to the Americans (over and above the French and British titles to it, through which it also had passed into United States hands) in 1795 in the Treaty of Greenville. After their recent experience with the Michigan Indian tribes, it would seem that neither Cass nor the War Department wanted to negotiate for this strip yet again.

The worst expectations of Cass and the Americans were confirmed when the expedition arrived at the Sault. The Saulteur chiefs were uniformly in a nasty mood. In twenty-five years the Americans had not showed up to claim their territory, the Greenville Treaty was becoming a vague memory, and their British friends remained in place at Drummond. At a council during which Cass asked the Indians to confirm the 1795 cession, the principal chief, Sassaba, appeared in the red coat of a British officer and denounced the Americans loudly, kicked aside the presents brought for him, and returned to his camp where in a gesture of defiance he raised the Union Jack. The Indians of the north were clearly less than happy with America's military presence at Mackinac and increasing dominance in the fur trade, yet their British Father, whose presence Sassaba's performance was clearly intended to evoke, was seemingly powerless. Just as Pontiac had done his job and held steady before the gates of Detroit, waiting futilely for the French to reappear, so now the Saulteur Chippewas made their stand before a modest party of Americans; once again their European friends failed the Indians. Cass's response to all of this was as brazenly impudent as Sassaba's pageant was pretentious. With a single interpreter he marched on the Indian camp, pulled down the Union Jack, and informed the chief in no uncertain terms that no foreign flag could be flown over American territory.[1] His point was made; the territory was American.

John Johnston, a former British trader at the Sault who had participated in Captain Roberts's surprise attack on Fort Michilimackinac in 1812 but was now reconciled with the United States and serving as American Indian agent there, was absent at this time; but his wife, the full-blooded daughter of a Chippewa chief, was present and interceded in what was unquestionably a dangerous situation. Cass's party was small, and the Chippewas could pull together a large force quickly—and use their British guns. But Mrs. Johnston was wise enough to understand that the British (who were few enough at Drummond, did not intend to join in an engagement with the Americans for the benefit of a few disgruntled Indians. She knew that without benefit of British arms and munitions the Indians could not hope to challenge the American position in the north, and that a bloody incident inflicted on the Cass party would surely call out a war, either of territorial acquisition or of extinction—neither of which could be welcome to the Indians, whose mere subsistence was by now dependent on their relationship with the Americans. At length the chiefs met with Cass, accepted American sovereignty, and reaffirmed the Greenville Treaty that had given the Americans the tract along the St. Marys. Fort Brady was built there only two years later, without incident. The text of the Treaty at Sault Ste. Marie begins on page 178.

It is interesting and a bit ambiguous that Sassaba did not sign the treaty. It is important that this is the first of only two treaties of cession in what would become Michigan that specifically mention Indian fishing rights (the second is the last of the 1855 treaties at Detroit, with the same Saulteur Chippewa band, that revokes the same right to fish in deference to the new locks). The right is written as a right of access and encampment as a land easement provided that the Indians will not interfere with the construction and garrisoning of the fort contemplated for the location. The right is very specific about the location of the fishery set aside for the Indians and the language of the treaty is also specific about who is securing what and to whom: the United States government, having reaffirmed acquiring the territory and with it, presumably, the littoral, riparian, and usufructuary rights to to adjacent water, now gives back specific rights of usage to the Indians.

The party continued west along the south shore of Lake Superior; along the route Schoolcraft took mineralogical samples and made notes. He also ascended the Ontonagon River to examine the huge copper boulder that had been reported by earlier travelers. They continued westward from what is now Duluth, following the network of rivers, streams, and portages to the Mississippi, which they ascended hoping to find its source; in this they failed.[2] As summer ended, the expedition turned downstream and returned east via the Wisconsin and Fox rivers route. Cass turned south from Green Bay to Fort Dearborn (at what would be Chicago), from there he traveled by horseback to Detroit, but he sent Schoolcraft and Douglas and a contingent northward across the top of Lake Michigan to pass through the Mackinac Straits and return to Detroit via Lake Huron. Cass had seen the beauty and promise of he north; Schoolcraft reported many traces of copper and iron. It would be years before interest in the ores would have them mined and a means of transporting them developed. But probably the most important by-product of the expedition was Schoolcraft's interest in the Indians he met. With Cass's influence he was appointed United States Indian agent for the Ottawa and Chippewa tribes in the north and in this position returned to the Sault in 1822. A year later he married Jane Johnston, half-breed daughter of John Johnston and his Indian wife. With Jane's help and half a lifetime of intense study, Schoolcraft gained recognition as the greatest authority in his century on the North American Indian.[3] He also negotiated with and for the Chippewa and Ottawa tribes the Treaty of Washington in 1836, perhaps the most important of the treaties of cession involving lands that were to become the state of Michigan.

The story of Michigan's struggle to statehood (1837), together with the failure of the fur harvest in the north, is the context of that treaty. The Northwest Ordinance (Article V) had created a hypothetical and imperfect (also poorly surveyed and therefore improperly mapped) boundary line running east and west from the southernmost "bend" of Lake Michigan to the Lake Erie shore as the line separating the northern from the southern tier of the states destined to be carved out of the Northwest Territory. In 1805, when Michigan was created a territory, Congress decreed that its southern boundary should be that set in the Northwest Ordinance. (In Ohio's petition for statehood she had set her own northern boundary, but that erupted into an issue only later.) The maps of the time were so imperfect that they showed the southern extremity of Lake Michigan to be farther north than it is; this would have enormous consequences when Michigan petitioned for statehood. For the moment, however, in the west the issues were slightly different.

When Indiana was ready for statehood in 1816, her citizens petitioned Congress to move their upper line ten miles north. The reason for this is apparent on a glance at a midwestern map: a line running east and west from the southern extremity of Lake Michigan and serving as the northern boundary for Ohio, Indiana, and Illinois would cut Indiana and Illinois completely off from access to the Great Lakes and remove the Maumee River port of Toledo from Ohio, giving what would become Michigan control of the access to that river—which became the tremendous issue in 1836. In 1818 the residents of Illinois were even more ambitious; they asked for a sixty-mile-wide strip of the Michigan Territory to their north. In a spirit of fairness and to guarantee some access for everyone to the great natural inland waterway—the common highway established in and promised by the Northwest Ordinance—Congress granted both requests (thereby affirming also the method by which that "compact" between the federal government and the people of the states that would be created in the Old Northwest could be modified). In so doing it set the stage for the absurd melodrama of Michigan's entry into the union—more on which later.

The ownership of land near Detroit, except for the French title to the ribbon farms extending north and east from the town center into what is now Grosse Pointe and the shores of Lake St. Clair, was pretty well clarified and organized after the 1805 fire that devastated the community and the federal land grant that Governor Hull secured to reorganize after it. None of the lands, however, secured by Hull in 1807 were surveyed until after the War of 1812. The first surveys of public lands in

Michigan were put up for contract in the spring of 1815, when Edward Tiffin issued contracts to Alexander Holmes for a base line from a point north of Detroit west to the Indian border and Benjamin Hough for a "true meridian" north from Fort Defiance, Ohio, to the base line.[4] Reports from these survey teams induced Tiffin to condemn Michigan so terribly in November of the same year; the team working north from Fort Defiance indeed had to work through the "Black Swamp" to the west of Frenchtown (Monroe).

Once the base line and principal meridian were run to an intersection, the surveyors could block the state out into townships and sections. This work was begun also in 1815, all according to the plan set forth in the Ordinance of 1785, for the government was interested in opening the new territory for sale and settlement as soon as possible to recoup money spent acquiring and organizing. The market for these lands, however, was not brisk and the survey process was slow; a government land office was not opened in Detroit until 1818. The preliminary survey of the Lower Peninsula was still not complete in 1840 (after title to the northern lands had been cleared from Indian claims by the Treaty of Washington, 1836), when William Austin Burt ran the principal meridian across Bois Blanc Island and into the Upper Peninsula, and the survey of the whole state was not complete until the 1850s.[5]

Michigan's progress toward statehood was as slow as the early growth of her population. As late as 1819 the territory did not have the five thousand free adult males required by the Northwest Ordinance to become a territory of the second grade (her totlal non-Indian population in 1820 was 8,765).[6] So popular was the prospect of settlement on her lands. Michigan labored pathetically toward political organization for statehood until 1835. In the fall of that year state government was formed and placed in operation, though Michigan did not become the twenty-sixth state of the Union until January of 1837. The reason for the delay has been facetiously called the "Toledo War" and the "Maumee Melee" and it is the background for the Treaty of Washington in 1836.

What it was was the territorial dispute that anyone with sense could have seen developing since the early maps were found wanting, Ohio drafted her constitution in 1802, and Indiana petitioned to have her border moved north in 1816. Until that date the southern boundary of Michigan Territory had been set as a line drawn directly east from the southern extremity of Lake Michigan. The faulty early maps on which the framers of the Northwest Ordinance had relied had misplaced Lake Michigan slightly to the north and thus the line *intended* by the ordinance should have run east to Lake Erie just north of the mouth of the Maumee River on which is now Toledo. When the surveyors and cartographers relocated Lake Michigan, however, the line was found to run into Lake Erie south of the Maumee and Toledo on about the east-west line that now separates the Ohio counties of Ottawa and Wood, to the south, and Lucas, to the north—thus placing what is now Toledo and the access to the Maumee in Michigan.[7]

It would have been extremely sensible if Ohio had joined in Indiana's 1816 petition, before Michigan had any significant population, pretensions about becoming a state, and therefore political clout; doing so would have solved the problem that was otherwise destined to erupt and give Michigan a uniform southern border. Instead of this, however, the Ohioans simply stuck by their 1802 constitution in which, without federal authority or assent of Congress, they had recognized the dubious quality of the maps of the day and moved their border north by unilateral claim. Congress admitted Ohio to the Union in 1803, but without specifically addressing the issue of the wandering state line and in so doing left the boundary question to fester.

In the meantime, Ohio had embarked on an ambitious internal improvements program, an important (and expensive) feature of which was to have been a system of canals ultimately to connect the Ohio River with Lake Erie via the Maumee. This is what she had at stake. Michigan saw the value in the proposition also; if she could control the northern access she could share in an easy route for commerce and immigration that would connect her directly with the Ohio Valley, the Mississippi, and so finally the Gulf of Mexico—almost all at Ohio's expense. This is what she had at stake. Her case rested on the fact that Congress had failed *specifically* to acknowledge and so ratify Ohio's border nor had it followed the proper steps to modify the provisions of the Northwest Ordinance, which was the law of the land and by which provisions (despite Indiana's encroachment to the north) Michigan wanted to abide. But despite the law, her case as a practicality was pretty weak from the beginning. The importance of it all was at the extreme north end of the issue; for the political maneuverings around and about the disputed Toledo strip gained for Michigan some other territory that she did not then want. The conditions for statehood as they came to be laid down forced Michigan to accept responsibility for the entire Upper Peninsula.

When Michigan was organized as a territory in 1805, Congress, disregarding the constitution under which Ohio had been admitted to the Union, fixed as its southern boundary the Lake Michigan line as stipulated in the Northwest Ordinance. The Ohioans in Washington continued to press for an altered line (which should have been possible, after all, if one considers the ease with which Indiana and Illinois altered their northern borders), but the matter was largely ignored until 1812. In that year a congressional resolution called for a survey of the line as set forth in the Northwest Ordinance, apparently trying to determine decisively how far south Lake Michigan extended and so where exactly enacted law placed the line, which might then be discussed intelligently. The war intervened, so the survey was put off until 1817.

By this time Edward Tiffin, former governor of Ohio, had been named to the surveyor general's office; he directed his surveyor, William Harris, to run the line— but exactly according to the constitution of the state of Ohio, disregarding the mandate of the federal government to clarify its own law. Tiffin evidently wanted to take no chances for his Ohio friends and by now no one was playing exactly fair. This provoked a lively protest from Michigan's Governor Cass to President Monroe, who ordered a resurvey in 1818. It was executed by John A. Fulton according to the provisions of the Northwest Ordinance and, predictably, came out into Lake Erie to the south of the Maumee. Now, though at the western end of it Indiana's border had been moved ten miles into Michigan, at least the line mandated by the Northwest Ordinance was established and everyone knew for the first time where Lake Michigan was. And at least for the moment it looked as if Michigan owned Toledo.

For several years the matter seems to have been settled, more or less. The Ohio legislature declared the Harris line to be the official and legal one—ignoring the mandate of federal law in place—while Michigan quietly moved in to administer the Toledo strip. A Michigan land company invested in the strip and two towns were laid out, which were merged in 1833 to become Toledo. Michigan courts were held there and the residents voted in Michigan territorial elections and were counted in the Michigan census preliminary to application for statehood. In the meantime, Governor Cass even tried to negotiate a compromise with the Ohioans by which they might retain control of the Maumee River mouth. That would have been too sensible to fly; on the other hand, it would also have been an instance of a state and a territory messing with a line run according to federal law and so surely would have been unacceptable to someone—someone who lives in Washington and has never seen Toledo. So Ohio kept herself busy with her internal improvements, smugly sticking to her constitution.

In 1833 Michigan presented her first petition to Congress for admission to statehood—and someone (in Ohio) discovered a technical shortcoming in the Fulton survey. A new survey was ordered, performed by Capt. Andrew Talcott assisted by Lt. Robert E. Lee, that accomplished nothing beyond confirming the Fulton survey. The Senate then debated and passed a bill supporting Ohio's claim and the Harris line. This was sent to the House where it was referred to committee, which tabled it until the session adjourned. In the next session (1834-35) the Ohio senators revived the bill and appended to it a section confirming the northern boundaries of Indiana and Illinois. They explicitly sought support from their neighbors to the west by implying that if Ohio's territorial claims failed, Michigan might well challenge the legality of the northward drifting borders of those two states. The Senate again passed the amended bill and again the House failed to act on it.

Back in Ohio the comedic soap opera proceeded. Acting Gov. Stevens T. Mason was in power in Michigan and he directed the territorial council to appoint three commissioners to negotiate with Ohio. Gov. Robert Lucas refused to negotiate, ordered the Harris line permanently marked, and organized an area including the eastern end of the disputed strip into a county that would finally bear his name. Michigan countered by passing a resolution imposing a large fine and five years imprisonment on any other than Michigan or federal officials who might attempt to exercise any office in the strip. Lucas answered this by appointing a sheriff and a panel of judges to hold court in his new county, and at this Governor Mason called out the territorial militia, asked for volunteers, placed himself at the head of this unlikely army, and headed for the Toledo strip. There he arrested a party of surveyors who were marking the Harris line and any other Ohio officials he could find. Meanwhile, a team of federal commissioners arrived to attempt to mediate the issue and accomplished exactly nothing.

The Ohio legislature voted $300,000 for the military defense of the strip, which the Michigan Territorial Council answered by voting $315,000 for the same purpose. Governor Lucas ordered the session of court for which he had already prepared to be held within the strip (to provide a record of Ohio's administration there), which was accomplished by a single judge and a recorder at midnight under an armed guard of Ohio militiamen, after which all fled to the sanctuary of undisputed territory. There was even a wound, the only recorded one of the "war": a Michigan sheriff was cut with a jackknife in a tavern scuffle with an Ohio militiaman.

In retrospect the whole affair seems mostly humorous if not downright silly. At the time, however, the prospect of armed conflict between the territory and the state posed grave problems echoing far beyond the "battlefield" melodrama and led to brave solutions of immense consequence to the citizens of Michigan. From a strictly legal point of view, Michigan and Mason were probably in the right; the Northwest Ordinance was the law of the land and the Fulton-Talcott line was the manifestation of that law. This was the view presented to President Jackson (and not to his great pleasure) by the attorney general of the United States. From the other point of view, it is not difficult to see Ohio's point—an early example of the assertion of states' rights. She had, after all, long been accepted into statehood with an approved state constitution, which included, even if somewhat brashly, a modified northern border and had proceeded with internal improvements under the aegis of that constitution. She also had population, state government, and so political clout in Washington—especially so considering her alliance with Indiana and Illinois. Michigan did not. Both the problem and its solution thus became explicitly political. Former President John Quincy Adams commented: "Never in the course of my life have I known a controversy of which all the right was so clear on one side and all the power so overwhelmingly on the other.[8]

President Jackson had a political party and therefore an election to worry about in 1836—and there were a lot of votes to consider in Ohio, Indiana, and Illinois that he would surely lose for the Democrats if he took Michigan's side in the dispute while she was still a slightly populated territory struggling toward statehood. He thus compromised himself in favor of his party and tried to cool Michigan down by removing Mason from power and appointing John. S. Horner as territorial governor, which did not work, as Horner was snubbed both socially and politically and quickly moved on to Wisconsin. He also exercised his enormous power to influence Congress to resolve the issue in favor of the three states already formed.

The compromise that would finally end, if not resolve, the issue was engineered by a Senate committee chaired by Jackson's man, Sen.Thomas Hart Benton of Missouri. By 1836 it was clear that Michigan was about to become the fourth state carved out of the Northwest Territory, and there was substantial concern that the territory remaining was too large to be politically manageable as a single state. The Northwest Ordinance had stipulated that out of the original territory would emerge not less than three nor more than five states; this part of the ordinance seems to have remained in fashion. Thus when the Wisconsin Territory was established in April of 1836, its eastern limit was fixed along the lines of the Menominee and Montreal rivers, at the western extremity of what is now Michigan's Upper Peninsula.

The problem remained of what to do with this far northern tract: the people who lived in the areas of Mackinac and Sault Ste. Marie (its only populated areas, and these sparse) had already petitioned to become a separate Territory of Huron, fearing (with good reason, as it has turned out) that their land and their life was so far removed from the population at and around Detroit that they could not hope to be properly represented downstate—and the people who lived in Detroit and elsewhere to the south wanted nothing to do with it. The Upper Peninsula, once regarded as the gateway to the west and the point of greatest strategic importance in the interior, owing to the development of Ohio and a working international peace on the Lakes, had deteriorated in almost everyone's estimation to a veritable no man's land. The northern peninsula, now destined to be Michigan's unwanted consolation prize in her dispute with Ohio, was styled a "sterile region on the shores of Lake Superior, destined by soil and climate to remain forever a wilderness," and "a region of perpetual snows—the *Ultima Thule* of our national domain in the north.[9]

But two factors, the one political and the other logistical, determined that the Upper Peninsula would be appended to Michigan. First, there had to be a trade-off for the short shrift Michigan had received in the settlement of the dispute over the Toledo strip; second, in the Treaty of Washington signed in March of 1836 between the United States and the northern Michigan Chippewa and Ottawa tribes, the United States had secured a huge tract of land in the northern Lower Peninsula together with the Upper Peninsula as far west as what is now Escanaba. Though geographically attached to the emerging Wisconsin Territory, it was clearly practical, wanted or unwanted, to attach these lands to the new state for administration—that is, survey and organization to prepare for marketing, which was already going on in the Michigan Territory and through which continued the process of civilizing and so controlling the Indians.

Originally the people of Michigan, through a convention of their representatives called to Ann Arbor in September of 1836, flatly rejected the proposed compromise, even those favoring it doing so only with the stipulation that the boundary issue be arbitrated by the United States Supreme Court. Hardly had the convention been adjourned, however, before second thoughts began to creep in: it turned out there was money at stake—not to mention statehood. The application for statehood was being held up pending acceptance of the compromise. Statehood, beyond being desirable in itself, meant a five percent share in the profits starting (finally) to come in from the sale of public lands in Michigan, a share (calculated to be worth about $400,000) in the distribution of excess from the United States treasury, and several paid federal appointments that would be made among state residents. Acting Governor Mason, back in power after temporary Governor Horner departed for Wisconsin, would not himself reconvene the convention but advised that the people had the right to do so in order to reverse their previous decision. Thus it was that the people, feeling for the second time the weight of federal pressure and recognizing the value to them of federal dollars, called a Convention of Assent in December of 1836. In the meantime, Governor Cass had moved on to Washington as President Jackson's secretary of war, and Henry Schoolcraft had spent almost a year there setting up negotiations for his Indian treaty. These two men, who had explored together and written about the Upper Peninsula and recognized the potential of its resources, may have been the only prominent Michiganians who knew how good a bargain the United States was offering Michigan and they worked hard to push the deal, unwanted both at home and in Washington, through. Finally the Convention of Assent came to its decision and sent it to Washington: Michigan conceded the Toledo strip, and the Upper Peninsula as we know it was attached to the state of Michigan. Cass and Schoolcraft were part of a minority equipped to understand what a brilliant compromise it all was; most of the first generation of state residents knew only that they now owned something they did not want—their own white elephant in the north. On January 26, 1837, President Jackson signed the bill joining the state of Michigan with the Union.

CHAPTER ELEVEN

TREATY
OF WASHINGTON (1836)

As Michigan was edging slowly and painfully toward statehood by fighting her absurd little border war with Ohio, other events were taking shape in the north that would have immense consequences in negotiating and completing the Treaty of Washington (March 28, 1836) and thus on Michigan's becoming a state. From almost every point of view the Treaty of 1836 is the most important of the several treaties ceding Indian lands in the state of Michigan. Not only does it account for the largest tract acquired by the United States in Michigan (all the Lower Peninsula north of the Grand River in the west and west and north of the Thunder Bay River in the east, together with the Upper Peninsula to the west as far as the Escanaba River), it also marks a massive turning of the tide of Indian affairs and the Indians' recognition and acceptance of the dominant American culture on which they had become all but completely dependent.

In 1834 John Jacob Astor sold his trading interests in Michigan and the American Fur Company moved its center of operations to St. Louis; the heyday of the fur trader in the Great Lakes was over. The utter relentlessness of the Indian trapper in his quest for white man's goods in trade coupled with the enthusiasm of the American trader in his quest for profit had so diminished a supposedly inexhaustible resource that the territory being opened in the far west offered greater trading efficiency. Though Ramsay Crooks continued trading at Mackinac under the old company name, both volume and demand were down and supply was dwindling. Not only was the resource, therefore, becoming harder to harvest, but the market value of it was eroding. At the same time, the Indians' demand for and need of trading goods did not diminish; they had no industry of their own, no commercial alternative, and yet had become habitual consumers—now without a livelihood in the economy on which they depended. They were thus leaping heavily into debt to the American traders and had no means of discharging their obligations or comprehending their situation. This state of affairs was not good.

Nor was it helped by the fact that the federal government was then clearly content with its land holdings in Michigan; there was not even an appointed commissioner in the territory to negotiate with an eye to further acquisitions. Once again the land to the north was held in low enough esteem that no one wanted to own it. The people of Michigan did not want it attached to their evolving political entity, and the federal government did not want to invest in it because there was no identifiable market for it—and it as yet both contained and defined the Indian problem. This left the Indians doubly in a bad way; they had only two things of value that they could trade with the white man, and the value of both was declining dramatically. Some sort of relief was necessary. The Indians had unwittingly become wards of an evolving American economy and thus the first candidates for federal welfare compensation; the industry to which they were attached (and there was no other to which they could be attached) called for a government bailout.

This was the situation into which Henry Rowe Schoolcraft injected himself in the fall of 1835. He writes: "Circumstances had now inclined the Chippewa and Ottawa tribes of Indians to cede to the United States a portion of *their* extensive territory. Game had failed in the greater part of it, and they had no other method of raising funds to pay their large outstanding credits to the class of traders."[1] The Indians petitioned Schoolcraft as their agent for help out of a dismal state of affairs, and Schoolcraft betook himself as their representative to Washington in the fall of 1835 hoping to arrange a land cession to benefit them. His mission in Washington was explicitly neither approved nor much appreciated by Congress (or anyone else, for that matter), which at the time was busy enough with other aspects of the Michigan problem and so little inclined toward acquiring more land there.[2] Nor were the congressmen happily disposed toward discussing a corporate bailout or providing welfare benefits for noncitizens, the only legal means of financing which could be the sale of unmarketable property.

There are thus several clear objectives in the 1836 treaty quite separate from acquisition of unwanted land and arranging for compensation for it. Partly because of their improvidence and, to be sure, partly because of the success of the Yankee trader, the Indians had trapped themselves out of the one medium of exchange they understood: they knew the land to have some value—because they had already ceded, traded, and even sold parcels of it, some several times (which seemed a good deal)—but they still could not translate the value of it into a practicality. Owing largely to population dynamics, intranational wars, choice of life-style, and, thus, the necessity of annual migrations to hunting and fishing grounds, the Michigan Indians had long been nomadic by the time the Europeans arrived in the Great Lakes; they had only vague memories of town dwelling, mound building, metalworking, and other evidences of permanency of location. Their sense of agriculture was extremely primitive, and regressive: corn, squash, and perhaps some beans planted in natural clearings that would be left untended and then revisited later during the annual migration.

Then, like an animal being domesticated, they learned to depend on the white man, and so visits to his posts became a regular feature of the migration until alliances were formed and more or less permanent homes grew as appendages to white settlements. In all of this, though he shared it with his brothers, the land was something the Indian moved across and harvested from as he moved; it was not something he lived on and depended on in a particular location—which location itself could then provide for him and assume a value of its own. His meat was always running free and on the hoof; if he failed to catch it he did not eat. Fencing it in and husbanding it and fattening it for slaughter was utterly foreign to him. This concept he would have to learn. In it is implied a system of life within which the land assumes a practical value by the acre; he would need to become a part of this system or face being extinguished by it. It was for nothing less than this that Schoolcraft went to Washington in 1835.

The earlier treaties, going back as far as Greenville (1795) but especially Governor Cass's at Saginaw (1819), had introduced the idea of civilizing the Indians by withholding cash and offering American values and so participation in our economic and political system. By 1836 the northern Ottawas and Chippewas needed as well as wanted not just to ally with (as in the cases of the French and the British), but to join and participate in the American economy. The 1836 Treaty of Washington stands as a monument to this desire and this need. It is the first truly significant mutual attempt, important also because the Indians themselves initiated it, to take Indian land and alchemize it into an investment capable of providing enough return to sustain a living income. The text of the 1836 treaty begins on page 178.

As negotiated, signed, amended, ratified, and again agreed to in the also signed "Articles of Assent," the treaty provides for: cession, extinction thereby of Indian claim to title, removal as might be requested or required (by the Indians), disbanding of tribes, civilization, and integration of the Indian community with the American one.[3] In its design, then, the treaty suggests several clear phases of Indian-American relations. The first is securing of complete title to that "tract of country" including "all the lands and islands" within the tract described (Article First), extinction of title, and the option (and that only, and only if requested) of removal. For their lands the Indians were to receive up front $150,000 in goods and provisions "to be delivered at Michilimackinac on the ratification of this treaty" (Article Fourth) together with a payment of $300,000 designated to pay Indian obligations to the traders (which gives some idea of Indian indebtedness at Mackinac), and other good and valuable considerations—all designed to ease the Indians' passage into a new kind of life.

With the cash, they received the government promise, "as soon as the said Indians desire it" (Article Eighth), of suitable lands to the west of the Mississippi where, without as yet the threat of serious white intrusion, those who wished could carry on in their accustomed mode of life—engaging, it may be presumed, once again in the fur trade at its new center in St. Louis. This is but one of two provisions inviting the option of the Indian maintaining his old ways; for this treaty, like the earlier one at Saginaw, also preserves large tracts of land within the cession itself to be held by tribal councils as reservations inviolate—to be unsurveyed and undeveloped save at the discretion of the Indians. There are also stipulated payments to individuals, most often according to tribal rank, as both annuities and cash in hand.

Not including costs of some items that would be extremely hard to calculate, though up-front cash may appear low, the cash value of the cession of unwanted land—at a time and place where there was limited use for cash—comes to $1,537,148, a remarkable sum considering the values of the day and the state of the national treasury. This figure does not include the costs attached to agricultural, mechanical, and educational help, or the other promised goods and services.

The second phase implemented in the 1836 treaty, which also followed the pattern that evolved at Saginaw, had to do with the civilizing process. As surely as the treaty provided for annual payments to help sustain the Indians, so it also provided for: teachers, missions, schoolhouses, books, agricultural tools, mechanics tools, blacksmith shops, cattle, and, as at Saginaw, "such other objects as the President shall deem proper"—not to mention vaccine matter, medicines, physicians, tobacco, salt, and fish barrels (Article Seventh). Once again, but here more extensively, the intent of the treaty is clear: rather than a simple arm's length purchase contract (which could promise nothing more than to recommence the sad economic spiral), the United States government agreed to subsidize the Indians while they learned to accommodate themselves to the more advanced economic and social system within which they needed to learn to function to become self-sustaining citizens. There was thus room within the agreement, either by removal or by retreat to the reservations, for the Indians who wanted to accept only the cash in hand and the annuities and continue in their old ways.

But there was also generous encouragement for those who might choose to integrate with the dominant white culture. Insofar and as fast as it might prove possible, the Americans intended to get the land surveyed and recorded so that it could be assigned a practical value and marketed. Only then could the treaty pay for itself, the land be given back to the Indians as individuals by the section, the annuities cease, and the Indians who chose to participate be integrated with the American economy and society equally with all other residents on the land. Then each would have something of value, either to be again sold or to be worked for a livelihood— which was to be the principal business of the 1855 treaty, concluded on July 31 at Detroit, clearly anticipating the twenty-year deadlines set in the Treaty of Washington, to make sure all obligations on both sides had been properly met.

One intent of the whole process, to be sure, was the breaking down of tribal affiliation as a way of life; but the process also offered the only equitable alternative the Americans could give: ultimately, political affiliation with local, state, and federal government. This was the reason the 1836 treaty was amended by Congress during review and returned to the Indians for assent in slightly altered form. As negotiated by Schoolcraft and the council of chiefs that traveled to Washington, for instance, it "reserved for the use of the Chippeways, living north of the Straits of Michilimackinac, the following tracts, that is to say . . . the Islands of the Chenos with a part of the adjacent north coast of Lake Huron, corresponding in length and one mile in depth."[4] When the treaty was reviewed and ratified by Congress and the president in May, however, this reservation and the several others like it were restricted to a five-year period. After this period the Indians could occupy this and other territory not otherwise specifically included in the large system of permanent reservations only with the continuing permission of the federal government. The reasons for the change are clear enough and have little to do with the criticism that is often implied in concluding that this was just another instance of the white man capriciously working his wiles on the hapless Indian.[5]

When Schoolcraft and the chiefs were framing the 1836 treaty, Michigan's petition for statehood, with all its problems—even ones with military implications—was very much on the table and Congress was busy trying to deal with it. Securing complete title to more Indian lands in Michigan added yet another and significant dimension to these problems: not only did the federal government have to finance the acquisition, it also had to found a social welfare system to support and benefit the Indians while the land to be acquired was organized so as to have value for all the residents on it, including the Indian ones. The boundaries of the new state were also to be determined, as was the description of the lands being negotiated for acquisition from the tribes.

Once a deal was struck in that quarter and the large area of what was to become the Upper Peninsula could be known as included in it, it would be immensely to the advantage of the Washington types to begin doing something with their acquisition. Government surveyors were already pushing north in Michigan, and it would clearly be both wise and prudent to proceed with the surveys to their earliest possible conclusion, even if there was no known market for the land—the larger part ofwhich was not successfully marketed until the timber boom later in the century. For these reasons also, though it was more logically connected geographically with the new Wisconsin Territory, the Upper Peninsula was destined to be attached to Michigan *and* organized in all haste to determine the latest and best use for it and to organize the Indians who lived on it and were rapidly approaching destitution.

Thus Congress put in place the five-year limit to Indian lands not designated for perpetual reservation; the perpetual reservations, because they were to remain the inviolate property of tribal councils, were not scheduled for survey, but all remaining lands were to be surveyed as soon as possible. It might take five years for the survey teams to reach the eastern Upper Peninsula, but when they got there, when the principal meridian of the state came ashore at what is now Cedarville in the Les Cheneaux Islands group, the area had to be ready for survey without local contest. Ultimate ownership was not yet even a sensible question; organizing the land, and in the process the civilizing of the Indians, was a necessary and immediate concern. The Les Cheneaux reservation, thus, like the other reservations specified in Article Third, was temporary and transitional—though Shab-wa-way (the principal chief in the area and a signer of the treaty) and his band of Chippewas were never asked to leave and ended up with substantial, individually owned tracts of land among the islands and on the mainland adjacent.[6] As a chief of the "first class," Shab-wa-way also received a cash payment of five hundred dollars and an annuity. The Chippewas of the eastern Upper Peninsula were also promised and given a dormitory on Mackinac Island for use when they might wish to visit there (to trade or visit their agent; the building still stands and is historically marked) and the assistance of farmers and mechanics.

In the summer of 1836 the Indian contingent returned from Washington to the Great Lakes well pleased with the work they had accomplished. As recently as the previous fall they had found themselves deeply in debt and without a means of extricating themselves; with Schoolcraft's help they had discovered a way out of their hole and, against all odds at the time (and with help from the circumstances surrounding Michigan's petition for statehood), worked out a way into the future. The Treaty of Washington offered the Indians economic opportunity equal to that of any other citizen-settler. The amended treaty, ratified and ready for approval by the Indians, was returned to Michigan and sent to Mackinac, where the Indians were assembled to consider and sign the Articles of Assent. Schoolcraft was present and records that "its principles were freely and fully discussed," after which the Indians assented to the treaty as amended by Congress and received, as promised, their first distribution of goods and cash—to their "joy and satisfaction." Which, Schoolcraft concludes, "will shut their mouths forever with regard to the oft-repeated scandal of the stinginess and injustice of the American Government."[7] Twenty-six years later Shab-wa-way still carried proudly and showed to friends the medallion-portrait of President Jackson that was his memento of the trip to Washington.[8] In his biography of Schoolcraft, Richard Bremer gives a good account of the negotiations in Washington and the signing of the amended treaty. Of the various parties involved in its provisions, only the traders were unhappy with it; some of the debts to them were discharged by the government agent responsible at rates as low as fifty cents to the dollar.[9]

CHAPTER TWELVE

TREATIES
AT DETROIT (1855)

The logic of the series of treaties by which the federal government secured lands occupied by Indians in Michigan and extinguished Indian claim to title to them was begun at Greenville and Detroit and Saginaw, and graven in rock in Washington in 1836; it was brought to its conclusion at Detroit in 1855. The last of the Michigan land cessions, in what is now the western end of the Upper Peninsula, were completed in the treaties of Cedar Point (1836) and La Pointe (1842); by 1842 the surveys had been extended into the eastern Upper Peninsula. There is nothing remarkable about these treaties; they follow the pattern now well established: each is a land cession, and that only, to which was attached some up-front cash to be paid as annuities to help the Indians along, each provides for the satisfaction of Indian debt to the traders, and each provides the by now customary goods and services, all for a specified time (twenty years at Cedar Point, twenty-five at La Pointe), to help integrate the tribesmen with the American system of civilization that was by now destined for them.

Once again the adjoining waters of the Great Lakes are nowhere an issue. The land only, and the usual privileges of occupancy on it (again for a specified time—until the land was needed for settlement) was at issue, including islands in waters still imperfectly charted, some virtually unknown. The waters carried boundary lines, but that only; what was perceived as ownable, and therefore valuable, was strictly above the high-water mark—together with the mineral and other material rights that attached to it.

Uniformly through the treaties of cession in Michigan, the United States government negotiated with the North American Indians as foreign nations with all the rights and responsibilities that that implies. Having won our part of the continent from the British, we then set about securing it from its aboriginal inhabitants in as orderly a fashion as was possible under rapidly changing circumstances. This ultimately became far more complex than exchanging cash for title; it became integration, the end of which was to accommodate the Indians within our socioeconomic system. To accomplish this we had to arrange for them to own something, land in the first instance, of assignable value so that they would have a means of participating in the system. This and the naturalization of the Michigan Indians were important objects of the 1855 Treaties at Detroit.[1]

The Treaty of Washington set three time limits, five years for the temporary reservations, ten years for the services of mechanics and farmers, twenty years for most of the annuity payments. In 1855, then, the scheduled payments were winding down, so the tribes again sent a delegation to Washington—not to modify any standing agreements, but now to make sure that all treaty agreements had been properly met. The broadest purpose, thus, of the 1855 treaties was to confirm that the government obligations incurred in 1836 had been discharged and that the Indians were well on their way to the social integration promised in the twenty-year feature of the Treaty. Just as in 1836, the Indians called for the negotiations, in part because they wanted to extend some of the social services devised to help them in transition, as well as to get an accounting of what was given or due or both before the provisions of the 1836 treaty lapsed in the following year.

What was written at Detroit in 1855 was a series of treaties between the United States government and the various bands of Ottawa and Chippewa Indians who had exercised claims on land within the state of Michigan before or under the extant treaties of cession of the land that became the state. The first and most important of these, because it is the most general and most noted and quoted, is with the Ottawa and Chippewa Indians of the state, who were parties to the Treaty of Washington.The second is with the Chippewas of Sault Ste. Marie, who were parties to Governor Cass's treaty there in 1820, which specifically gave the tribes the right to camp and fish at the Sault rapids. The third is with the Chippewas of Saginaw, party to a separate treaty in 1837, and of Swan Creek and Black River, parties to the Treaty of Washington, but now living in the state of Michigan. The intent of the 1855 treaties could not be more clear: the Indian matter in Michigan was to be settled once and for all. The texts of the treaties of 1855 begin on page 188.

Though the treaty with the Saulteur Chippewas has a precise and single point—extinguishing fishing rights specifically granted in Cass's treaty—all three treaties clearly try to reach a final solution. (The Sault tribe treaty was done in August and the Sault locks had been opened to traffic in June; it was necessary to clear the waters for that traffic as well as to unencumber the land in favor of the city growing beside the locks.) In each the United States government pledges payment of final compensation to cover all debt to the indians; in each the annuities guaranteed in 1836 for twenty years were to end and the United States government was to be released from any further liability. In the two more general treaties the civilizing process is carried forward in the award of lands, by the section to individual Indians, services, funds, and structures—the grist and sawmills for the Saginaw types, for instance.

Justice Lindemer, in his dissenting opinion in *People v. LeBlanc* considers carefully the notes from the treaty negotiations before the 1855 treaty session. He correctly infers that the Chippewas were eager for the treaty as their means to a new life within the American rural and agrarian economy. He quotes, for instance, the Indian negotiator Was-son: "We have all come to the question in regard to the lands. We know our great father will give us these lands for a homestead. I have abandoned the woods for a maintenance & am now a farmer. I no longer go into the woods & look for wild animals when I want to eat; but I kill one of the cattle I raise for myself." Similarly, As-sa-gon, another Indian negotiator, expressed his concern over selecting good agricultural lands because so much of the land in his territory was swampy and unsuitable for agriculture. The Indians clearly expected assimilation into the white society and regarded that prospect as the last and greatest gift of their "great father." As-sa-gon was also concerned over the slow progress of Indian children in learning English and asked that better trained schoolmasters be engaged, while Mene-a-du-pe-na-se requested additional money for college tuition for Indian boys. It is clear, Justice Lindemer concludes, that both parties intended to provide for the future and the future was to be the end of the traditional life-style of the Indians.

The general survey of the state had been largely completed by the end of the 1851 season and this, together with the twenty-year feature of the 1836 treaty, made possible a final disposition of the Indian problem within Michigan's borders. The 1855 treaty conferred citizenship, land, and seed money for investment and development upon the Indians. The land was now surveyed, described, recorded in the public land offices; the theory was now to withdraw various tracts of it from public sale to further benefit the Indians. Frank R. Grover writes:

> This treaty granted to each Chippewa and Ottawa Indian the head of a family eighty acres of land; to each single person over twenty-one years of age, forty acres and to each family of orphan children under that age and consisting of two or more persons eighty acres of land. Further providing "Each Indian entitled to land under this article may make his own selection of any land within the tract reserved herein for the band to which he may belong." Provision was further made for the preparation of a list of the Indian grantees by the Indian agent; that such selection of land by the Indians should by made within five years after the preparation of such a list and be filed with the Indian agent at Detroit to be transmitted to Washington; that the Indians making such selection should take immediate possession, receiving non-assignable certificates, prohibiting sales by the certificate holders; that after ten years such restrictions should be withdrawn and patents issued, subject, however, to the right of the President in special cases, on the recommendation of the Indian agent to appoint guardians for those incapable of managing their own affairs and, in special cases to permit sales prior to the expiration of such ten years. The lands not so selected were to then be open again to general sale by the government and the resident

homesteaders at the date of the treaty were protected in their occupancy and existing rights. Also provided for the payment to the Indians in annuities and cash and in expenditures for them during a term of ten years, for educational purposes, agricultural implements, cattle, household goods and otherwise, the sum of $573,{400}.[2]

Having acquired the land twice from Great Britain and then extinguished Indian claim to title to it, the United States government proceeded to give it back to the Indians by the parcel. In the process the government attempted to integrate them with the American economy while also continuing to instruct them in the management of it and protecting them throughout—by restricting their ability to sell their new and individually owned assets for a reasonable time during which a fair market value could be established. The final intent of the treaties was to break down tribal affiliations, for which the Indians were given a new affiliation. They who had been regarded as equal and often belligerent foreign nationals were now to be treated as equal partners in the enterprise of national development—even if they would require substantial help in upholding their end of the partnership. Too, in creating this sense of partnership, in conferring upon the Indians something of value and teaching them how to use it, the United States sought to discharge all legal claims the nations, tribes, or bands might have on the government communally. For this, the Indians received ownership, citizenship, participation—with all its individual rights and prerogatives.

CHAPTER THIRTEEN

INTO THE TWENTIETH CENTURY

The controversy over Indian fishing rights in the Michigan waters of the Great Lakes began in April 1971. The Michigan Supreme Court ruled in *People v. Jondreau* (Appendix 2, page 192) that descendants of any Indian tribe that once ceded lands in Michigan to the United States have the right to hunt and fish on the ceded land and its adjacent waters free from any encumbrance of state law or regulation.[1] The tribes moved quickly to take advantage of this windfall and by the end of 1971 were fishing commercially in northern waters without regard for state imposed protective regulations.

At the time, the Great Lakes had only narrowly survived the double disaster of the intrusions of the sea lamprey and the alewife. The lamprey was a new, foreign, formidable, and highly successful predator/parasite. The alewife further upset the already staggering biological balance of the lakes because, though a small species, it is aggressive. It adapted well, bred copiously and, most important, as a foreign species it had no natural predator to keep it in balance. The predator species, mostly game fish, then present in the lakes were slow to learn to forage on it. These intrusions began about the end of World War II and the nosedive they precipitated resulted, only ten years later in 1955, in the almost unbelievable statistic that fourteen hundred miles of commercial nets set in the Michigan waters of Lake Michigan took exactly eight lake trout with a total weight of thirty-four pounds—down six million pounds in a decade.[2]

In the 1960s the Michigan Department of Natural Resources (DNR), led by Howard Tanner, moved firmly to restore the fishery. The DNR found chemicals with which to combat the lamprey and introduced the Pacific salmon species, natural predators for the alewife. The turnabout was as dramatic as had been the decline.

The aggressive programs were begun in 1964 and by 1970, just a year before the Jondreau case, waters that had been barren of game fish ten years ago were again among the most productive in the world. The new charter boat industry alone added hundreds of millions of dollars to the state's economy. The lakes again had value, and one can only surmise that that restored value took the Jondreau case to court. It proved a landmark in Michigan law and laid the foundation in the state for the better known, more fully developed, and more often discussed *People v. LeBlanc* (Appendix 2, page 199).

But the blockbuster case, important because it was taken up in a federal district court in Grand Rapids that effectively found in its own favor in deregulating tribal commercial fishing and seriously restricted the state's ability to manage its own resources, is *United States v. Michigan* (Appendix 2, page 218), Judge Noel P. Fox presiding. The litigation was begun in 1973 by the federal government (the Bureau of Indian Affairs, an agency of the Department of the Interior), on its own behalf and on behalf of the Bay Mills Indian Community, against the State of Michigan and several named officials of the DNR, all in their official positions; the United States argued as trustee for the tribes that unrelinquished (indeed, unspecified) rights to fish the waters of the Great Lakes were guaranteed the Indians through the land cessions represented in the nineteenth century Michigan Indian treaties—and in such documents as the Northwest Ordinance (1787) and the Treaty of Ghent, which ended the War of 1812. Subsequently, the Bay Mills Indian Community (in 1974), the Sault Ste. Marie Tribe of Chippewa Indians (in 1975), and the Grand Traverse Band of Ottawas and Chippewas (in 1979) intervened as party plaintiffs.

Though filed in 1973 the case was not argued at trial until February 1978, though it was delayed until September. Meantime, in December of 1976, the Supreme Court of Michigan issued its split decision in *People v. LeBlanc*. District Court Judge Nicholas J. Lambros in Sault Ste. Marie had convicted the Chippewa Indian leader, Abe LeBlanc, of fishing in Pendills Bay (a small bay within Lake Superior's Whitefish Bay) in September 1971, without a commercial fishing license and with a gill net, because a gill net kills indiscriminately, prohibited by state law. The conviction was taken to Chippewa County Circuit Court, where Judge William F. Hood upheld it. It then went to the Michigan Court of Appeals, where it was in part reversed and remanded, and from there to the Supreme Court of Michigan.

There Judge G. Mennen Williams wrote the majority opinion, reversing the earlier convictions and holding that the Chippewa Indians reserved for themselves fishing rights in off-reservation waters according to the Treaty of Washington (1836), that these fishing rights were not relinquished in the Treaty of Detroit (1855), and that, therefore, save for a rule of reason inserted to preserve a species from extinction, the Indians could fish where and with what they pleased in waters demarked within the cession lines of the 1836 treaty. Though the burden of proof seems excessive and it falls on the State, because the remands attached to Judge Fox's ruling suggest that this part of *LeBlanc* stands as law, the rule of reason remains important. It also precedes Judge Fox's opinion by three years, and it is clear that in the actions leading to his arrest Abe LeBlanc intended to test the Jondreau opinion issued just five months earlier in 1971.

In each of the cases cited the judges recur to the mandates set forth by the United States Supreme Court (echoing through many Indian cases, but apparently founded in *Jones v. Mehan* [1899]) as governing the legal construction of United States treaties with North American Indian nations. Both broadly and explicitly, the Supreme Court of the land requires applying historical method to the nterpretation of the treaties and so their implications in our century. Broadly, the Supreme Court recognizes the self-evident: the northern Indians were, until assimilation into European-American civilization began, an unlettered people; they had no written language, lexicon, or system of calculation; they had no currency or other medium of exchange; they had no calendar or accurate means of reckoning time or keeping records. Only the other party could possibly have written any treaty with them—and it is remarkable how far the federal government attempted (even if it may not always have been a success) to treat with the tribes fairly. Therefore, the Supreme Court dictates, the treaties must be construed quite literally and in the simplest meaning of the words contained in them as the Indians would have understood them at the time—not as the words might be understood by learned and subtle and ambiguous lawyers and judges, especially at some later date. More explicitly, because of the inequity in literacy, the Court demands that any ambiguity be resolved in favor of the Indians.

As much to the point is the implied mandate, if the judges are to be held to construing the treaties as the Indians would have understood them at the time of their framing, to understand the historical period in which the individual treaties were put together, the historical context from which they emerged in which context only can the least ambiguous meaning of the language be determined. It would not be fair, thus, to apply the language of the 1855 treaty to construing the 1836 one, though it would be perfectly proper to apply the language of previous treaties to it—and to construe the Treaty of Detroit (1855) in the context of the treaties that preceded and fed into it. This is historical method and certainly seems to be what the Supreme Court calls for.

The language of the treaties (and the ordinances) is self-evidently simple and direct—and this for the same reasons that the twentieth-century judges demand that it be construed simply and directly. The ordinances were writtens to direct the organization, both geographic and legal and governmental, of territory as yet unsurveyed and largely unsettled to benefit and protect the unsophisticated agriculturalists expected to commence the settlement of it and the remnant French Canadians and Indians already on it alike. The treaties were written as both land cessions and extinguishments of claim to title in the most basic possible terms so as to be comprehensible to both the unlettered aboriginals and the anticipated settlers. No one in the early stages of territorial development was expected to be terribly subtle or learned; simplicity was therefore mandatory and the emphasis was on basics. Thus the very first legal provisions of the Northwest Ordinance (Section 2) are to protect private property (estates) and dower rights; the land was perceived as having value, as was familial responsibility, even before the other niceties of law and order. The territory was to be no refuge for family deserters and the resident Indians were to be dealt with fairly; the provision for education was surely to encourage a sophistication that would allow the evolving states to become fully participatory with the original thirteen—and to encourage the civilizing process among the Indian *and other* unlettered inhabitants.

Unfortunately, though they pretend to it, in their opinions the judges are a little lean on history. In his lengthy opinion, for instance, though he roundly interprets very selective historical matter, Judge Fox refers to only two published histories: Samuel Eliot Morison's *Oxford History of the American People* (1965) and the *American Heritage Pictorial History of the Presidents* (1968). Both are deliberately and popularly liberal—written, that is, with a subjective bias—and therefore slanted and both lack certain authority for that reason. It may not be necessary or even appropriate for a judge to admit published books as evidence but, especially given the Supreme Court mandate for applying historical method to treaty construction, should he choose to do so one would hope that he might build a more comprehensive and objective bibliography than the one Judge Fox leaves behind.

The judge cites both Morison and the American Heritage volume as his authority on the bankruptcy of federal Indian removal policy that resulted in the tribal march west along a "trail of tears" after the Black Hawk War. His is a very nice and dramatic exercise in liberal historical generalization in which he roundly condemns the federal government for its policy of removal. He deemphasizes the fact that, though removal was an option (and that only) in the earlier Michigan treaties, removal was seldom if ever forced on the Indian tribes of Michigan. His argument works only by remote analogy and has no place in a consideration of the Michigan treaties—except, perhaps, in a note allowing that in Michigan removal was never taken seriously as policy. Trading land that was unwanted because it was barren for other land in the west that had not as yet been overtrapped and thus might be presumed to have greater value as a place of understood commerce was an option, but the Indians found the western lands unsuitable on inspection and there the matter ended.

The judges are equally fallacious in their ethnological characterization of the Indian peoples in Michigan. Federal policy from very early on (the Northwest Ordinance, for instance, as well as the treaties) dictated that the United States government as well as the governments of the states in evolution treat the tribes with all possible tolerance, kindness, fairness, and consideration as sovereign foreign nations that happened to play by rules deriving from a foreign and unlettered culture. That makes it attractive to characterize the postcontact Indians as gentle and simple souls led astray and set upon by unscrupulous Europeans—then American Europeans. The argument just does not hold water. As Ted Williams points out:

> Throughout most of the continent the Asian invaders [very certainly in the northern climes] found a harsh, cruel land and became, not surprisingly, harsh and cruel themselves. "Noble," as we define it now, doesn't quite fit a society that taught its children the art of torturing captives all night, using such implements as clam shells to remove skin and muscle, taking great pains to prevent their victims from lapsing into unconsciousness, then eating the hearts of those who did not cry out.[3]

Evidence of the barbaric side of Indian social behavior, in both the precontact and the postcontact periods, is extremely well documented in both Parkman and the *Jesuit Relations,* as it is in most of the authoritative histories and ethnological studies—including several reputable ones written by Indian historians.

It is sad that Judge Fox, though he happily and proudly introduces the Northwest Ordinance as the "backdrop" for his decision and promises a full discussion of it in his opinion, then shies away from this extremely important document. Clearly he is fond of Article III, which promises fairness in all matters to the Indians; he probably does not much like Article IV, which defines the waters. Nevertheless, he gives us the fact that the new Congress of the United States, fully armed with a constitution in 1789 (two years after the passage of the ordinance by the Congress of the Confederation in 1787), made it a primary object to reenact the ordinance in its very first session. That suggests that the document, insofar as it defines rights and responsibilities and protections in the territory destined to be carved into states, carries the weight of a constitutional contract—all of it, including parts he does not quote or cite—that can be legally altered only by consent of the parties to it: the federal government and the peoples of the states in formation and, later, formed. The treaties themselves, in honoring the commitment promised in the ordinance, clearly reflect its philosophy toward the natives. They also reflect its definition of the waters.

The Northwest Ordinance was enacted by the Congress of the Confederation in New York in 1787. Though revolutionary hostilities had ceased with the Treaty of Paris in 1783, government in the newly conceived United States was far from settled. An international border between the United States and what would become Canada was tentatively agreed upon as a line to be drawn through the Great Lakes and their navigable connections to the junction of the forty-fifth parallel and the St. Lawrence River, but the line was not surveyed and published until the Ashburton Treaty was completed in 1828. British and American relations in North America, thus, remained tenuous at best. Pointedly, though both the French and Indian War and the American Revolutionary War were over and decided by international European treaty, the Indians of the Old Northwest were never legally brought to peace by treaty process. Just as they remained belligerents favoring and waiting for the French in the years after the Plains of Abraham (1759) and the first Treaty of Paris (1763), so after the American Revolution they remained belligerents favoring the British. And the British, owing in part to the lack of American enthusiasm (which begins to account for the lack of a financed standing postwar army), stayed on in their military and trading posts in the upper Great Lakes. From these posts, Detroit and Michilimackinac prominent among them, they supplied and incited the Indians—as they did from slightly modified positions through the War of 1812, at the end of which the Treaty of Ghent (1814) finally settled the matter, though even then the Indians were not legally and by treaty brought to peace.

The Indians could not understand the tactical and economic considerations that informed the treaties at Paris and at Ghent, and were not invited to participate in them. It was thus left to the United States, finally formed after the Constitutional Convention in 1789, to bring the Indians of the Old Northwest legally to terms in a separate peace. Through all these years it was the job of the other side, first French, then British, to keep them supplied and at war. It was an expensive process and, especially because the Indians were naturally predisposed against a negotiated peace and settlement, it worked. Winning and losing a battle or a war was, for the tribes, engaging the enemy, killing, dying, and then figuring out who won—simple as that. This is the context in which Gen. Anthony Wayne's Ohio and Indiana campaign, the Treaty of Greenville, Governor Hull's 1807 treaty at Detroit, and the Treaty of Ghent must be understood. It is remarkable that the United States did not consider the Indians at Greenville a defeated nation, for surely they were—and still armed and belligerent, which they showed well enough through the years leading into the War of 1812, continuously armed and incited by the British who continued to seem, thus, not so very friendly either, though they were surely vanquished by treaty. No one was sure if the new government of the United States could make it and almost everyone was willing to wager that it would not. One finds little understanding of this background in the judges' arguments.

Every bit as dangerous is the judicial consideration of the background of the Treaty of Washington (1836). Only Judge Williams in *LeBlanc* (Appendix 2, page 199) so much as pays lip service to the fact that what was to become Michigan was struggling toward statehood in that year, and that it was not a very nice struggle; nor do the judges mention that what was destined to become the northern part of it was completely unwanted territory—anathema to the residents of Michigan and the federal government alike, and useless to the tribes because they had trapped out their means of livelihood on it and so could not even begin to pay their immense debt to the traders at Mackinac. The residents of Michigan did not want it because they saw no short term value to it; the federal government did not want it for the same reason and because it could not easily, therefore, find the dollars with which to pay for the survey of it so that it could be sold to a private buyer who did not yet want it. There was just no perceived value to it, at least in the short run, because it was not desirable for settlement. That would come much later in the century—and it would have to be paid for, organized, and managed in the meantime.

Nor do the judges so much as mention the fact that it was the Indians who petitioned Henry R. Schoolcraft, as their agent, to negotiate the cession of 1836 as their way out of their debts to the traders and into an uncertain future in the context of a little understood American and largely agrarian economy. That is why all parties placed such emphasis on treaty items that had other than cash value. Beyond paying off the traders and procuring some staples, money had little relevance to the Indians of the north; homestead lands, blacksmiths, agricultural education and help, and livestock, on the other hand, were the means to a new kind of subsistence and way of life within a system that would accommodate them if they could learn about it. The old ways were already doomed and all parties seem to have understood that. The problem was to find a way to include the Indians and help them into an economy they could barely comprehend. In considerng the treaty background, especially Judge Fox performs as great a job of slander on Schoolcraft and Secretary Cass, and in the same spirit, as the War Department worked on General Hull after the fall of Detroit in 1812.

The issue in the north in the latter twentieth century remains Indian fishing rights and that issue focuses on the nineteenth-century treaties and the recent judicial interpretations of them. In fact, only two Michigan treaties address the issue of fishing at all. In 1820 Governor Cass negotiated a treaty with the Saulteur Chippewas in which was reaffirmed the multiple purchase of the six-mile strip along the St. Marys River by the United States and in which the United States secured to the Indians an easement to encamp and fish at the rapids. In 1855, in a treaty separate from the other treaties signed at Detroit in that year, George W. Manypenny and Henry C. Gilbert, commissioners, concluded a treaty of agreement with the same Salteur band that goes straight to the same point. "ARTICLE I. The said Chippewa Indians surrender to the United States the right of fishing at the falls of the St. Mary's and of encampment, convenient to the fishing-ground, secured to them by the treaty of June 16, 1820."[4]

In the first instance the federal government granted to the Indians an easement for camping and fishing at the rapids; in the second, they bought back the privilege for just compensation to be determined later by a separate presidential commissioner, the determination to be "final and conclusive, and the amount awarded shall be paid to said Indians, as annuities are paid, and shall be received by them in full satisfaction for the right hereby surrendered: *Provided,* that one-third of said award shall, if the Indians desire it, be paid to such of their half-breed relations as they may indicate" (Article 2). The Sault lock canal had recently been completed and the St. Marys rapids were now open for navigation between Lakes Superior and Huron; Sault Ste. Marie would be developing and the Indian right to camp and fish had to be extinguished as a practical necessity.

These two treaties are particularly interesting, not only because the judges virtually ignore the implications of them, but because they clearly set forth the nineteenth-century understanding of who gave (and retained) what to whom in the earlier treaties. The right to fish was thus firmly attached to the ownership of the adjacent camping and fishing grounds and was granted as an easement by the owners of the land *to* the Indians so that they might continue to sustain themselves in their traditional fashion there as long as might be possible. There is no evidence that Indian fishing at the Sault had a commercial dimension at the time of the 1820 treaty.

In fact, the earliest evidence of commercial fishing, predictably enough, is around Detroit—where there was population (and therefore a market), salt (with which to preserve the fish), coopers, blacksmiths, and therefore barrels (in which to pack them), and a growing fleet of Great Lakes vessels (in which to ship them). Silas Farmer records that in 1818 whitefish, the most desirable species at the Detroit area fisheries, were so plentiful that they were worth only $3.00 per barrel and boatloads were sold for fifty cents per hundred. In 1822, he notes, the Hog Island fishery packed twelve hundred barrels, worth $4.00 to $5.00 per barrel, but in 1823 the catch was not so large and the price was $2.00 to $3.00 per hundred. In the early part of one week in October in 1824 the fishery at Grosse Isle brought in between twenty-five and thirty thousand whitefish in a single day. By 1825 the fish were worth between $6.00 and $7.00 per barrel and thousands of barrels were shipped out to Ohio and New York. In 1827 there were so many fish that fifteen thousand were taken with a single seine in five hauls. The catch in the Detroit River between 1836 and 1840 "averaged about thirty-five hundred barrels per year, worth eight dollars per barrel."[5] As late as 1880 the Detroit River fishery averaged about twelve thousand half-barrels, worth $4.75 each. In 1873 the State Fish Commission was established and operated its first hatchery during its first year in business. The only truly significant population in the state, thus, was well enough served by the Detroit River non-Indian commercial fishery that it not only provided for its own needs but exported packed fish by 1825 and was still doing so late in the century.

There was hardly a need for a developed commercial fishery in the north, certainly not in the early decades of the nineteenth century. There was no significant market, no efficient means of preserving the catch, and only limited means of moving it to other developing markets. There was thus no commercial fishing in the north, at either Mackinac Island or Sault Ste. Marie, until the American Fur Company began to break down and Irish immigrants brought with them both fishing and cooper's skills—and a Great Lakes transportation system brought salt north from Detroit. Although it is true that John Johnston's widow operated a small fishing operation at Sault Ste. Marie in the 1830s, she barely got by with it, together with the manufacture of maple sugar.[6] There was almost surely no significant Indian participation in a northern fishery that can in any way be regarded as commercial, except as employees for the likes of Mrs. Johnston and the American Fur Company under Ramsay Crooks when it entered into the fishing business as the fur trade was faltering. The Indians were traditionally skilled at netting fish; there is no doubt about that. And there is evidence that the Indians shared fish and other game with both the French and the British (as the Europeans shared liquor and other gifts as a condition of the trade). But there is no hard evidence that there was ever an Indian trade in fish with either the whites or one another in which we can realistically define a market—as with the market in furs.

In fact, during the winter of 1778-79, when the British were preparing their new fort on the island of Michilimackinac, Patrick Sinclair detached a sergeant and six privates for fishing and they caught enough to feed all the Michilimackinac Indians and had a thousand-pound surplus to ship to Niagara. The Indians ate fish and corn, while the soldiers ate bread, pork, and peas—which they preferred, to the detriment of any potential northern market in fish. Sinclair judged that three expert Canadian fishermen could produce enough to sustain a limited commercial harvest.[7] Clearly in this year the Indians indulged no commercial dimension to their catch. Instead, the Indians fished seasonally for subsistence and shared their bounty when successful while the soldiers of the garrison fished, probably through the ice, to sustain the Indians. Commerce was wholly in furs, though Schoolcraft enthusiastically projected a productive commercial fishery at the Sault as a possible means to Indian livelihood at the time when he was negotiating the 1836 treaty (in *People v. LeBlanc,* Appendix 2, page 199).

And that is the reason for the inclusion of the fish barrels and the barrels of salt in the fourth article of the Treaty of 1836. Though the Indians were skilled fishers, especially with their traditional gill nets, they had no commerce in fish—no means of packing, preserving, or transporting the product they could well harvest. They just did not have, and never did, coopers or barrels or salt or an efficient means of transport. They did have skill in fishing, at a modest subsistence level, and places in which to fish. It was reasonable for the federal government to expect that, given the missing elements to this potential commerce, the Indians might develop the harvest of that resource, seemingly endless, into a modest livelihood within the new American economy—just as they might be expected to use land by the parcel as a means to a living. It can only be fair to conclude that the provision for barrels and salt was intended to set the Indians up in business in competition with the American Fur Company and Mrs. Johnston at the Sault—who received no such subsidies.

APPENDIX I

THE TEXT OF THE NORTHWEST ORDINANCE AND THE TEXTS OF THE MICHIGAN INDIAN TREATIES

Notes on the Texts

The ordinances appear in the *Journals of the Continental Congress , 1774-1789*, ed. John C. Fitzpatrick (Washington, D. C.: United States Government Printing Office, 1933). I have adopted an edited version of the text of the Northwest Ordinance that appears as an appendix in *The Northwest Ordinance: Essays on Its Formulation, Provisions, and Legacy,* ed. Frederick D. Williams (Lansing: Michigan State University Press, 1989). The text varies only in format and minor editorial decisions from that in the *Journals.*

The texts of the earlier treaties are taken from *The Public Statutes at Large of the United States of America,* Vol. 7, ed. Richard Peters, and published by the authority of Congress (Boston: Charles C. Little and James Brown, 1848). Texts of all and later treaties may be found in Charles J. Kappler's *Indian Affairs: Laws and Treaties, 1778-1883,* Vol. 2, *Treaties* (New York: Interland Publishing Company, 1972 [U.S. Government Printing Office, 1904]). For all the older texts that make up the appendix I am deeply indebted to my colleague George M. Covington, and his colleagues in the law firm Gardner, Carton & Douglas, Chicago. In each case I have followed the best treaty text available in every detail possible, omitting only editorial marginalia, schedules of payment, and the often long lists of signers. There are no significant variations among the texts other than details of typography and format.

It is my hope that bringing these important texts out from the stacks of legal and academic libraries will help demystify them and guide the ordinary student and reader toward an understanding of them as the historical documents that precede the applied law and so inform important contemporary judicial and political opinions and decisions.

The Northwest Ordinance: An Ordinance for the Government of the Territory of the United States North West of the River Ohio

Be it Ordained by the United States in Congress Assembled that the said territory for the purposes of temporary government be one district, subject however to be divided into two districts as future circumstances may in the Opinion of Congress make it expedient.

Be it ordained by the authority aforesaid, that the estates both of resident and non resident proprietors in the said territory dying intestate shall descend to and be distributed among their children and the descendants of a deceased child in equal parts; the descendants of a deceased child or grandchild to take the share of their deceased parent in equal parts among them; and where there shall be no children or decendants then in equal parts to the next of kin in equal degree and among collaterals the children of a deceased brother or sister of the intestate shall have in equal parts among them their deceased parent's share and there shall in no case be a distinction between kindred of the whole and half blood; saving in all cases to the widow of the intestate her third part of the real estate for life, and one third part of the personal estate; and this law relative to descents and dower shall remain in full force until altered by the legislature of the district. And until the governor and judges shall adopt laws as hereinafter mentioned estates in the said territory may be devised or bequeathed by wills in writing signed and sealed by him or her in whom the estate may be, being of full age, and attested by three witnesses, and real estates may be conveyed by lease and release or bargain and sale signed, sealed and delivered by the person being of full age in whom the estate may be and attested by two witnesses provided such wills be duly proved and such conveyances be acknowledged or the execution thereof duly proved and be recorded within one year after proper magistrates, courts and registers shall be appointed for that purpose and personal property may be transferred by delivery saving however to the french and canadian inhabitants and other settlers of the Kaskaskies, Saint Vincents and the neighboring villages who have heretofore professed themselves citizens of Virginia, their laws and customs now in force among them relative to the descent and conveyance of property.

Be it ordained by the authority aforesaid that there shall be appointed from time to time by Congress a governor, whose commission shall continue in force for the term of three years, unless sooner revoked by Congress; he shall reside in the district and have a freehold estate therein, in one thousand acres of land while in the exercise of his office. There shall be appointed from time to time by Congress a secretary, whose commission shall continue in force for four years, unless sooner revoked; he shall reside in the district and have a freehold estate therein in five hundred acres of land while in the exercise of his office; It shall be his duty to keep and preserve the acts and laws passed by the legislature and the public records of the district and the proceedings of the governor in his executive department and transmit authentic copies of such acts and proceedings every six months to the Secretary of Congress. There shall also be appointed a court to consist of three judges any two of whom to form a court, who shall have a common law jurisdiction and reside in the district and have each therein a freehold estate in five hundred acres of land while in the exercise of their offices, and their commissions shall continue in force during good behavior.

The governor, and judges or a majority of them shall adopt and publish in the district such laws of the original states criminal and civil as may be necessary and best suited to the circumstances of the district and report them to Congress from time to time, which laws shall be in force in the district until the organization of the general assembly therein, unless disapproved of by Congress; but afterwards the legislature shall have authority to alter them as they shall think fit.

The governor for the time being shall be Commander in chief of the militia, appoint and commission all officers in the same below the rank of general Officers; All general Officers shall be appointed and commissioned by Congress.

Previous to the Organization of the general Assembly the governor shall appoint such magistrates and other civil officers in each county or township, as he shall find necessary for the preservation of the peace and good order in the same. After the general Assembly shall be organized, the powers and duties of magistrates and other civil officers shall be regulated and defined by the said Assembly; but all magistrates and other civil officers, not herein otherwise directed shall during the continuance of this temporary government be appointed by the governor.

For the prevention of crimes and injuries the laws to be adopted or made shall have force in all parts of the district and for the execution of process criminal and civil, the governor shall make proper divisions thereof, and he shall proceed from time to time as circumstances may require to lay out the parts of the district in which the indian titles shall have been extinguished into counties and townships subject however to such alterations as may thereafter be made by the legislature.

So soon as there shall be five thousand free male inhabitants of full age in the district upon giving proof thereof to the governor, they shall receive authority with time and place to elect representatives from their counties or townships to represent them in the general assembly, provided that for every five hundred free male inhabitants there shall be one representative and so on progressively with the number of free male inhabitants shall the right of representation encrease until the number of representatives shall amount to twenty five after which the number and proportion of representatives shall be regulated by the legislature; provided that no person be eligible or qualified to act as a representative unless he shall have been a citizen of one of the United States three years and be a resident in the district or unless he shall have resided in the district three years and in either case shall likewise hold in his own right in fee simple two hundred acres of land within the same; provided also that a freehold in fifty acres of land in the district having been a citizen of one of the states and being resident in the district; or the like freehold and two years residence in the district shall be necessary to qualify a man as an elector of a representative.

The representatives thus elected shall serve for the term of two years and in case of the death of a representative or removal from office, the governor shall issue a writ to the county or township for which he was a member, to elect another in his stead to serve for the residue of the term.

The general assembly or legislature shall consist of the governor, legislative council and a house of representatives. The legislative council shall consist of five members to continue in Office five years unless sooner removed by Congress any three of whom to be a quorum and the members of the council shall be nominated and appointed in the following manner, to wit; As soon as representatives shall be elected, the governor shall appoint a time and place for them to meet together, and when met they shall nominate ten persons residents in the district and each possessed of a freehold in five hundred acres of Land and return their names to Congress; five of whom Congress shall appoint and commission to serve as aforesaid; and whenever a vacancy shall happen in the council by death or removal from office, the house of representatives shall nominate two persons qualified as aforesaid, for each vacancy, and return their names to Congress, one of whom Congress shall appoint and commission for the residue of the term, and every five years, four months at least before the expiration of the term of service of the Members of Council, the said house shall nominate ten persons qualified as aforesaid, and return their names to Congress, five of whom Congress shall appoint and commission to serve as Members of the council five years, unless sooner removed. And the Governor, legislative council, and house of representatives, shall have authority to make laws in all cases for the good government of the district, not repugnant to the principles and Articles in this Ordinance established and declared. And all bills having passed by a majority in the house, and by a majority in the council, shall be referred to the Governor for his assent; but no bill or legislative Act whatever, shall be of any force without his assent. The Governor shall have power to convene, prorogue and dissolve the General Assembly, when in his opinion it shall be expedient.

The Governor, Judges, legislative Council, Secretary, and such other Officers as Congress shall appoint in the district shall take an Oath or Affirmation of fidelity, and of Office, the Governor before the president of Congress, and all other Officers before the Governor. As soon as a legislature shall be formed in the district, the Council and house assembled in one room, shall have authority by joint ballot to elect a Delegate to Congress, who shall have a seat in Congress, with a right of debating, but not of voting, during this temporary Government.

And for extending the fundamental principles of civil and religious liberty, which form the basis whereon these republics, their laws and constitutions are erected; to fix and establish those principles as the basis of all laws, constitutions and governments, which forever hereafter shall be formed in the said territory; to provide also for the establishment of States and permanent government therein, and for their admission to a share in the federal Councils on an equal footing with the original States, at as early periods as may be consistent with the general interest, It is hereby Ordained and declared by the authority aforesaid, That the following Articles shall be considered as Articles of compact between the Original States and the people and States in the said territory, and forever remain unalterable, unless by common consent, *to wit,*

ARTICLE THE FIRST. No person demeaning himself in a peaceable and orderly manner shall ever be molested on account of his mode of worship or religious sentiments in the said territory.

ARTICLE THE SECOND. The Inhabitants of the said territory shall always be entitled to the benefits of the writ of habeas corpus, and of the trial by Jury; of a proportionate representation of the people in the legislature, and of judicial proceedings according to the course of the common law; all persons shall be bailable unless for capital offences, where the proof shall be evident, or the presumption great; all fines shall be moderate, and no cruel or unusual punishments shall be inflicted; no man shall be deprived of his liberty or property but by the judgment of his peers, or the law of the land; and should the public exigencies make it necessary for the common preservation to take any persons property, or to demand his particular services, full compensation shall be made for the same; and in the just preservation of rights and property it is understood and declared; that no law ought ever to be made, or have any force in the said territory, that shall in any manner whatever interfere with, or affect private contracts or engagements, bona fide and without fraud previously formed.

ARTICLE THE THIRD. Religion, Morality and knowledge being necessary to good government and the happiness of mankind, Schools and the means of education shall forever be encouraged. The utmost good faith shall always be observed toward the Indians, their lands and property shall never be taken from them without their consent; and in their property, rights and liberty, they never shall be invaded or disturbed, unless in just and lawful wars authorised by Congress; but laws founded in justice and humanity shall from time to time be made, for preventing wrongs being done to them, and for preserving peace and friendship with them.

ARTICLE THE FOURTH. The said territory, and the States which may be formed therein shall forever remain a part of this Confederacy of the United States of America, subject to the Articles of Confederation, and to such alterations therein as shall be constitutionally made; and to all the Acts and Ordinances of the United States in Congress Assembled, conformable thereto. The Inhabitants and Settlers in the said territory, shall be subject to pay a part of the federal debts contracted or to be contracted, and a proportional part of the expences of Government, to be apportioned on them by Congress, according to the same common rule and measure by which apportionments thereof shall be made on the other States; and the taxes for paying their proportion, shall be laid and levied by the authority and direction of the legislatures of the district or districts or new States, as in the original States, within the time agreed upon by the United States in Congress Assembled. The Legislatures of those districts, or new States, shall never interfere with the primary disposal of the Soil by the United States in Congress Assembled, nor with any regulations Congress may find necessary for securing the title in such soil to the bona fide purchasers. No tax shall be imposed on lands the property of the United States; and in no case shall non resident proprietors be taxed higher than residents. The navigable Waters leading into the Mississippi and St. Lawrence, and the carrying places between the same shall be common highways, and forever free, as well to the Inhabitants of the said territory, as to the Citizens of the United States, and those of any other States that may be admitted into the Confederacy, without any tax, impost or duty therefor.

ARTICLE THE FIFTH. There shall be formed in the said territory, not less than three nor more than five States, and the boundaries of the States, as soon as Virginia shall alter her act of cession and consent to the same, shall become fixed and established as follows, to wit: The Western State in the said territory, shall be bounded by the Mississippi, the Ohio and Wabash rivers; a direct line drawn from the Wabash and post Vincents due North to the territorial line between the United States and Canada, and by the said territorial line to the Lake of the Woods and Mississippi. The middle State shall be bounded by the said direct line, the Wabash from post Vincents to the Ohio; by the Ohio, by direct line drawn due North from the mouth of the great Miami to the said territorial line, and by the said territorial line. The eastern State shall be bounded by the last mentioned direct line, the Ohio, Pennsylvania, and the said territorial line; provided however, and it is further understood and declared, that the boundaries of these three States, shall be subject so far to be altered, that if Congress shall hereafter find it expedient, they shall have authority to form one or two States in that part of the said territory which lies north of an east and west line drawn through the southerly bend or extreme of lake Michigan; and whenever any of the said States shall have sixty thousand free Inhabitants therein, such State shall be admitted by its Delegates into the Congress of the United States, on an equal footing with the original States, in all respects whatever; and shall be at liberty to form a permanent constitution and State government, provided the constitution and government so to be formed, shall be republican, and in conformity to the principles contained in these Articles; and so far as it can be consistent with the general interest of the Confederacy, such admission shall be allowed at an earlier period, and when there may be a less number of free Inhabitants in the State than sixty thousand.

ARTICLE THE SIXTH. There shall be niether Slavery nor involuntary Servitude in the said territory otherwise than in the punishment of crimes, whereof the party shall have been duly convicted; provided always that any person escaping into the same, from whom labor or service is lawfully claimed in any one of the original States, such fugitive may be lawfully reclaimed and conveyed to the person claiming his or her labor or service as aforesaid.

Be it Ordained by the Authority aforesaid, that the Resolutions of the 23d of April 1784 relative to the subject of this ordinance be, and the same are hereby repealed and declared null and void.

Fort Greenville, in the Ohio Country
A Treaty of Peace

Between the United States of America and the Tribes of Indians, called the Wyandots, Delawares, Shawanoes, Ottawas, Chipewas, Putawatimes, Miamis, Eel-river, Weeas, Kickapoos, Piankashaws, and Kaskaskias.

To put an end to a destructive war, to settle all controversies, and to restore harmony and a friendly intercourse between the said United States, and Indian tribes; Anthony Wayne, major-general, commanding the army of the United States, and sole commissioner for the good purposes above mentioned, and the said tribes of Indians, by their Sachems, chiefs, and warriors, met together at Greenville, the head quarters of the said army, have agreed on the following articles, which, when ratified by the President, with the advice and consent of the Senate of the United States, shall be binding on them and the said Indian tribes.

ARTICLE I. Henceforth all hostilities shall cease; peace is hereby established, and shall be perpetual; and a friendly intercourse shall take place, between the said United States and Indian tribes.

ARTICLE II. All prisoners shall on both sides be restored. The Indians, prisoners to the United States, shall be immediately set at liberty. The people of the United States, still remaining among the Indians, shall be delivered up in ninety days from the date hereof, to the general or commanding officer at Greeneville, Fort Wayne or Fort Defiance; and ten chiefs of the said tribes shall remain at Greeneville as hostages, until the delivery of the prisoners shall be effected.

ARTICLE III. The general boundary line between the lands of the United States, and the lands of the said Indian tribes, shall begin at the mouth of the Cayahoga river, and run thence up the same to the portage between that and the Tuscarawas branch of the Muskingum; thence down that branch to the crossing place above Fort Lawrence; thence westerly to a fork of that branch of the great Miami river running into the Ohio, at or near which fork stood Loromie's store, and where commences the portage between the Miami of the Ohio, and the St. Mary's River, which is a branch of the Miami, which runs into Lake Erie; thence a westerly course to Fort Recovery, which stands on a branch of the Wabash; then south-westerly in a direct line to the Ohio, so as to intersect that river opposite the mouth of the Kentucke or Cuttawa river. And in consideration of the peace now established; of the goods formerly received from the United States; of those now to be delivered, and of the yearly delivery of goods now stipulated to be made hereafter, and to indemnify the United States for the injuries and expenses they have sustained during the war; the said Indian tribes do hereby cede and relinquish forever, all their claims to the lands lying eastwardly and southwardly of the general boundary line now described; and these lands, or any part of them, shall never hereafter be made a cause or pretence, on the part of the said tribes or any of them, of war or injury to the United States, or any of the people thereof.

And for the same considerations, and as an evidence of the returning friendship of the said Indian tribes, of their confidence in the United States, and desire to provide for their accommodation, and for that convenient intercourse which will be beneficial to both parties, the said Indian tribes do also cede to the United States the following pieces of land; to wit. (1.) One piece of land six miles square at or near Loromie's store before mentioned. (2.) One piece two miles square at the head of the navigable water or landing on the St. Mary's river, near Girty's town. (3.) One piece six miles square at the head of the navigable water of the Au-Glaize river. (4.) One piece six miles square at the confluence of the Au-Glaize and Miami rivers, where Fort Defiance now stands. (5.) One piece six miles square at or near the confluence of the rivers St. Mary's and St. Joseph's, where Fort Wayne now stands, or near it. (6.) One piece two miles square on the Wabash river at the end of the portage from the Miami of the lake, and about eight miles westward from Fort Wayne. (7.) One piece six miles square at the Ouatanon or old Weea towns on the Wabash river. (8.) One piece twelve miles square at the British fort on the Miami of the lake at the foot of the rapids. (9.) One piece six miles square at the mouth of the said river where it empties into the Lake. (10.) Oned piece six miles square upon Sandusky lake, where a fort formerly stood. (11.) One piece two miles square at the lower rapids of Sandusky river. (12.) The post of Detroit and all the land to the north, the west and the south of it, of which the Indian title has been extinguished by gifts or grants to the French or English governments; and so much more land to be annexed to the district of Detroit as shall be comprehended between the river Rosine on the south, lake St. Clair on the north, and a line, the general course whereof shall be six miles distant from the west end of lake Erie, and Detroit river. (13.) The post of Michillimackinac, and all the land on the island, on which that post stands, and the main land adjacent, of which the Indian title has been extinguished by gifts or grants to the French or English governments; and a piece of land on the main to the north of the island, to measure six miles on lake Huron, or the streight between lakes Huron and Michigan, and to extend three miles back from the water of the lake or streight, and also the island of De Bois Blanc, being an extra and voluntary gift of the Chipewa nation. (14.) One piece of land six miles square at the mouth of the Chikago river emptying into the south-west end of Lake Michigan, where a fort formerly stood. (15.) One piece twelve miles square at or near the mouth of the Illinois river, emptying into the

Mississippi. (16) One piece six miles square at the old Piorias fort and village, near the south end of the Illinois lake on said Illinois river: And whenever the United States shall think proper to survey and mark the boundaries of the lands hereby ceded to them, they shall give timely notice thereof to the said tribes of Indians, that they may appoint some of their wise chiefs to attend and see that the lines are run according to the terms of this treaty.

And the said Indian tribes will allow the people of the United States a free passage by land and by water, as one and the other shall be found convenient, through their country, along the chain of posts herein before mentioned; that is to say, from the commencement of the portage aforesaid at or near Loromie's store, thence along said portage to the St. Mary's, and down the same to Fort Wayne, and then down the Miami to lake Erie: again from the commencement of the portage at or near Loromie's store along the portage from thence to the river Au-Glaize, and down the same to its junction with the Miami at Fort Defiance: again from the commencement of the portage aforesaid, to Sandusky river, and down the same to Sandusky bay and Lake Erie, and from Sandusky to the post which shall be taken at or near the foot of the rapids of the Miami of the lake: and from thence to Detroit. Again from the mouth of Chikago to the commencement of the portage, between that river and the Illinois, and down the Illinois river to the Mississippi, also from Fort Wayne along the portage aforesaid which leads to the Wabash, and then down the Wabash to the Ohio. And the said Indian tribes will also allow to the people of the United States the free use of the harbours and mouths of rivers along the lakes adjoining the Indian lands, for sheltering vessells and boats, and liberty to land their cargoes where necessary for their safety.

ARTICLE IV. In consideration of the peace now established and of the cessions and relinquishments of lands made in the preceding article by the said tribes of Indians, and to manifest the liberality of the United States, as the great means of rendering this peace strong and perpetual; the United States relinquish their claims to all other Indian lands northward of the river Ohio, eastward of the Mississippi, and westward and southward of the Great Lakes and the waters uniting them, according to the boundary line agreed on by the United States and the king of Great-Britain, in the treaty of peace made between them in the year 1783. But from this relinquishment by the United States, the following tracts of land, are explicitly excepted. 1st. The tract of one hundred and fifty thousand acres near the rapids of the river Ohio, which has been assigned to General Clark, for the use of himself and his warriors. 2d. The post of St. Vincennes on the river Wabash, and the lands adjacent, of which the Indian title has been extinguished. 3d. The lands at all other places in possession of the French people and other white settlers among them, of which the Indian title has been extinguished as mentioned in the 3d article; and 4th. The post of fort Massac toward the mouth of the Ohio. To which several parcels of land so excepted, the said tribes relinquish all the title and claim which they or any of them may have.

And for the same considerations and with the same views as above mentioned, the United States now deliver to the said Indian tribes a quantity of goods to the value of twenty thousand dollars, the receipt whereof they do hereby acknowledge; and henceforward every year forever the United States will deliver at some convenient place northward of the river Ohio, like useful goods, suited to the circumstances of the Indians, of the value of nine thousand five hundred dollars; reckoning that value at the first cost of the goods in the city or place in the United States, where they shall be procured. The tribes to which those goods are to be annually delivered, and the proportions in which they are to be delivered, are the following.

1st. To the Wyandots, the amount of one thousand dollars. 2d. To the Delawares, the amount of one thousand dollars. 3d. To the Shawanese, the amount of one thousand dollars. 4th. To the Miamis, the amount of one thousand dollars. 5th. To the Ottawas, the amount of one thousand dollars. 6th. To the Chippewas, the amount of one thousand dollars. 7th. To the Putawatimes, the amount of one thousand dollars. 8th. And to the Kickapoo, Weea, Eel-river, Piankashaw and Kaskaskias tribes, the amount of five hundred dollars each.

Provided, That if either of the said tribes shall hereafter at an annual delivery of their share of the goods aforesaid, desire that a part of their annuity should be furnished in domestic animals, implements of husbandry, and other utensils convenient for them, and in compensation to usefull artificers who may reside with or near them, and be employed for their benefit, the same shall at the subsequent annual deliveries be furnished accordingly.

ARTICLE V. To prevent any misunderstanding about the Indian lands relinquished by the United States in the fourth article, it is now explicitly declared, that the meaning of that relinquishment is this: The Indian tribes who have a right to those lands, are quietly to enjoy them, hunting, planting, and dwelling thereon so long as they please, without any molestation from the United States; but when those tribes, or any of them, shall be disposed to sell their lands, or any part of them, they are to be sold only to the United States; and untill such sale, the United States will protect all the said Indian tribes in the quiet enjoyment of their lands against all citizens of the United States, and against all other white persons who intrude upon the same. And the said Indian tribes again acknowledge themselves to be under the protection of the said United States and no other power whatever.

ARTICLE VI. If any citizen of the United States, or any other white person or persons, shall presume to settle upon the lands now relinquished by the United States, such citizen or other person shall be out of the protection of the United States; and the Indian tribe, on whose land the settlement shall be made, may drive off the settler, or punish him in such manner as they shall think fit; and because such settlements made without the consent of the United States, will be injurious to them as well as to the Indians, the United States shall be at liberty to break them up, and remove and punish the settlers as they shall think proper, and so effect that protection of the Indian lands herein before stipulated.

ARTICLE VII. The said tribes of Indians, parties to this treaty, shall be at liberty to hunt within the territory and lands which they have now ceded to the United States, without hindrance or molestation, so long as they demean themselves peaceably, and offer no injury to the people of the United States.

ARTICLE VIII. Trade shall be opened with the said Indian tribes; and they do hereby respectively engage to afford protection to such persons, with their property, as shall be duly licensed to reside among them for the purpose of trade, and to their agents and servents; but no person shall be permitted to reside at any of their towns or hunting camps as a trader, who is not furnished with a license for that purpose, under the hand and seal of the superintendant of the department north-west of the Ohio, or such other person as the President of the United States shall authorise to grant such licenses; to the end, that the said Indians may not be imposed on in their trade. And if any licensed trader shall abuse his privilege by unfair dealing, upon complaint and proof thereof, his license shall be taken from him, and he shall be further punished according to the laws of the United States. And if any person shall intrude himself as a trader, without such license, the said Indians shall take and bring him before the superintendant or his deputy, to be dealt with according to law. And to prevent impositions by forged licenses, the said Indians shall at least once a year give information to the super-intendant or his deputies, of the names of the traders residing among them.

ARTICLE IX. Lest the firm peace and friendship now established should be interrupted by the misconduct of individuals, the United States, and the said Indian tribes agree, that for injuries done by individuals on either side, no private revenge or retaliation shall take place; but instead thereof, complaint shall be made by the party injured, to the other: By the said Indian tribes, or any of them, to the President of the United States, or the superintendant by him appointed; and by the superintendant or other person appointed by the President, to the principal chiefs of the said Indian tribes, or of the tribe to which the offender belongs; and such prudent measures shall then be pursued as shall be necessary to preserve the said peace and friendship unbroken, until the Legislature (or Great Council) of the United States, shall make other equitable provision in the case, to the satisfaction of both parties. Should any Indian tribes meditate a war against the United States or either of them, and the same shall come to the knowledge of the before-mentioned tribes, or either of them, they do hereby engage to give immediate notice thereof to the general or officer commanding the troops of the United States, at the nearest post. And should any tribe, with hostile intentions against the United States, or either of them, attempt to pass through their country, they will endeav-or to prevent the same, and in like manner give information of such attempt, to the general or officer commanding, as soon as possible, that all causes of mistrust and suspicion may be avoided between them and the United States. In like manner the United States shall give notice to the said Indian tribes of any harm that may be meditated against them, or either of them, that shall come to their knowledge; and do all in their power to hinder and prevent the same, that the friendship between them may be uninterrupted.

ARTICLE X. All other treaties heretofore made between the United States and the said Indian tribes, or any of them, since the treaty of 1783, between the United States and Great Britain, that come within the purview of this treaty, shall henceforth cease and become void.

In testimony whereof, the said Anthony Wayne, and the Sachems and War Chiefs of the before-mentioned Nations and Tribes of Indians, have hereunto set their Hands, and affixed their seals. Done at Greenville, in the Territory of the United States, north-west of the river Ohio, on the third day of August, one thousand seven hundred and ninety-five.

Detroit, in the Territory of Michigan
Articles of a Treaty

Made at Detroit, this seventeenth day of November, in the year of our Lord, one thousand eight hundred and seven, by William Hull, governor of the territory of Michigan, and superintendant of Indian affairs, and sole commissioner of the United States, to conclude and sign a treaty or treaties, with the several nations of Indians, north west of the river Ohio, on the one part, and the sachems, chiefs, and warriors of the Ottoway, Chippeway, Wyandotte, and Pottawatamie nations of Indians, on the other part. To conform and perpetuate the friendship, which happily subsists between the United States and the nations aforesaid, to manifest the sincerity of that friendship, and to settle arrangements mutually beneficial to the parties; after a full explanation and perfect understanding, the following articles are agreed to, which, when ratified by the President, by and with the advice and consent of the Senate of the United States, shall be binding on them, and the respective nations of Indians.

ARTICLE I. The sachems, chiefs, and warriors of the nations aforesaid, in consideration of money and goods, to be paid to the said nations, by the government of the United States as hereafter stipulated; do hereby agree to cede and forever quit claim, and do in behalf of their nations hereby cede, relinquish, and forever quit claim, unto the United States, all right, title, and interest, which the said nations now have, or claim, or ever had, or claimed, in, or unto, the lands comprehended within the following described lines and boundaries: Beginning at the mouth of the Miami river of the lakes, and running thence up the middle thereof, to the mouth of the great Au Glaize river, thence running due north, until it intersects a parallel of latitude, to be drawn from the outlet of lake Huron, which forms the river Sinclair; thence running north east the course, that may be found, will lead in a direct line, to White Rock, in lake Huron, thence due east, until it intersects the boundary line between the United States and Upper Canada, in said lake, thence southwardly, following the said boundary line, down said lake, through river Sinclair, lake St. Clair, and the river Detroit, into lake Erie, to a point due east of the aforesaid Miami river, thence west to the place of beginning.

ART. II. It is hereby stipulated and agreed on the part of the United States, as a consideration for the lands, ceded by the nations aforesaid, in the preceding article, that there shall be paid to the said nations, at Detroit, ten thousand dollars, in money, goods, implements of husbandry, or domestic animals (at the option of the said nations, seasonably signified, through the superinendant of Indian affairs, residing with the said nations, to the department of war), as soon as practicable, after the ratification of the treaty, by the President, with the advice and consent of the Senate of the United States; of this sum, three thousand three hundred and thirty three dollars thirty three cents and four mills, shall be paid to the Ottaway nation, three thousand three hundred and thirty three dollars thirty three cents and four mills, to the Chippeway nation, one thousand six hundred sixty six dollars sixty six cents and six mills, to the Wyandotte nation, one thousand six hundred sixty six dollars sixty six cents and six mills, to the Pottawatamie nation, and likewise an annuity forever, of two thousand four hundred dollars, to be paid at Detroit, in manner as aforesaid: the first payment to be made on the first day of September next, and to be paid to the different nations, in the following proportions: Eight hundred dollars to the Ottaways, eight hundred dollars to the Chippeways, four hundred dollars to the Wyandottes, and four hundred dollars to such of the Pottawatamies, as now reside on the river Huron of lake Erie, the river Raisin, and in the vicinity of the said rivers.

ART. III. It is further stipulated and agreed, if at any time hereafter, the said nations should be of the opinion, that it would be more for their interest, that the annuity aforesaid should be paid by instalments, the United States will agree to a reasonable commutation for the annuity, and pay it accordingly.

ART. IV. The United States, to manifest their liberality, and disposition to encourage the said Indians, in agriculture, further stipulate, to furnish the said Indians with two *blacksmiths* one to reside with the Chippeways, at Saguina, and the other to reside with the Ottaways, at the Miami, during the term of ten years; said blacksmiths are to do such work for the said nations as shall be most useful to them.

ART. V. It is further agreed and stipulated, that the said Indian nations shall enjoy the privilege of hunting and fishing on the lands ceded as aforesaid, as long as they remain the property of the United States.

ART. VI. It is distinctly to be understood, for the accommodation of the said Indians, that the following tracts of land within the cession aforesaid, shall be, and hereby are reserved to the said Indian nations, one tract of land six miles square, on the Miami of lake Erie, above *Roche de Boeuf,* to include the village, where *Tondaganie,* (or the Dog) now lives. Also, three miles square on the said river, (above the twelve miles square ceded to the United States by the treaty of Greenville) including what is called *Presque Isle* also four miles square on the Miami bay, including the villages where *Meshkemau* and Wau-gau now live; also, three miles square on the river *Raisin,* at a place called *Macon,* and where the river *Macon* falls into the river *Raizin* which place is about fourteen miles from the mouth of said river *Raizin;* also, two sections of one mile square each, on the river *Rouge,* at *Seginsiwin's* village; also two sections of one mile square each, at *Tonquish's* village, near the river *Rouge;* also three miles square on lake St. Clair, above the river Huron, to include *Machonce's* village; also, six sections, each section containing one mile square, within the cession aforesaid, in such situations as the said Indians shall elect, subject, however, to the approbation of the President of the United States, as to the places of location. It is further understood and agreed, that whenever the reservations cannot conveniently be laid out in squares, they shall be laid out in *paralelograms* or other figures, as found most practicable and convenient, so as to contain the area specified in miles, and in all cases they are to be located in such manner, and in such situations, as not to interfere with any improvements of the French or other white people, or any former cessions.

ART. VII. The said nations of Indians acknowledge themselves to be under the protection of the United States, and no other power, and will prove by their conduct that they are worthy of so great a blessing.

IN TESTIMONY WHEREOF, the said William Hull, and the sachems, and war chiefs representing the said nations, have hereunto set their hands and seals.

Done at Detroit, in the territory of Michigan, the day and year first above written.

At Ghent, Belgium, Treaty of Peace and Amity
Between His Britannic Majesty and the United States of America

His Britannic Majesty and the United States of America, desirous of terminating the war which has unhappily subsisted between the two countries, and of restoring, upon the principles of perfect reciprocity, peace, friendship, and good understanding between them, have, for that purpose, appointed their respective plenipotentiaries, that is to say: His Britannic Majesty, on his part, has appointed the right honorable James Lord Gambier, late admiral of the white, now admiral of the red squadron of His Majesty's fleet, Henry Goulburn Esquire, a member of the imperial Parliament, and under Secretary of State, and William Adams, Esquire, Doctor of Civil Laws:—And the President of the United States, by and with the advice and consent of the Senate thereof, has appointed John Quincy Adams, James A. Bayard, Henry Clay, Jonathan Russell and Albert Gallatin, citizens of the United States, who, after a reciprocal communication of their respective full powers, have agreed upon the following articles:

ARTICLE THE FIRST. There shall be a firm and universal peace between His Britannic Majesty and the United States, and between their respective countries, territories, cities, towns, and people, of every degree, without exception of places or persons. All hostilities, both by sea and land, shall cease as soon as this treaty shall have been ratified by both parties, as hereinafter mentioned. All territory, places, and possessions whatsoever, taken by either party from the other, during the war, or which may be taken after the signing of this treaty, excepting only the islands hereinafter mentioned, shall be restored without delay, and without causing any destruction, or carrying away any of the artillery or other public property originally captured in the said forts or places, and which shall remain therein upon the exchange of the ratifications of this treaty, or any slaves or other private property. And all archives, records, deeds, and papers, either of a public nature, or belonging to private persons, which, in the course of the war, may have fallen into the hands of the officers of either party, shall be, as far as may be practicable, forthwith restored and delivered to the proper authorities and persons to whom they respectively belong. Such of the islands in the Bay of Passamaquoddy as are claimed by both parties, shall remain in the possession of the party in whose occupation they may be at the time of the exchange of the ratifications of this treaty, until the decision respecting the title to the said islands shall have been made in conformity with the fourth article of this treaty. No disposition made by this treaty, as to such possession of the islands and territories claimed by both parties, shall, in any manner whatever, be construed to affect the right of either.

ARTICLE THE SECOND. Immediately after the ratifications of this treaty by both parties, as hereinafter mentioned, orders shall be sent to the armies, squadrons, officers, subjects and citizens, of the two powers, to cease from all hostilities. And to prevent all causes of complaint which might arise on account of the prizes which may be taken at sea after the said ratifications of this treaty, it is reciprocally agreed, that all vessels and effects which may be taken after the space of twelve days from the said ratifications, upon all parts of the coast of

North America, from the latitude of twenty-three degrees north, to the latitude of fifty degrees north, and as far eastward in the Atlantic ocean, as the thirty-sixth degree of west longitude from the meridian of Greenwich, shall be restored on each side: That the time shall be thirty days in all other parts of the Atlantic ocean, north of the equinoctial line or equator, and the same time for the British and Irish channels, for the Gulf of Mexico and all parts of the West Indies: Forty days for the North seas, for the Baltic, and for all parts of the Mediterranean: Sixty days for the Atlantic ocean south of the equator, as far as the latitude of the Cape of Good Hope: Ninety days for every other part of the world south of the equator: And one hundred and twenty days for all other parts of the world, without exception.

ARTICLE THE THIRD. All prisoners of war taken on either side, as well by land as by sea, shall be restored as soon as practicable after the ratifications of this treaty, as hereinafter mentioned, on their paying the debts which they may have contracted during their captivity. The two contracting parties respectively engage to discharge, in specie, the advances which may have been made by the other for the sustenance and maintenance of such prisoners.

ARTICLE THE FOURTH. Whereas it was stipulated by the second article in the treaty of peace, of one thousand seven hundred and eighty-three, between His Britannic Majesty and the United States of America, that the boundary of the United States should comprehend all islands within twenty leagues of any part of the shores of the United States, and lying between lines to be drawn due east from the points where the aforesaid boundaries, between Nova Scotia, on the one part, and East Florida on the other, shall respectively touch the bay of Fundy, and the Atlantic ocean, excepting such islands as now are, or heretofore have been, within the limits of Nova Scotia; and whereas the several islands in the Bay of Passamaquoddy, which is part of the Bay of Fundy, and the island of Grand Menan in the said Bay of Fundy, are claimed by the United States as being comprehended within the aforesaid boundaries, which said islands are claimed as belonging to his Britannic Majesty, as having been at the time of, and previous to, the aforesaid treaty of one thousand seven hundred and eighty-three, within the limits of the province of Nova Scotia: In order, therefore, finally to decide upon these claims, it is agreed that they shall be referred to two commissioners to be appointed in the following manner, viz: one commissioner shall be appointed by his Britannic Majesty, and one by the president of the United States, by and with the advice and consent of the Senate thereof, and the said two commissioners so appointed shall be sworn impartially to examine and decide upon the said claims according to such evidence as shall be laid before them on the part of his Britannic Majesty and of the United States respectively. The said commissioners shall meet at St. Andrews, in the province of New Brunswick, and shall have power to adjourn to such other place or places as they shall think fit. The said commissioners shall, by a declaration or report under their hands and seals, decide to which of the two contracting parties the several islands aforesaid do respectively belong, in conformity with the true intent of the said treaty of peace of on thousand seven hundred and eighty-three. And if the said commissioners shall agree in their decision, both parties shall consider such decision as final and conclusive. It is further agreed, that in the event of the two commissioners differing upon all or any of the matters so referred to them, or in the event of both or either of the said commissioners refusing, or declining, or wilfully omitting, to act as such, they shall make jointly or spearately, a report or reports, as well to the Government of his Britannic majesty as to that of the United States, stating in detail the points on which they differ, and the grounds upon which their respective opinions have been formed, or the grounds upon which they, or either of them, have so refused, declined, or omitted to act. And his Britannic majesty, and the government of the United States, hereby agree to refer the report or reports of the said commissioners, to some friendly sovereign or state, to be then named for that prupose, and who shall be requested to decide on the differences which may be stated in the said report or reports, or on the report of one commissioner, together with the grounds upon which the other commissioner shall have refused, declined, or omitted to act, as the case may be. And if the commissioner so refusing, declining, or omitting to act, shall also wilfully omit to state the grounds upon which he has so done, in such manner that the said statement may be referred to such friendly sovereign or state, together with the report of such other commissioner, then such sovereign or state shall decide ex parte upon the said report alone. And his Britannic majesty and the government of the United States engage to consider the decision of such friendly sovereign or state to be final and conclusive on all the matters so referred.

ARTICLE THE FIFTH. Whereas neither that point of the high lands lying due north from the source of the river St. Croix, and designated in the former treaty of peace between the two powers as the northwest angle of Nova-Scotia, nor the northwesternmost head of the Connecticut river, has yet been ascertained; and whereas that part of the boundary line between the dominions of the two powers which extends from the source of the river St. Croix directly north to the abovementioned northwest angle of Nova-Scotia, thence along the said highlands that divide those rivers that empty themselves into the river St. Lawrence from those which fall into the Atlantic ocean to the northwesternmost head of the Connecticut river, thence down along the middle of that river to the forty-fifth degree of north latitude; thence by a line due west on said latitude until it strikes the river Iroquois or Cataraguy, has not yet been surveyed: it is agreed, that for these several purposes two commissioners shall be appointed, sworn, and authorized to act exactly in the manner directed with respect to those mentioned in the next preceding article, unless otherwise specified in the present article. The said commissioners shall meet at St. Andrews, in the province of New-Brunswick, and shall have power to adjourn to such other place or places as they shall think fit. The said commissioners shall have power to ascertain and determine the points abovementioned, in conformity with the provisions of the said treaty of peace of one thousand seven hundred and eighty three, and shall cause the boundary aforesaid, from the source of the river St. Croix to the river Iroquois or Cataraguy, to be surveyed and marked according to the said provisions. The said commissioners shall make a map of the said boundary, and annex to it a declaration under their hands and seals, certifying it to be the true map of the said boundary, and particularizing the latitude and longitude of the northwest angle of Nova-Scotia, of the northwesternmost head of the Connecticut river, and of such other points of the said boundary as they may deem proper. And both parties agree to consider such map and declaration as finally and conclusively fixing the said boundary. And in the event of the said two commissioners differing, or both, or either, of them, refusing, declining, or wilfully omitting to act, such reports, declarations, or statements, shall be made by them, or either of them, and such reference to a friendly sovereign or state, shall be made, in all respects, as in the latter part of the fourth article is contained, and in as full a manner as if the same was herein reported.

ARTICLE THE SIXTH. Whereas, by the former treaty of peace that portion of the boundary of the United States from the point where the forty-fifth degree of north latitude strikes the river Iroquois or Cataraguy to the lake Superior, was declared to be "along the middle of said river into lake Ontario, through the middle of said lake until it strikes the communication by water between that lake and lake Erie, thence along the middle of said communication into lake Erie, through the middle of said lake until it arrives at the water communication into the lake Huron, thence through the middle of said lake to the water communication between that lake and lake Superior." And whereas doubts have arisen what was the middle of the said river, lakes, and water communications, and whether certain islands lying in the same were within the dominions of his Britannic majesty or of the United States: In order, therefore, finally to decide these doubts, they shall be referred to two commissioners, to be appointed, sworn, and authorized to act exactly in the manner directed with respect to those mentioned in the next preceding article, unless otherwise specified in this present article. The said commissioners shall meet, in the first instance, at Albany, in the state of New-York, and shall have the power to adjourn to such other place or places as they shall think fit: The said commissioners shall, by a report or declaration, under their hands and seals, designate the boundary through the said river, lakes, and water communications, and decide to which of the two contracting parties the several islands lying within the said rivers, lakes, and water communications, do respectively belong, in conformity with the true intent of the said treaty of one thousand seven hundred and eighty-three. And both parties agree to consider such designation and decision as final and conclusive. And in the event of the said two commissioners differing, or both, or either of them, refusing, declining, or wilfully omitting to act, such reports, declarations or statements, shall be made by them, or either of them, and such reference to a friendly sovereign or state shall be made in all respects as in the latter part of the fourth article is contained, and in as full a manner as if the same was herein repeated.

ARTICLE THE SEVENTH. It is further agreed that the said two last-mentioned commissioners, after they shall have executed the duties assigned to them in the preceding article, shall be, and they are hereby authorized, upon their oaths impartially to fix and determine, according to the true intent of the said treaty of peace, of one thousand seven hundred and eighty-three, that part of the boundary between the dominions of the two powers, which extends from the water communications between lake Huron, and lake Superior, to the most north-western point of the Lake of the Woods, to decide to which of the two parties the several islands lying in the lakes, water communications, and rivers, forming the said boundary, do respectively belong, in conformity with the true intent of the said treaty of peace, of one thousand seven hundred and eighty-three; and to cause such parts of the said boundary, as require it, to be surveyed and marked. The said commissioners shall, by a report or declaration under their hands and seals, designate the boundary aforesaid, state their decision on the points thus referred to them, and particularize the latitude and longitude of the most north-western point of the lake of the Woods, and of such other parts of the said boundary as they may deem proper. And both parties agree to consider such designation and decision as final and conclusive. And, in the event of the said two commissioners differing, or both, or either of them refusing, declining, or wilfully omitting to act, such reports, declarations, or statements, shall be made by them, or either of them and such reference to a friendly sovereign or state, shall be made in all respects, as in the latter part of the fourth article is contained, and in as full a manner as if the same was herein repeated.

ARTICLE THE EIGHTH. The several boards of two commissioners mentioned in the four preceding articles, shall respectively have power to appoint a secretary, and to employ such surveyors or other persons as they shall judge necessary. Duplicates of all their respective reports, declarations, statements and decisions, and of their accounts, and of the journal of their proceedings, shall be delivered by them to the agents of his Britannic majesty, and to the agents of the United States, who may be respectively appointed and authorized to manage the business on behalf of their respective governments. The said commissioners shall be respectively paid in such manner as shall be agreed between the two contracting parties, such agreement being to be settled at the time of the exchange of the ratifications of this treaty. And all other expenses attending the said commissions shall be defrayed equally by the two parties. And in the case of death, sickness, resignation, or necessary absence, the place of every such commissioner, respectively, shall be supplied in the same manner as such commissioner was first appointed, and the new commissioner shall take the same oath of affirmation, and do the same duties. It is further agreed between the two contracting parties, that in case any of the islands mentioned in any of the preceding articles, which were in the possession of one of the parties prior to the commencement of the present war between the two countries, should, by the decision of any of the boards of commissioners aforesaid, or of the sovereign or state so referred to, as in the four next preceding articles contained, fall within the dominions of the other party, all grants of land made previous to the commencement of the war, by the party having had such possession, shall be as valid as if such island or islands had, by such decision or decisions, been adjudged to be within the dominions of the party having had such possession.

ARTICLE THE NINTH. The United States of America engage to put an end, immediately after the ratification of the present treaty, to hostilities with all the tribes or nations of Indians with whom they may be at war at the time of such ratification; and forthwith to restore to such tribes or nations, respectively, all the possessions, rights, and privileges, which they may have enjoyed or been entitled to in one thousand eight hundred and eleven, previous to such hostilities: Provided always, That such tribes or nations shall agree to desist from all hostilities, against the United States of America, their citizens and subjects, upon the ratification of the present treaty being notified to such tribes or nations, and shall so desist accordingly. And his Britannic majesty engages, on his part, to put an end immediately after the ratification of the present treaty, to hostilities with all the tribes or nations of Indians with whom he may be at war at the time of such ratification, and forthwith to restore to such tribes or nations, respectively, all the possessions, rights, and privileges, which they may have enjoyed or been entitled to, in one thousand eight hundred and eleven, previous to such hostilities: Provided always, That such tribes or nations shall agree to desist from all hostilities against his Britannic majesty, and his subjects, upon the ratification of the present treaty being notified to such tribes or nations, and shall so desist accordingly.

ARTICLE THE TENTH. Whereas the traffic in slaves is irreconcileable with the principles of humanity and justice, and whereas both his Majesty and the United States are desirous of continuing their efforts to promote its entire abolition, it is hereby agreed that both the contracting parties shall use their best endeavors to accomplish so desirable an object.

ARTICLE THE ELEVENTH. This treaty, when the same shall have been ratified on both sides, without alteration by either of the contracting parties, and the ratifications mutually exchanged, shall be binding on both parties, and the ratifications shall be exchanged at Washington, in the space of four months from this day, or sooner, if practicable.

IN FAITH WHEREOF, we, the respective plenipotentiaries, have signed this treaty, and have thereunto affixed our seals.

Done, in triplicate, at Ghent, the twenty-fourth day of December, one thousand eight hundred and fourteen.

In the Saginaw River Valley Chippewas

Articles of a treaty made and concluded at Saginaw, in the Territory of Michigan, between the United States of America, by their commissioner, Lewis Cass, and the Chippewa Nation of Indians.

ARTICLE 1. The Chippewa Nation of Indians, in consideration of the stipulations herein made on the part of the United States, do hereby, forever, cede to the United States the land comprehended within the following lines and boundaries: Beginning at a point in the the present Indian boundary-line, which runs due north from the mouth of the Great Auglaize River, six miles south of the base line, so called, intersects the same; thence west sixty miles; thence in a direct line to the head of the Thunder Bay River; thence down the same, following the courses thereof, to the mouth; thence northeast to the boundary-line between the United States and the British Province of Upper Canada; thence with the same to the line established by the Treaty of Detroit, in the year one thousand eight hundred and seven; thence with the said line to the place of beginning.

ARTICLE 2. From the cession aforesaid the following tracts of land shall be reserved for the use of the Chippewa Nation of Indians:

One tract, of eight thousand acres, on the east side of the river Au Sable, near where the Indians now live.

One tract, of two thousand acres, on the river Mesagwisk.

One tract, of six thousand acres, on the north side of the river Kawkawling, at the Indian village.

One tract, of five thousand seven hundred and sixty acres, upon the Flint River, to include Reaum's village and a place called Kishkawbawee.

One tract, of eight thousand acres, on the head of the river Huron, which empties into the Saginaw River at the village of Otusson.

One island in the Saginaw Bay.

One tract, of two thousand acres, where Nabobask formerly lived.

One tract, of one thousand acres, near the island in the Saginaw River.

One tract, of six hundred and forty acres, at the bend of the river Huron, which empties into the Saginaw River.

One tract, of two thousand acres, at the mouth of Point Augrais River.

One tract, of one thousand acres, on the river Huron, at Menoequet's village.

One tract, of ten thousand acres, on the Shawassee River, at a place called the Big Rock.

One tract, of three thousand acres, on the Shawassee River, at Ketchewaundaugenink.

One tract, of six thousand acres, at the Little Forks on the Tetabawasink River.

One tract, of six thousand acres, at the Black Bird's town, on the Tetabawasink River.

One tract, of forty thousand acres, on west side of the Saginaw River, to be hereafter located.

ARTICLE 3. There shall be reserved, for the use of each of the persons hereinafter mentioned and their heirs, which persons are all Indians by descent, the following tracts of land: For the use of John Riley, the son of Menawcumegoqua, a Chippewa woman, six hundred and forty acres of land, beginning at the head of the first marsh above the marsh above the mouth of the Saginaw River, on the east side thereof. For the use of Peter Riley, the son of Menawcumegoqua, a Chippewa woman, six hundred and forty acres of land, beginning above and adjoining the apple-trees on the west side of the Saginaw River, and running up the same for quantity. For the use of James Riley, the son of Menawcumegoqua, a Chippewa woman, six hundred and forty acres, beginning on the east side of the Saginaw River, nearly opposite to Campeau's trading-house, and running up the river for quantity. For the use of Kawkawiskou, or the Crow, a Chippewa chief, six hundred and forty acres of land, on the east side of the Saginaw River, at a place called Menitego, and to include, in the said six hundred and forty acres, the island opposite to the said place. For the use of Nowokeshik, Metawaunene, Mokitchenoqua, Nondashemau, Petabonaqua, Messawwakut, Checbalk, Kitchegeequa, Sagosequa, Annoketoqua, and Tawcumegoqua, each, six hundred and forty acres of land, to be located at and near the grand traverse of the Flint River, in such manner as the President of the United States may direct. For the children of Bokowtonden, six hundred and forty acres, on the Kawkawling River.

ARTICLE 4. In consideration of the cession aforesaid, the United States agree to pay to the Chippewa Nation of Indians, annually, forever, the sum of one thousand dollars in silver; and do also agree that all annnuities due by any former treaty to the said tribe shall be hereafter paid in silver.

ARTICLE 5. The stipulation contained in the treaty of Greenville, relative to the right of the Indians to hunt upon the land ceded, while it continues the property of the United States, shall apply to this treaty; and the Indians shall, for the same term, enjoy the privilege of making sugar upon the same land, committing no unnecessary waste upon the trees.

ARTICLE 6. The United States agree to pay to the Indians the value of any improvements which they may be obliged to abandon, in consequence of the lines established by this treaty, and which improvements add real value to the land.

ARTICLE 7. The United States reserve to the proper authority the right to make roads through any part of the land reserved by this treaty.

ARTICLE 8. The United States engage to provide and support a blacksmith for the Indians, at Saginaw, so long as the President of the United States may think proper, and to furnish the Chippewa Indians with such farming utensils and cattle, and to employ such persons to aid them in their agriculture, as the President may deem expedient.

ARTICLE 9. This treaty shall take effect, and be obligatory on the contracting parties, as soon as the same shall be ratified by the President of the United States, by and with the advice and consent of the Senate thereof. Proclaimed March 25, 1820.

At Sault Ste. Marie, Michigan Territory
Articles of a Treaty

Made and concluded at the Sault de St. Marie, in the Territory of Michigan, between the United States, by their Commissioner Lewis Cass, and the Chippeway tribe of Indians.

ART. 1. The Chippeway tribe of Indians cede to the United States the fillowing tract of land: Beginning at the Big Rock, in the river St. Mary's, on the boundary line between the United States and the British Province of Upper Canada; and running thence, down the said river, with the middle thereof, to the Little Rapid; and, from those points, running back from the said river, so as to include sixteen square miles of land.

ART. 2. The Chippeway tribe of Indians acknowledge to have received a quantity of goods in full satisfaction of the preceding cession.

ART. 3. The United States will secure to the Indians a perpetual right of fishing at the falls of St. Mary's, and also a place of encampment upon the tract hereby ceded, convenient to the fishing ground, which place shall not interfere with the defences of any military work which may be erected, nor with any private rights.

ART. 4. This treaty, after the same shall be ratified by the President of the United States, and by the advice and consent of the Senate thereof, shall be obligatory on the contracting parties.

In witness whereof, the said Lewis Cass, Commissioner as aforesaid, and the Chiefs and Warriors of the said Chippeway tribe of Indians, have hereunto set their hands, at the place aforesaid, this sixteenth day of June, in the year of our Lord one thousand eight hundred and twenty.

At Washington, District of Columbia
Treaty with the Ottawa, etc., 1836

Articles of a treaty made and concluded at the city of Washington in the District of Columbia, between Henry R. Schoolcraft, commissioner on the part of the United States, and the Ottawa and Chippewa nations of Indians, by their chiefs and delegates.

ARTICLE FIRST. The Ottawa and Chippewa nations of Indians cede to the United States all the tract of country within the following boundaries: Beginning at the mouth of Grand river of Lake Michigan on the north bank thereof, and following up the same to the line called for, in the first article of the treaty of Chicago of the 29th of August 1821, thence, in a direct line, to the head of Thunder-bay river, thenced with the line established by the treaty of Saginaw of the 24th of September 1819, to the mouth of said river, thence northeast to the boundary line in Lake Huron between the United States and the British province of Upper Canada, thence northwestwardly, following the same line, as established by the commissioners acting under the treaty of Ghent, through the straits, and river St. Mary's, to a point in Lake Superior north of the mouth of *Gitchy Seebing,* or Chocolate river, thence south to the mouth of said river and up its channel to the source thereof, thence, in a direct line to the head of the *Skonawba* river of Green bay, thence down the south bank of said river to its mouth, thence, in a direct line, through the ship channel into Green bay, to the outer part thereof, thence south to a point in Lake Michigan west of the north cape, or entrance of Grand river, and thence east to the place of beginning, at the cape aforesaid, comprehending all the lands and islands, within these limits, not hereinafter reserved.

ARTICLE SECOND. From the cession aforesaid the tribes reserve for their own use, to be held in common the following tracts for the term of five years from the date of the ratification of this treaty, and no longer; unless the United States shall grant them permission to remain on said lands for a longer period, namely: One tract of fifty thousand acres to be located on Little Traverse bay: one tract of twenty thousand acres to be located on the north shore of Grand Traverse bay, one tract of seventy thousand acres to be located on, or, north of the *Pieire Marquetta* river, one tract of one thousand acres to be located by Chingassanoo,—or the Big Sail, on the Cheboigan. One tract of one thousand acres, to be located by Mujeekewis, on Thunder-bay river.

ARTICLE THIRD. There shall also be reserved for the use of the Chippewas living north of the straits of Michilimackinac, the following tracts for the term of five years from the date of the ratification of this treaty, and no longer, unless the United States shall grant them permission to remain on said lands for a longer period, that is to say: Two tracts of three miles square each, on the north shores of the said straits, between *Point-au-Barbe* and *Mille Coquin* river, including the fishing grounds in front of such reservations, to be located by a council of the chiefs. The Beaver islands of Lake Michigan for the use of the Beaver-island Indians. Round island, opposite Michilimackinac, as a place of encampment for the Indians, to be under the charge of the Indian department. The islands of the *Chenos,* with a part of the adjacent north coast of Lake Huron, corresponding in length, and one mile in depth. Sugar island, with its islets, in the river of St. Mary's. Six hundred and forty acres, at the mission of the Little Rapids. A tract commencing at the mouth of the *Pississowining* river, south of Point Iroquois, thence running up said stream to its forks, thence westward, in a direct line to the Red water lakes, thence across the portage to the Tacquimenon river, and down the same to its mouth, including the small islands and fishing grounds, in front of this reservation. Six hundred and forty acres, on Grand Island, and two thousand acres, on the main land south of it. Two sections, on the northern extremity of Green bay, to be located by a council of the chiefs. All the locations, left indefinite by this, and the preceding articles, shall be made by the proper chiefs, under the direction of the President. It is understood that the reservation for a place of fishing and encampment, made under the treaty of St. Mary's of the 16th of June 1820, remains unaffected by this treaty.

ARTICLE FOURTH. In consideration of the foregoing cessions, the United States engage to pay to the Ottawa and Chippewa nations, the following sums, namely. 1st. An annuity of thirty thousand dollars per annum, in specie, for twenty years; eighteen thousand dollars, to be paid to the Indians between Grand River and the Cheboigun; three thousand six hundred dollars, to the Indians on the Huron shore, between the Cheboigan and Thunder-bay river; and seven thousand four hundred dollars, to the Chippewas north of the straits, as far as the cession extends; the remaining one thousand dollars, to be invested in stock by the Treasury Department and to remain incapable of being sold, without the consent of the President and the Senate, which may, however, be given, after the expiration of twenty-one years. 2nd. Five thousand dollars per annum, for the purpose of education, teachers, school-houses, and books in their own language, to be continued twenty years, and as long thereafter as Congress may appropriate for the object. 3rd. Three thousand dollars for missions, subject to the conditions mentioned in the second clause of this article. 4th. Ten thousand dollars for agricultural implements, cattle, mechanics' tools, and such other objects as the President may deem proper. 5th. Three hundred dollars per annum for vaccine matter, medicines, and the services of physicians, to be continued while the Indians remain on their reservations. 6th. Provisions to the amount of two thousand dollars; six thousand five hundred pounds of tobacco; one hundred barrels of salt, and five hundred fish barrels, annually, for twenty years. 7th. One hundred and fifty thousand dollars, in goods and provisions, on the ratification of this treaty, to be delivered at Michilimackinac, and also the sum of two hundred thousand dollars, in consideration of changing the permanent reservations in article two and three to reservations for five years only, to be paid whenever their reservations shall be surrendered, and until that time the interest on said two hundred thousand dollars shall be annually paid to the said Indians.

ARTICLE FIFTH. The sum of three hundred thousand dollars shall be paid to said Indians to enable them, with the aid and assistance of their agent, to adjust and pay such debts as they may justly owe, and the overplus, if any, to apply to such other use as they may think proper.

ARTICLE SIXTH. The said Indians being desirous of making provision for their half-breed relatives, and the President having determined, that individual reservations shall not be granted, it is agreed, that in lieu thereof, the sum of one hundred and fifty thousand dollars shall be set apart as a fund for said half-breeds. No person shall be entitled to any part of said fund, unless he is of Indian descent and actually resident within the boundaries described in the first article of this treaty, nor shall any thing be allowed to any such person, who may have received any allowance at any previous Indian treaty. The following principles, shall regulate the distribution. A census shall be taken of all the men, women, and children, coming within this article. As the Indians hold in higher consideration, some of their half-breeds than others, and as there is much difference in their capacity to use and take care of property, and, consequently, in their power to aid their Indian connexions, which furnishes a strong ground for this claim, it is, therefore, agreed, that at the council to be held upon this subject, the commissioner shall call upon the Indian chiefs to designate, if they require it, three classes of these claimants, the first of which, shall receive one-half more than the second, and the second, double the third. Each man woman and child shall be enumerated, and an equal share, in the respective classes, shall be allowed to each. If the father is living with the family, he shall receive the shares of himself, his wife and children. If the father is dead, or separated from the family, and the mother is living with the family, she shall have her own share, and that of the children. If the father and mother are neither living with the family, or if the children are orphans, their share shall be retained till they are twenty-one years of age; provided, that such portions of it as may be necessary may, under the direction of the President, be from time to time applied for their support. All other persons at the age of twenty-one years, shall receive their portions agreeably to the proper class. Out of the said fund of one hundred and fifty thousand dollars, the sum of five thousand dollars shall be reserved to be applied, under the direction of the President, to the support of such of the poor half breeds, as may require assistance, to be expended in annual instalments for the term of ten years, commencing with the second year. Such of the half-breeds, as may be judged incapable of making a proper use of the money, allowed them by the commissioner, shall receive the same in instalments, as the President may direct.

ARTICLE SEVENTH. In consideration of the cessions above made, and as a further earnest of the disposition felt to do full justice to the Indians, and to further their well being, the United States engage to keep two additional blacksmith-shops, one of which, shall be located on the reservation north of Grand river, and the other at *Sault Ste. Marie.* A permanent interpreter will be provided at each of these locations. It is stipulated to renew the present dilapidated shop at Michilimackinac, and to maintain a gunsmith, in addition to the present smith's establishment, and to build a dormitory for the Indians visiting the post, and appoint a person to keep it, and supply it with fire-wood. It is also agreed, to support two farmers and assistants, and two mechanics, as the President may designate, to teach and aid the Indians, in agriculture, and in the mechanic arts. The farmers and mechanics, and the dormitory, will be continued for ten years, and as long thereafter, as the President may deen this arrangement useful and necessary; but the benefits of the other stipulations of this article, shall be continued beyond the expiration of the annuities, and it is understood that the whole of this article shall stand in force, and inure to the benefit of the Indians, as long after the expiration of the twenty years as Congress may appropriate for the objects.

ARTICLE EIGHTH. It is agreed, that as soon as the said Indians desire it, a deputation shall be sent to the southwest of the Missouri River, there to select a suitable place for the final settlement of said Indians, which country, so selected and of reasonable extent, the United States will forever guaranty and secure to said Indians. Such improvements as add value to the land, hereby ceded, shall be appraised, and the amount paid to the proper Indian. But such payment shall, in no case, be assigned to, or paid to, a white man. If the church on the Cheboigan, shall fall within this cession, the value shall be paid to the band owning it. The net proceeds of the sale of the one hundred and sixty acres of land, upon the Grand River upon which the missionary society have erected their buildings, shall be paid to the said society, in lieu of the value of their said improvements. When the Indians wish it, the United States will remove them, at their expence, provide them a year's subsistence in the country to which they go, and furnish the same articles and equipments to each person as are stipulated to be given to the Pottowatomies in the final treaty of cession concluded at Chicago.

ARTICLE NINTH. Whereas the Ottawas and Chippewas, feeling a strong consideration for aid rendered by certain of their half-breeds on Grand river, and other parts of the country ceded, and wishing to testify their gratitude on the present occasion, have assigned such individuals certain locations of land, and united in a strong appeal for the allowance of the same in this treaty; and whereas no such reservations can be permitted in carrying out the special directions of the President on this subject, it is agreed, that, in addition to the general fund set apart for half-breed claims, in the sixth article, the sum of forty-eight thousand one hundred and forty-eight dollars shall be paid for the extinguishment of this class of claims, to be divided in the following manner: To Rix Robinson, in lieu of a section of land, granted to his Indian family, on the Grand river rapids, (estimated by good judges to be worth half a million) at the rate of thirty-six dollars an acre: To Leonard Slater, in trust for Chiminonoquat, for a section of land above said rapids, at the rate of ten dollars an acre: To John A. Drew, for a tract of one section and three quarters, to his Indian family, at Cheboigan rapids, at the rate of four dollars; to Edward Biddle, for one section to his Indian family at the fishing grounds, at the rate of three dollars: to John Holiday, for five sections of land to five persons of his Indian family, at the rate of one dollar and twenty-five cents; to Eliza Cook, Sophia Biddle, and Mary Holiday, one section of land each, at two dollars and fifty cents: To Augustin Hamelin junr, being of Indian descent, two sections, at one dollar and twenty-five cents; to William Lasley, Joseph Daily, Joseph Trotier, Henry A. Levake, for two sections each, for their Indian families, at one dollar and twenty-five cents: To Luther Rice, Joseph Lafrombois, Charles Butterfield, being of Indian descent, and to

George Moran, Louis Moran, G. D. Williams, for half-breed children under their care, and to Daniel Marsac, for his Indian child, one section each, at one dollar and twenty-five cents.

ARTICLE TENTH. The sum of thirty thousand dollars shall be paid to the chiefs, on the ratification of this treaty, to be divided agreeably to a schedule hereunto annexed. *[Schedule deleted.]*

ARTICLE ELEVENTH. The Ottawas having consideration for one of their aged chiefs, who is reduced to poverty, and it being known that he was a firm friend of the American Government, in that quarter, during the late war, and suffered much in consequence of his sentiments, it is agreed, that an annuity of one hundred dollars per annum shall be paid to Ningweegon or the Wing, during his natural life, in money or goods, as he may choose. Another of the chiefs of said nation, who attended the treaty of Greenville in [1795], and is now, at a very advanced age, reduced to extreme want, together with his wife, and the Government being apprized that he has pleaded a promise of Gen. Wayne, in his behalf, it is agreed that Chusco of Michilimackinac shall receive an annuity of fifty dollars per annum during his natural life.

ARTICLE TWELFTH. All expenses attending the journey of the Indians from, and to their homes, and their visit at the seat of Government, together with the expenses of the treaty, including a proper quantity of clothing to be given them, will be paid by the United States.

ARTICLE THIRTEENTH. The Indians stipulate for the right of hunting on the lands ceded, with the other usual privileges of occupancy, until the land is required for settlement. In testimony whereof, the said Henry R. Schoolcraft, commissioner on the part of the United States, and the chiefs and delegates of the Ottawa and Chippewa nation of Indians, have hereunto set their hands, at Washington the seat of Government, this twenty-eighth day of March, in the year one thousand eight hundred and thirty-six.

SUPPLEMENTAL ARTICLE. To guard against misconstruction in some of the foregoing provisions, and to secure, by further limitations, the just rights of the Indians, it is hereby agreed: that no claims under the fifth article shall be allowed for any debts contracted previous to the late war with Great Britain, or for goods supplied by foreigners to said Indians, or by citizens, who did not withdraw from the country, during its temporary occupancy by foreign troops, for any trade carried on by such persons during the said period. And it is also agreed: that no person receiving any commutation for a reservation, or any portion of the fund provided by the sixth article of this treaty, shall be entitled to the benefit of any part of the annuities herein stipulated. Nor shall any of the half-breeds, or blood relatives of the said tribes, commuted with, under the provisions of the ninth article, have any further claim on the general commutation fund, set apart to satisfy reservation claims, in the said sixth article. It is also understood, that the personal annuities, stipulated in the eleventh article, shall be paid in specie, in the same manner that other annuities are paid. Any excess of the funds set apart in the fifth and sixth articles, shall, in lieu of being paid to the Indians, be ratained and vested by the Government in stock under the conditions mentioned in the fourth article of this treaty. In testimony whereof, the parties above recited, have hereunto set their hands, at Washington the seat of Government, this thirty-first day of March, in the year one thousand eight hundred and thirty-six.

At the City of Detroit, in the State of Michigan Treaty with the Ottawa and Chippewa, 1855

Articles of agreement and convention made and concluded at the city of Detroit, in the State of Michigan, this the thirty-first day of July, one thousand eight hundred and fifty-five, between George W. Manypenny and Henry C. Gilbert, commissioners on the part of the United States, and the Ottawa and Chippewa Indians of Michigan, parties to the treaty of March 28, 1836.

In view of the existing condition of the Ottawas and Chippewas, and of their legal and equitable claims against the United States, it is agreed between the contracting parties as follows:

ARTICLE 1. The United States will withdraw from sale for the benefit of said Indians as hereinafter provided, all the unsold public lands within the State of Michigan embraced in the following descriptions, to wit:

First. For the use of the six bands residing at and near Sault Ste. Marie, sections 13, 14, 23, 24, 25, 26, 27, and 28, in township 47 north, range 5 west; sections 18, 19, and 30, in township 47 north, range 4 west; sections 11, 12, 13, 14, 15, 22, 23, 25, and 26, in township 47 north, range 3 west, and section 29 in township 47 north, range 2 west; sections 2, 3, 4, 11, 14, and 15 in township 47 north, range 2 east, and section 34 in township 48 north, range 2 east; sections 6, 7, 18, 19, 20, 28, 29, and 33 in township 45 north, range 2 east; sections 1, 12, and 13, in township 45 north, range 1 east, and section 4 in township 44 north, range 2 east.

Second. For the use of the bands who wish to reside north of the Straits of Mackinac townships 42 north, ranges 1 and 2 west; township 43 north, range 1 west, and township 44 north, range 12 west.

Third. For the Beaver Island Band—High Island, and Garden Island, in Lake Michigan, being fractional townships 38 and 39 north, range 11 west —40 north, range 10 west, and in part 39 north, range 9 and 10 west.

Fourth. For the Cross Village, Middle Village, L'Arbrechroche and Bear Creek bands, and of such Bay du Noc and Beaver Island Indians as may prefer to live with them, townships 34 to 39, inclusive, north, range 5 west—townships 34 to 38, inclusive, north, range 6 west-townships 34, 36, and 37 north, range 7 west, and all that part of township 34 north, range 8 west, lying north of Pine River.

Fifth. For the bands who usually assemble for payment at Grand Traverse, townships 29, 30, and 31 north, range 11 west, and townships 29, 30, and 31 north, range 12 west, and the east half of township 29 north, range 9 west.

Sixth. For the Grand River bands, township 12 north, range 15 west, and townships 15, 16, 17 and 18 north, range 16 west.

Seventh. For the Cheboygan band, towsnships 35 and 36 north, range 3 west.

Eighth. For the Thunder Bay band, section 25 and 36 in township 30 north, range 7 east, and section 22 in township 30 north, range 8 east.

Should either of the bands residing near Sault Ste. Marie determine to locate near the lands owned by the missionary society of the Methodist Episcopal Church at Iroquois Point, in addition to those who now reside there, it is agreed that the United States will purchase as much of said lands for the use of the Indians as the society may be willing to sell at the usual Government price.

The United States will give to each Ottawa and Chippewa Indian being the head of a family, 80 acres of land, and to each single person over twenty-one years of age, 40 acres of land, and to each family of orphan children under twenty-one years of age containing two or more persons, 80 acres of land, and to each single orphan child under twenty-one years of age, 40 acres of land to be selected and located within the several tracts of land hereinbefore described, under the following rules and regulations:

Each Indian entitled to land under this article may make his own selection of any land within the tract reserved herein for the band to which he may belong—*Provided,* That in case of two or more Indians claiming the same lot or tract of land, the matter shall be referred to the Indian agent, who shall examine the case and decide between the parties.

For the purpose of determining who may be entitled to land under the provisions of this article, lists shall be prepared by the Indian agent, which lists shall contain the names of all those persons entitled, designating them in four classes. Class 1st, shall contain the names of heads of families; class 2d, the names of single persons over twenty-one years of age; class 3d, the names of orphan children under twenty-one years of age, comprising families of two or more persons, and class 4th, the names of single orphan children under twenty-one years of age, and no person shall be entered in more than one class. Such lists shall be made and closed by the first day of July, 1856, and thereafter no applications for the benefits of this article will be allowed.

At any time within five years after the completion of the lists, selections of lands may be made by the persons entitled thereto, and a notice thereof, with a description of the land selected, filed in the office of the Indian agent in Detroit, to be by him transmitted to the Office of Indian Affairs at Washington City.

All sections of land under this article must be made according to the usual subdivisions; and fractional lots, if containing less than 60 acres, may be regarded as forty-acre lots, if over sixty and less than one hundred and twenty acres, as eighty acre lots. Selections for orphan children may be made by themselves or their friends, subject to the approval of the agent.

After selections are made, as herein provided, the persons entitled to the land may take immediate possession thereof, and the United States will thenceforth and until the issuing of patents as hereinafter provided, hold the same in trust for such persons, and certificates shall be issued, in a suitable form, guaranteeing and securing to the holders their possession and an ultimate title to the land. But such certificates shall not be assignable and shall contain a clause expressly prohibiting the sale or transfer by the holder of the land described therein.

After the expiration of ten years, such restriction on the power of sale shall be withdrawn, and a patent shall be issued in the usual form to each original holder of a certificate for the land described therein, *Provided* That each restriction shall cease only upon the actual issuing of the patent; *And provided further* That the President may in his discretion at any time in individual cases on the recommendation of the Indian agent when it shall appear prudent and for the welfare of any holder of a certificate, direct a patent to be issued. *And provided also,* That after the expiration of ten years, if individual cases shall be reported to the President by the Indian agent, of persons who may then be incapable of managing their own affairs from any reason whatever, he may direct the patents in such cases to be withheld, and the restrictions provided by the certificate, continued so long as he may deem necessary and proper.

Should any of the heads of families die before the issuing of the certificates or patents herein provided for, the same shall issue to the heirs of such deceased persons.

The benefits of this article will be extended only to those Indians who are at this time actual residents of the State of Michigan, and entitled to participate in the annuities provided by the treaty of March 28, 1836; but this provision shall not be construed to exclude any Indian now belonging to the Garden River band of Sault Ste. Marie.

All the land embraced within the tracts hereinbefore described, that shall not have been appropriated or selected within five years shall remain the property of the United States, and the same shall thereafter, for the further term of five years, be subject to entry in the usual manner and at the same rate per acre, as other adjacent public lands are then held, by Indians only; and all lands, so purchased by Indians, shall be sold without restriction, and certificates and patents shall be issued for the same in the usual form as in ordinary cases; and all lands remaining unappropriated by or unsold to the Indians after the expiration of the last-mentioned term, may be sold or disposed of by the United States as in the case of all other public lands.

Nothing contained herein shall be so construed as to prevent the appropriation, by sale, gift, or otherwise, by the United States, of any tract or tracts of land within the aforesaid reservations for the location of churches, school-houses, or for other educational purposes, and for such purposes purchases of land may likewise be made from the Indians, the consent of the President of the United States, having, in every instance, first been obtained therefor.

It is also agreed that any lands within the aforesaid tracts now occupied by actual settlers, or by persons entitled to pre-emption thereon, shall be exempt from the provisions of this article; provided, that such pre-emption claims shall be proved, as prescribed by law, before the first day of October next.

Any Indian who may have heretofore purchased land for actual settlement, under the act of Congress known as the Graduation Act, may sell and dispose of the same; and, in such case, no actual occupancy or residence by such Indians on lands so purchased shall be necessary to enable him to secure a title thereto.

In consideration of the benefits derived to the Indians on Grand Traverse Bay by the school and mission established in 1838, and still continued by the Board of Foreign Missions of the Presbyterian Church, it is agreed that the title to three separate pieces of land, being parts of tracts Nos. 3 and 4, of the west fractional half of section 35, township 30 north, range 10 west, on which are the mission and school buildings and improvements, not exceeding in all sixty-three acres, one hundred and twenty-four perches, shall be vested in the said board on payment of $1.25 per acre; and the President of the United States shall issue a patent for the same to such person as the said board shall appoint.

The United States will also pay the further sum of forty thousand dollars, or so much thereof as may be necessary, to be applied in liquidation of the present just indebtedness of the said Ottawa and Chippewa Indians; provided, that all claims presented shall be investigated under the direction of the Secretary of the Interior, who shall prescribe such rules and regulations for conducting such investigation, and for testing the validity and justness of the claims, as he shall deem suitable and proper; and no claim shall be paid except upon the certificate of the said Secretary that, in his opinion, the same is justly and equitably due; and all claimants, who shall not present their claims within such time as may be limited by said Secretary within six months from the ratification of the treaty, or whose claims, having been presented, shall be disallowed by him, shall be forever precluded from collecting the same, or maintaining an action thereon in any court whatever; and provided, also, that no portion of the money due said Indians for annuities, as herein provided, shall ever be appropriated to pay their debts under any pretence whatever; provided, that the balance of the amount herein allowed, as a just increase of the amount due for the cessions and relinquishments aforesaid, after satisfaction of the awards of the Secretary of the Interior, shall be paid to the said Chippewas or expended for their benefit, in such manner as the Secretary shall prescribe, in aid of any of the objects specified in the second article of this treaty.

ARTICLE 2. The United States will also pay to the said Indians the sum of five hundred and thirty-eight thousand and four hundred dollars, in the manner following, to wit:

First. Eighty thousand dollars for educational purposes to be paid in ten equal annual instalments of eight thousand dollars each, which sum shall be expended under the direction of the President of the United States; and in the expenditure of the same, and the appointment of teachers and management of schools, the Indians shall be consulted, and their views and wishes adopted so far as they may be just and reasonable.

Second. Seventy-five thousand dollars to be paid in five equal annual instalments of fifteen thousand dollars each in agricultural implements and carpenters' tools, household furniture and building materials, cattle, labor, and all such articles as may be necessary and useful for them in removing to the homes herein provided and getting permanently settled thereon.

Third. Forty-two thousand and four hundred dollars for the support of four blacksmith-shops for ten years.

Fourth. The sum of three hundred and six thousand dollars in coin, as follows: ten thousand dollars of the principle, and the interest on the whole of said last-mentioned sum remaining unpaid at the rate of five per cent. annually for ten years, to be distributed *per capita* in the usual manner for paying annuities. And the sum of two hundred and six thousand dollars remaining unpaid at the expiration of ten years, shall be then due and payable, and if the Indians then require the payment of said sum in coin the same shall be distributed *per capita* in the same manner as annuities are paid, and not in less than four equal annual instalments.

Fifth. The sum of thirty-five thousand dollars in ten annual instalments if three thousand and five hundred dollars each, to be paid only to the Grand River Ottawas, which is in lieu of all permanent annuities to which they may be entitled by former treaty stipulations, and which sum shall be distributed in the usual manner *per capita.*

ARTICLE 3. The Ottawa and Chippewa Indians hereby release and discharge the United States from all liability on account of former treaty stipulations, it being distinctly understood and agreed that the grants and payments hereinbefore provided for are in lieu and satisfaction of all claims, legal and equitable on the part of said Indians jointly and severally against the United States, for land, money or other thing guaranteed to said tribes or either of them by the stipulations of any former treaty or treaties; excepting, however, the right of fishing and encampment secured to the Chippewas of Sault Ste. Marie by the treaty of June 16, 1820.

ARTICLE 4. The interpreters at Sault Ste. Marie, Mackinac, and for the Grand River Indians, shall be continued, and another provided at Grand Traverse, for the term of five years, and as much longer as the President may deem necessary.

ARTICLE 5. The tribal organization of said Ottawa and Chippewa Indians, except so far as may be necessary for the purpose of carrying into effect the provisions of this agreement, is hereby dissolved; and if at any time hereafter, further negotiations with the United States, in reference to any matters contained herein, should become necessary, no general convention of the Indians shall be called; but such as reside in the vicinity of any usual place of payment, or those only who are immediately interested in the questions involved, may arrange all matters between themselves and the United States, without the concurrence of other portions of their people, and as fully and conclusively, and with the same effect in every respect, as if all were represented.

ARTICLE 6. This agreement shall be obligatory and binding on the contracting parties as soon as the same shall be ratified by the President and Senate of the United States. In testimony whereof the said George W. Manypenny and the said Henry C. Gilbert, commissioners as aforesaid, and the undersigned chiefs and headmen of the Ottawas and Chippewas, have hereto set their hands and seals, at the city of Detroit the day and year first above written.

At the City of Detroit, in the State of Michigan
Treaty with the Chippewa of Sault Ste. Marie, 1855

Articles of agreement made and concluded at the city of Detroit, in the State if Michigan, the second day of August, 1855, between George W. Manypenny and Henry C. Gilbert, commissioners on the part of the United States, and the Chippewa Indians of Sault Ste. Marie.

ARTICLE 1. The said Chippewa Indians surrender to the United States the right of fishing at the falls of the St. Mary's and of encampment, convenient to the fishing-ground, secured to them by the treaty of June 16, 1820.

ARTICLE 2. The United States will appoint a commissioner who shall, within six months after the ratification of this treaty, personally visit and examine the said fishery and place of encampment, and determine the value of the interest of the Indians therein as the same originally existed. His award shall be reported to the President, and shall be final and conclusive, and the amount awarded shall be paid to said Indians, as annuities are paid, and shall be received by them in full satisfaction for the right hereby surrendered: *Provided,* That one-third of said award shall, if the Indians desire it, be paid to such of their half-breed relations as they may indicate.

ARTICLE 3. The United States also give to the chief, O-shaw-waw-no, for his own use, in fee-simple, a small island in the river St. Mary's, adjacent to the camping-ground hereby surrendered, being the same island on which he is now encamped, and said to contain less than half an acre: *Provided,* That the same has not been heretofore otherwise appropriated or disposed of; and in such case, this grant is to be void, and no compensation is to be claimed by said chief or any of the Indians, parties hereto, in lieu thereof.

ARTICLE 4. This agreement shall be obligatory and binding on the contracting parties as soon as the same shall be ratified by the President and Senate of the United States. In testimony whereof, the said George W. Manypenny and the said Henry C. Gilbert, commissioners as aforesaid, and the undersigned chiefs and headmen of the Chippewa Indians of Sault Ste. Marie, have hereto set their hands and seals at the city of Detroit the day and year first above written.

At the City of Detroit, in the State of Michigan, Treaty with the Chippewa of Saginaw, etc., 1855

Articles of agreement and convention, made and concluded at the city of Detroit, in the State of Michigan, this second day of August, one thousand eight hundred and fifty-five, between George W. Manypenny and Henry C. Gilbert, commissioners on the part of the United States, and the Chippewa Indians of Saginaw, parties to the treaty of January 14, 1837, and that portion of the band of Chippewa Indians of Swan Creek and Black River, parties to the treaty of May 9, 1836, and now remaining in the State of Michigan.

In view of the existing conditions of the Indians aforesaid, and of their legal and equitable claims against the United States, it is agreed between the contracting parties as follows, viz:

ARTICLE 1. The United States will withdraw from sale, for the benefit of said Indians, as herein provided, all the unsold public lands within the State of Michigan embraced in the following description, to wit:

First. Six adjoining townships of land in the county of Isabella, to be selected by said Indians within three months from this date, and notice thereof given to their agent.

Second. Townships Nos. 17 and 18 north, ranges 3, 4, and 5 east.

The United States will give to each of the said Indians, being a head of a family, eighty acres of land; and to each single person over twenty- one years of age, forty acres of land; and to each family of orphan children under twenty-one years of age, containing two or more persons, eighty acres of land; and to each single orphan child under twenty-one years of age, forty acres of land; to be selected and located within the several tracts of land hereinbefore described, under the same rules and regulations, in every respect, as are provided by the agreement concluded on the 31st day of July, A.D. 1855, with the Ottawas and Chippewas of Michigan, for the selection of their lands.

And the said Chippewas of Saginaw and of Swan Creek and Black River, shall have the same exclusive right to enter lands within the tracts withdrawn from sale for them for five years after the time limited for selecting the lands to which they are individually entitled, and the same right to sell and dispose of land entered by them, under the provisions of the Act of Congress known as the Graduation Act, as is extended to the Ottawas and Chippewas by the terms of said agreement.

And the provisions therein contained relative to the purchase and sale of land for school-houses, churches, and educational purposes, shall also apply to this agreement.

ARTICLE 2. The United States shall also pay to the said Indians the sum of two hundred and twenty thousand dollars, in manner following, to wit:

First. Thirty thousand dollars for educational purposes, to be paid in five equal annual instalments of four thousand dollars each, and in five subsequent equal annual instalments of two thousand dollars each, to be expended under the direction of the President of the United States.

Second. Forty thousand dollars, in five equal annual instalments of five thousand dollars each, and in five subsequent equal annual instalments of three thousand dollars each, in agricultural implements and carpenters' tools, household furniture and building materials, cattle, labor, and all such articles as may be necessary and useful for them in removing to the homes herein provided, and getting permanently settled thereon.

Third. One hundred and thirty-seven thousand and six hundred dollars in coin, in ten equal instalments of ten thousand dollars each, and in two subsequent equal annual instalments of eighteen thousand and eight hundred dollars each, to be distributed *per capita* in the usual manner for paying annuities.

Fourth. Twelve thousand and four hundred dollars for the support of one blacksmith-shop for ten years. The United States will also build a grist and saw mill for said Indians at some point in the territory, to be selected by them in said county of Isabella, provided, a suitable water-power can be found, and will furnish and equip the same with all necessary fixtures and machinery, and will construct such dam, race, and other appurtenances as may be necessary to render the water-power available: *Provided,* That the whole amount for which the United States shall be liable under this provision, shall not exceed the sum of eight thousand dollars.

The United States will also pay the further sum of four thousand dollars for the purpose of purchasing a saw-mill, and in repair of the same, and in adding thereto the necessary machinery and fixtures for a run of stone for grinding grain—the same to be located on the tract described in clause "second," Article 1.

The United States will also pay the further sum of twenty thousand dollars, or so much thereof as may be necessary, to be applied in liquidation of the present just indebtedness of the said Indians; *Provided,* That all claims presented shall be investigated under the direction of the Secretary of the Interior within six months, who shall prescribe such rules and regulations for conducting such investigation, and for testing the validity and justice of the claims as he shall deem suitable and proper. And no claim shall be paid except on the certificate of the said Secretary that, in his opinion, the same is justly and equitably due; and all claimants, who shall not present their claims within such time as may be limited by said Secretary, or, whose claims having been presented, shall be disallowed by him, shall be forever precluded from collecting the same, or maintaining an action thereon in any court whatever; *And, provided, also,* That no portion of the money due said Indians for annuities, as herein provided, shall ever be appropriated to pay their debts under any pretence whatever; *Provlded,* That the balance of the amount herein allowed as a just increase for the cessions and relinquishments aforesaid, after satisfaction of the awards of the Secretary of the Interior, shall be paid to the said Indians, or expended for their benefit in such a manner as the Secretary shall prescribe, in aid of any of the objects specified in this treaty.

ARTICLE 3. The said Chippewas of Saginaw, and of Swan Creek and Black River, hereby cede to the United States all the lands within the State of Michigan heretofore owned by them as reservations, and whether held for them in trust by the United States or otherwise; and they do hereby, jointly and severally, release and discharge the United States from all liability to them, and to their, or either of their said tribes, for the price and value of all such lands, heretofore sold, and the proceeds of which remain unpaid.

And they also hereby surrender all their, and each of their permanent annuities, secured to them, or either of them by former treaty stipulations, including that portion of the annuity of eight hundred dollars payable to "the Chippewas," by the treaty of November 17, 1807, to which they are entitled, it being distinctly understood and agreed, that the grants and payments hereinbefore provided for, are in lieu and satisfaction of all claims, legal and equitable on the part of said Indians, jointly and severally, against the United States for land, money, or other thing guaranteed to said tribes, or either of them, by the stipulations of any former treaty or treaties.

ARTICLE 4. The entries of land heretofore made by Indians and by the Missionary Society of the Methodist Episcopal Church for the benefit of the Indians, on lands withdrawn from sale in townships 14 north, range 4 east, and 10 north, range 5 east, in the State of Michigan, are hereby confirmed, and patents shall be issued therefor as in other cases.

ARTICLE 5. The United States will provide an interpreter for said Indians for five years, and as much longer as the President may deem necessary.

ARTICLE 6. The tribal organization of said Indians, except so far as may be necessary for the purpose of carrying into effect the provisions of this agreement, is hereby dissolved.

ARTICLE 7. This agreement shall be obligatory and binding on the contracting parties as soon as the same shall be ratified by the President and Senate of the United States. In testimony whereof, the said George W. Manypenny and the said Henry C. Gilbert, commissioners as aforesaid, and the undersigned, chiefs and headmen of the Chippewas of Saginaw, and of Swan Creek and Black River, have hereto set their hands and seals at the city of Detroit, the day and year first above written.

APPENDIX II

THE JUDICIAL OPINIONS

A Note on Reading the Opinions

The three opinions here included focus on the "treaty waters" of the northern Great Lakes, span the decade of the 1970's, and so are of extraordinary interest to all who would understand the tumultuous shift in the legal interpretation of "rights" to fish in northern Great Lakes waters that has led to the misunderstandings and confrontations between Indians and non Indians that characterized the decade of the 1980's and promise to define the decade of the 1990's.

It all began innocently enough and the early judicial history is summarized by Justice Swainson in the *Jondreau* case. As early as the 1830's Chief Justice Marshall's Supreme Court established liberal guidelines to govern the construction of federal treaties with the North American Indians according to which the federal government of the United States assumed full responsibility as trustee for the well-being of its wards under treaty, the Indians. This benevolent relationship under law prevailed in theory throughout the nineteenth and into the early twentieth century; no matter how well or ill it may have worked itself out in practice, the principles stood.

In the course of the twentieth century, however, very much in accordance, it would appear, with the theories of integration and amalgamation expressed in the nineteenth century Michigan Indian treaties, the Indians came to be generally regarded as citizens of the United States—with all of the ordinary rights, privileges, prerogatives, and responsibilities attached thereto. But latterly, more liberal courts, notably of the 1970's, returned to the earlier emphases by re-assigning special status to tribal communities as separate sovereign nations with special rights to self-determination even within the geographical and political boundaries of the United States—rights guaranteed, it is said, by last century's treaties. These are the "rights" that have dominated the courtrooms for the past two decades.

In the opinions here presented, Judge Swainson, writing for the Michigan State Supreme Court in the matter of *People v. Jondreau,* approaches a liberal decision cautiously and moderately (not to mention, relatively speaking, briefly). He keeps his eye firmly on the judicial history of the matter, on the pertinent cases in precedent, and on the documents that lead most directly to his court's decision. Nevertheless, his opinion handed down, the tribes quite suddenly possessed hunting and fishing prerogatives that were not previously recognized.

Within months, to test the case it must be assumed, Abe LeBlanc cast his unlicensed and supposedly illegal nets into Pendills Bay and thus initiated *People v. LeBlanc*. Judge G. Mennon Williams wrote the majority opinion of the same State Supreme Court in this matter in 1976. The nineteenth century United States Supreme courts had called for the application of historical method in the approach to litigation growing out of federal treaty law. Accordingly, the Williams Court, in an early instance in Michigan, considered carefully the principle treaties themselves (as well as related documents, such as the minutes of the negotiations), and came to a decision that reaffirmed that of the Swainson Court. The Williams Court is to be commended for its effort to consider straightforwardly these important historical documents. Many will find, however, the dissenting opinions of justices Lindemer, Coleman, and Ryan as compelling and persuasive as is the majority opinion.

Well before the *LeBlanc* case was reported out, however, in 1973 the federal government filed in Federal District Court on behalf of itself and the Bay Mills Indian Community, and thus *United States v. Michigan* came before Judge Noel P. Fox. Judge Fox duly documents his obligation to apply historical method and enthusiastically approaches his responsibility— at some length, one can fairly observe. His opinion fully affirms and then extends the liberal opinions handed down in the earlier-published cases. Unfortunately, the judge ranges himself, and apparently permits the federal government's expert witnesses to range, far beyond the documents that are central to the matter (even beyond the history that correctly pertains to it), and in so doing loses touch almost entirely with the actual historical background and the important documents that emerge from it. What he produces is an extensive document that will survive as a significant contribution to laws still in formation and not yet fully tested in the courts. It will also stand as a perfect example of the imperfect application of historical method.

People v. Jondreau [384 Mich 539] Opinion of the Court

I.

The interpretation of Indian treaties by the courts has varied greatly depending upon the precise wording of the treaties. Hence, a close examination of the treaty involved in this case is imperative. Under the Chippewa Treaty of 1854, the Federal government agreed under Article 2:

> "1st. For the L'Anse and Vieux De Sert bands, all the unsold lands in the following townships in the State of Michigan: Township fifty-one north range thirty-three west; township fifty-one north range thirty-two west; the east half of township fifty north range thirty three west; the west half of

township fifty north range thirty-two west; and all of township fifty-one north range thirty-one west, lying west of Huron Bay."

Article 11 of the treaty states:

" * * * And such of them as reside in the territory hereby ceded shall have the right to hunt and fish therein, until otherwise ordered by the President."

When Mr. Jondreau came ashore on June 1, 1965, he alleged he was within T 51 N, R 33 W. If a line were extended from the boundaries into the Bay, the area where he was fishing would have been within T 51 N, R 33 W. The people correctly contend that under Michigan law the boundaries of the township do not extend into the Great Lakes. *People v. Bouchard* (1890), 82 Mich 156 [46 N.W. 232]. Thus, they assert, that Jondreau was not within T 51 N, R 33 W. They further assert that title to the waters and submerged lands in the Great Lakes vested in the State of Michigan when it became a State in 1837. Thus, they contend, that the Indians did not have title to the waters and submerged lands and, therefore, could not cede them to the United States government.

Defendant contends that the title to the waters and submerged lands did not pass to the State of Michigan in 1837 and, thus, were part of the ceded land under the treaty.

Both parties have done an excellent job of discussing in detail the numerous United States Supreme Court cases involving title to submerged lands, beginning with *Martin v. Waddell* (1842), 41 US (16 Peters) 367 (10 L.Ed. 997), and ending with *United States v. California* (1947), 332 US 19 (67 S.Ct. 1658, 91 L.Ed. 1889). However, after a thorough analysis of these cases, we believe that the interpretation of the treaty does not depend on the title to the waters and submerged lands of Keweenaw Bay. Hence, we will not discuss the question of title to these lands and waters.

Under Article 2, section 2, of the United States Constitution, the President has the power to make treaties, provided that two-thirds of the Senate concur. This, of course, was the procedure that was followed when the Chippewa Indian Treaty of 1854 was made.

Article 6 of the United States Constitution states in part:

"This Constitution, and the Laws of the United States which shall be made in Pursuance thereof; and all Treaties made, or which shall be made, under the Authority of the United States, shall be the supreme Law of the Land; and the Judges in every State shall be bound thereby, any Thing in the Constitution or Laws of any State to the contrary notwithstanding.*

[*note. *See, e.g.,* Whitney v. Robertson *(1888), 124 U.S. 190 (8 S.Ct. 456, 31 L.Ed. 386), and* Cooper v. Aaron *(1958), 358 U.S. 1 (78 S.Ct. 1401, 3 L.Ed. 2d 5).]*

Thus, as Judges of a state court, we are bound by this Chippewa Indian Treaty of 1854, and, to the extent that any state law or regulation conflicts with the treaty, the state law or regulation is invalid. We, therefore, must determine what was meant by the statement in the treaty "and such of them as reside in the territory hereby ceded shall have the right to hunt and fish therein, until otherwise ordered by the President."

Although there is no legislative history available on the making of this treaty, we are aided by the fact that the United States Supreme Court has laid down general rules of construction in cases involving Indian treaties. In *Worcester v. Georgia* (1832), 31 U.S. (6 Peters) 515, (8

L.Ed. 483), Justice McLean stated (p. 582):

> "The language used in treaties with the Indians should never be construed to their prejudice. * * * How the words of the treaty were understood by this unlettered people, rather than their critical meaning, should form the rule of construction."

In *Choctaw Nation v. United States* (1886), 119 U.S. 1 (7 S.Ct. 75, 30 L.Ed. 306), after quoting the above statement, the court said (p. 28):

> "The parties are not on an equal footing, and that inequality is to be made good by the superior justice which looks only to the *substance of the right,* without regard to technical rules framed under a system of municipal jurisprudence, formulating the rights and obligations of private persons, equally subject to the same laws." (Emphasis added.)

See, also, *Jones v. Meehan* (1899), 175 U.S. 1 (20 S.Ct. 1, 44 L.Ed. 49); *United States v. Winans* (1905), 198 U.S. 371, 380, 381 (25 S.Ct. 662, 49 L.Ed. 1089); *Kennedy v. Becker* (1916), 241 U.S. 556, 563 (36 S.Ct. 705, 60 L.Ed. 1166); and *Menominee Tribe v. United States* (1968), 391 U.S. 404, 406 (fn 2) (88 S.Ct. 1705, 20 L.Ed. 2d 697).

The substance of the right to fish must have included the right to fish on the Keweenaw Bay. For the L'Anse band of Chippewa Indians (See Map, Appendix A [*omitted*]), the fishing right on the Keweenaw Bay was clearly a valuable right. Any other construction of the treaty would make the right granted by the treaty without substance. The Indians did not have knowledge of the laws concerning municipal boundaries or sovereignty disputes between the Federal and state governments. Since they were living on land bordering the Keweenaw Bay, as "an unlettered people" they would assume that the right to fish meant the right to fish on the Keweenaw Bay.

II.

In the case of *Worcester v. Georgia, supra,* where the court struck down a state law which attempted to regulate certain actions of white persons and Indians, Chief Justice Marshall stated (p. 561):

> "The *whole intercourse* between the United States and this [Indian] nation, is, by our constitution and laws, *vested in the government of the United States."* (Emphasis added.)

Following this case, the courts retreated from this position for almost a century. State laws which limited the rights of Indians under the various treaties were upheld as valid exercises of the police power. However, in recent years, the courts have again accorded Indians full rights under the treaties. Thus, while the court stated in *Ward v. Race Horse* (1896), 163 U.S. 504, 507, 509, 513 (16 S.Ct. 1076, 41 L.Ed. 244):

> "The power of a State to control and regulate the taking of game cannot be questioned. * * * To suppose that the words of the treaty intended to give to the Indian the right to enter into already established States and seek out every portion of unoccupied government land and there exercise the right of hunting, in violation of the municipal law, would be to presume that the treaty was so drawn as

to frustrate the very object it had in view. * * * the States have full power to regulate within their limits matters of internal police * * *."

and in *Kennedy v. Becker* (1916), 241 U.S. 556 (36 S.Ct. 705, 60 L.Ed. 1166) (pp. 563, 564):

> "* * * we [are] of the opinion that the clause is fully satisfied by considering it a reservation of a privilege of fishing and hunting upon the granted lands in common with the grantees, and others to whom the privilege might be extended, but subject nevertheless to that necessary power of appropriate regulation, as to all those privileged, which inhered in the sovereignty of the State over the lands where the privilege was exercised."

These views have, however, been limited by implication in recent years by United States Supreme Court decisions. For example, in *Tulee v. Washington* (1942), 315 U.S. 681 (62 S.Ct. 862, 86 L.Ed. 1115), the court held that the State could not require a fishing license fee without violating a treaty made in 1859 (12 Stat. 951 [1859]). Likewise, in *Menominee Tribe v. United States, supra,* the court held that an act of Congress in 1954 did not terminate by implication the Wolf River Treaty of 1854 (10 Stat. 1064 [1854]). The court held that valuable hunting and fishing rights given by a treaty were not easily extinguished without a specific statement on the subject. These cases, while not directly on point, do demonstrate a decisive trend in the decisions of the Federal courts toward granting Indians expanded rights under the various treaties. See, also, *Metlakatla Indian Community v. Egan* (1962), 369 U.S. 45 (82 S.Ct. 552, 7 L.Ed.2d 562); *Makah Indian Tribe v. Schoettler* (CA9 1951), 192 F.2d 224, and *Maison v. Confederated Tribes of Umatilla Indian Reservation* (CA9, 1963), 314 F.2d 169.

Both parties have done an exceedingly fine job of analyzing in great detail the numerous cases dealing with Indian treaties. While these cases are instructive, they are not binding for two reasons: First, these cases do not involve construction of the Chippewa Indian Treaty of 1854. Second, because of the change in judicial attitude over the past 30 years, we have two lines of conflicting precedent that are not conclusive to our determination of this case. We do, however, have one case directly on point.

People v. Chosa (1930), 252 Mich 154 [233 N.W. 205], involved an identical fact situation. Chosa and Attikons, members of the L'Anse band of Chippewa Indians, were convicted of violating fish and game laws. This Court affirmed. The Court stated (p. 160 [233 N.W. p. 207]):

> "The treaties evidently established a servitude of the right to hunt and fish on the ceded land in favor of the Indians and against the exclusive dominion of private ownership, *but they provided no immunity from operation of game laws, as against the State." (Emphasis added.)

The people cite *Chosa* as determinative of the decision in this case. If *Chosa* is good law, then undoubtedly the people are correct. We believe that *Chosa* no longer states the applicable law. When *Chosa* was decided in 1930, our Court properly relied on the governing authorities as of that date. However, through the passage of time, the foundations upon which *Chosa* rested are no longer sustained as valid.

Chosa rested on two basic premises. Defendant Chosa had argued that the clause giving the President the power to abrogate the treaty was the only limit on the hunting and fishing rights. The Court answered, at p. 160 [233 N.W. at p. 207]:

> "As a restriction on operation of State game laws, it would be foreign to our system of government in providing control of sovereign powers of the State by an officer of another sovereignty."

This view, however, does not display a proper deference for the treaty power granted to the President by Article 2 of the United States Constitution, and under Article 6 of the United States Constitution, as stated supra, we, as State Court Judges must respect any treaty as superior to our state laws.

A somewhat similar conflict between state laws and the Federal treaty power arose in the case of *Missouri v. Holland* (1920), 252 U.S. 416 (40 S.Ct. 382, 64 L.Ed. 641, 11 A.L.R. 984). In 1916, the United States had made a treaty with Great Britain (39 Stat. 1702 [1916]) for the protection, by closed hunting seasons and in other ways, of migratory birds in the United States and Canada. It bound each country to take the necessary measures for carrying out the treaty. Thereupon, Congress prohibited (Act of July 3, 1918, ch. 128, 40 Stat. 755 [1918]) killing, capturing, or selling any of the migratory birds designated by the terms of the treaty, except as permitted by regulations made by the Secretary of Agriculture. The State of Missouri filed a bill in equity to prevent Holland, a United States game warden, from attempting to enforce this act and the regulations made pursuant to it. The state claimed it was an unconstitutional interference with the rights reserved to the state by the Tenth Amendment and that the acts of the defendant invaded the sovereign powers of the state as owner of the wild birds. Mr. Justice Holmes, in upholding the treaty and the act passed pursuant thereto, stated (p. 434 [40 S.Ct. p. 384]):

> "No doubt it is true that as between a State and its inhabitants the State may regulate the killing and sale of such birds, but it does not follow that its authority is exclusive of paramount powers. * * * Valid treaties of course 'are as binding within the territorial limits of the States as they are elsewhere throughout the dominion of the United States.' *Baldwin v. Franks* [1887], 120 U.S. 678, 683 7 S.Ct. 656, 30 L.Ed. 766. *No doubt the great body of private relations usually fall within the control of the State, but a treaty may override its power."* (Emphasis added.)

Thus, under the treaty power, the President may make determinations that affect the powers normally reserved to the state.

Second, our Court in *Chosa* relied on the fact that Indians were United States citizens and, thus, subject to all state laws. The Court stated (p. 162 [233 N.W. p. 207]):

> "When one becomes a citizen of the United States, he casts off both the rights and obligations of his former nationality and takes on those which pertain to other citizens of the country. 11 C.J. p. 786.

> "Both because of the new citizenship and by the express terms of the statute under which the allotments were made, defendants became subject to the laws of the State, civil and criminal."

This contention was rejected by the United States Supreme Court in *Puyallup Tribe v. Department of Game of Washington* (1968), 391 U.S. 392 (88 S.Ct. 1725, 20 L.Ed. 2d 689). Mr. Justice Douglas, speaking for the Court, stated (p. 398):

> "The right to fish 'at all usual and accustomed' places *may, of course, not be qualified by the State, even though all Indians born in the United States are now citizens of the United States."* (Emphasis added.)

Thus, the foundations upon which *Chosa* rested have not stood the test of time. We think the better view is expressed by the court in *State v. Arthur* (1953), 74 Idaho 251 (261 P.2d 135), which involved the prosecution of members of the Nez Perce Tribe of Indians for having killed deer out of season on national forest lands. The deer were within the exterior boundaries of land ceded to the Federal government under a treaty of 1855 (12 Stat. 957 [1855]). The state contended that the game and fish regulations did apply to the ceded land. The district court sustained defendant's demurrer and entered an order dismissing the action. The state Supreme Court affirmed. The court pointed out that the holdings in such cases as *Ward v. Race Horse, supra,* and *Kennedy v. Becker, supra,* have been repudiated by later cases. The court stated (pp. 261 [-262, P.2d p. 141]):

> "If the right exists in the State to regulate the killing of game upon open and unclaimed lands ceded by the Nez Perce Indians to the United States, it follows that such right is to be exercised under the police power of this state. Generally stated, the police power under the American constitutional system has been left to the states. * * * That the State has and may exercise such power generally is not the question. * * *

> "[T]he statute of any state enacted pursuant to its police power which conflicts with any treaty of the United States constitutes an interference with matters that are within the exclusive scope of federal power and, hence, cannot be permitted to stand. 16 C.J.S., Constitutional Law, 196, page 565; the treaty being superior to a particular state law and regulation, though the state law and regulation involved is otherwise within the legislative power of the state, the rights created under the treaty cannot thus be destroyed."

At pages 264, 265 [261 P.2d at pages 142-143], the court further stated:

> "One of the primary purposes of licensing in reference to fishing and hunting is to conserve wild life; the law is essentially a regulatory act rather than a revenue act. * * * While both fishing and hunting are primarily sport and recreation for most fishermen and hunters, this is not so with respect to the Indians; they have always fished and hunted to obtain food and furs necessary for their existence and have been controlled as to the time when and the area where and the amount of catch or kill by the exigencies of the occasion; while no doubt this was more so in 1855 than it is now, the fact remains that it is to a lesser extent also true today; be that as it may, their rights reserved in this respect should be determined in the light of conditions existing at the time of the treaty and the manifest intent of all contracting parties at that time. * * * If the position of the State is sustained the assurance given by Governor Stevens that they could kill game when they pleased and the provision of the treaty reserving to them the right to hunt upon open and unclaimed lands is no right at all. Out of the solemn obligations of the treaty, and the express reserved property right which never passed from the Indians to anyone and which the federal government has never extinguished but has expressly recognized before and after Idaho was admitted to the Union, the Nez Perce would now have no right in any respect different than that enjoyed by all others, except perhaps the freedom from the burden of a license fee. This was never intended under the broad, fair and liberal construction of the treaty. The Supreme Court of the United States has recognized and expressly held that the Indian treaty fishing provisions accorded to them rights which do not exist for other citizens. * * * What are such rights under the State's theory? Perhaps to hunt without a license. If such rights exist as to fishing most assuredly they exist as to hunting. If the State can regulate the time of year in which they may hunt then they are accorded no greater rights in this respect than exist for other citizens.

> "We are not here concerned with the wisdom of the provisions of the treaty under present conditions nor with the advisability of imposing upon the Indians certain regulatory obligations in the interest of conserving wild life; that is for the Federal Government, the affected tribe, and perhaps the State of Idaho to resolve under appropriate negotiations; our concern here is only with reference to protecting the rights of the Indians which they reserved under the Treaty of 1855 to hunt upon open and unclaimed land without limitation, restriction or burden."

While this case is not binding upon our Court, we believe that it expresses the proper balance between the rights of the Chippewa Indians and the police powers of the state under the treaty of 1854.

The people point out the fact that unlimited fishing rights could deplete our limited national resources. They rely on *Puyallup, supra,* where the court held that the state could provide regulations that were reasonably necessary for the conservation of fish. In an age of growing awareness of the need to preserve and protect our environment, this is an important consideration. However, unlike the treaty of 1855 considered in the *Arthur* case, the Chippewa Indian Treaty of 1854 does provide a safeguard. Under Article 11, the President may issue an order limiting or extinguishing the hunting and fishing rights of the Indians. The four fish involved in this case will not upset the ecological balance. However, if in the future the number of fish being taken does constitute such a threat, we are convinced that the President would take appropriate action.

We, therefore, overrule *People v. Chosa,* supra, and hold that the game regulations are invalid as applied to the defendant Jondreau and other Indians who are protected by the Chippewa Indian Treaty of 1854.

Judgment reversed.

BLACK, J. (concurring).

I agree with and have endorsed the opinion Justice SWAINSON has prepared, yet would step a bit farther.

In the majestic phrasing of the Doxology, the supremacy clause [Article VI (2), Constitution of the United States] was from the beginning and is now really regnant. Its prospective force and effect upon the states, and "the Judges in every State," came to conception and birth when Michigan was both trackless and primeval. Binding us now, as in 1930 when *People v. Chosa,* 252 Mich. 154 [233 N.W. 205] came to judicial attention, it says imperatively that "all Treaties made"—along with the other components therein listed—"shall be the supreme Law of the Land." Now as in *Chosa* the same treaty of 1854 is before us, along with the same appeal to its overriding impact.

Today we find definitely that this same treaty of 1854 provided and now provides "a specific condition of enjoyment of the reservation" which to this day tolerates no challenge by Michigan and the courts of Michigan. No like finding, and no opposing finding, was made by the *Chosa* Court. Irrelevant reasons only were assigned for refusal to support the treaty-stipulated right of *Chosa* and *Attikons* to hunt and fish on the reservation. See pages 160 and 161 of *Chosa*'s report.

In that setting *People v. Chosa* was released to our books a little over 40 years ago. This Court attempted then in contravention of the treaty and the supremacy clause to interpose subordinate interests of the state, and the never exercised revocatory power of the President, to block the enforcement of that treaty. This was something more than judicial error. It was pure nullity.

There is no occasion for overrulement or distinguishment of *Chosa*. It never became law in the first place, both its judgment and the statute applied there having spent their whole force in the utterance of worthless words. *People v. Chosa* was, when handed down December 2, 1930, like the earth before it was made, "without form, and void." (Genesis ch. 1:2.)

399 Mich. 31

People of the State of Michigan, Plaintiff, Appellant and Appellee,

v.

A. B. Le Blanc, Defendant, Appellee and Appellant.

Nos. 6, 7, March Term, 1976.
Supreme Court of Michigan. Dec. 27, 1976.
[248 N.W. 2d 199]

Frank J. Kelley, Atty. Gen., Robert A. Derengoski, Sol. Gen., Jerome Maslowski, Stewart H. Freeman, Asst. Attys. Gen., Lansing, for the People.

Kathryn L. Tierney, Bay Mills Indian Community, Brimley, William J. James, Director, Upper Peninsula Legal Services, Inc., Sault Ste. Marie, Bruce R. Greene, Native American Rights Fund, Boulder, Colo., for A. B. LeBlanc.

Freihofer, Hecht, Oosterhouse & DeBoer, P.C. by Peter W. Steketee, Grand Rapids, for amici curiae.

WILLIAMS, Justice.

Defendant A. B. LeBlanc, a Chippewa Indian and an enrolled member of the Bay Mills Indian Community, was arrested on September 28, 1971 in Pendills Bay of Lake Superior about 20 miles west of Sault Ste. Marie by a conservation officer for the Michigan Department of Natural Resources and charged with fishing commercially without a license and with fishing with an illegal device, a gill net. He was convicted of both charges in district court.

Defendant's appeal of these convictions presents complex issues involving, on the one hand, the existence and continued vitality of fishing rights for Chippewa Indians under the Treaty of 1836 and the Treaty of 1855,*

[*7 Stat. 491 (1836), 11 Stat. 621 (1856). The Indian treaties are compiled in Indian Treaties: 1778-1883 (Kappler, 2d ed, Interland Publishing, Inc., 1972), which was originally published as 2

Indian Affairs: Laws and Treaties (Kappler, Washington, DC, United States Government Printing Office, 1904), herein cited as "2 Kapp."—Reporter]

and, on the other hand, the authority of the State of Michigan in the conservation of natural resources to regulate the exercise of whatever fishing rights remain reserved by the Chippewas under those treaties.

Specifically, three central issues require resolution:
(1) Did the Chippewa Indians, pursuant to the Treaty of 1836, in ceding their title to the territory involved, reserve the right to fish in the waters where defendant was arrested?
(2) If such fishing rights were reserved by the Chippewas in the Treaty of 1836, were these rights relinquished by the Treaty of 1855?
(3) If the Chippewas continue to possess reserved fishing rights, may the State of Michigan regulate the exercise of those rights, and if so, to what extent? We hold that the Chippewa Indians did reserve fishing rights in the waters where defendant was arrested pursuant to the Treaty of 1836, that these fishing rights were not relinquished by the Treaty of 1855, and that the State of Michigan has limited authority to regulate those rights, as described below.

Specifically, with regard to the State's authority to regulate off-reservation fishing rights, the state regulation is valid only if:
1) it is necessary for the preservation of the fish protected by the regulation;
2) the application of the regulation to the Indians holding the off-reservation fishing right is necessary for the preservation of the fish protected;
3) and the regulation does not discriminate against the treaty Indians.

Pursuant to these holdings, we affirm the Court of Appeals reversal of defendant LeBlanc's conviction for fishing without a commercial license, and affirm the Court of Appeals remand to the district court on the charge of fishing with an illegal device for a determination of whether the state prohibition of gill nets meets the standards for state regulation of off-reservation fishing rights and whether defendant LeBlanc's second conviction must stand or fall. The standards for these determinations are outlined in this opinion.

I—FACTS

Defendant LeBlanc has not disputed that he was fishing commercially without a license and with a gill net at the time of his arrest.

That arrest took place on September 28, 1971 in Pendills Bay of Lake Superior, a part of Whitefish Bay. [See Appendix-Map I] *(here omitted)*

At trial before District Court Judge Lambros, defendant's sole defense was that he had a right to fish free from State regulations and control pursuant to the Treaty of 1836.

He was found guilty of engaging in commercial fishing without a license under M.C.L.A. § 308.22; M.S.A. § 13.1513 and of fishing with an illegal device under M.C.L.A. § 302.1; M.S.A. § 13.1602.

These convictions were affirmed by the Circuit Court of Chippewa County on December 27, 1972.

The Court of Appeals, however, granted leave, and in October of 1974 reversed defendant's conviction for fishing commercially without a license, holding that the application of the license requirement conflicted with defendant's treaty rights, and remanded the case to district court for a determination of whether the prohibition of gill nets is necessary to prevent a substantial depletion of the fish supply. Under the Court of Appeals decision, if the State does not meet the burden of proving that the prohibition against gill nets is necessary to prevent a substantial depletion of the fish supply on remand, then the defendant's conviction under M.C.L.A. § 302.1; M.S.A. § 13.1602 must also be reversed.

Both the People and defendant LeBlanc applied for leave to appeal to the Supreme Court, leave being granted on February 26, 1975.

The People appeal the Court of Appeals holding that the Chippewas reserved "* * * fishing rights in all the waters adjoining those lands ceded by the treaty [of 1836] and that such rights were not relinquished by any provision of the Treaty of 1855." Defendant LeBlanc challenges the Court of Appeals holding that the State may regulate the manner of taking fish if the regulation is " * * * necessary to prevent a substantial depletion of the fish supply * * *."

II—RESERVED FISHING RIGHTS
UNDER THE TREATY OF 1836

The Treaty of 1836 was negotiated by the United States with the Chippewa and Ottawa Indians in Michigan as part of an official policy of removing Indians from their traditional homelands and resettling them west of the Mississippi, beyond the borders of the rapidly expanding civilization of non-Indian Americans.*

[*By the act of May 28, 1830, 4 Stat. 411, Congress officially established the policy of exchanging federal lands west of the Mississippi for other lands then held by Indian tribes.]

In Article First of this particular treaty, the Chippewas and the Ottawas ceded to the United States territory now constituting roughly the northern third of Michigan's Lower Peninsula and the eastern half of its Upper Peninsula.* [See Appendix—Map II] *(map omitted)*

[Article First of the Treaty of 1836 is quoted in its entirety in footnote 7, infra.]

In exchange, the Chippewas and Ottawas were to receive certain monetary payment for a period of years, and certain land to the southwest of the Missouri river where they were to find their "final settlement."

Under the treaty, the Chippewas reserved certain rights. Defendant LeBlanc based his claim of treaty fishing rights on two alternative grounds arising out of two separate treaty provisions, Article Thirteenth and Article Third.

In Article Thirteenth, the Chippewas retained certain rights in the area ceded pursuant to Article First:

"*Article Thirteenth.* The Indians stipulate for the right of hunting on the lands ceded, with the other usual privileges of occupancy, until the land is required for settlement."

Defendant LeBlanc argues first that rights reserved in Article Thirteenth include the right to fish.

In Article Third, the Chippewas reserved certain areas along the coast of the Great Lakes, including a large area in the Upper Peninsula which encompassed the present day site of the Bay Mills Reservation, home of defendant LeBlanc. It is argued second that Pendills Bay, where defendant was arrested, was included in the area reserved by the Chippewas in Article Third and is part of the present day Bay Mills Reservation.*

[*Defendant first raised the argument that he was within the confines of the Bay Mills Reservation when arrested on application to the Court of Appeals for rehearing. This application was denied.]

The District Court and the Court of Appeals concluded that defendant LeBlanc did hold off-reservation fishing rights pursuant to Article Thirteenth.*

[*The lower courts reached no conclusion as to the effect of Article Third because defendant did not raise this issue before them.]

We agree with this conclusion and reject defendant's argument that Pendills Bay is part of the present day Bay Mills Reservation.

A. ARTICLE THIRTEENTH OF THE TREATY OF 1836.

In construing Article Thirteenth of the Treaty of 1836, we are constrained to follow certain well-settled rules of construction for interpretation of Indian treaties established by the United State[s] Supreme Court.

[1] First, the Supreme Court has held that, so far as is possible, Indian treaties must be interpreted as the Indians would have understood them. The foundation of this rule of construction was explained in *Jones v. Meehan,* 175 U.S. 1, 10-11, 20 S.Ct. 1, 44 L.Ed. 49 (1899), as follows:

> "In construing any treaty between the United States and an Indian tribe, it must always * * * be borne in mind that the negotiations for the treaty are conducted, on the part of the United States, an [sic] enlightened and powerful nation, by representatives skilled in diplomacy, masters of a written language, understanding the modes and forms of creating the various technical estates known to their law, and assisted by an interpreter employed by themselves; that the treaty is drawn up by them and in their own language; that the Indians, on the other hand, are a weak and dependent people, who have no written language and are wholly unfamiliar with all forms of legal expression, and whose only knowledge of the terms in which the treaty is framed is that imparted to them by the interpreter employed by the United States; and that the *treaty must therefore be construed,* not according to the technical meaning of its words to learned lawyers, but *in the sense in which they would naturally be understood by the Indians."* (Emphasis added.) 175 U.S. 1, 10-11, 20 S.Ct. at 5.

The United States Supreme Court has recently reaffirmed this rule of construction in *Choctaw Nation v. Oklahoma,* 397 U.S. 620, 631, 90 S.Ct. 1328, 25 L.Ed.2d 615; *reh. den.* 398 U.S. 945, 90 S.Ct. 1834, 26 L.Ed.2d 285 (1970).

[2] Second, the United States Supreme Court has directed that ambiguities found in Indian treaties are to be resolved in favor of the Indians. See *McClanahan v. Arizona State Tax Commission,* 411 U.S. 164, 174, 93 S.Ct. 1257, 36 L.Ed.2d 129 (1973); *Carpenter v. Shaw,* 280 U.S. 363, 367, 50 S.Ct. 121, 74 L.Ed. 478 (1930); *Winters v. United States,* 207 U.S. 564, 576-577, 28 S.Ct. 207, 52 L.Ed. 340 (1908); *People v. Jondreau,* 384 Mich. 539, 544, 185 N.W.2d 375 (1971). As explained in these cases, the Indians were an unlettered people who were not on equal footing with the United States government in their treaty negotiations. It should therefore not be expected that they would have protected themselves against ambiguities in the treaty language. Given this inequitable bargaining situation, fairness demands that any ambiguity be resolved in favor of the Indians.

[3] Applying these rules of construction to the language of Article Thirteenth of the Treaty of 1836, we can only come to the conclusion that the Chippewas reserved their fishing rights

in the territory ceded to the United States.

The record below clearly indicates that fishing was central to the Chippewa way of life at the time the Treaty of 1836 was negotiated. Part of the extensive and uncontroverted evidence of this fact included a 1836 report by the Acting Superintendent of Michigan for Indian Affairs to the Commissioner of Indian Affairs stating in part as follows:

> "The Chippewas cultivate corn and potatoes to a limited extent, but devote most of their time in quest of food in the chase or in fishing." [District Court transcript, p. 57]

Clearly too, Chippewa fishing had a commercial dimension. In fact, Article Fourth of the Treaty of 1836 provided for the delivery of 10,000 fish barrels and 2,000 barrels of salt to the Indians over a twenty year period to be used in the fishing business.*

> [*The pertinent portion of Article Fourth reads as follows:
> "In consideration of the foregoing cessions, the United State engage to pay to the Ottawa and Chippewa nations, the following sums, namely . . . 6th . . . one hundred barrels of salt, and five hundred fish barrels, annually, for twenty years."
> The importance of commercial fishing in this area at the time of the Treaty of 1836 is well-described in a letter from Henry Schoolcraft, author of "Personal Memoirs of a Residence of Thirty Years with the Indians Tribes . . . A.D. 1812 to A.D. 1842."
> "The number of fishing stations about the coast is numerous, and the points where fish are taken are annually increasing, under the incipient enterprise of the inhabitants. It would be difficult to estimate the present value of this trade to commerce. Several thousands of barrels of fish are put up annually. One thousand barrels were brought from Lake Superior to the present season. The waters of this lake are probably destined to yield an exhaustless supply of this article. Twenty thousand dollars worth of fish may be expected to be barreled in the upper lakes the present year. (District Court transcript, pp. 55-56)]

Given the central position of fishing, both subsistence and commercial, in the Chippewa culture during the time period of the Treaty of 1836, there can be little doubt that the Indian stipulation in Article Thirteenth "for the right of hunting on the lands ceded, with the other usual privileges, of occupancy" was understood by the Chippewas to include the right to fish.

This conclusion is buttressed by the recognition that provisions allowing the Indians to fish on ceded lands were included in treaties with Michigan Indian tribes as a matter of course.*

> [*For example, in the Treaty of Detroit, November 17, 1807 (7 Stat. 105, 2 Kapp 92, Article V provided: ". . . Indian nations shall enjoy the privilege of hunting and fishing on the lands ceded as aforesaid, as long as they remain the property of the United States."
> For similar provisions see: Treaty of Greenville, August 3, 1795 (7 Stat. 49, 2 Kapp 39), Article VII; Treaty of Fort Industry, July 4, 1805 (7 Stat. 87, 2 Kapp 77), Article VI; Treaty of Brownstown, November 25, 1808 (7 Stat. 112, 2 Kapp 99), Article IV; Treaty of Miami Rapids, September 29, 1817 (7 Stat. 160, 2 Kapp 145), Article 11; Treaty of Saginaw, September 24, 1819 (7 Stat. 203, 2 Kapp 185) Article 5; Treaty of Chicago, August 29, 1821 (7 Stat. 218, 2 Kapp 198), Article 5.]

Moreover, our interpretation of Article Thirteenth is consistent with the United States Supreme Court's holding in *Menominee Tribe of Indians v. United States,* 391 U.S. 404, 405-406, 88 S.Ct. 1705, 1707, 20 L.Ed.2d 697 (1968), that the phrase ". . . to be held as Indian lands are held . . ." in the Treaty of Wolf River included the right to hunt and fish.

The People argue that even if this interpretation of Article Thirteenth is correct, defendant LeBlanc does not possess reserved fishing rights pursuant to the Treaty of 1836 for two reasons:

(1) The Chippewas and the Ottawas did not hold aboriginal title to the waters of the Great Lakes within the boundaries outlined in Article First of the Treaty of 1836, and therefore did not cede the waters of the Great Lakes to the United States in the Treaty of 1836. Since defendant LeBlanc was arrested in a bay in Lake Superior, it is argued that he cannot claim to be protected from state regulation by fishing rights reserved in the lands ceded in the Treaty of 1836.

(2) Any fishing rights reserved in territory ceded in the Treaty of 1836 have terminated pursuant to the phrase "until the land is required for settlement" in Article Thirteenth.

With regard to the People's first claim, we conclude that the Chippewas did in fact hold aboriginal title at least to the area in which defendant LeBlanc was arrested.

[4] The concept of aboriginal title, sometimes called Indian title, describes the non-treaty possessory rights of American natives to territory which they had continually occupied before the advent of white civilization.

The principles of aboriginal title were first put forth by Chief Justice Marshall in *Johnson v. McIntosh,* 21 U.S. 543, 8 Wheat 543, 5 L.Ed. 681 (1823) in terms that were recently reaffirmed by the United States Supreme Court in *Oneida Indian Nation v. County of Oneida,* 414 U.S. 661, 667, 94 S.Ct. 772, 777, 39 L.Ed.2d 73 (1974), as follows

> "It very early became accepted doctrine in this Court that although fee title to the lands occupied by Indians when the colonists arrived became vested in the sovereign—first the discovering European nation and later the original States and the United States—a right of occupancy in the Indian tribes was nevertheless recognized. That right, sometimes called Indian title and good against all but the sovereign, could be terminated only by sovereign act. Once the United States was organized and the Constitution adopted, these tribal rights to Indian lands became the exclusive province of the federal law. Indian title, recognized to be only a right of occupancy was extinguishable only by the United States."

[5] The corollary of the power of the United States to extinguish the Indian's aboriginal title is the power of the United States to determine which Indian tribes rightfully held aboriginal title. *Cramer v. United States,* 261 U.S. 219, 227, 43 S.Ct. 342, 67 L.Ed. 622 (1923), quoted with approval in *United States v. Santa Fe Pacific R. Co.,* 314 U.S. 339, 345, 62 S.Ct. 248, 86 L.Ed.2d 260 (1941), and *Oneida Indian Nation v. County of Oneida, supra.* This determination was often made in treaties either extinguishing or recognizing the aboriginal title of a certain tribe of Indians.

[6] In examining Article First and Article Third of the Treaty of 1836, it is undeniable that the United States, in negotiating that treaty, recognized the aboriginal title of the Ottawa and the Chippewa in at least certain waters of the Great Lakes. For example, in the segment of Article Third quoted above, it is written that the Chippewas reserve certain territory "including the small islands and the fishing grounds, in front of this reservation." The fishing grounds referred to are in Lake Superior.

Moreover, the area described in Article First, that being the territory ceded by the Ottawas and the Chippewas to the United States, extends well into the Great Lakes.*

> [*Article One in its entirety reads as follows:
> "The Ottawa and Chippewa nations of Indians cede to the United States all the tract of country within the following boundaries: Beginning at the mouth of Grand river of Lake Michigan on the

north bank thereof and following up the same to the line called for, in the first article of the treaty of Chicago of the 29th of August 1821, thence, in a direct line, to the head of Thunder-bay river, thence with the line established by the treaty of Saginaw of the 24th of September 1819, to the mouth of said river, thence northeast to the boundary line in Lake Huron between the United States and the British province of Upper Canada, thence northwestwardly following the said line, as established by the commissioners acting under the treaty of Ghent, through the straits, and river St. Mary's, to a point in Lake Superior north of the mouth of Gitchy Seebing, or Chocolate river, thence south to the mouth of said river and up its channel to the source thereof, thence, in a direct line to the head of the Skonawba river of Green bay, thence down the south bank of said river to its mouth, thence, in a direct line, through the ship channel into Green bay, to the outer part thereof, thence south to a point in Lake Michigan, west of the north cape, or entrance of Grand river, and thence east to the place of beginning, at the cape aforesaid, comprehending all the lands and islands, within these limits, not hereinafter reserved." [*See Map 11*] (map omitted; same as in *United States v. Michigan*, below)

For example, the ceded area is bounded in part by a line traveling from the mouth of the Thunder-Bay river, "thence northeast to the boundary line *in Lake Huron* * * * thence northwestwardly, * * * *through the straits,* and river St. Mary's, *to a point in Lake Superior* north of the mouth of *Gitchy Seebing,* or Chocolate river * *" (emphasis added).

While we have no difficulty in concluding that the aboriginal title of the Indians did in fact extend into the Great Lakes, contrary to the allegations of the People, we cannot conclude that the Chippewas *alone* had aboriginal title in the *entire* area described in Article First of the Treaty of 1836.

[7] The difficulty is that two different Indian "nations" ceded the described territory to the United States, the Chippewas and the Ottawas. Unfortunately, it is not at all evident from the language of the treaty which ceded areas had been occupied by the Ottawas and which by the Chippewas.

In such a circumstance, the existence of aboriginal title in a particular Indian tribe becomes a question of fact involving a judicial determination that the tribe claiming such title occupied exclusively the territory at issue. *United States v. Santa Fe Pacific R. Co., supra,* 314 U.S. 339, 345, 62 S.Ct. 248, 86 L.Ed. 260. This determination is to he made with reference to the habits and modes of life of the Indian tribes involved. *Mitchel v. United States,* 34 U.S. (9 Pet.) 711, 746, 9 L.Ed. 283 (1835).

[8] In the instant case, it is not necessary to determine all the segments of the ceded area to which the Chippewas, as opposed to the Ottawas, had held aboriginal title. Defendant LeBlanc was arrested in Pendills Bay, a part of Whitefish Bay about 20 miles West of Sault Ste. Marie. Judge Lambros concluded that the Chippewas had retained fishing rights pursuant to their aboriginal title in Pendills Bay, and that conclusion is both reasonable and sufficient for this case.

The record developed at trial and the language of the Treaty of 1836 itself leave no doubt that Pendills Bay was part of that area of the Upper Peninsula that the Chippewas had long occupied exclusive of other tribes.

In this regard, for example, it is significant that evidence was presented at trial that the Indian legend of the genesis of the Chippewas tribe is rooted in the Sault Ste. Marie area. In that legend, a pair of cranes created by the great spirit chose the Sault Ste. Marie area as their nesting place because of the plentiful supply of fish to be found there. Upon coming to rest, the two cranes were transformed into a man and a woman who were the progenitors of the

Chippewa clan in that area.*

> [*See District court transcript pp. 52-53. This legend is recited in Indian Myths, a book by Ellen Russel Emerson published in 1965 (Ross & Haines, Minneapolis).]

The aboriginal title of the Chippewas in the area was recognized in the Treaty of June 16, 1820 where the Chippewas ceded to the United States sixteen square miles on the St. Mary's River while reserving a "permanent reserve" and "perpetual fishing right" at the falls of St. Mary's.*

> [*See Article 3 of the Treaty of 1820:
>
> "The United States will secure to the Indians a perpetual right of fishing at the falls of St. Mary's and also a place of encampment upon the tract hereby ceded, convenient to the fishing ground, which place shall not interfere with the defences of any military work which may be erected, nor with any private rights."]

Finally the aboriginal title of the Chippewas in the Pendills Bay area was recognized by the United States in the Treaty of 1836 itself. As noted above, Article Third of the Treaty of 1836 reserved certain areas for the Chippewas alone,*

> [*Article Second of the Treaty of 1836 reserved certain territory for the Ottawas and Chippewas in common.]

which included a reservation encompassing Pendills Bay.*

> [*See the quoted segment of Article Third on (the following pages) of this opinion.]

The location of this reservation was in obvious recognition of the long standing occupancy of the Chippewas of this area.

It is little wonder, then, that in the face of this, and other evidence, the People did not dispute at trial that the area in which defendant had been arrested had been Chippewa country at the time of the Treaty of 1836.

We thus conclude with the district court that the area in which defendant was arrested was territory in which the Chippewas had reserved fishing rights pursuant to the Treaty of 1836, and reject the People's argument to the contrary.

There remains, however, the People's second contention, i.e., that any fishing rights reserved under Article Thirteen have been terminated pursuant to the phrase "* * * until the land is required for settlement."

[9] Undoubtedly this clause was intended to protect the right of non-Indians to settle in the ceded area without interference from Chippewas claiming "the usual privileges of occupancy," and has limited the rights of the Chippewas to hunt. However, the ceded water areas of the Great Lakes have obviously not been required for settlement, and therefore the fishing rights reserved by the Chippewas in these areas have not been terminated.

In sum then, we hold, in agreement with the District Court and the Court of Appeals, that the Treaty of 1836, pursuant to Article Thirteenth reserved for the Chippewas fishing rights in the waters where defendant was arrested.

B. ARTICLE THIRD OF THE TREATY OF 1836.

[10] Defendant LeBlanc has argued in the alternative before this court that when arrested in Pendills Bay, he was within the Bay Mills Reservation, was thus exercising on-reservation fishing rights, and was therefore protected from the application of the state regulations he has been convicted of breaking.*

> [*We recognize that this argument was not raised or argued before the district court. It was

raised for the first time by the defendant upon application for rehearing to the Court of Appeals.

Ordinarily, we do not consider legal theories not raised at trial. However, where, as here, the legal theory rests upon undisputed facts (i.e. defendant's arrest in Pendills Bay), the parties have had the opportunity to fully brief the legal issue involved (i.e. the continued validity of the reservations created in Article Third of the Treaty of 1836), and the reviewing court can reach a reasonable conclusion upon evidence contained in the record, the reviewing court may decide the issue in the interest of justice and judicial efficiency. As stated in Dation v. Ford Motor Co., *314 Mich. 152, 160-161 22 N.W.2d 252, 255 (1946): "The general rule that a question may not be raised for the first time on appeal to this Court is not inflexible. When consideration of a claim sought to be raised is necessary to a proper determination of a case, such rule will not be applied." See also* Felcoskie v. Lakey Foundry Corporation, *382 Mich. 438, 442, 170 N.W.2d 129 (1969);* Dolske v. Gormley, *58 Cal.2d 513, 25 Cal.Rptr. 270, 375 P.2d 174 (1962);* Panopulos v. Maderis, *47 Cal.2d 337, 303 P.2d 738 (1956);* In re Lee's Estate, *49 Wash.2d 254, 299 P.2d 1066 (1956).*

In the instant case, it is necessary to determine whether defendant was on a reservation or not when arrested because it might affect the right of the state to regulate his fishing activity. See, for example, Menominee Tribe v. United States, *supra;* Kimball v. Callahan, *493 F.2d 564 (CA 9, 1974);* Moore v. United States, *157 F.2d 760 (CA 9, 1946), cert. den. 330 U.S. 827, 67 S.Ct. 867, 91 L.Ed 1277 (1947)]*

This argument is grounded in Article Third of the Treaty of 1836 which established nine reservations for the Chippewas along the coast of the Great Lakes. One of the reservations created was a large area in the Upper Peninsula apparently including Pendills Bay. That reservation was created in Article Third as follows:

"ARTICLE THIRD. There shall also be reserved for the use of the Chippewas living north of the straits of Michilimackinac, the following tracts for the term of five years from the date of the ratification of this treaty, and no longer, unless the United States shall grant them permission to remain on said lands for a longer period, that is to say * * * A tract commencing at the mouth of the *Pississowining* river, south of Point Iroquois, thence running up said stream to its forks, thence westward, in a direct line to the Red water lakes, thence across the portage to the Tacquimenon river, and down the same to its mouth, *including the small islands and fishing grounds, in front of this reservation.*" (Emphasis added.) *[footnote reference to Map II omitted.]*

Defendant argues that the portion of the reservation created in the quoted language of Article Third constituting the "fishing grounds in front of this reservation" was not terminated after the five year period provided for, given the continued presence of the Chippewas in the area since the Treaty of 1836 and that Article Third remain effective to the extent that it established Pendills Bay as part of the present day Bay Mills Reservation.

We reject this argument and conclude that Pendills Bay is not part of the Bay Mills Reservation.

Defendant is correct in stating that the United States at least tacitly permitted the Chippewas to remain on the reservations created in Article Third of the Treaty of 1836 long after the five year period set out in that provision. Evidence of this fact is found in a letter written by George Manypenny, Commissioner of Indian Affairs, on May 21, 1855 urging a new treaty:

"Firstly, as regards the Ottawas and Chippewas in the State of Michigan, that I am of the opinion that an officer or officers of this Department should be designated by the President, to negotiated [sic] with the Indians, with a view of adjusting all matters now in an unsettled condition; and making proper arrangements for their permanent residence in that State.

"It was anticipated that after a few years, these Indians would remove southwest of the Mississippi, hence the provision of a home for them there, as per Article 8 of the treaty and the Senate's amendment thereto, *but they were not limited by the treaty to any time within which they should remove to avail themselves of the homes thus provided.*

"They have never emigrated west, but have continued to hold the reservations described in the 2d and 3d articles of the treaty which have accordingly been withheld from sale, to accommodate the Indians.

"Measures should now be taken in my judgment to secure permanent homes to the Ottawas and Chippewas either on the reservations, or on other lands in Michigan belonging to the government. * * *" [See Supplement Appendix, p. 7b] (Emphasis added.)

However, the permission to remain on the reservations created in Article Third of the Treaty of 1836 ended with the Treaty of 1855. In the Treaty of 1855, the United States recognizing the failure of its removal policy, moved to create permanent homes for the Chippewas pursuant to Article One of that treaty as is indicated in the letter quoted above.

In accordance with Article One of the Treaty of July 31, 1855 and the Indian Appropriation Act of June 19, 1860 (12 Stat. 58), the United States government purchased 527.85 acres of land within the area reserved in Article Third of the Treaty of 1836 from the Methodist Mission Society to be held in trust for the Chippewa Indians. This land, along with 1053.91 acres purchased in 1937 pursuant to Indian Reorganization Act, 48 Stat. 984 (1934) constitutes the Bay Mills Reservation. Pendills Bay is about 10 miles west of the westernmost boundary of the Bay Mills Reservation.

[11] In establishing new homes for the Chippewas pursuant to the Treaty of July 31, 1855, the United States terminated its permission to retain the reservations created in Article Third of the Treaty of 1836, including the reservation apparently containing Pendills Bay.

We hold then, that Pendills Bay is not part of the present-day Bay Mills Reservation, and that defendant LeBlanc was not exercising an on reservation fishing right when arrested.

III—The Treaty of July 31, 1855

[12] The People argue that any fishing rights reserved by the Chippewas in the Treaty of 1836 under Article Thirteenth were extinguished by the Treaty of 1855 pursuant to Article Three of that treaty.

The pertinent language from the Treaty of 1855 reads as follows:

"In view of the existing condition of the Ottawas and Chippewas, and of their legal and equitable claims against the United States, it is agreed between the contracting parties as following:

Article 3. *The Ottawa and Chippewa Indians hereby release and discharge the United States from all liability on account of former treaty stipulations,* it being distinctly understood and agreed that the grants and payments hereinbefore provided for are *in lieu and satisfaction of all claims, legal and equitable on the part of said Indians* jointly and severally against the United States, *for land, money or other thing guaranteed to said tribes* or either of them by the stipulations of any former treaty or treaties, excepting, however, the right of fishing and encampment secured to the Chippewas of Sault Ste. Marie by the treaty of June 16, 1820." (Emphasis added.)

It is the theory of the People that any fishing rights reserved under Article Thirteenth of the Treaty of 1836 constitute a "liability" or "claims * * * for land, money or other thing" released in Article Three of the Treaty of 1855.

The Court of Appeals found that such an interpretation gave the treaty language "* * * a meaning wholly at odds with what appears to have been intended by the parties to be encompassed within the terms of this provision." 55 Mich.App. 684, 688, 223 N.W.2d 305, 307 (1974). Moreover, the Court of Appeals concluded that an interpretation which strained to equate a reserved fishing right with a liability or claim for land, money or other thing would be completely at odds with the rules of construction mandated by the United States Supreme Court in *Worcester v. Georgia,* 31 U.S. (6 Pet.) 515, 8 L.Ed. 483 (1832), and by this Court in *People v. Jondreau, supra:*

> "The language used in treaties with the Indians should never be construed to their prejudice. * * * How the words of the treaty were understood by this unlettered people, rather than their critical meaning, should form the rule of construction." 384 Mich. 539, 544, 185 N.W.2d 375, 377, quoting from *Worcester v. Georgia, supra.*

We fully agree with the Court of Appeals on this issue. An examination of the minutes of the negotiations preceding the Treaty of 1855 clearly indicate that the interpretation of Article Three of that treaty asserted by the People would conflict not only with the rules of construction mandated for Indian treaties, but also the clear intent of the parties.

The Treaty of 1855 was negotiated within the context of the failure of the removal policy of the United States and the dissatisfaction of the Chippewas and the Ottawas with the perceived failure of the United States to fulfill certain promises made.

The tenor of the treaty negotiations was set in the introductory remarks of the Commissioner of Indian Affairs, Hon. Geo. W. Manypenny:

> "There were two delegations of Ottawas and Chippeways at Washington last winter, each making nearly the same enquiries concerning the affairs of their people. They each had the impression that there was unsettled business under the older treaties running back as far as 1795. * * * I directed the acting commissioner, when I left Washington from which place I have been absent four or five weeks, to examine & if he found any default in the fulfillment of the old treaties by Government, to advise me of it. The fact in relation to your business, accords with the fair presumption, because it is a fair presumption, that when the treaty of 1836 was made all questions, growing out of previous treaties, of an unsettled character, were adjusted. With this general remark I now say, that notwithstanding this fair presumption, if it shall appear that there is still anything actually due to you under the old treaties, you may rely upon my efforts to obtain it for you." (pp. 3-4 of typed transcript of the negotiation of the Treaty of 1855)

After listening to the inquiries and complaints of the Indians present, Agent Henry C. Gilbert responded on behalf of the United States as follows:

> "Listen to me until I reply to your questions. We have talked a great deal today. What we could, we have answered & explained to you.
>
> But after all the interests you are here to take care of are in a small compass. I have examined

the old treaties carefully & can find nothing in them that you are entitled to except, the amount of $1700 permanent annuity, referred to this morning. With that exception all your claims against the U. S. are based upon the treaty of 1836. And now I will state what we think is due to you under that treaty.

"1st. The sum of $200,000 for your reservations.

"Then comes the sum of $20,000 reserved annuity, with the Interest. Then there is the value of their improvements as appraised. There may be something due on that fund.

"These are all the funds, on which anything remains unpaid in which you have any interest & the manner in which the gross amount shall be paid is one of the most important things we have come here to consider. Then there is the question in regard to lands. The Government is willing to provide you with homes & is willing that those homes shall be in the State of Michigan." (pp. 20-21 of typed transcript of the Treaty minutes)

There is not the slightest indication in this portion of the negotiations, or in the minutes of the negotiations in their entirety that the Treaty of 1855 would affect hunting or fishing rights reserved under the Treaty of 1836.

The same may be said of an excerpt of a letter sent by the Indian agents negotiating the Treaty of 1855 to the Acting Commissioner of Indian Affairs summarizing the impact of the treaty as follows:

"In consideration therefore of the difference of the value of the western lands, and the home now secured to the Indians in Michigan and in the release and discharge of the United States from all claims or demands on account thereof, or on account of removal thereto and subsistence, or an account of the claims for 'articles and equipments to each person' and also in discharge and full satisfaction of the $200,000 stipulated to be paid them in lieu of the reservations by the Senate's amendment to the 4th Article of the treaty of 1836, and in like discharge of the sum which has accumulated from the investment of the $1,000 per annum, provided for by the 4th article of the treaty aforesaid, and in discharge of the $1,700 permanent annuity due to the Ottawas and heretofore specifically allud-èd to; in fact, in lieu and satisfaction of all claims, legal or equitable, on the part of said Indians joint-ly and severally against the United States for land, money or other things guaranteed to them or either of them by the stipulations of any former treaty or treaties (excepting the right of fishing and encamp-ment secured to the Chippewas of Sault Ste. Marie by the treaty of June 16, 1820) the United States are to pay them or expend for their benefit, the sum of $534,400 in manner following, viz:— * * *

[*The special exclusion of the right of fishing and encampment secured in this letter and in Article Three of the Treaty of 1855 might be here explained.*

The Chippewas in the Sault Ste. Marie area had long been concerned about maintaining access to their fishing site at St. Mary's Falls, for this site was not only a superb fishery, but also served as an ancestral bury-ing ground. In recognition of this important area to the Chippewas the United States guaranteed a "perma-nent" right to fish and encamp here in the Treaty of 1820. See fn. 9, supra.

However, the fishing site and encampment were destroyed twenty three years later when the St. Mary's ship canal was constru[ct]ed, leading to demands for compensation by the Chippewas. See the letter from George H. Manypenny and Henry c. Gilbert, Commissioners, to the Department of the Interior, Office of Indian Affairs, dated August 7, 1855.

The controversy was not settled in the Treaty of July 31, 1855, as the quoted exclusion clause makes clear. A separate agreement, on August 2, 1855, dealt with this issue.]

While it is conceivable that the United States intended "claims * * * for other things" in the Treaty of 1855 to refer to fishing rights reserved by the Chippewas in the Treaty of 1836, such seems highly unlikely given the complete absence of any discussion of the termination of such rights in the treaty negotiations.

In any case, it is clear that the Chippewas and the Ottawas would not have understood Article Three of the Treaty of 1855 to terminate hunting and fishing rights reserved in the Treaty of 1836 given the absence of any mention of such prospect.

The Indian representatives present at the discussions preceding the Treaty of 1855 put their trust in the white men who represented the President of the United States, whom they referred to as "great father," as is indicated by the following statements found in the treaty minutes:

> *"Pay bah me say* [one of the Chippewa representatives] I have listened to all that has been said. In regard to this proposal I have the lost the light. As you have listened to what the Chippeways say in regard to this tax matter, we have the same views upon that point. *You are wise. You know what is right. We therefore present ourselves to you to take what you regard best."* (pp. 31-32 of typed transcript of the minutes of the treaty negotiations, emphasis added)

> *"Pay bah me say.* I wish to say a few words more to my father [*i. e.* the Commissioner of Indian Affairs]. I wish to tell him, what our older chiefs determined, before I went to see him at Washington last winter. Before we went we had council and consulted about the treaties and about what we should ask of you, and we all said we were ignorant like children, lost in the woods that we knew not where to go nor how far it is to the water or the prairie. And the chiefs in those meetings said we are not anything, but the white man is like a tall tree; he can see the prairie and the water over everything afar off.

> He can look and behold all the nations of the world. And we further said that we had an agent now whom we like, because he has treated us well since he has been with us. * * * I speak the mind of all the Indians and not mine own alone."

People such as these certainly would not have expected the white men whom they perceived as wise, trustworthy and concerned about their best interest, to terminate important rights preserved in the Treaty of 1836 without so much as mentioning such termination. Given, then, the rules of construction mandating that a treaty should be interpreted as the Indians understood it, and that the language of the treaty should not be read to the prejudice of the Indians, we will not strain the language of Article Three of the Treaty of 1855 to mean that reserved fishing rights pursuant to the Treaty of 1836 were terminated.

[13] Our conclusion is buttressed by the directive of the United States Supreme Court that "the intention to abrogate or modify a treaty is not to be lightly imputed." *Menominee Tribe v. United States, supra,* 391 U.S. 404, 413, 88 S.Ct. 1705, 1711, 20 L.Ed.2d 697.

IV—The Authority of the State to Regulate Chippewa Fishing Rights

Having determined that the Chippewa Indians reserved fishing rights in the waters where defendant was arrested pursuant to the Treaty of 1836, and that those rights survived the Treaty of 1855, we must now determine the proper scope of State regulation of these rights.

The scope of proper state regulation of off-reservation rights has been the subject of a good deal of controversy.*

[*For the discussion of commentators on the scope of Indian fishing rights, see the following: Comment, Indian Treaty Analysis and Off-Reservation Fishing Rights: A Case Study, 51 Wash.L.Rev. 61 (1975); R. Johnson, The State Versus Indian Off-Reservation Fishing: A United States Supreme Court Error, 47 Wash.L. Rev. 207 (197Z); Comment, Indian Law—State Regulation—Hunting and Fishing Rights, 18 N.Y.L., Forum 442 (1972); Comment, State Power and the Indian Treaty Right to Fish, 59 Cal.L.Rev. 485 (1971); Hobbs, Indian Hunting and Fishing Rights, 32 Geo.Wash.L.Rev. 504 (1964).]

However, for purposes of this case, two important United States Supreme Court cases should be the focus of our attention, *Tulee v. Washington,* 315 U.S. 681, 62 S.Ct. 862, 86 L.Ed. 1115 (1942), and *Puyallup Tribe v. Department of Game,* 391 U.S. 392, 88 S.Ct. 1725, 20 L.Ed.2d 689 (1968).

In *Tulee,* defendant, a Yakima Indian, was charged and convicted of catching salmon with a net without first having obtained a license. Defendant argued that a treaty between the United States and the Yakima tribe entitled him to fish without a license off the reservation in the areas specified by the treaty.

The Supreme Court agreed, holding that the state was without power to charge a Yakima Indian a fee for exercising his off-reservation treaty fishing rights.*

[*The holding of the Court was expressed as follows:

"Viewing the treaty in this light, we are of the opinion that the state is without power to charge the Yakimas a fee for fishing. A stated purpose of the licensing act was to provide for 'the support of the state government and its existing public institutions.' Laws of Washington. 1937, c. 149, pp. 529, 534. The license fees prescribed are regulatory as well as revenue producing. But it is clear that their regulatory purpose could be accomplished otherwise, that the imposition of license fees is not indispensable to the effectiveness of a state conservation program. Even though this method may be both convenient and, in its general impact, fair, it acts upon the Indians as a charge for exercising the very right their ancestors intended to reserve. We believe that such exaction of fees as a prerequisite to the enjoyment of fishing in the 'usual and accustomed places' cannot be reconciled with a fair construction of the treaty. We therefore hold the state statute invalid as applied in this case." 315 U.S. 681, 685, 62 S.Ct. 862, 864, 86 L.Ed. 1115.]

In *Puyallup Tribe,* the Department of Game of Washington brought suit against the Puyallup Indians seeking declaratory relief and an injunction. In the Treaty of Medicine Creek, the Puyallup's off-reservation fishing rights were expressed as follows:

"The right of taking fish, at all usual and accustomed grounds and stations, is further secured to said Indians, in common with all citizens of the Territory * * *."

The United States Supreme Court held as follows:

"[T]he right to fish at those respective places is not an exclusive one. Rather, it is one 'in common with all citizens of the Territory.' Certainly the right of the latter may be regulated. And we see no reason why the right of the Indians may not also be regulated by an appropriate exercise of the police power of the State. The right to fish 'at all usual and accustomed' places may, of course not be qualified by the State, even though all Indians born in the United States are now citizens of the United States. * * * But the manner of fishing, the size of the take, the restriction of commercial fishing, and the like may be regulated by the State in the interest of conservation, provided the regulation meets appropriate standards and does not discriminate against the Indians." 391 U.S. 392, 398, 88 S.Ct. 1725, 1728, 20 L.Ed.2d 689.

Tulee and *Puyallup Tribe* establish the following when applied to the instant case.

[14] First, since the defendant when arrested was exercising off-reservation fishing right pursuant to Article Thirteenth of the Treaty of 1836, the conviction for fishing without a commercial license cannot stand under the authority of *Tulee v. Washington, supra.* Such was the holding of the Court of Appeals, and we affirm that court in its holding on this issue.

[15] Second, defendant's conviction for fishing with an illegal device may stand only if the prohibition of the gill net as applied to the Chippewas meets the standards established in *Puyallup Tribe, supra.*

With regard to this second point, defendant LeBlanc asserts that *Puyallup Tribe* is distinguishable from the instant case in that the treaty in Puyallup provided for off-reservation fishing rights "in common with all citizens of the territory," which the treaty provision in the instant case contains no such stipulation.

[16] We disagree. Article Thirteenth of the Treaty of 1836 provides: "The Indians stipulate for the right of hunting on the lands ceded, with the other usual privileges of occupancy, until the land is required for settlement." Even under the most liberal construction of this language, we cannot conclude that the rights reserved here were *exclusive*. The proviso, ". . . until the land was required for settlement," indicates that the interests and rights of the other citizens of the territory were to be taken into account. Moreover, the Treaty of 1836 had been negotiated with an awareness that statehood was soon forthcoming for Michigan. Michigan in fact became a state in 1837. Certainly then, the territory acquired from the Indians so as to facilitate statehood would not have been so heavily encumbered as to allow the treaty Indians the exclusive "privileges of occupancy."

Thus, in the instant case, as in *Puyallup Tribe, supra,* the Indians hold their off-reservation fishing rights in common with the citizens of the State of Michigan.*

[*This does not imply that the Chippewas are in the same position as all other citizens of Michigan with regard to their fishing rights. The sources of the fishing rights of Chippewas and the rest of the citizenry of Michigan are different, and as stated in Puyallup Tribe, "[t]o construe the treaty as giving the Indians no rights but such as they would have without the treaty' (198 U.S. at 380, 25 S.Ct. at 664) would be 'an impotent outcome to negotiations and a convention, which seemed to promise more and give the word of the Nation for more.'" 391 U.S. 392, 397, 88 S.Ct. 1725, 1728, 20 L.Ed.2d 689. See also Antoine v. Washington, infra.]

Given the applicability of *Puyallup Tribe, supra,* we must remand the second charge to the district court for a determination of whether the prohibition of gill nets as applied to the Chippewas passes muster under the standards of that case. The difficulty in this regard is divining precisely what the State is required to show to successfully defend the constitutionality of its regulation.

The recent case of *Antoine v. Washington,* 420 U.S. 194, 95 S.Ct. 944, 43 L.Ed.2d 129 (1975), helped clarify the standards established in *Puyallup Tribe.* In *Antoine,* defendant

Indians appealed a conviction for hunting and possession of deer during the closed season in an area of a former Indian reservation that the tribe had ceded to the government. In discussing the power of the State to regulate the hunting rights of the Indians, the United States Supreme Court construed *Puyallup Tribe* as follows:

> "In *Puyallup I, supra,* [391 U.S.] at 398, 88 S.Ct. 1725, we held that although the rights 'may * * * not be qualified by the State * * * the manner of fishing [and hunting], the size of the take, the restriction of commercial fishing [and hunting], and the like may be regulated by the State in the interest of conservation, provided the regulation meets appropriate standards and does not discriminate against the Indians.' The 'appropriate standards' requirement means that the State must demonstrate that its regulation is a reasonable and necessary conservation measure [citations omitted] *and that its application to the Indians is necessary in the interest of conservation.*" 420 U.S.194, 207, 95 S.Ct. 944, 952, 43 L.Ed.2d 129.

Thus, under *Antoine v. Washington*, the question in the instant case becomes, first, whether the prohibition of gill nets is a reasonable and necessary conservation measure, and second, whether the prohibition of the use of gill nets by the Chippewas is necessary in the interest of conservation.*

[**In defining "appropriate standards" in these terms, the United States Supreme Court apparently rejected the approach of the 9th Circuit in* Maison v. Confederated Tribes, *314 F.2d 169 (CA 9, 1963), where it was held that the state regulation was required to be indispensable for conservation.*]

A recent Ninth Circuit opinion, *United States v. State of Washington,* 520 F.2d 676 (CA 9, 1975), is significant in that it helped define when a state regulation is necessary for conservation and when such regulation was discriminatory.

In *Washington,* the United States brought suit against the State of Washington to enforce the state's compliance with certain treaties between the United States and various tribes of western Washington.

The court first held that a state regulation was serving conservation of fish under *Puyallup Tribe* only if the regulation served to perpetuate the fish to be protected.*

[* *In* United States v. Washington, *supra, the fishing sites involved were on a river. The state proposed a definition of conservation encompassing three objectives: 1) to allow sufficient escapement of fish to perpetuate the fish run; 2) to assure the maximum sustained harvest of fish; and 3) to provide for an orderly fishery.*

The court rejected the proposed definition as follows:

"[T]he only rationale for permitting state interference with Indian fishing precludes adoption of this definition and restricts the meaning of conservation to insuring optimum spawning escapement for perpetuation of the run. 'Rights can be controlled by the need to conserve a species . . . .' Department of Game of Washington v. Puyallup Tribe (Puyallup 11), *414 U.S. 44, 49, 94 S.Ct. 330, 334, 38 L.Ed.2d 254 (1973)." 520 F.2d 676, 686.*]

Moreover, the court held that the state cannot discriminate against the treaty Indians by forcing treaty Indians to yield their own protected interests in order to promote the welfare of the state's other citizens. Direct regulation of treaty Indian fishing rights is permissible only after the state has proven that it cannot serve conservation by regulating the rights of citizens not possessing treaty fishing rights. 520 F.2d 676, 686.*

[**As noted above this case dealt with fish runs in a river which necessitated the equitable apportionment of the opportunity to fish in order to protect the rights of the treaty Indians and the other citizens of Washington, 520 F.2d 676, 687-88. Such apportionment may not be a necessary* *consideration in the circumstances of this case.*]

See also *Sohappy v. Smith* 302 F.Supp. 899 (D.Or., 1969), for an example of another case taking the approach used in *U.S. v. Washington, supra.*

Finally, in 1971, this Court was confronted with the question of the scope of the state's authority to regulate Indian off-reservation fishing rights in *People v. Jondreau,* 384 Mich. 539, 185 N.W.2d 375 (1971). In this case, defendant Jondreau, a Chippewa Indian, was arrested for possession of trout out of season. Noting that *Puyallup Tribe, supra,* provided that the state could provide for regulation of off-reservation fishing rights which were reasonably necessary for the conservation of fish, we held that the regulation of the time in which the Chippewas exercised their fishing rights was not a valid application of state power, particularly in view of the fact that the treaty in question specifically provided a mechanism for federal regulation of the fishing rights of the Chippewas.

In the light of these cases, we conclude that on remand, the district court should uphold defendant's conviction for fishing with an illegal device only if:

(1) the prohibition of the gill net is necessary for the preservation of the fish protected by the regulation;

(2) the application of this prohibition to the Chippewas is necessary for the preservation of the fish protected;

(3) and the regulation does not discriminate against the Chippewas.

V—Conclusion

We affirm the Court of Appeals reversal of defendant LeBlanc's conviction for fishing without a commercial license. We also affirm the Court of Appeals remand to the District Court on the charge of fishing with an illegal device. The determination on remand of whether the application of the state prohibition against gill nets to the Chippewas is valid should be made in accordance with the standards set out in this opinion.

T. G. KAVANAGH, C. J., and FITZGERALD and RYAN, JJ., concur.

See following illustrations [here omitted]

LINDEMER, Justice (dissenting).

With Justice Williams we agree that the Treaty of 1836 granted the Chippewa Indians the right to fish in Pendills Bay.

We cannot conclude, however, that that Treaty secured that right indefinitely. The rights arising under Article Third were limited "for the term of five years from the date of ratification of this treaty, and no longer; unless the United States shall grant them permission to remain on said lands for a longer period." We are in agreement with Justice Williams that those rights were extinguished by the Treaty of July 31, 1855.

In like manner, the rights established by Article Thirteenth were limited by the language "until the land is required for settlement." Our understanding that these rights were meant to be temporary is also supported by the language of Article Eighth.

"It is agreed, that as soon as the said Indians desire it, a deputation shall be sent to the southwest of the Missouri River, there to select a suitable place with the final settlement of said Indians, which country, so selected in reasonable extent, the United States will forever guaranty and secure to said Indians. * * * When the Indians wish it, the United States will remove them, at their expense, provide them a year's subsistence in the country to which they go, and furnish the same articles and equipments to each person as are stipulated to be given to the Pottowatomies in the final treaty of cession concluded at Chicago."

Article Eighth is a reflection of the United States' policy of removing Indians from their native lands in order to make available new territories for white settlements and to avoid conflicts between Indians and settlers. In light of the Federal government's removal policy and those limitations placed in the Treaty, we must conclude that the fishing rights secured under the Treaty of 1836 were temporary in nature and meant to expire in a short time.

Article Thirteenth fishing rights arise from the language "usual privileges of *occupancy* until the *land* is required for settlement." In our opinion, Article Thirteenth is susceptible of only one interpretation, that is, settlement of the *land* terminates all usual privileges of occupancy associated with the land. In construing Article Thirteenth to include the right to fish we had to conclude that fishing was a usual privilege of occupancy of land. To hold that "the ceded water areas of the Great Lakes have obviously not been required for settlement and therefore the fishing rights reserved by the Chippewas in these areas have not been terminated" is logically inconsistent and strains the treaty language beyond the breaking point. We seriously doubt that the Chippewas would have understood the term "usual privileges of occupancy" to have two different meanings. Nor, considering the Indians' way of life, do we believe that the Chippewas would have thought that the privilege of fishing in a body of water could be separated from the privilege of using the land surrounding or abutting it.

We further conclude that Article 3 of the Treaty of July 31, 1855, extinguished any fishing rights that existed pursuant to Article Thirteenth of the Treaty of 1836. Article 3 reads:

"The Ottawa and Chippewa Indians hereby release and discharge the United States from all liability on account of former treaty stipulations, it being distinctly understood and agreed that the grants and payments hereinbefore provided for are in lieu and satisfaction of all claims, legal and equitable on the part of said Indians jointly and severally against the United States, for land, money or other thing guaranteed to said tribes or either of them by the stipulations of any former treaty or treaties; excepting, however, the right of fishing and encampment secured to the Chippewas of Sault Ste. Marie by the Treaty of June 16, 1820."

We wholeheartedly agree with the Circuit Judge's opinion in that "[s]ince the Treaty of July 31, 1855, specifically provided that grants and payments were in lieu and satisfaction of all claims for land, money or other thing guaranteed by the 'stipulations' of any former treaty, it is difficult to conceive how it could have been made more clear that any special right provided for in a 'stipulation' in the treaty of 1836 was canceled."

The Treaty of July 31, 1855, reflects a marked departure from the policy of removal of the 1836 treaty. The Treaty of 1855 provides for the dissolution of the tribal structure of the Chippewa, sums of money and individual allotments of land to individual Indians, and assistance in the settlement and assimilation of the Chippewa into their new life style as settlers. It provides them with schools, blacksmith shops, agricultural implements, carpenter's tools, household furniture, building materials and cattle.

In *Tulee v. Washington,* 315 U.S. 681, 62 S.Ct. 862, 86 L.Ed. 1115 (1942), the United States Supreme Court examined the negotiations preceding the treaty agreement therein reached and was "impressed by the strong desire the Indians had to retain the right to hunt and fish in accordance with the immemorial customs of their tribes." 315 U.S. at 684, 62 S.Ct. at 864. Here, we have examined the treaty negotiations and find they are bereft of any mention of fishing rights, immemorial or otherwise. Rather, both parties anticipated that the Chippewa were no longer to live as they historically had.

That the Chippewa were to adopt the life style of the citizens of Michigan is indicated not only in the language of the treaty, but also by the expressed anticipations of both parties during the treaty negotiations. Indian agent Henry C. Gilbert told the Indians that it was the object of the government "to induce you to settle upon the soil and procure a livelihood by agriculture." The Indians expressed great concern in selecting the lands they were to receive and securing good title to those lands. As-sa-gon, an Indian negotiator, observed that many of his native lands were not good. He added:

> "Much of them are heavy and swampy and we must select only such as are good for agriculture."

Another Indian negotiator, Was-son, remarked:

> "We have all come to the question in regard to the lands. We know our great father will give us these lands for a homestead. I have abandoned the woods for a maintenance & am now a farmer. I no longer go into the woods & look for wild animals when I want to eat; but I kill one of the cattle I raise for myself."

Was-son's remarks were the only reference to hunting or fishing during the treaty negotiations.

The Chippewa clearly expected that they were to be assimilated into the white society. As-sa-gon expressed concern over the slow progress of the Indian children in learning the English language and requested that more competent schoolmasters be hired. Mene-a-du-pe-na-se asked that additional educational funds be earmarked for college tuition for the Indian boys.

The intent of both Parties was to plan for the future in light of present realities. "We are," As-sa-gon stated, "now acting for our children." The future contemplated was an end to the traditional life style of the Chippewa. The reason no hunting or fishing rights were retained by the treaty was that such rights were not intended to be retained.

We would affirm the convictions.

COLEMAN, J., concurs.

RYAN, Justice (dissenting).

I agree that the "usual privileges of occupancy" referred to in Article Thirteenth of the Treaty of 1836 included the right to fish in the abutting waters of Lake Superior. However, I concur with Justice Lindemer that Article Thirteenth must be interpreted to mean that "settlement of the *land* terminates all usual privileges of occupancy associated with the land." It being manifest that the land in Michigan's Upper Peninsula is required for settlement, the fishing rights acquired under the treaty are extinguished.

However, I cannot subscribe to my brother's second conclusion because I agree with Justice Williams that the decisions of the United States Supreme Court regarding the construction of Indian treaties requires us to conclude on this record that the Treaty of July 31, 1855 did not extinguish any of the fishing rights granted the Chippewas in the Treaty of 1836.

I would affirm the convictions.

<h1 style="text-align:center">United States of America et al., Plaintiffs,</h1>

v.

<h1 style="text-align:center">State of Michigan et al., Defendants.
No. M26-73 C.A.</h1>

<h1 style="text-align:center">United States District Court, W. D. Michigan, N. D.
May 7, 1979.</h1>

James S.Brady, U.S. Atty., J. Terrance Dillon, Asst. U.S. Atty., Dept. of Justice, Grand Rapids, Mich., Elmer T. Nitzschke, Dept. of Interior, St. Paul, Minn., Bruce R. Greene, Native American Rights Fund, Boulder, Colo., Kathryn L. Tierney, Bay Mills Indian Community, Brimley, Mich., William J. James, James Jannetta, Legal Services, and Daniel T. Green, Sault Ste. Marie Tribe Bay Mills Indian Community, Sault Ste. Marie, Mich., for plaintiffs. Gregory T. Taylor, Asst. Atty. Gen., Lansing, Mich., for defendants

<h1 style="text-align:center">Opinion</h1>

<h2 style="text-align:center">Preface</h2>

FOX, Chief Judge

"No one can deny that the constitution of the United States is the supreme law of the land; and consequently, no act of any state legislature, or of congress, which is repugnant to it, can be of any validity. Now, if an act of a state legislature be repugnant to the constitution of the state, the state court will declare it void; and if such act be repugnant to the constitution of the Union, or a law made under that constitution, which is declared to be the supreme law of the land, is it not equally void? And under such circumstances, *if this court should shrink from a discharge of their duty, in giving effect to the supreme law of the land, would they not violate their oath, prove traitors to the constitution, and forfeit all just claim to the public confidence?" Worcester v. Georgia,* 31 U.S. (6 Pet.) 515, 571-2, 8 L.Ed. 483 (1832) (McLean,

J., concurring) (emphasis supplied).

When matters of great public and constitutional significance involving fundamental duties of the United States come here for resolution, this court assumes an extra duty of care in explaining the reasons for its decision. As always, the court states the factual basis and legal standards on which its conclusion rests so that the appellate court will know the legal grounds for this court's decision. Equally important, however, this court assumes also an affirmative obligation to attempt to educate the public concerning the basic principles underlying our constitutional democracy and the practical application of these principles in our public affairs. See, *Oliver v. Kalamazoo Bd. of Education,* 368 F.Supp. 143 (W.D. Mich. 1973).

NORTHWEST ORDINANCE

THE NORTHWEST TERRITORIAL GOVERNMENT—1787

THE CONFEDERATE CONGRESS, JULY 13, 1787

AN ORDINANCE FOR THE GOVERNMENT OF THE TERRITORY
OF THE UNITED STATES NORTHWEST OF THE RIVER OHIO

ARTICLE III

Religion, morality, and knowledge being necessary to good government and the happiness of mankind, schools, and the means of education shall forever be encouraged. *The utmost good faith shall always be observed towards the Indians; their lands and property shall never be taken from them without their consent; and in their property rights, and liberty they never shall be invaded or disturbed, unless in just and lawful wars authorized by Congress; but laws founded in justice and humanity shall, from time to time, be made, for preventing wrongs being done to them, and for preserving peace and friendship with them.* (Emphasis supplied.)

The above language, taken from the Northwest Ordinance, first enacted by the Confederated Congress in 1787 and reenacted by the First Congress of the United States at its very first session in 1789, is the backdrop for this action. It will be discussed in detail in the course of this opinion.

Also a backdrop of this case is the history of the American treatment of the Indians. In 1869 President Grant appointed a commission (pursuant to Act of Congress of April 10, 1869) composed of "nine men, representing the influence and philanthropy of six leading States, to visit the different Indian reservations, and to 'examine all matters appertaining to Indian affairs.'" Their report includes the following language:

While it cannot be denied that the government of the United States, in the general terms and temper of its legislation, has evinced a desire to deal generously with the Indians, it must be admitted that the actual treatment they have received has been unjust and iniquitous beyond the power of words to express. Taught by the government that they had rights entitled to respect; when those rights have been assailed by the rapacity of the white man, the arm which should have been raised to protect them has been ever ready to sustain the aggressor. The history of the government connections with the Indians is a shameful record of broken treaties and unfulfilled promises.

The history of the border white man's connection with the Indians is a sickening record of murder, outrage, robbery, and wrongs committed by the former as the rule, and occasional savage outbreaks and unspeakably barbarous deeds of retaliation by the latter as the exception.

The class of hardy men on the frontier who represent the highest type of the energy and enterprise of the American people, and are just and honorable in their sense of moral obligation and their appreciations of the rights of others, have been powerless to prevent these wrongs, and have been too often the innocent sufferers from the Indians' revenge.

That there are many good men on the border is a subject of congratulation, and the files of the Indian Bureau attest that among them are found some of the most earnest remonstrants against the evils we are compelled so strongly to condemn. *The testimony of some of the highest military officers of the United States is on record to the effect that, in our Indian wars, almost without exception, the first aggressions have been made by the white man, and the assertion is supported by every civilian of reputation who has studied the subject.*

In addition to the class of robbers and outlaws who find impunity in their nefarious pursuits upon the frontiers, there is a large class of professedly reputable men who use every means in their power to bring on Indian wars, for the sake of the profit to be realized from the presence of troops and the expenditure of government funds in their midst. They proclaim death to the Indians at all times, in words and publications, making no distinction between the innocent and the guilty. They incite the lowest class of men to the perpetration of the darkest deeds against their victims, and, as judges and jurymen, shield them from the justice due to their crimes. Every crime committed by a white man against an Indian is concealed or palliated; every offense committed by one Indian against a white man is borne on the wings of the post or the telegraph to the remotest corner of the land, clothed with all the horrors which the reality or imagination can throw around it. Against such influences as these the people of the United States need to be warned. The murders, robberies, drunken riots, and outrages perpetrated by Indians in time of peace—taking into consideration the relative population of the races on the frontier—do not amount to a tithe of the number of like crimes committed by white men in the border settlements and towns. Against the inhuman idea that the Indian is only fit to be exterminated, and the influence of the men who propagate it, the military arm of the government cannot be too strongly guarded.

It is hardly to be wondered at that inexperienced officers, ambitious for distinction, when surrounded by such influences, have been incited to attack Indian bands without adequate cause, and involve the nation in an unjust war. It should, at least, be understood that in the future such blunders should cost the officer his commission, and that such destruction is an infamy. [Footnote to a 1978 Detroit *Free Press* article by Tom Opre documenting contemporary violence omitted.]

Report of Commission of Citizens (November 23, 1869), cited in Report of Commission of Indian Affairs, 47-48 (1869). (Emphasis supplied.)

Senator Clay made similar points on the floor of the Senate in 1835. Speaking of the Cherokee Indians of Georgia, he said, as reported in the *Congressional Globe* for February 4, 1835:

Mr. C. said he wished to turn the attention of the Senate to the nature of the wrongs this people had suffered—to the present condition of the Cherokees, whose lands had been guaranteed by the United Sates. He went into the examination with the utmost feelings of sorrow and regret at the miserable state to which these tribes were reduced by the laws of the States. But he would assure the honorable Senators from Georgia he was actuated by no hostile intentions to that State. Georgia was the first that made these encroachments; she originated the plan of invading the Indian rights, and she had carried it far beyond all others. He had not all these various laws before him. It was not necessary to go into details; it was sufficient to notice the results. By the first act Georgia abolished the Government of the Cherokee nation. No nation (said Mr. C.) can exist without a Government of some kind. These people had formed and established a Government in imitation of our own. But it was wholly immaterial what the humble form of that Government might be. Georgia had abolished it. She next proceeded to divide their territories into counties, and distribute them by lotteries among their citizens—every head of a family being entitled to the land drawn against his number. She did indeed reserve a small pittance of a few acres for those Indians who wished to remain within her limits, but under circumstances that rendered them worthless. She gave them no rights, no franchise, no single privilege. They were denied the power of testifying in courts of justice. No Indian could be a witness in favor of his fellows.

The present case is not a 14th Amendment case, as defendants advocate. It is an Indian treaty case in which the State asks the court to abrogate the Indians' aboriginal rights which have survived for over 12,000 years and are valid to this day, and which were guaranteed to the Indians by the Treaty of Ghent and the Treaties of 1836 and 1855. This case deals only with the jurisdiction of the Federal government over the Indians and its authority to enter into treaties which bind the states. Const. Art. 6, cl. 2; Art. 1, 8.

Michigan would take the Indians' subsistence and livelihood, their right to fish, and divide it by a modern-day lottery, the Indians being permitted to compete for licenses equally with those who have taken their rights from them.

I. Introduction

On April 9, 1973, the United States of America in its own behalf and in behalf of the Bay Mills Indian Community, initiated this litigation in order to protect the tribe's rights to fish in certain waters of the Great Lakes vested in the tribe by virtue of aboriginal occupation and use, the Treaty of Ghent of 1814, and the Treaty with the Ottawa and Chippewa Nation of 1836. In its complaint, the United States asked that the State be enjoined from interfering with the Indians' treaty—confirmed rights to fish in the Great Lakes.

The Bay Mills Indian Community intervened in the action on December 12, 1974, and added certain individual officials of the Michigan Department of Natural Resources as defendants in its complaint. Bay Mills also expanded the scope of the complaint by alleging that it possessed a reserved exclusive fishing right in Whitefish Bay of Lake Superior and a right to fish in the remaining waters of Lake Superior free of state regulation. Accordingly, Bay Mills asked the court for declaratory and injunctive relief to prohibit the State from interfering with these fishing rights, and an affirmative order that the State must exercise its police power to regulate any non-Indian fishing which would be in derogation of these rights. Bay Mills amended its complaint on October 28, 1975, added the Michigan Department of Natural Resources as a defendant, and again expanded the scope of the complaint by alleging a treaty-protected, reserved right to fish in all of the area of the Great Lakes ceded to the United States in a treaty signed in 1836. This ceded area covered large portions of Lakes Michigan, Superior, and Huron.

The Sault Ste. Marie tribe of Chippewa Indians, a tribe organized in 1975 under the Indian Reorganization Act, 25 U..S.C. . § 476, intervened in this action and filed a complaint against the above-named defendants on December 12, 1975. In its complaint, the tribe alleged a treaty–protected, reserved right to fish in Lake Superior free from state regulation. On June 17, 1976, the Chippewa tribe filed an amended complaint in which it alleged an exclusive right to fish in the waters reserved to the Indians in the Treaty of 1836, and a right to fish in the ceded waters of the Great Lakes free from state regulation.

The United States amended its complaint in June of 1976 to comply with the intervenors' complaints, with minor differences. The United States did not allege that there existed "ceded waters" under the 1836 treaty, but instead alleged that the Indians had an aboriginal right to fish in the waters adjacent to the lands ceded under the 1836 treaty and adjacent to the lands reserved in that treaty. Also, the United States did not ask for a declaratory judgment that the tribes have exclusive fishing rights in all the waters adjacent to land reservations contained in the 1836 treaty, but instead asked the court to determine that the State had no jurisdiction to regulate anyone fishing within the Bay Mills Indian Community reservation, which it alleges included Whitefish Bay. In effect, the United States' complaint excluded the Chippewa tribe's allegation that it has exclusive fishing rights in certain waters of the Great Lakes adjacent to 1836 treaty reservation areas in addition to Whitefish Bay.

The plaintiffs' pleas for relief are grounded in the Supremacy Clause of the United States Constitution, Article 6, Clause 2.

The State of Michigan, in its answer, disputed the interpretation given the Treaty of 1836 by the plaintiffs, questioned the continued existence of the tribes which were signatories to the Treaty, and alleged as defenses: (1) that the treaty was a removal treaty, and therefore the Indians intended to relinquish any aboriginal fishing rights they may have held in 1836; (2) a subsequent treaty in 1855 discharged all prior rights under the 1836 treaty; (3) this 1855 treaty was an accord and satisfaction extinguishing all prior rights; (4) the Indians did not have any aboriginal rights over the Great Lakes; (5) Article 13th of the 1836 Treaty—which granted the Indians the right to use the fruits of the land until the land is required for settlement—acted as a reservation upon a condition subsequent, and that condition having occurred, the use is extinguished; (6) the land reservations made in the 1836 Treaty have expired by the terms of the Treaty; (7) even though there may be a treaty-protected right to fish, the State of Michigan may still regulate this right in the interest of conservation or under other state police powers; (8) the expansion of the Sault Ste. Marie Chippewa reservation may be done only with the consent of the state; (9) the Chippewa Tribe was dissolved by the 1855 Treaty, and the Chippewa tribe from Sault Ste. Marie is not in privity with the original signatories to the treaty.

The State of Michigan set forth a counterclaim in its answer in which it asked the court to declare that the Indians involved in this action are not exempt from state regulation. The Court views this counterclaim as a repetition of the denials and defenses set forth above, however.

The Michigan United Conservation Clubs (MUCC), a sportsman's group, petitioned this court for permission to intervene in the action. That petition was denied for reasons set forth in an earlier opinion of this court; MUCC has been permitted to act as an amicus curiae, however.

After numerous pretrial motions were disposed of, trial began on February 27, 1978. The Court heard extensive historical evidence and received voluminous documentation meant to provide a basis for interpreting the often ambiguous treaties in issue in this case. Extensive briefs and arguments considered the issue of whether the State of Michigan or the United States alone has the right to regulate fishing by the plaintiff tribes in the Upper Great Lakes.

[1] Before the filing of the complaint and continuously during the Course of these proceedings, the State of Michigan and certain individually named state officials have acted in derogation of the vested aboriginal and federal rights of the plaintiff Indian tribes. The conflict between the state and tribal fisherman is notorious; scarcely a day goes by without an article appearing in one or more of the state's major newspapers concerning the controversy. That it is a passionate issue is exemplified by a recent wholly improper attempt to influence this Court through the circulation of petitions amongst sports fishermen which urged that the court rule against the Indians. The circulation of petitions is an action diametrically at odds with the methods of access to the courts mandated by the Federal rules of Civil Procedure. This misguided action gave thousands of people the erroneous impression that constitutional rights are a matter of popular contest. This was a corruption of the concept of the Federal Judicial system. In a democracy, many times people violate Constitutional and Inalienable rights. The United States Courts exist to ensure guaranteed constitutional rights against the TYRANNY OF POPULAR MAJORITIES. Federal Court Judges are, or ought to be, custodians of secured constitutional right.

Before giving my specific findings of fact and conclusions of law, and in the effort to foster public understanding, I present the following more exhaustive statement of the issues and law involved in this case.

The United States, guided by the Nixon administration and acting in its role as trustee for the Indians, filed this action against the State of Michigan to secure Indian rights which it says were reaffirmed by an 1836 Treaty with the Ottawa and Chippewa Indians. In so doing it was merely accepting obligations imposed by the Northwest Ordinance, *supra.* The Northwest Ordinance not only provided for Michigan's first government but simultaneously set the standard by which the territorial government and the United States would be obliged to deal with the Indians of the Territory.

By this enactment, the Founding Fathers declared a guardian-ward relationship between the United States and the Michigan Indians. Trained as they were in denominational schools, where their routine assignments included translation of the bible from English to Latin and from Latin to Greek, the Founding Fathers did not hesitate to found this relationship on moral and religious principles, the principles which, generally, they transformed into political principles when they formulated our present government, including them in the Declaration of Independence and the Preamble to the Constitution as well as here in the Northwest Ordinance. It is these principles which must be applied here in interpreting the treaties and in measuring the transactions between the United States and its wards, the Indians. To do otherwise would be in violation not only of the laws of man but also of the laws of "nature and nature's God," which are, or ought to be the Supreme Law of this land.

Also, before Michigan's statehood, the United States entered into a treaty with Great Britain in which it offered its most solemn word as a nation, in formal treaty, to honor all rights of the Michigan Indians.

ARTICLE THE NINTH

The United States of America engage to put an end, immediately after the ratification of the present treaty, to hostilities with all tribes of nations of Indians with whom they may be at war at the time of such ratification; and forthwith to restore to such tribes or nations, respectively, all the possessions, rights, and privileges, which they may have enjoyed or been entitled to in one thousand eight hundred and eleven, previous to such hostilities: Provided always, That such tribes or nations shall agree to desist from all hostilities, against the United States of America, their citizens and subjects, upon the ratification of the present treaty being notified to such tribes or nations, and shall so desist accordingly. And his Britannic majesty engages, on his part, to put an end immediately after the ratification of the present treaty, to hostilities with all the tribes or nations of Indians with whom he may be at war at the time of such ratification, and forthwith to restore to such tribes or nations, respectively, all the possessions, rights, and privileges, which they may have enjoyed or been entitled to, in one thousand eight hundred and eleven, previous to such hostilities; *Provided always,* That such tribes or nations shall agree to desist from all hostilities against his Britannic majesty, and his subjects, upon the ratification of the present treaty being notified to such tribes or nations, and shall so desist accordingly.

This provision of the Treaty of Ghent, signed on December 24, 1814 (8 Stat. 218), was not mere rhetoric; it was a compromise position secured from Britain, which threatened indefinite continuation of the War of 1812 unless the United States restored the rights of Britain's Indian allies. Both nations pledged to restore to such tribes or nations all the possessions, rights and privileges which they may have enjoyed or been entitled to in 1811, before such hostilities. Both nations assumed the guardianship of the Indians and acknowledged all aboriginal Indian rights to use land, sea and air in the New World, excluding all whites from their territory until and unless the United States had secured the lands from the Indians by valid, just, humane treaties. As guardian, the United States was obliged to acquire the lands and other property not on the best terms it could get for itself, but on the best terms it could get for the Indians. At all times it was required to protect the Indians' interests. In the Treaty of Ghent, Britain effected its duty as guardian of the Indians of the lands it surrendered to the United States by securing a promise from the United States to assume a guardian relationship toward those Indians. The United States agreed to treat these Indians not as a defeated enemy, but as a ward fully possessed of all rights arising by virtue of original occupancy and use of the lands. The United States accepted this obligation in exchange for an identical promise by Great Britain and in order to end the War of 1812. Indians of the Northwest Territory who had allied with Great Britain were possessed of aboriginal rights, vested by virtue of original occupancy and use and International treaty and protected by the obligations of their guardian, the United States.

[2, 3] In our constitutional system of government the states cannot enter into treaties with foreign governments—only the federal government can. When acting within its power to deal with foreign governments, the federal government can make treaties which give it authority in areas which otherwise would belong solely to the states. In such cases the state no longer has authority in areas governed by the treaty. Federal control of migratory waterfowl, for instance, derives from a treaty with Great Britain. In this case the federal government has entered into a treaty with Indians, a matter which, like foreign affairs, is within its sole jurisdiction. One question presented here is whether this treaty with the Indians deprives the state

of all authority to regulate matters covered by the treaty, specifically Indian fishing in certain waters of the Great Lakes.

From the earliest times the United States has been ambivalent about its assumed role as trustee for the Indians, expressing noble sentiments executed by ignoble actions. During the 18th and 19th centuries the United States typically dealt with the Indians by treaty, as co-sovereign nations. Typically also, the United States secured Indian lands on terms which were little short of conquest and carried out the treaty in such fashion as to complete the vanquishment.

Michigan has staked most of its case on an 1830 Act of Congress called "An Act to provide for an exchange of lands with the Indians residing in any of the states or territories, and for their removal west of the river Mississippi," (4 Stat. 411) and referred to as the "Removal Act." Congress did nothing in this Act to lessen the obligation of the Executive toward the Indians. *(American Heritage Pictorial History of the Presidents,* Vol. I, p. 224 [1968]) The principal authorization of the Act is to make it lawful for the President to offer lands belonging to the United States west of the Mississippi to the Indians who chose to exchange their present lands. Section 7 of the Act indicates that the Act does not contemplate any variation in Indian policy: "*Provided,* That nothing in this act contained shall be construed as authorizing or directing the violation of any existing treaty between the United States and any of the Indian tribes."

Of necessity, this court has had an opportunity to review the actions of almost every administration in the history of our country. The removal policy in question began during the Presidency of Thomas Jefferson. Piecemeal removal began during Monroe's administration but slowed down during the administration of John Quincy Adams, who had a humane and paternal attitude toward the Indians. Andrew Jackson ran for office supporting the policy and received authorization from Congress to implement it. During Jackson's term Henry Schoolcraft was appointed to secure from the Indian bands, whose progeny make up the plaintiff tribes, lands which would become the State of Michigan. During Van Buren's presidency, pressure for removal of Indians to lands west of the Mississippi waned. The Indians stayed in Michigan, but were deprived of their rights under the 1836 treaty, and many others, almost as quickly as they were signed. By the time Pierce became President, even many of the eastern states wanted to keep Indians on their ancestoral homes. A new treaty was signed with the Michigan Indians during his administration which gave the Indians permanent reservations (most of which no longer exist) in exchange for releasing the United States from its unfulfilled financial and personal property obligations under earlier treaties.

In an effort to provide a perspective on the Removal Policy of the United States, I quote the following accounts of noted historians who the State's own expert testified are authoritative and reliable. (Tr. 1716.)

3. Removal of the Eastern Indians

An American journalist who had spent several years in India, and whose small children had come to love the Indians, came home in 1958. Shortly thereafter he found the boys crying as they watched a TV "Western" because, as one moaned, "They're killing Indians !" Papa had to explain that these were not Indians of India but Red Indians, and that to kill them was part of the American Way of Life.

The only extenuation of American policy toward the natives of North America is that it continued an old-world process of one race or people pushing a weaker one out of an area that it wanted. Almost every European today is a descendant of Asiatic intruders into Europe; almost every North African the descendant or Arab intruders. "The country is a land for cattle," said the children of Reuben to Moses when they saw the land of Gilead, "and thy servants have cattle; wherefore, said they, if we have found grace in thy sight, let this land be given unto thy servants for a possession." In the United States, as elsewhere in the nineteenth century, this process of conquest and expansion took the form of a relatively highly developed civilization pushing out a backward people who could not or would not be absorbed, and who were too few in number and weak in technique long to resist. But some of the Indians put up a very good fight.

The problem of United States-Indian relations, which for many years had involved international rivalries, became localized after the Florida treaty was ratified in 1821. "Foreign interference" could no longer be used as an excuse for abusing the Indians. And there was no more need to placate them to prevent their siding with the British, French, or Spanish.

Efforts to maintain Indian reservations within the Eastern states were generally unsuccessful, although a few small ones, such as that of the Abnaki in Oldtown, Maine, and the Tuscarora reservation near Niagara Falls, still endure, menaced or sliced away by the bulldozer. Conditions for a reservation's lasting were a partial adoption by Indians of the American Way of Life, and a strong government service to protect them from the white man's trickery and alcohol. But, for fifty years after American independence, the Indians did not wish to conform, many federal agents were political hacks, government trading posts were unable to compete with unauthorized private traders who supplied the Indians with liquor, and frontiersmen everywhere coveted the Indians' land.

Monroe's administration bowed to demands of the West by adopting a removal policy. Plans for concentrating the tribes west of the Mississippi now began to take shape, and piecemeal removal began in the 1820's from the Old Northwest and the lower South, to segments of what had been the domains of the Caddo, the Quapaw, and the Osage. Tribesmen with well-developed farms, especially influential halfbreeds, were given the choice of removal, or staying put and becoming American citizens. Those who preferred to leave, exchanged their property for new lands in the West and were promised payment for travel expenses and the value of improvements on their relinquished property. The assent of the Indians was often merely nominal; federal commissioners bribed important chiefs, and, if necessary, got them drunk enough to sign anything. "Persuasion" often took the form of urging the Indians to sell improvements for cash with which to pay off debts to white traders. This removal policy slowed down during the administration of John Quincy Adams, whose attitude toward the Indians was humane and paternal, but picked up momentum and was carried to a successful conclusion (from the white point of view) under Jackson. The President, having negotiated several removal treaties during his military career, knew very well the hardship involved, but regarded this as the only possible way to save the Indians from extinction. They were faced with the irresistible force of a white expansion which the Democrats had no intention of checking.

Soon after Jackson's inauguration, Georgia, Alabama, and Mississippi asserted jurisdiction over Indian reservations, in contemptuous disregard of federal treaties, and even set up county governments to be put in operation as soon as the rightful owners of the soil were expelled. Congress then passed an Indian Removal Act (1830), appropriating half a million dollars for the purpose. The President was authorized to grant lands in the unorganized part of the Louisiana Purchase in exchange for those relinquished in the East, to protect the Indians in their new reservations, to pay expenses of removal and one year's subsistence, and compensate them for improvements on the relinquished land.

The liquidation of Indian reservations in the Old Northwest was largely accomplished between 1829 and 1843. Mixed bands of Shawnee, Delaware, Wyandot, and others were persuaded to accept new reservations west of Missouri. Their numbers were drastically reduced by disease on the journey. Theft by federal officials of what was due to the Indians, and funeral rites for those who died en route, exhausted their resources long before this "trial of tears," [sic] as it was aptly called by later writers sympathetic to the Indians, came to an end. Many groups were unable to make the journey in one season and suffered intensely at improvised winter quarters. A cholera epidemic broke out in 1832; measles took hundreds of lives. Further trials awaited the survivors, especially those who hoped to till the soil; the cost of equipment reduced them to penury or debt long before they could raise a crop or draw upon tribal annuities. Money from the sale of improvements at the old village ordinarily went into the expenses of travel, if it did not stick in the pockets of federal agents.

At one point during these removals, hostilities broke out. Black Hawk, chief of the Sauk and Fox, who had fought on the British side in 1812, tried to retain his ancient tribal seat at the mouth of Rock river, Illinois, opposite Davenport, Iowa. White squatters encroached on the village and enclosed the Indians' cornfields. After the governor of Illinois had threatened him, Black Hawk agreed that after crossing the Mississippi for his annual winter hunt, he would never return. But his people, threatened by hostile Sioux, ran out of food. Hoping to find a vacant prairie in which to plant a corn crop, Black Hawk recrossed the Mississippi in the spring of [1832] with about 1000 members of his tribe. The governor of Illinois, assuming this to be a hostile expedition, called out the militia (Abraham Lincoln commanding a company) and pursued the starving Indians up the Rock river into the Wisconsin wilderness. It was a disgraceful frontier frolic, stained by wanton massacre of Indians, including women and children. The only redeeming feature was the chivalrous consideration of Black Hawk by Lieutenant Jefferson Davis of the regular army, when the captured chief was placed in his charge; forty years later, Davis referred to Black Hawk's rear-guard action at Wisconsin Heights as the most gallant fight he had ever witnessed. Black Hawk subsequently visited the "Great White Father" in Washington and was presented with a sword and a medal by President Jackson. But he lost his tribal lands.

The four great Indian nations of the Old Southwest, the Chickasaw, Creek, Choctaw, and Cherokee, were Jackson's particular problem. In 1830 the Choctaw of Mississippi signed a treaty providing for their removal within three years. As with others, this migration brought death, suffering, and poverty. In 1832 a treaty was signed with the Creek nation to wind up their large reservation in Alabama. Some members kept individual allotments and faced the cunning of new white neighbors who poured into their reservation before they could leave. Many died on the journey. By 1860 the Creek nation had lost about 40 per cent of its population. The rest settled in the Indian Territory, near the Choctaw. The Chickasaw of Mississippi, a fairly small group, fared better and obtained fairly good prices for their improvements, since their land was desirable for cotton plantations.

These three nations were agricultural and sedentary; some even held Negro slaves. The Cherokee, whose nation spread over northwest Georgia into Alabama and around Chickamauga, Tennessee, were even more advanced, by European standards. It had always been a white grievance against the Indians that they rejected "civilization." The Cherokee, unfortunately for themselves, took the palefaces at their word. George Gist, a halfbreed whose Indian name was anglicized as Sequoyah, provided the necessary spark. Convinced that literacy was the key to Indian survival, Sequoyah invented a simple form of writing and printing the Cherokee language; Bibles, other books and even a weekly newspaper The Cherokee Phoenix were printed. These Indians welcomed Christian missionaries, built roads, houses, and churches, adopted a constitution for the Cherokee nation and elected a legislature. They became more civilized than the Georgia "crackers" and "hill-billies" who coveted their lands. Nor, for that matter, do the inhabitants of Faulkner's Yoknapatawoha [sic] County appear to be an improvement over the Chickasaw whom they replaced.

The independence of the Cherokee nation had been guaranteed by the United States in a treaty of 1791, but the State of Georgia had been chopping away at their lands for over thirty years, and regarded the treaty as obsolete. Discovery of gold in the Cherokee country in 1828 brought this controversy to a head, and a rough class of whites to the spot. Here was a case of federal supremacy against the state rights, as clear at [sic] that of South Carolina; but President Jackson let Georgia have her own way. His secretary of war, Peggy Eaton's husband, informed the Cherokee that they were mere tenants at will. The federal troops sent by President Adams to protect the Indians were withdrawn, and Major Ethan Allen Hitchcock, sent by the war department to investigate frauds against them, made so devastating a report that the department suppressed it. Chief Justice Marshall decided, in a test case brought by a missionary (the Reverend Samuel C. Worcester of Vermont), that the laws of Georgia rightly had no force within Cherokee territory. Jackson commented, "John Marshall has made his decision. Now let him enforce it." As Georgia held a lottery to dispose of their lands, and no friends in power appeared to help them, the Cherokee were forced to accept removal. Agents of the Indian administration negotiated a treaty with a small minority of the chiefs in 1835, but most of them refused to attend the negotiations, and few departed within the three-year limit set by the treaty. A protest to President Van Buren, signed by 15,665 Indians, was blandly ignored. So, in 1838, regular troops under General Winfield Scott rounded up the Cherokee and started them on the long trial [sic] to Indian Territory. This journey cost them one-quarter of their number, but the remainder reorganized their national government, prospered, and have retained their language and alphabet to the present day. Several hundred diehards in the Great Smokies, who resisted removal, were eventually given the Qualla reservation in North Carolina.

A similar controversy with the Seminole of Florida ended in war. A tricky treaty of removal, negotiated in 1832 with a few chiefs, was repudiated by the greater portion of the tribe, led by a brave chieftain named Osceola. Secure in the fastness of the Everglades, Osceola baffled the United States Army for years, and was only captured by treachery at a truce conference. Many Seminoles were rounded up and sent west, but others kept up the fight until 1842. By that time they had cost the United States some $20 million and 1500 lives. A few thousand remained in the Everglades. Their descendants, known as the Miccosukee Seminoles, are the only occupants of some 200,000 acres of swampland north of the Tamiami trail. They live, like their ancestors, by hunting, fishing, and a little agriculture. Never having made peace with the United States, they are currently threatened by drainage and development projects, and a "progress" which they do not want.

The only Western statesman to denounce these shabby and dishonorable proceedings was Henry Clay. His speech in the Senate on 14 February 1835 is the more praiseworthy because the Indians had no votes, and because his Kentucky constituents cared nothing for them. He quoted the long list of treaties guaranteeing to the Cherokee their lands, and the still longer list of acts of the State of Georgia which violated not only these treaties, but the most elementary principles of justice and decency. He drew tears from the eyes of the senators, but they did nothing for the Cherokee except to expedite their removal.

President Jackson seems to have kept a good conscience about all this, and several friends of the Indians, such as Lewis Cass and Thomas L. McKenney, head of the war department's bureau of Indian affairs, supported removal as the only alternative to extermination. Jackson's rationale of Indian removal appears in his Farewell Address of March 1837: "The states which had so long been retarded in their improvement by the Indian tribes residing in the midst of them are at length relieved from the evil, and this unhappy race—the original dwellers in our land—are now placed in a situation where we may well hope that they will share in the blessings of civilization." Lewis Cass went the General one better, piously invoking the theory that God intended the earth to be cultivated. Cherokee cultivation evidently did not count.

By the end of Van Buren's presidential term, it was assumed, at least by the Democrats, that the Indian question had been solved. All important Eastern tribes—those who, in Jackson's phrase, had "retarded improvement" (i.e. resisted white land grabbers)—had been provided for behind a barrier that ran from Lake Superior through Wisconsin and Iowa Territories, thence along the western boundaries of Missouri and Arkansas to the Red river on the Texas border. Behind this line the tribes were guaranteed possession "as long as grass grows and water runs"; and thence most of them were eventually ousted, when the tide of white settlement lapped around them and slaughtered their game. But, in a sense, the removal policy was justified by the later history of the "five civilized Indian Nations"—Creek, Cherokee, Choctaw, Chickasaw, and Seminole—in Oklahoma. Removal gave them the necessary respite to recover their morale, and until the Civil War they succeeded in keeping white men out.

Looking backward, it is now evident that, in view of the irresistible push of the westward movement, Indian removal was the lesser evil. It had to be, but, the process was carried out with unnecessary hardship to the victims.

In many instances missionaries and other individuals managed to protect the Indians. The Ojibway or Chippewa had a reservation along the Bad river of Wisconsin, which was taken under the protection of the Reverend L. H. Wheeler, a Protestant missionary at La Pointe. When, in 1850, white pioneers began lobbying Congress to remove these Indians west of the Mississippi and acquire their lands, Wheeler visited the proposed site of the resettlement and reported that it would be a deed of mercy to shoot every Ojibway rather than send them there. Congress reconsidered, and in 1854 guaranteed these Indians three small reservations on the south shore of Lake Superior, which they still hold in 1964. Other tribes were not so fortunate. Between 1853 and 1856 the United States negotiated no fewer than fifty-two treaties, mostly with nations in the Mississippi valley or west of the great river, by virtue of which it added 174 million more acres to the public domain.

Remnants of the Six Nations who had been guaranteed possession or reservations in New York State, by treaties concluded as far back as 1784, have been fighting a losing battle. Chief Red Jacket of the Seneca long managed to preserve the integrity of his people in their reservation, which is now covered by the City of Buffalo. After his death in 1830, a group of New York speculators known as the Ogden Land Company began an intensive drive to get possession of the Seneca reservation. By bribing greedy individuals to act as "chiefs" and sign away land, this company managed to rob the tribe of almost their entire heritage. President Van Buren, to his credit, denounced the subsequent "treaty" as a steal, but it passed the Senate, by the casting vote of Vice President Johnson, the reputed slayer of Tecumseh.

Samuel Eliot Morison, *The Oxford History of the American People* (1965) at 445-52.

Similarly, the *American Heritage Pictorial History of the Presidents* (1968). Vol. 1, states:

TRAIL OF TEARS

Although the Indian Removal Act of 1830 simply authorized the President to negotiate for land, Andrew Jackson's "requests" were in fact orders. Resigned to their fate, the Choctaw and Chickasaw began the long journey from the Southeast to Arkansas and Oklahoma. But the Creek, who had disastrously encountered Jackson in 1813 and 1817, knew better than to believe his promise of guaranteed territory west of the Mississippi. Standing their ground in 1832, they extracted a treaty that said "they shall be free to go or stay, as they please." Four years later, their chiefs in chains and guns at their backs, the Creek joined the exodus. In 1832, the Sauk were driven from their Illinois villages and across the Mississippi, leaving possessions and food stores behind. When Chief Black Hawk sent his braves to negotiate with the military, their white flags were ignored. After several skirmishes, the desperate leader tried to lead his starving people back home, but they were stopped at the river. That pathetic series of events, known as the Black Hawk War, cost hundreds of Indian lives. In Georgia, the peaceful Cherokee sought and won from the Supreme Court a favorable decision, to which neither the state officials nor President Jackson paid any attention. Like the other Indian tribes, the Cherokee embarked on a long journey to the West, along a "trail of tears."

During the 20th century these Indians attempted to secure rights previously denied them. During Theodore Roosevelt's presidency, Congress passed a law which permitted them to appear before the Court of Claims to settle the ownership of monies held in trust by the United States at the time of the 1855 Treaty. The Ottawas and Chippewas filed suit, and, in 1907, were able to show that the United States still owed them monies which were to have been paid twenty years after the signing of the original treaty. *Ottawa and Chippewa Indians v. United States,* 42 Ct.Cl. 240 (1907). In 1946, during the Truman administration, Congress established the Indian Claims Commission. The Bay Mills Indians filed suit and proved that their land had been worth approximately seven times what they were paid in the 1836 treaty. *Bay Mills Indians v. United States,* 26 I.C.C. 538 (1971), Indian Claims Commission Docket # 18E and 58.

The present action marks the first time during the long history of these Indian peoples that the United States has not been the opposing party in their effort to secure rights granted to them by solemn treaties. The action was initiated by the United States during the Nixon administration, was pressed during the Ford administration, and carried forward during the Carter administration. As the case presently stands, the United States and the plaintiff Indian tribes, the parties to the two treaties here in question, have come to this court agreeing that their treaties reserved Indian fishing rights in the Upper Great Lakes.

That there are persons within the state whose rights to fish derive from federal (as opposed to state) law has been totally unacceptable to the state and its Department of Natural Resources. The state's position on this fundamental concept was stated by its counsel in his opening argument:

> There is no question but that the State now and always has stood ready to provide fishing privileges to all our citizens, commercial fishing privileges to all our citizens on an equal basis, including Indians or others of whatever race or ethnic background.

(Tr. 1210.) The state obdurately adheres to this position despite the fact that the Supreme Court of the United States long ago rejected the identical contention. In *United States v. Winans,* 198 U.S. 371, 25 S.Ct. 662, 49 L.Ed. 1089 (1905), the Supreme Court reviewed a lower court decision which held, in effect, that the Indians were to be treated just like any other citizen of the State of Washington, notwithstanding their treaty reserved the right to fish at their usual and accustomed sites. The Court first stated the lower court's ruling and then articulated unambiguously its disapproval:

> In other words, it was decided [by the lower court] that the Indians acquired no rights but what any inhabitant of the territory or state would have. Indeed, acquired no rights but such as they would have without the treaty. This is certainly an impotent outcome to negotiations and a convention which seemed to promise more, and give the word of the nation for more.

Id. at 380, 25 S.Ct. at 644. See also *Seufert Bros. Co. v. United States,* 249 U.S. 194, 39 S.Ct. 203, 63 L.Ed. 555 (1919).

Although the United States before 1836 exercised dominion over the area which was later to become the State of Michigan, it had not as of that time taken steps to extinguish aboriginal title in the Ottawas and Chippewas. The southern portion of the Michigan territory was becoming settled in the early 1800's and there could be no assurance of cloudless title in non-Indian settlers so long as the Indians' aboriginal title to the land remained unextinguished. While the United States had several options available to it in order to accomplish an extinction of Indian title, it chose the most common method of that time and negotiated a treaty of cession with the Ottawa and Chippewa living in the northwestern portion of the lower peninsula and eastern half of the Upper Peninsula of what is now the State of Michigan.

[4,5] Central to the plaintiffs' contentions and rooted in *United States v. Winans, supra,* is the concept that under the treaty the Indians were the grantors of a significant land cession and the United States was the grantee. As in any land transaction (not just those involving the Indians), the grant extends only to those interests and rights specifically conveyed and to none others. When the Indians granted to the United States their ownership in the land and waters of the Great Lakes described in Article First of the 1836 treaty, they retained all those rights not specifically conveyed. Among the retained rights was their aboriginal right to continue to fish in the ceded waters of the Great Lakes.

[6, 7] A misunderstanding quickly arises if the transaction between the United States and the Indians is thought of as the ordinary land transaction where the seller conveys all of his rights in the property he sells. Under this interpretation, it would be necessary for the Indians to be able to show that the United States granted them the right to fish. The transaction is better understood if the focus is upon the concept of "reservation." The Indians gave up some rights, reserving all those not specifically conveyed. In a Washington treaty, for instance, the Indians explicitly reserved a right to fish at "all usual and accustomed places." They then conveyed their land, without conveying to the United States the right to exclude the Indians from the land adjoining the places where they fished. The owners who purchased the land adjoining these fishing places did not have the right to exclude Indians from the land because the Indians implicitly reserved a right to cross it, there being no other way to exercise their fishing right. The white owners only had the right to exclude non-Indian trespassers. Likewise, certain Western Indian tribes explicitly reserved land for agricultural purposes, the treaty not specifically conveying all the water of adjacent rivers to the United States. The tribes reserved whatever water they needed to make use of their land. White settlers with similarly arid lands were not provided for by the treaties, and were not entitled to any water used by the Indians. The reservation was implied from the fact that the Indians could not otherwise use their lands for agriculture. The Michigan Indians here claim that they never granted their right to fish to the United States, but reserved it so that they could continue to exercise their way of life while living in Michigan, a right they reserved under the treaty. They are not obliged to show that the United States granted *them* the right to fish, but only that they reserved it. They need not show that they explicitly reserved it.

[8, 9] Of course, not every treaty of cession leaves the Indian grantors with reserved fishing rights. In order for the right to exist in the first instance, it must be shown that the Indians were in fact using the resource, i.e., that they exercised this right, subsumed within their larger, aboriginal right to their land and water. Thus, the factual predicate for the reserved fishing right is the documented historic, ethno-historic, anthropologic and archaeologic evidence proving that commercial and subsistence fishing was of significance to the Indians during treaty times. Plaintiffs' testimony at trial overwhelmingly established this factual predicate. Having established these facts, the reserved right to fish arises by implication. Thus, the Indians impliedly reserved the right to subsistence and commercial fishing because of this resource's importance to the Indian community at and before the time they entered into the treaty.

[10] In addition to the implied right to fish, plaintiffs also rely on explicit language in the treaty in support of their claims. Article XIII provides that:

The Indians stipulate for the right of hunting on the lands ceded, with the other usual privileges
of occupancy, until the land is required for settlement.

7 Stat. 495. This language constitutes an explicit reservation of a right broad enough to include
the taking of fish from the Great Lakes for subsistence and commercial purposes.

Because the language of the treaties is general, vague and ambiguous, the issues before
this court involve not only the treaties themselves but also the history of their negotiation and
the entire history of the Michigan Indians. This is the way the case has been tried by the parties. The plaintiffs submitted evidence that, in this northern region of the present United States,
where agriculture has always been difficult but fish have been in abundance, Indians have
relied upon fishing as basic to their livelihood since 10,000 years before Christ. They submitted evidence that the Indians adopted gill nets from their eastern cousins shortly after the
birth of Christ, and used them productively for centuries, even though, as defendants said,
white men could not get a catch from such nets unless made of much finer materials. The
plaintiffs presented experts who testified that the Michigan Indians grew to depend upon the
fisheries to secure European goods and that their earliest participation in the European market economy rested upon their expertise at fishing. It is this sort of evidence which this court
had to evaluate in order to determine whether the Ottawas and Chippewas so depended upon
subsistence and commercial fishing at the time they signed the treaty of 1836 that they could
not have knowingly signed away their right to fish.

The lands ceded by the treaty of 1836 were less explored than many regions of the far
west. More desirable lands in Michigan had been secured by prior treaties.*

[*The Treaty of Saginaw of 1819, 7 Stat. 203 (1819), secured the area around the thumb of the
lower peninsula. The negotiation of that treaty is not only typical of treaty negotiations, but also
reveals how General Lewis Cass, Secretary of War in 1836, dealt with the Indians in 1819, when he
was a commissioner. When General Cass was leaving for the negotiations in which he planned to
"procure a cession of that valuable territory," he realized he had a very difficult assignment because
the Indians had not received the annuity they had been promised in an 1807 Treaty. Treaty of Nov.
17, 1807 (7 Stat. 105.) Accordingly, he secured a personal bank loan for the amount of the "annuity" (which was in fact a grant) so that he might have silver to place before the Indians during the
negotiation. As Cass put it, he got the money so that he would "be able to comply with past engagements before I call upon the Indians lo perform others." F. Dustin, The Saginaw Treaty of 1819, 8
(1919). He displayed the silver during the negotiations and gave it to the Indians only after they
signed the new treaty. Thus, the consideration from the first treaty served to secure not only the first
treaty, but the second also.

Although Cass had made extensive preparations to ensure that the Indians would be there when
he arrived, few Indians had come. He sent out runners to gather missing chiefs and tribal leaders,
but did not wait for them to arrive. He began negotiations at once. S. Gross. Indians, Jack and Pines,
1962, at p. 17. Cass' actions were an aggressive pursuit of his objective of acquiring "that valuable
land." The Indians were primitive and uncivilized, but they knew what they wanted, and they did not
want to move out of Michigan beyond the Mississippi. They wanted to stay on their hunting grounds.

The Chief. O-Ge-maw-ke-to. addressed Cass' proposal of cession as follows: " 'You do not know
our wishes. Our people wonder what has brought you so far from your homes. Your young men have
invited us to come and light the council fire. We are here to smoke the pipe of peace, but not to sell
our lands. Our American Father Wants them. Our English Father treats us better. He has never
asked for them. Your people trespass upon our hunting grounds. You flock to our shores. Our waters
grow warm; our land melts like a cake of ice. Our possessions grow smaller and smaller. The warm
wave of the white man rolls in upon us and melts us away. Our women reproach us. Our children

want homes.

Shall we sell from under them the spot where they spread their blankets? We have not called you here. We smoke with you the pipe of peace.'" History of Saginaw County, *151 (1881).*

The account of Cass' speech reads as follows: "To this the Commissioner replied with earnestness, reproving the speaker for arrogant assumption, that their Great Father at Washington had just closed a war in which he had whipped their Father, the English king, and the Indians too; that their lands were forfeited in fact by the rules of war, but that he did not purpose to take them without rendering back an equivalent, notwithstanding their late acts of hostility; that their women and children should have secured to them ample tribal reserves on which they could live, unmolested by their white neighbors, where they could spread their blankets and be aided and instructed in agriculture." History of Saginaw County, *151 (1881).*

This humiliation was in fact contrary to the provisions of the Treaty of Ghent with Great Britain ending the War of 1812. Under that treaty the Indians regained in full the rights which Cass, impelled by the zest of his heroism, declares do not exist. After this initial session, negotiations continued in the presence of Cass' soldiers and 60 other whites, until a treaty was signed in ceremony for which Cass supplied 5 barrels of whiskey. Saginaw Treaty of 1819, 17 (1919).

To meet the resistance brought about by the Indians' desire to retain their hunting grounds, Cass assured them they could continue to hunt in the forests. S. Gross, supra, at 17. By this deception and by granting them the silver vested under the earlier treaty, Cass induced the Indians to believe, mistakenly, that they had won a victory and could retain their lands and their earlier treaty rights.

It is reported that in other negotiations Cass told Ohio Indians he would take a cession of their lands from Michigan Indians if the Ohio Indians did not sell. He brought the Michigan Indians to Ohio for the negotiations. (Tr. 493.)]

The lands of Upper Michigan were bypassed by settlers who sought agricultural lands further west. Only a few thousand Indians, organized into bands, inhabited the entire area along with a few traders and military men. These Indians used the land and water, seasonally migrating over the land to secure the resources of the area.

In the 1830's some of the Indians wanted to acquire annuities like their Potawatomie brothers and realized that the United States would give such payments in exchange for land. One group indicated that it would cede Drummond Island in Lake Huron; chiefs of questionable authority offered to cede lands belonging to other Indians in order to get an annuity. Even these groups had so little understanding of American property law that they expected to continue using the land as before even after a cession.

Lewis Cass, Secretary of War, and Henry Schoolcraft, Indian Agent in Michigan, were not interested in such proposals. They ordered representatives of all area Indian bands to Washington, escorted by traders chosen because of their known influence over the Indians and who were rewarded by the terms of the subsequent treaty. Away from their forest homes for over four months, many for the first time in their lives, unable to engage in their ordinary pursuits, housed in buildings and transported over streets, the Indians signed a treaty written by white traders, explained to them by white interpreters and fostered by men who had supplied them with firewater for years. They were then permitted to return to their homes.*

[*Similar coercion was effected in different fashion in treaty negotiations with the Osages: On the 8th of November, 1808, Peter Chouteau, the United States' agent for the Osages, arrived at Fort Clark. On the 10th he assembled the Chiefs and warriors of the Great and Little Osages in council and proceeded to state to them the substance of a treaty, which, he said, Governor Lewis had deputed him to offer the Osages, and to execute with them. Having briefly explained to them the purport of the treaty, he addressed them to this effect, in my hearing, and very nearly in the following words: "You have heard this treaty explained to you. Those who now come forward and sign it, shall be considered friends of the United States and treated accordingly. Those who refuse to come forward and sign it shall be considered enemies of the United States, and treated accordingly." The Osages replied in substance, "that if their great American father wanted a part of their land he must have it, that he was strong and powerful, they were poor and pitiful, what could they do? He had demand-ed their land and thought proper to offer them something in return for It. They had no choice, they must either sign the treaty or be declared enemies of the United States." George C. Silbey, factor at Fort Osage, cited in Schmeckebier, the* Office of Indian Affairs, Its History, Activities, and Organization *(1927), pp. 59-60.*]

Before and during its negotiation and by the language of the treaty, they were assured that they could continue to use the land when they returned to their homes, as before. Had they felt anxious about their fishing grounds before the negotiations, those fears were allayed: areas sought by whites were granted exclusively to the Indians, and no mention was made that the treaty might take any other fishing rights away.

By the terms of the treaty monies granted to the Indians for their land were assigned to traders to pay for Indian debts, and Henry Schoolcraft negotiated over $50,000 for his rela-tives. The Indians got their annuities, certain services, reservations at their traditional fishing grounds and a promise of land in the West.

But, the white men were not through with the Indians. The Senate ratified the treaty with an amendment limiting the terms of the reservations to five years or longer, as the United States might permit. This put the Indians on notice that things had not gone as they had under-stood them. But, Schoolcraft allayed their fears by assuring them they could continue to use all of their lands as before, leading them to understand that this use would go on without limit. Satisfied, the Indians signed the pact.

The United States did not pay all of the annuities promised; took the most important of the fishing grounds to build a canal and permitted settlers to come into the territory to such an extent that the Indians feared they would lose their reservations and there would be no land left for them. The United States wanted to secure clear title over Indian lands so that they could be sold to settlers and to concentrate the Indians in fewer locations on less land. These motivations led to a new treaty in 1855. In that treaty, signed in Detroit, the United States granted the Indians reservations and assumed specific obligations to provide services and benefits in exchange for a release from the prior treaty financial and personal property obligations it had not fulfilled. The reservations were again placed near traditional fishing grounds. In a separate treaty, the United States offered compensation for the fishing grounds granted in perpetuity and which it had destroyed at Sault Ste. Marie.

After the 1855 treaty, the United States dealt with the treaty Indians on a local basis, no longer pretending that there was an Ottawa and Chippewa Nation. More recently, it recog-nized the Bay Mills tribe under the Indian Reorganization Act as an Indian tribe entitled to the benefits of prior Indian treaties. Most recently, it did the same for the Sault Ste. Marie band of Chippewa Indians.

[11] When a court is called upon to construe an Indian treaty, the Supreme Court has man-dated that it employ the following principles which flow from the guardian-ward relation-ship of the United States to the Indians: The treaty must be construed as the Indians would have understood it; doubtful expressions must be resolved in favor of the Indians, and treaties must be construed liberally in favor of the Indians. Generally, these principles are laid down so that Indian tribes, usually numbering little more than a few thousand, are not wholly dis-advantaged by the strength and resources of the United States. In this case every justification

ever given in support of these principles is satisfied. The treaty was imposed by subtle, invidious and incidious [sic] negotiators who sought only signatures without regard for whether they were a product of free consent; the treaties binding the Indians were written in English, although the Indians knew no English and their language arose out of a hunting and fishing tradition without a concept of property; interpreters could only describe general outlines of the agreement; details were left to the good faith of the drafters; the final version of the treaty was drafted behind closed doors by Henry Schoolcraft and the traders who escorted the Indians to Washington; these men had conflicts of interest and each was rewarded handsomely by the treaty, altogether receiving over a quarter of a million dollars.

[12] From the history of the negotiations of the 1836 and 1855 treaties, evidence of the sort of use the Indians made of the Great Lakes fisheries at the time of the 1836 Treaty, and bound as I am to construe the treaties as they would have been understood by the Indians, I am compelled to conclude that the Ottawa and Chippewa Indians, and the plaintiff tribes as their successors, reserved an aboriginal right to fish in the waters of the Great Lakes ceded by the Treaty of 1836, which right they may exercise without regulation by the State of Michigan.

Specific findings of fact and conclusions of law are contained in a following section of this opinion.

Insofar as any motion has been of significance, it has been ruled upon at the appropriate time. Certain insubstantial motions remain and will be dealt with summarily.

[13] The State has before the court a motion to require the joinder of all necessary and indispensable parties. It argued that this order was necessary to bring into the action all Indians claiming fishing rights as descendants of the signatories to the 1836 Treaty. The court recognizes the position that the State finds itself in is difficult. However, a substantially similar argument was advanced by the State in support of its second motion for partial summary judgment. In that motion, the State asked that the court bring into the action all individuals who may possess any individual fishing rights as a result of the dissolution of the tribal organizations by the Treaty of 1855. The court denied that motion, and indicated that the present parties were sufficient to enable the court to pass on Phase I issues before it.

[14] The individual defendants have petitioned this court for the right to a jury trial. Because this action involves prospective injunctive relief sought by plaintiffs, and because plaintiffs have not presented any evidence of tortious conduct by any of the named individual defendants, there is no basis for requiring a jury trial, and defendants' motion is denied.

[15] The State's motion for a three-judge court is likewise easily disposed of.*

[*Because this action commenced before the repeal of 28 U.S.C. § 2281 on August 12, 1976, that statute and interpretative case law applies to this motion. See, Pub.L. 94-381, 7.]

The sole basis upon which plaintiffs have prosecuted this action is that the Indians possess an aboriginal fishing right which has been confirmed by treaty with the United States. Under the United States Constitution, Article VI, clause 2, a treaty made under the authority of the United States becomes the supreme law of the land. Consequently, because a treaty provision maintains the same status as a federal statute, the State cannot regulate what federal law preempts. This is the foundation of plaintiffs' allegation that the State of Michigan may not regulate federally protected fishing rights. Obviously, the plaintiffs are relying upon the Supremacy Clause of the Constitution to support their claim. The Supreme Court of the United States has indicated that a three-judge court is not necessary where the action is based on the Supremacy Clause.*

[*Swift v. Wickham, *382 U.S. 111, 122, 124-29, 86 S.Ct. 258, 15 L.Ed.2d 194 (1965); see also,* Moe v. Confederated Salish and Kootenia Tribes, *425 U.S. 463, 481 n. 17, 96 S.Ct. 1634, 48 L.Ed.2d 96 (1976).*]

Further, any relief plaintiffs request is also premised on that constitutional ground. For these reasons, the State's motion is denied.

The State has indicated that several motions to compel discovery have not been ruled upon. To the contrary, the court ruled in an Order of July 30, 1976 that these motions were moot and need not be decided.

I have not considered plaintiffs' Exhibits P-1, P-2 or P-3 in my deliberations in this matter or in this opinion.

II. Jurisdiction, Issues and Parties

(1) Jurisdiction is vested in this Court by virtue of: (a) 28 U.S.C. § 1345, in that the United States brings this action on its own behalf and on behalf of the Bay Mills Indian Community and the Sault Ste. Marie Tribe of Chippewa Indians, federally recognized Indian tribes, in connection with its administration of Indian affairs and in fulfillment of its fiduciary duties; (b) 28 U.S.C. § 1331, in that the matter in controversy involves the fishing rights of the plaintiff tribes, which in both instances have a value in excess of $10,000, exclusive of interests and costs, which are claimed to exist and to be secured under the Constitution, laws and treaties of the United States; and (c) 28 U.S.C. § 1362, in that this action is brought by Indian tribes with governing bodies duly recognized by the Secretary of the Interior alleging violations of their rights under the Constitution, laws and treaties of the United States.

(2) Each of the plaintiffs has standing to maintain the claims asserted in this action.

(3) An actual controversy exists between each of the plaintiffs on the one hand and the defendants on the other, as to the meaning of the treaties at issue herein and the existence of any tribal right to fish in the Michigan waters of the Great Lakes under those treaties.

(4) A declaratory judgment is properly sought pursuant to 28 U.S.C. § 2201 and 2202, and this court may grant such relief.

(5) Venue is properly laid in this court under 28 U.S.C. § 1391(b) in that all defendants reside within the Western District of Michigan.

(6) This trial has been limited to the issues identified for separate trial by this Court in its Order of July 30, 1976, which are: (a) Whether the Indians reserved or retained fishing rights in the Great Lakes waters purportedly ceded by them under the Treaty of 1836 (7 Stat. 491); (b) If the Indians reserved rights to fish in those waters, were those rights abrogated in whole or in part by the Treaty of 1855 (11 Stat. 621); and (c) Assuming those reserved fishing rights were not abrogated, does the State possess any jurisdiction to regulate the exercise of those rights by treaty tribe members?

The United States of America is a party plaintiff which brought this suit in its own behalf and in behalf of plaintiff-intervenor Bay Mills Indian Community and Sault Ste. Marie Tribe of Chippewa Indians pursuant to its federal trust responsibility toward those tribes.

The Sault Ste. Marie Tribe of Chippewa Indians is a present-day tribal entity which, with respect to the matters which are the subject of this litigation, is a political successor in interest to the Indians who were party to the Treaty of 1836. It is recognized by the United States as a currently functioning Indian tribe maintaining a tribal government. This tribe is organized pursuant to Section 16 of the Indian Reorganization Act, 25 U.S.C. 476. Its membership is determined in accordance with its Constitution and By Laws, and the membership criteria require proof that the member is an Indian of the treaty area. (Tr. 1127-29; Ex. P-120.)

The Bay Mills Indian Community is a present-day tribal entity which, with respect to the matters that are the subject of this litigation, is a political successor in interest to the Indians who were party to the Treaty of 1836. It is recognized by the United States as a currently functioning Indian tribe maintaining a tribal government on the Bay Mills Reservation. This tribe is organized pursuant to the Indian Reorganization Act, 25 U.S.C. 476. Its membership is determined in accordance with its Constitution and By-Laws and the membership criteria require proof that the member is an Indian of the treaty area. (Tr. 1059-62; Ex. P-119.)

Defendants in this cause are the State of Michigan, its Natural Resources Commission, and certain officials of the Michigan Department of Natural Resources. The State of Michigan exercises regulatory power over the Great Lakes fishery within its borders. This power is exercised by and through defendant Natural Resources Commission, which is the state administrative agency with responsibility for regulating the Great Lakes fishery.

Defendant Howard Tanner is the Director of the Department of Natural Resources. As such he is the chief executive officer of the Department, with overall responsibility for administering the state's fisheries program and enforcing state fishing laws and regulations. John Scott is the Chief of the Fisheries Division of the Department, and as such is responsible for the administration of the state's fisheries program. Louis Gray is the Acting Chief of the Law Enforcement Division of the Department, and as such is responsible for the enforcement of state fishing laws and regulations.*

[*The Department of Natural Resources officers were sued in their official capacities. Names of the current holders of the positions have been substituted for those named in the Amended Complaint. See Fed.R.Civ.P. 25(d)(1).]

Together those officials are responsible for administering and enforcing the statutes, regulations, orders and policies governing the Great Lakes fishery which are challenged by plaintiffs in this case.

III. Witnesses

Plaintiffs' expert witness Helen Hornbeck Tanner is an ethnohistorian who has studied American Indian tribes for approximately thirty years, and who has concentrated for the last sixteen years on the study of Indian tribes of the Upper Great Lakes. She has testified as an expert witness in other cases involving issues of Indian culture and history. Her training and experience have been concentrated in analyzing and interpreting the history, culture and lifestyle of Upper Great Lakes Indian tribes. (Tr. 53-56, 66-74; Ex. P-130.)

Plaintiffs' expert witness Charles E. Cleland is an anthropologist specializing in archaeology and ethnozoology. he has spent the majority of his professional career in personally investigating and analyzing Upper Great Lakes Indian tribes and their relationship to the animal species found in that area in historical and prehistoric times. (Tr. 658-92; Ex. P-141.)

Plaintiffs' expert witness James A. Clifton is an anthropologist and ethnohistorian who has specialized in the study of Indian tribes' responses to changes in their aboriginal culture brought about by European contact and dominance. He has spent more than half of his professional career in the particular study of Indian tribes of the Upper Great Lakes and the Ohio valley, including the removal policy and its implementation in that area. Further, he has extensive experience in the analysis of Algonquian personal names as written by Europeans and Americans in order to determine the pronunciation and identity of the named persons. The testimony showed that from his early training at the University of Chicago he did not follow the traditional subject matter breakdowns of American higher education but prepared to engage in the broad, reliable cultural investigations which were especially helpful to this court. The defendants' effort to impeach him for lack of compartmentalized academic certifications was comparable to an effort to disqualify Thomas Edison as an expert on electricity. (Tr. 2058-2109; Ex. P-177.)

Defendants' expert witness Phillip P. Mason is an historian and archivist whose academic training and research have concentrated on American social and economic history. The witness is not, by either training or experience, thoroughly familiar with the culture of the Upper Great Lakes Indians. His familiarity with the facts in this case rests primarily upon his work in editing the papers of Henry Schoolcraft and upon examination of documents since being retained by defendants. The limited perspective of his experience and his academic discipline, limited as they are to written accounts of the matters in issue here, prevented him from enlightening the court as to the total circumstances of the treaties. (Tr. 1214-25, 1237-47, 1252-55, D. Ex. 291.)

Defendants' witness Asa T. Wright is a fisheries biologist who has been employed by defendants in that capacity for most of his professional career. He has no educational background or experience in either history or anthropology, nor has he been trained in the research or analysis of historic documents. This lack of training, background and familiarity permitted him to offer opinions from his field of expertise which are at odds with the facts. (Tr. 1844-53, 1859-63, D. Ex. 313.)

The oral testimony of the tribal witnesses educated in the history and customs of their people by tribal elders is found to be reasonable and credible factual data regarding certain relevant aspects of Indian life at and after treaty times. (Tr. 130-32, 776-77, 1066-70, 1095-98, 1105-06, 1113-15, 1129-33.)

IV. Findings of Fact

A. THE INDIANS OF THE TREATY AREA.

While the term "Ottawa and Chippewa Nations" is used in the treaty and by this court in its opinion, the term is a non-Indian term used to describe Indian peoples of a similar culture, and was not used by the Indians themselves in describing their political organization. The primary unit of political and economic organization was the band, which was frequently associated with a village. Political authority was weak; decisions were usually reached by consensus, and persons became "chiefs" for ad hoc purposes based upon skill. From both a political and Indian cultural perspective, there was no such thing as an Ottawa-Chippewa tribe or nation. (Tr. 100-02, 596, 772-76, 779-81.)

Four different but related tribes of Indians have been associated with the area later included within the State of Michigan—the Ottawa, Chippewa (or Ojibway), Potawatomi and Wyandot (or Huron). (Tr. 93.) The Ottawa, Chippewa and Potawatomi had an early tradition of closeness and referred to themselves as the Three Fires. (Tr. 93.) The Ottawa and Chippewa share a common language. According to Chippewa tradition, they were located originally in the valley of the St. Lawrence River and migrated westward to the northern peninsula of Michigan somewhere near the year 1500. Some Chippewa bands moved farther west to Wisconsin. (Tr. 93) The Ottawas, which means "traders," were historically identified with Manitoulin Island in Lake Huron, which is a part of Canada. (Tr. 94.) The Ottawas too advanced westward and settled in the lower peninsula of Michigan with concentrations near the Straits of Mackinac. (Tr. 94.) The Wyandots lived in the area of present day Detroit since at least the early 1700's. The Potawatomis of Michigan have been identified with the southern portion of the state.

Of the four tribes discussed, only the Ottawa and Chippewa were signatories of the Treaty of 1836. (Tr. 96.) The names of the bands and their locations are as follows: In the Upper Peninsula, there was a band on Lake Superior opposite Grand Island which bore that name (Tr. 97); the eastern end of Whitefish Bay was the home of the Tahquamenon Bay band (Tr. 97); closer to Sault Ste. Marie, but still in Whitefish Bay, was the Waishkee Bay band (Tr. 123); the Sault Ste. Marie band was located in and around the city of the same name (Tr. 97); there was a Garden River band whose members spent much time in Canada and on Sugar Island located in the St. Mary's River (Tr. 98). Also near the St. Mary's River in Lake Huron was the Drummond Island band. (7 Stat. 495.) On the northern shore of Lake Michigan there was a band at the Les Cheneaux Islands (Tr. 98); there were bands at Big and Little Bay de Noc (Tr. 98); at the Beaver Islands (Tr. 98); at Little and Grand Traverse Bays (Tr. 98); and on Lake Huron there were bands at St. Ignace, Thunder Bay and Cheboygan. (Tr. 98.) The southern portion of the ceded area was the home of the Grand River bands (Tr. 98). Included among these bands were beneficiaries of the Treaty of Ghent, which ended the War of 1812. (Tr. 1060-61, 1064, 1128, 1179.)

The bands located within the area of cession were Ottawa, Chippewa and a mixture of both. (Tr. 98.) Henry Schoolcraft described the Indians of the Treaty area as "intercalated," a minerological [sic] term to describe stratified layers of rock. (Tr. 99.) In other words, there were some distinct Ottawa groups, some distinct Chippewa groups and some groups consisting of both. (Tr. 99.) It was not possible before 1836 to draw a precise line on a map showing distinct areas occupied exclusively by either Ottawa or Chippewa. (Tr. 100.) The Ottawa and Chippewa lived at peace together in their intercalated relationship. (Tr. 94-100, 177, Ex. P-17.)

The first significant American contact with the Indians of the treaty area probably began in 1820 with the Cass expedition. (Tr. 105.) Lewis Cass led an expedition into the northern portion of the Lower Peninsula and the Upper Peninsula of Michigan at a time before its exploration by any other Americans. (Tr. 105.) Before the Americans, the Indians of the treaty area had contact with the French, beginning in the middle seventeenth century, followed by the British. (Tr. 106.)

The life style of the Ottawa and Chippewa during the period leading up to the 1836 Treaty was cyclical in nature. Springtime activity was devoted to the making of maple sugar. Sometimes the sugar was their only source of food during the harsh months of February and March. (Tr. 111.) In early May, the spring fishing season started and some agricultural activities were conducted, depending upon the location of a band. (Tr. 111.) The 140-day growing season line extends across Michigan at a point south of Traverse City. Thus, Indians north of that line were engaged in very limited agricultural pursuits. (Tr. 111.)

Canoe making was another springtime activity because this was the best time of the year for removing the bark from birch trees. (Tr. 111.) In the summer, food gathering occurred. In August, those crops available were harvested and shortly thereafter berries were gathered. (Tr. 112.)

In the fall, there was another significant fishing season and substantial time was devoted to this activity. (Tr. 112) Before departing for winter hunting stations, supplies were procured from traders which were often advanced against the furs the Indians expected to trap. (Tr. 112.) The Indians dealt with traders on the basis of barter. (Tr. 112.) They traded furs and fish for supplies the traders carried. (Tr. 112-13.) It was not until after the 1836 Treaty with its provisions for annuities that the Indians had cash available to use for obtaining supplies. (Tr. 113.)

Indians were traders, of course, even before European contact. (Tr. 106.) As previously stated, the word "Ottawa" means "trader." One of the principal trade centers in the treaty area was at the Straits of Mackinac. (Tr. 106.) Early trade routes extended from Montreal down to the Gulf of Mexico and were dependent upon the Great Lakes and the Mississippi River for transportation. (Tr. 107.) After European contact, trading by the Indians continued and expanded because the Indians were then able to obtain manufactured goods like iron kettles, hooks, axes, hatchets, needles, awls and firearms. (Tr. 109.)

B. *ROLE OF FISHING IN THE LIFESTYLE OF THE INDIANS OF THE TREATY AREA.*

The prehistoric and historic record of the Upper Great Lakes shows a long evolutionary sequence extending back at least 12,000 years during which fishing in the Great Lakes has been of increasing importance to the Indian people of the treaty area. The nature of the fishery resource has helped to shape the Indian culture of this area. Ecologically, the Upper Great Lakes area is a transitional area between the pine forest to the north and the hardwood forest to the south. It was low in many natural resources, including mammals. (Tr. 697-98.) The Great Lakes contained a productive fishery, however, which was characterized by Rostlund in his authoritative monograph on the aboriginal fisheries of North America as the "Inland Shore Fishing Complex." This fishery (shown on the map, Ex. P-143) lies generally north at a line demarcating 140 frost-free days. As prehistoric Indian culture evolved after the retreat of the glaciers, the Indians south of that line turned increasingly to agriculture as the main subsistence activity, while those north of the line turned increasingly to fishing. Though fish did not occur in the Great Lakes in the abundance that characterized other aboriginal fisheries, the fish did concentrate in relatively small areas in the spring and fall, primarily to spawn. This bi-modal cycle with its periods of concentration allowed the Indians to utilize the fishery resource. (Tr. 699-703.)

The earliest Indians of northern Michigan were big game hunters. The first evidence of Indian fishing in the Upper Great Lakes occurs in Late Archaic Period with archaeological sites dated between 2000 and 1000 B.C. Although the Indians of this period were primarily hunters, they began coming to the shores of the Great Lakes in the spring, when spring spawners such as sturgeon were gathered, and took fish by hook, gorge and spear. (Tr. 728-30.)

Even before this time, however, a new fishing technology was being developed and applied on the Atlantic coast which would eventually alter drastically the subsistence and lifestyle of the Indians of the Upper Great Lakes. Fishing nets originated on the Atlantic coast around 6000 B.C. and began spreading slowly westward through the process of cultural diffusion. By 2500 B.C. nets were in use on the Lower Great Lakes. From there they spread to the Upper Great Lakes, where they appeared during the Middle Woodland Period at around the time of the birth of Christ. (Tr. 744-45.) As with the earlier fishing techniques, which remained in use, nets were first applied to the spring fishery. However, during the Late Woodland Period (which immediately preceded European contact), the primary fishery shifted from the spring to the fall, when species such as lake trout and whitefish were taken. With this major change the fishery continued to become more important and more productive. (Tr. 739-40)

The introduction of nets and the shift of the fall fishery led to the development of the Late Woodland Period settlement pattern which was encountered by the first Europeans to enter the Upper Great Lakes. In the spring the Indians would gather in large fishing villages of around 200 persons, where they would remain until the onset of winter. In winter the village would break up into small family groups which would disperse inland to hunt. When spring came the cycle would be renewed. The warm weather fishing villages were located on the shores of the Upper Great Lakes throughout the treaty area in locations with convenient access to productive fishing grounds. (Tr. 121-23, 236-38, 733-43, 760-63, 825-30.)

By the time of first European contact around 1650 A.D. fishing had come to be of enormous importance to the Upper Great Lakes Indians. All traditional fishing methods were still in use, but the most productive was gill netting from canoes. The Indians caught both spring- and fall-spawning species, including sturgeon, suckers, pike, whitefish and lake trout. (Tr. 130, 758-60.) Fish was a very crucial item in the Indian diet, comprising about 65% of the usable meat consumed in the warm months. (Tr. 768-71.) British and French settlements in the same area show significantly less dependence upon fish in the European diet. (Tr. 769-71.) At first contact, as in earlier and later times, fishing was the key to understanding the subsistence and settlement patterns of the Upper Great Lakes Indians.

A written record of the Indians of the treaty area began with the arrival of Europeans, though of course this record was not kept by the Indians, but by the newcomers encountering a strange culture. Nevertheless, these European and later, American observers amply documented the continued extreme importance of fishing to the Indians. Throughout the period from first contact to the 1830's, missionaries, explorers, traders, and military and governmental officials wrote of the Indian gill net fishery in the Great Lakes and of its importance to the Indian inhabitants. For example, the Frenchman Joutel wrote this detailed description of Indian gill netting at the Straits of Mackinac in 1687 (Tr. 784-85):

> They are very skillful at fishing and the fishing is very good in those parts. There are fish of various kinds which they catch with nets, made with a very good mesh; and although they only make them of ordinary sewing thread, they will nevertheless stop fish weighing over ten pounds. They go as far as a league out into the lake to spread their nets, and to enable them to find them again, they leave marks, namely, certain pieces of cedar wood which they call "aquantiquants," which serve the same purpose as buoys or anchors. They have nets as long as 200 fathoms and about 2 feet deep. At the lower part of those nets they fasten stones to make them go to the bottom, and on the upper part they put pieces of cedar wood which the French people who were then at this place called floats. Such nets are spread in the water, like snares among crops, the fish being caught as they pass, like partridge and quails in snares. The nets are sometimes spread in a depth of more than 30 fathoms, and when bad weather comes, they are in danger of being lost.

Cadillac in 1695 described the same fishery as a "daily manna, which never fails." (Tr. 785.) Many similar accounts were placed on the record. (Tr. 105-08, 154, 113-20, 782-89, 791-94.) These historic and ethnographic materials were summarized by Rostlund in his authoritative work in this fashion (Tr. 796):

> [A] gill net fishery par excellence in native North America was found in this region of great interior lakes inhabited by the whitefish family; and it may be added that this great food resource could not have been adequately exploited had the gill net been unknown. * * * [A]s fishermen those people . . . were second to none in the aboriginal North America.

Long before European contact, the Indians of the Upper Great Lakes had participated in a far-flung trade and exchange network which extended at least as far south as the Gulf of Mexico. (Tr. 106-07; Ex. P-142) This was not, however, a proper commercial network, because commercial activity requires a market economy based upon a system of exchange using understood equivalents, and such a market economy was absent from the Upper Great Lakes in aboriginal times. The Europeans brought with them their market economy, and with it an opportunity for the Indians to participate in an entirely new aspect of the fishery—a commercial fishery. (Tr. 797-99.) From that time onward, the commercial fishery as well as the subsistence fishery was important to the Indians. As is also indicated by the Indians' adoption of nets, the Indians' participation in commercial fishing as soon as this opportunity presented itself, reveals that the Indians' participation in the Great Lakes fishery was never static, but evolved as new opportunities became available.

As early as the middle of the 18th century Indians were participating in a commercial fishery by trading fish to the French at Michilimackinac. (Ex. P-8, 9.) Before the 19th century, however, the main Indian commercial activity was in the fur trade. The fur trade was on the wane in the early 19th century. By that time the Indians had become dependent upon manufactured trade goods and needed to continue their participation in the market economy. The naturally turned to fish as a commodity which could produce a surplus for trade. (Tr. 124, 799-801) In the 1830's the fur companies began to turn to fish as well. Foremost among them was the American Fur Co., which operated a fishing enterprise on Lake Superior from 1835 through the early 1840's. Its principal fishing operations were west of the treaty area, but it did operate fishing stations at Whitefish Point and Grand Island. (State Ex. 309) The American Fur Co. and its rivals developed a market for Upper Great Lakes fish and provided a ready outlet for the purchase of Indian fish and employment of Indian fishermen. (Tr. 153-55, 437-43, 801-07.) The fishermen for the American Fur Co. were largely Indians, who were the major producers of fish in Northern Lake Michigan, Northern Lake Huron, and Lake Superior for the entire first half of the nineteenth century. (Tr. 281, 803-05, 807-09, 970, 973, 1559.) Indian names do not appear in the employee roles of the American Fur Co., however, probably because Indians fished as subcontractors. (Tr. 1781-82.)

The evidence firmly establishes that the Indians of the treaty area were heavily engaged in commercial fishing at the time of the Treaty of 1836, both as employees and as independent fishermen. The Blois *Gazeteer* of 1840 described one type of Indian participation in the commercial fishery (Tr. 804):

> At Mackinac, St. Mary's Strait, and Lake Superior, the fishermen are composed of French, Indians, and Mestizoes or halfbreeds. They are generally employed by capitalists and in Lake Superior

by the American Fur Company, furnished with necessary outfits, and paid in such goods as their necessities may require.

Grace Lee Nute, in her article on the American Fur Co., which was relied on by the experts on both sides, also indicates that the American Fur Co. engaged Indian fishermen (State Ex. 309, P. 489), and a contract between an Indian fisherman and the company for fishing at Whitefish Point in 1837 was also introduced. (State Ex. 226.) Indians also barrelled their own fish and sold them to traders (State Ex. 50), and traders contracted with intermediaries like Charles Butterfield to purchase fish from Indians. (Ex. P-176.) Indian commercial fishing is evidenced in the treaty itself as well; under the sixth provision of Article Fourth, the Indians were to receive 100 barrels of salt and 500 fish barrels annually for twenty years.

Subsistence fishing continued to be tremendously important to the Indians of the treaty area in the 1830's. The introduction of the market economy, the fur trade and the dependence of the Indians on trade goods did not alter the subsistence dependence of the Indians on the fishery; to the contrary, as Fitting reported in his "Patterns of Acculturation at the Straits of Mackinac," those factors actually increased and amplified the importance of fishing. (Tr. 766-67.) Fish remained the staple of the Indian diet. This factor was stressed by Lewis Cass, who in 1820 wrote that for the Indians of the treaty area fish "constitute a considerable part of the food of all the Indians upon this extensive frontier. Deprived of this means of support, they must absolutely perish." (Tr. P-20 and 20A.)

In 1836 the settlement pattern of the Indians was the same as it had been for centuries, since the introduction of nets: in the warm months the Indians were concentrated in large fishing villages, and in the winter the villages broke up into family groups who went inland to hunt and trap. The Indians were living on the shores of the Great Lakes throughout the treaty area adjacent to the productive fishing grounds. (Tr. 97-100, 121-23, 236-38, 760 760-68, 825-30.) This settlement pattern is shown in the Treaty of 1836 itself—in the location of the reservations and of the chiefs listed in the schedule supplemental to Article Tenth. It is also shown in Henry Schoolcraft's 1837 map and census (Ex. P-125; State Ex. 311) and in similar exhibits. (State Ex. 63, 284.)

Despite this settlement pattern and the concentration of fishing in the areas of settlement, Indian fishing was not confined to these areas. Indians of the treaty area, before and during treaty times, traveled extensively, and to the most remote areas of the Great Lakes. (Tr. 127-29, 753-54). They had various sizes of canoes, adapted to different purposes, and used these in their travels. (Tr. 469-71.)

In sum, in 1836, fishing in the waters of the Great Lakes for both subsistence and commercial purposes was extremely important to the Indians of the treaty area. (Tr. 559, 807, 1762-3, 1773, 1785, 1788-89, 1792-99, 1801, 1886.) Dr. Cleland described the Indian fishery in 1836 as a "vitally important resource for the survival of those people, and upon the advent of a commercial system, a means by which they made their principal living during a very difficult era" and as "the primary cornerstone of their cultural being." (Tr. 831.)

Fishing remained enormously important to the Indians of the treaty area up to the Treaty of 1855. This is amply documented by a variety of sources, from the Morman leader Strang of Beaver Island to the official reports by Indian agents. (Tr. 120-21, 156-63, 165-75, 808-09.) Store ledgers of local traders and merchants indicate that Indians were obtaining cash credits for barrels of fish on both a large and small scale. (Ex.P-166, 167, 168, 169, 170, 171,

172, 173, 174, 175.) A particularly fertile source for such evidence is the annual reports of the Commissioner of Indian Affairs to Congress, which include reports of local agents, subagents and the like. In the report for 1842, for instance, the Indian school at St. Ignace complains of poor attendance "caused by frequent absence of families from home, pursuing their calling as fishermen." (State Ex. 269, No. 36.) The report for 1844 states that an increased demand for fish has improved the economic position of Indian fishermen. (Ex. P-66.) In 1848 the Indians of the subagency at Sault Ste. Marie sold at least 1200 barrels of fish. (Ex. P-72.) In 1852 Rev. Pitezel reported to the Commissioner (Ex. P-75):

> One means of their subsistence must be, from the nature of things, fishing. Lake Superior abounds with the finest fish. As long as they reside about the lake, this occupation must be to them what the farm is to the farmer, or the trade to the mechanic.

Similar statements occur in other reports of the period. (Ex. P-67, 69, 70, 71, 73, 77, 79.) In 1855 fishing in the Great Lakes remained the primary Indian subsistence activity and was perhaps an even more important commercial activity than at earlier times. (Tr. 169-70, 824-25, 831-32.)

Fishing remained an important activity of the Indians of the treaty area throughout the remainder of the 19th century. The Mackinac Agency reported to the Commissioner of Indian Affairs in 1861: "Those bands residing near the Great Lakes still depend, to a great extent, on fishing for a livelihood." (Ex. P-98, p. 5) In 1860—the first year in which Indians were counted—the census for northern Michigan showed that Indians and half-breeds dominated the commercial fishery. (Tr. 809-14; Ex. P-156.) Indian participation remained high and actually increased slightly by the 1880 census. (Tr. 815-18; Ex. P-157, 158.) Smith and Snell's survey of commercial fishing in the Great Lakes in 1885 also showed heavy Indian participation in the fishery of the northern Upper Great Lakes. (Tr. 818-23; Ex. P-4.)

Indian involvement in the Great Lakes fishery has continued through this century to the present day. The Bay Mills Indian Community is a fishing community whose members have always fished for subsistence and commercial purposes. As one member, Don Parish, put it: "[F]ishing was our way of life, it was our livelihood, and fishing is our living, so we just had to fish." (Tr. 1116.) Other tribal witnesses expressed similar sentiments. (Tr. 1064-66, 1075-79, 1094-1102, 1129-37, 1160-64, 1184-86.) Indian fishermen still live in the same areas and fish on the same fishing grounds as did their ancestors for centuries past. (Tr. 1064-66, 1070-74, 1075-79, 1094-1102, 1113-16, 1138-39, 1161-62, 1171-73; Ex. P129E, 135, 135A, 136, 136A, 136B, 136C, 136D.) Indian fishing of today is remarkably like Indian fishing in 1836, and not much different from Indian fishing two millennia before that.

C. *NEGOTIATION OF THE TREATY OF 1836.*

When the United States negotiated treaties with the Indians of the Territory of Michigan, it was bound by certain responsibilities imposed by previous Treaties and Laws. The first of these is the Northwest Ordinance, discussed above. Additionally, the United States undertook certain obligations towards the Indians, and restored all aboriginal rights, through the treaty which ended the War of 1812 with Great Britain, the Treaty of Ghent, signed on December 24, 1814 (8 Stat. 218). This Treaty was referred to by Henry Clay, Senator from

Kentucky, in a speech before the Senate on a Resolution concerning the Cherokee Indians in
Georgia:

> He alluded to the negotiations between Great Britain and the United States, for the termination
> of the late war. The hinge on which the negotiation turned, he had a distinct recollection, was the
> claim brought forward by the British negotiators on behalf of the Indians, and which they held as a
> *sine qua non* to the conclusion of a treaty of peace—that the Indians, her allies, should have a per-
> manent boundary assigned them, and that neither party should be at liberty to purchase the lands
> they set apart. But the American commissioners would not listen to the proposition so much as to
> refer it to their Government, informing the British commissioners that, if they did so, they were sure
> it would meet with the most prompt rejection. They stated that the Indians lived under their own cus-
> toms, and not the laws of the United States, and that they were placed under the protection of the
> United States alone, whether they were subjects or otherwise. The correspondence finally terminat-
> ed in a proposition to which the American commissioners assented, that the United States should do
> their best endeavors to restore peace with the Indians with which they were at war, and restore to
> them all the rights and privileges they enjoyed prior to the commencement of hostilities. And he
> declared it to be his belief that, if the Indian rights had not been thus declared, there would have been
> a prolongation of the war.

The Congressional Globe, February 3, 1835, at 195. It should be noted that Henry Clay was
a negotiator and signatory of the Treaty of Ghent for the United States.*

> *[*The above comment on the negotiations on the Treaty of Ghent was placed in historical per-
> spective by Samuel Eliot Morison in* The Oxford History of the American People *(1965) at 397-98:*

> > *To the astonishment and distress of the American peace commissioners . . . their opposite numbers were
> > instructed to admit neither impressment nor neutral rights as even subjects of discussion. The United States
> > must abandon all claims to the Newfoundland fisheries, the northeastern boundary must be revised to pro-
> > vide a direct British road between St. John, N.B., and Quebec; and the northwest boundary must also be rec-
> > tified to give Canada access to the Upper Mississippi. Finally, the old project of an Indian satellite state north
> > of the Ohio river was revived. Adams, an experienced diplomat, expected the negotiations to terminate on this
> > point, and prepared to go home. Henry Clay, untrained in diplomacy but an expert poker player, was confi-
> > dent the British would recede, as they did. On 16 September, the British commissioners were instructed to
> > drop the Indian project.]*

A treaty can be analogized to a special kind of contract and, like all contracts, the motivations of the parties can, and often do, differ substantially. There were two principal parties
to the treaty—the United States and the Indians—but each party represented a collection of
individual interests. (Tr. 132.)

Some Indians in the treaty area were interested in obtaining annuities like their neighbors
the Potawatomis. (Tr. 133.) Others wanted to protect their special, customary fishing grounds
from non-Indian fishermen. (Tr. 133.) Still others, in particular the Indians in the Upper
Peninsula wanted to secure blacksmith services to make and repair metal equipment, especially implements used for fishing. (Tr. 133)

Representatives of the United States also had differing motivations for treating with the
Indians. Henry Schoolcraft, principal negotiator for the United States, was concerned about
national security and wanted to secure the Upper Peninsula against British encroachment.
(Tr. 134, 163-65.) As a mineralogist, Schoolcraft believed there were valuable mineral deposits
in the area, such as salt and coal, and he wanted to be sure there would be no impediments

to the government's exploitation of these minerals if rumors of their existence later proved accurate. (Tr. 134.) Traders, who played a major role in the treaty process, were owed large sums by the Indians and a treaty was the best way to be certain these debts were paid. (Tr. 136.) There was also significant pressure for statehood in the early 1830's. Early Michigan leaders, like Lewis Cass and Senator Lucius Lyons, wanted to attract settlers to the area and in order that there be available land, the Indians' title had to be extinguished. (Tr. 135, 1305.) Michigan territory in the early 1830's was not experiencing the same settlement rate as in Ohio, Indiana and Illinois. (Tr. 1294.) Reasons included the large Indian population in Michigan and settlers' fears of confrontation with them; a lack of roads to allow settlement of the interior; harsh weather conditions, and the like. (Tr. 1294.)

The dominant motive appears to have been to cheat the Indians out of their lands and reduce their holdings to the reservations. Thereby the Indians would be deprived of their natural habit of roaming the range of the lands on their summer and winter migrations. Thereby the Indians would be deprived of their lands before they realized their eventual value. The figure received for the land—$12\frac{1}{2}$–13 cents per acre—indicates that the Indians were cheated out of their land. (Tr. 210, 227, 275, 2134-36, 2380-84.)

By 1836, much of the Indians' aboriginal title to Michigan land had already been extinguished through various treaties. In 1807 the United States obtained the land around Detroit under the Treaty of Detroit. (Tr. 1295.) The United States acquired land in southwestern Michigan (below the Grand River) under the 1822 Treaty of Chicago. Under the Treaty with the Saginaw Chippewas in 1819, the United States acquired land in the eastern side of the Lower Peninsula up to Thunder Bay on Lake Huron. (Tr. 1295-96.)

In the fall of 1835, a small group of Indians (primarily Ottawas) made their way to Washington, D.C., to talk to government officials about a treaty. (Tr. 136.) The arrival of this group of chiefs with limited authority provided Schoolcraft with occasion to emulate Cass in the negotiation of the Treaty of Saginaw. Having found out about this group, Schoolcraft hastily departed for Washington, D.C., as well. (Tr. 139.) The United States seized upon these events as an opportunity to purchase lands from all the Indians of the area, and quickly expanded the scope of the purchase to include all of the area of Michigan eventually ceded in the Treaty of 1836. (Tr. 135-36, 606-07, 1315-26). Schoolcraft aggressively sought other chiefs in order to seize another tract of "that very valuable land." In early 1836, a larger delegation of Indians was escorted to Washington, D.C. in order to negotiate a treaty. (Tr. 139.) Most of the escorts were traders from throughout the area of cession. (Tr. 139.) The escorts were arranged for, in most instances, by Schoolcraft and other government officials. (Tr. 139.) Documents support the notion that the presence of traders was essential if the United States was to accomplish a cession of Indian lands. (Tr. 140; Ex. P-46 and 46A.) Some traders, such as Robert Stuart, John Drew and Edward Biddle, were associated with the American Fur Co. (Tr. 141-42.)

Dr. Helen Hornbeck Tanner, plaintiffs' principal ethnohistoric witness, testified that:

> Fur traders were widely used as mediators in effecting Indian treaties and were usually present, and in some cases, beneficiaries of the Treaty. Their personal contacts with the Indian people were important, in one way, and their influence over them appears to have been considerable. (Tr. 142.)*

> [*Defendants' Exhibit 312 contains a detailed list of the claims traders submitted for payment under the treaty. For example, Edward Biddle received more than $45,000 (Ex. 312, Claim No. 63,

Tr. 1621). Rix Robinson, Robert Stuart, John Holiday, John Hulbert and Henry Levake received, in toto, approximately $57,000 as claimants under the treaty. (Ex. 312, Tr. 1625-33.) Altogether, claimants or creditors received $220,954.57 under the treaty. (Ex P-321, Tr. 1633.) All these persons played a major role in the treaty process, including accompanying various bands to Washington, D.C. Most of these persons were listed at the end of the treaty signifying their attendance and participation in the negotiation process. Perhaps the most prominent figure in the treaty process was Henry Schoolcraft. His family members received approximately $53,000 under the treaty as creditors to the Indians. (Ex. P-132; Tr. 1636-42)]

In the spring of 1836, the process of selecting Indian representatives and transporting them to Washington began. The selection of the traders who accompanied the Indians was initiated and controlled largely by the United States, acting through Henry Schoolcraft and his agents. Schoolcraft sent for his relatives, Waishkee and his son Waw-be-geeg, to represent some of the Upper Peninsula bands. (Tr. 142.) At this same time, a power of sale was being circulated amongst the Indians for their signatures (marks) to be affixed. This power of sale (Ex. P-47 and 47A) was sent to Washington and arrived while the treaty negotiations were taking place. (Tr. 143.) Indian delegates came from Muskegon, Grand River, Michilimackinac, Sault Ste. Marie, L'Arbre Croche and Grand Traverse. One group from Grand River did not come under trader escort and a trader was summoned to attend the negotiations. While in Washington the Indian delegates were placed in charge of Rix Robinson, Robert Stuart, John Drew, H. A. Lavake, William Lasley, George Moran, Lewis Moran, Augustus Hamelin, and Leonard Slater. All were traders except Hamelin, an educated half-breed, and Slater, a missionary. (Tr. 96, 139-48, 145-47, 177-79, 1326-30, 1334-47; Ex. P-15, 46, 47.) The United States paid all of the expenses incurred by the Indians in order to transport them to Washington (Tr. 147), including providing them with clothes and other gifts. Once in Washington, the Indians were housed and fed at the expense of the government.

Lewis Cass was the Secretary of War in President Jackson's administration, and, being a military man, he knew full well that "Andrew Jackson's 'requests' were in fact orders," when it came to Indian matters. (*American Heritage Pictorial History of the Presidents,* Vol. 1, p. 224 [1968]). This attitude was in turn conveyed to Henry Schoolcraft in a letter authorizing him to treat with the Indians. (Ex. P-53.) Cass' instructions directed Schoolcraft to obtain a cession of Indian land, in part to facilitate the advancement of non-Indian settlers. He was told not to allow individual reservations but if reservations were provided for, the Indians should hold them in common until later ceded to the United States. (Tr. 149.) Other instructions required him to determine that the Indian representatives were genuine and authorized to cede land and to obtain as large a cession as possible. No claims for debts were to be settled in the treaty itself unless the Indians insisted upon it. Annuities of twenty years duration were to be provided. (Tr. 148-50, 1345-49; Ex. P-53, D. Ex. 16.)

Schoolcraft made an opening statement to the assembled group in which he explained why the treaty was to be negotiated with both the Ottawa and Chippewa rather than negotiating two separate treaties. Schoolcraft stated the President of the United States believed the Ottawa and Chippewa to be "brother tribes." Article First of the treaty refers to "the Ottawa and Chippewa nations of Indians." However, the Indians did not think of themselves as "nations" nor were they organized politically at the tribal level. (Tr. 773.) The term "nation" was coined by non-Indians to facilitate treating with the Indians. (Tr. 101.) Treaties, after all, were used to memorialize agreements between foreign countries. The analogue was applied to agreements between the United States and Indians until 1871 when it was outlawed by Congress. (25 U.S.C. 71) The Indians usually referred to themselves as "the People." (Tr. 101.)

The treaty minutes also reflect that some Ottawa bands from the Lower Peninsula did not want to sell their land while the Indians in the Upper Peninsula were more willing to sell. (Tr. 178.) The treaty commissioners tried to use the Chippewa's willingness to sell to shame the Ottawas into agreeing to a cession. (Tr. 178-79; Ex. P-17A, pp. 10-11.)

Interpreters, many of whom were inefficient, were always required during treaty negotiations because the Indians, with only minor exceptions, did not speak English. Of course, they could not read or write English either and those signing the treaty did so with a mark and not a signature. (Tr. 180.) In 1838 Schoolcraft commented on the incompetence of interpreters as follows: "The department is very much in the hands of ignorant and immoral interpreters, who frequently misconceive the point to be interpreted. Could we raise up a set of educated and moral men for this duty, the department would stand on high grounds." *Personal Memoirs,* p. 583, cited in Schmeckier, *The Office of Indian Affairs, Its History, Activities and Organization* (1927), p. 59.

The Indians referred to the treaty commissioners as "Father" which was a sign of respect. (Tr. 187.) They saw human relations in very personal terms (Tr. 187), and the term "Father" also signified the Indians' understanding that the treaty commissioners were authority figures. The Indians expected them to look out for Indian interests, as they were obliged to do as trustees for the Indians.

The 1836 treaty minutes also reveal an important matter which must not be overlooked. Discussions at the large sessions were concerned with generalities and concepts only. Each band designated its escort to sit down and formulate the actual treaty language and provisions out of the presence of the Indians. The escorts, with the sole exception of Augustus Hamelin, were all traders with a substantial pecuniary interest in seeing that the treaty negotiations were consummated. (Ex. P-17A, pp. 13-14; Tr. 183-87.) Unfortunately, there are no records reflecting the nature of these closed door drafting sessions. Dr. Tanner testified:

> . . . but it does appear that the Treaty was actually formulated when the traders got together. There is very little discussion in these Treaty Minutes, if any, about the actual provisions of the Treaty that was later presented to the Indian people, but there is no record of what transpired when the group of Indian traders were together in closed session and emerged with 13 articles of a Treaty that was presented to the Indians to sign.

(Tr. 183-84.)

The language in the Treaty of 1836 is the language of Henry Schoolcraft. (Tr. 183, 1367) From an examination of the transcript it can be determined that he was a subtle, invidious and insidious negotiator who convinced the Indians to trust him in these dealings. (Ex. P-17.)*

*[*Schoolcraft's behavior as a negotiator is also shown in another Michigan treaty. During the negotiations of an 1837 treaty with the Saginaw Chippewas Schoolcraft met an impasse. The Indians would not sign unless the treaty granted 640 acres to a doctor who served them during a smallpox epidemic. It did not: they refused to sign and left. Schoolcraft later recalled them and assured them the proposed version of the treaty contained the provision. They signed on the basis of this representation. It still did not.* History of Saginaw County *(1881) p. 157.*]

In shaming the reluctant Chippewas, Schoolcraft evidenced his disdain for the Indians' intentions and interests. The Ottawas declared: "We have decided we don't want to sell our land at all." To this Schoolcraft responded: "Well all right. I will deal with the Chippewa, and then they will go home with presents, and you will go home with nothing and you will all be ashamed." (Tr. 179.) Quite simply, he relied upon fraud and duress. (Tr. 493-96.) Judging from the amount of territory which they ceded to the United States, and the paltry sum which they received in exchange [*the price per acre of ceded land happens to coincide with the price traders charged per quart of whiskey at the time. (Tr. 245.)*], it is probable that when the Ottawa and Chippewa Indian Chiefs signed the Treaty of 1836, they were under the influence of alcohol and did not know what they were doing. Accounts by Henry Schoolcraft and others indicate that these Indians were no longer rational when the whites made alcohol available to them.

> It is the use of ardent spirits, however *(an article which is freely supplied),* that constitutes their chief bane, converting that which would otherwise be a season of plenty and good humor, into a gloomy and revolting scene of riot and drunkenness, followed not infrequently by disease, and sometimes by death. This is not the whole . . . of the evil. The facility with which the Indians part with their money becomes the secret motive of their being advised to call on the agents of the Government for their vested funds; and they thus become dupes of the artful and designing. (D. Ex. 252, p. 347.) (Emphasis supplied.)
>
> Could ardent spirits be kept from these unfortunate beings, it would be unnecessary ever to remove them.... A considerable number have joined that church, and appear to walk orderly, but some of the heathen portion of these bands are much degraded by the baneful effects of whiskey. They [sic.] American Fur Company, however, and some other respectable traders in that vicinity, have now determined to deal no more in spirituous liquors themselves, and are disposed to give every aid they can to the Government to put a stop to this nefarious traffic. (D. Ex. 269, p. 408.) Sir: I have the honor to report to you that the condition of the Indians at this sub-agency has been better than during the past year. There have been few instances of intoxication, and a greater disposition to provide for their families was evinced by many. (D. Ex. 269, p. 411.)

In *The Oxford History of the American People,* Morison describes the common practice at treaty signings: "The assent of the Indians was often merely nominal: federal commissioners bribed important chiefs and, if necessary, got them drunk enough to sign anything." (At 446.) This practice was not foreign to Michigan treaty negotiations nor to the principals responsible for the 1836 treaty. Lewis Cass, Secretary of War in 1836, negotiated the Treaty of Saginaw in 1819 and supplied 5 barrels of whiskey to the Indians on the day of the signing. F. Dustin, *The Saginaw Treaty of 1819,* 17 (1919). One of the traders representing the Indians in Washington in 1836 had engaged in extensive liquor trade with the treaty area Indians, claiming approximately $16,000 debt for liquor at the time. (Tr. 1621-23.) This man, Drew, and Rix Robinson, another of the escorts, were identified by Robert Stuart as the two men who were necessary for the success of the treaty negotiations. (Tr. 142.) In turn, Robert Stuart and Rix Robinson claimed debts for liquor on their own behalf or on behalf of the American Fur Co. (D. Ex. 312, pp. 40, 48, 50, 55.) It is unlikely the long-standing practice of supplying liquor to Indians stopped abruptly when these traders arrived in Washington, motivated as they were by the prospect of collecting thousands of dollars of purported debts created over a period of years. Use of liquor was one vehicle of the peonage they exercised over the Indians.

The convergence of such circumstances makes it reasonable to conclude that fueling the Indians with alcohol provided by traders was the final weapon Schoolcraft depended upon to effect the government purpose of evicting the Indians from their lands and to conquer the resistance of will he met when he sought cession of more than scattered parcels. Schoolcraft was, in the words of Dr. Tanner, prepared to use any means to achieve a treaty. (Tr. 494.) Besides using distortion, extortion and duress, he held out the carrot of silver and whiskey, relying on traders to supply whiskey during negotiations. The Indians' assent to the treaty was, accordingly, merely nominal.

The negotiation of this treaty is rent through with deception, manipulation and double dealing. The traders who accompanied the Indians to Washington were creditors for the Indians and would greatly profit from any provision which set aside money for the payment of Indian debts. (Tr. 262, 1731-32.) Some of these traders were dishonest. The fact that most of the traders who accompanied the Indians received money in payment of Indian debts from the treaty indicates that the Indians were improperly represented at the treaty negotiations, that the treaty does not contain their wishes or represent their best interests, and that much of the payment received by the Indians for their land was dishonestly and improperly dissipated in the payment of Indian debts. (Tr. 1616-33.) In addition, the traders, and Schoolcraft, struck upon the device of granting their own Indian families reservations in order to receive compensation of over $48,000. (Treaty of 1836, Article Ninth.) The American Fur Co. was a major creditor to the Indians of the area; it had a substantial interest in the form of the final treaty; it was in a position to have intimate knowledge of the treaty negotiations. The daughter of one of the interpreters at the treaty negotiations, John Holliday, wrote frequently, and often daily, to Ramsay Crooks, the President of the American Fur Co. Her father was also one of the seven partners of that company. The court takes this as evidence of improper influence over the Indians, and an indication that the terms of the Treaty of 1836 do not necessarily contain the intent or represent the true desires and agreements of the Indians. (Tr. 1333, 1340-45, 1633-36.)

Henry Schoolcraft led the treaty negotiations even though he had a conflict of interest. In its final form the treaty provided $53,000 to relatives of Henry Schoolcraft in payments of Indian debts. Some of his relatives were traders, a fact which surely influenced him in his negotiation of the provisions of the treaty. (Tr. 1636-41.) Further, some of Schoolcraft's relatives received payments under Article Ninth of the Treaty. It provides for payment of monies to half-breeds. Knowledge that the passage of a treaty would greatly benefit his family was inconsistent with Schoolcraft's involvement in the negotiations. (Tr. 1642–49.)

Later on in this opinion I will deal with the Indians' understanding of the treaty in greater depth. It is sufficient to note here that they apparently were led to believe that they were to receive land, not that they were to cede it away. (Tr. 321-23.) See, *Worcester v. Georgia,* 31 U.S. (6 Pet.) 515, 553, 8 L.Ed. 483 (1832). It is apparent from the testimony of the witnesses and the documentary evidence that the Indians of this area were devoted to a way of life which included, and was premised upon, hunting and fishing. It is inconceivable that they would have given up that way of life and signed a treaty which they understood to make that way of life impossible. (Tr. 267-75, 831-32.)*

*[*The dedication to the Indian way of life is illustrated by the Chippewa and Ottawa reaction upon seeing the land west of the Osage River to which the government wished the Indian tribes to remove. Once they saw that there were no "sugar bush," or sap bear-*

ing maple trees, an important part of their life, the Indians refused to consider removal any further. (Tr. 1414, D. Ex. 62, 95.)]

D. *PROVISIONS OF THE TREATY OF 1836.*

The precise boundary of the cession was not known in 1836 because most of the land area was uninhabited and had not been thoroughly explored. At the time of the treaty no one knew the shape of the northwestern side of Lake Michigan. (Tr. 191.) Some interior areas near Grand and Little Traverse Bays were not surveyed until 1855. (Tr. 191.) In Article First of the Treaty of 1836 the Indians of the treaty area ceded to the United States the following area:

> Beginning at the mouth of the Grand River of Lake Michigan on the north bank thereof, and following up the same to the line called for, in the first article of the treaty of Chicago of the 29th of August 1821, thence, in a direct line, to the head of Thunder-bay river, thence with the line established by the treaty of Saginaw of the 24th of September 1819, to the mouth of said river, thence northeast to the boundary line in Lake Huron between the United States and the British province of Upper Canada, then northwestwardly, following the said line, as established by the commissioners acting under the treaty of Ghent, through the straits, and river St. Mary's to a point in Lake Superior north of the mouth of *Gitchy Seebing,* or Chocolate river, thence south to the mouth of said river and up its channel to the source thereof, thence in a direct line to the head of the *Skonawba* river of Green bay, thence down the south bank of said river to its mouth, thence, in a direct line, through the ship channel into Green bay, to the outer part thereof, thence south to a point in Lake Michigan west of the north cape, or entrance of Grand river, and thence east to the place of beginning, at the cape aforesaid, comprehending all the lands and islands, within those limits, not hereinafter reserved.

This area includes the waters of the Great Lakes and the connecting waterway (St. Mary's River) out to the international or state borders. The area is shown on a map attached as Appendix 1. (7 Stat. 491; Tr. 188-93; Ex. P-129, 129A.) In Articles Second and Third of the Treaty of 1836 fourteen reservations in common were retained in the following locations: Little Traverse Bay, Grand Traverse Bay, on or north of the Pere Marquette River, on the Cheboygan River, on Thunder Bay, on the north shore of Lake Michigan between Point-au-Barbe and the Mille Coquin River, the Beaver Islands, Round Island in the Straits of Mackinac, the Les Cheneaux Islands and land in the Upper Peninsula adjacent thereto, Sugar Island, at the Little Rapids of the St. Mary's River, a large tract on Whitefish Bay of Lake Superior and westward in the Upper Peninsula, Grand Island and at the head of Bay Noc. These reservations are shown on the map attached hereto as Appendix 1. In addition, the reserve at the St. Mary's Rapids retained in the Treaty of 1820 was continued. In accordance with the treaty instructions, the reservations in the original treaty were of unlimited duration (7 Stat. 491; Tr. 148-49, 193-99, 246-47, 250-51, 610-12; Ex. P-41, 53, 125, 129B; D. Ex. 311.)

Two of the reservations retained by the Indians in the Treaty of 1836 specifically include the fishing grounds in the Great Lakes adjacent to the land reserve: The reserve on the north shore of Lake Michigan and the reserve on Whitefish Bay of Lake Superior. These two locations were the only fishing locations where friction had developed between Indians and whites before the Treaty of 1836. (7 Stat. 491; Tr. 236-45; Ex. P-21, 23, 27, 37.)

The reserved area described in Article Third at Whitefish Bay includes within it a portion of the Bay. There is a metes and bounds description of the land area followed by the words: ". . . including the small islands and fishing grounds in front of this reservation." Schoolcraft's 1837 map (Ex. P-125) shows a longitudinal line extending out into Whitefish Bay. Dr. Tanner testified:

> It is a matter of some interest, I conclude, that there is discernible on this map a line from the mouth of the Tacquimenon [sic.] River out to the International Border that would encompass the small islands and fishing grounds in front of the reservation that are referred to in the language of the Treaty. (Tr. 197)

> Q: [By Mr. Greene] So, in summary, then, that line on the Schoolcraft map adjacent to the land reserve at Whitefish Bay goes out into the water and includes some portion of Whitefish Bay, is that correct? A: [By Dr. Tanner] Yes, it does. (Tr. 198.) As originally negotiated there was no limitation on the period of time the land reserves might remain Indian lands. (Tr. 199.) Subsequent to the treaty negotiations in March, 1836, the United States Senate unilaterally added the following language to both Articles Second and Third:

> Article Two, line two, after the word, "tracts" insert the following words, to wit: "for the term of five years from the date of the ratification of this treaty, and no longer;" unless the United States grant them permission to remain on said lands for a longer period.
>
> Article Three, after the word "tracts," in the second line, insert the following words, to-wit: "For the term of five years from the date of the ratification of this treaty, and no longer, unless the United States grant them permission to remain on said lands for a longer period." (7 Stat. 497.)

In July, 1836, the Indians were summoned to Mackinac in order to obtain their assent to the Senate's unilateral amendment. (Tr. 202; Ex. P-57 and 57A.) On July 18, 1836, Henry Schoolcraft wrote a cover letter to Lewis Cass, Secretary of War, over the Indians' assent to the unilateral Senate amendments. In that letter he said:

> Sir: I have the honor herein to enclose to you articles of assent to the Senate's amendments of the Treaty of the 28th of March last, concluded in a general council of the Chippewa and Ottawa chiefs convened at this agency on the 12th, 14th, 15th and 16th instant. The cession of the reservations at the expiration of five years has been strenuously opposed by a part of the chiefs, but was finally yielded, on a consideration of the practical operation of the provision contained in the 13th article of the treaty, which seemed to them indefinitely the right of hunting on the lands ceded, with the other usual privileges of occupancy until the land is required for settlement. (Ex. P-18 and P-18A, p. 2.)

There was considerable Indian opposition to the insertion of the language adopted by the Senate. (Tr. 204.) However, the Indians apparently assented to the Senate amendment, because even though the language was in part motivated by those persons wanting to remove the Indians from Michigan, it appears the Indians' fears were assuaged by Schoolcraft's explanation of Article Thirteenth. Thus, despite the fact that the land reservations might not last indefinitely after the Senate amendment, the right to hunt, fish and gather the fruits from all the ceded territory (not just the reservations) would last *indefinitely.* (See Ex. P-18A, p. 2.) In Indian tradition it is said that the Indians retained the right to fish and hunt "as long as the sun rose and the waters flowed." (Tr. 1071)

Dr. James A. Clifton, plaintiffs' rebuttal expert on removal treaties, testified that he had read virtually every removal treaty, he had not recalled seeing the particular language of the

Senate amendment ever before. (Tr. 2267.) Relying on Schoolcraft's memoirs (State Ex. 304, p. 538), Clifton testified:

> Now his [Schoolcraft's] explanation, as nearly as I can make out what is going on here, is that Senator Hugh White [Chairman of the Indian Committee in the Senate] for personal political reasons, asserted these alterations in these alterations in these Treaties, and not for any other reason.... These alterations were inserted in the Treaty, not because of any practical consideration or because of any need for land in Michigan, but for internal political reasons involving the Senator and President Jackson. (Tr. 2271.)

Two of the nine tracts of land reserved by the Indians in Article Third explicitly include fishing grounds and small islands adjacent thereto—the reserve on Whitefish Bay and two tracts of land between Point-au-Barbe and the Mille Coquin River on the north shore of Lake Michigan near the Straits of Mackinac. Dr. Tanner testified that this explicit reference to fishing grounds underscored the importance of these fishing areas to the Indians. (Tr. 237.)

Regarding the Lake Michigan fishing grounds, there had been a controversy in 1832 resulting from an attempt by two white traders, Edward Biddle and John Drew, to gain exclusive rights to fish there. (See Ex. P-21 and P-21A; Tr. 238.) The Indians were angry because Messrs. Biddle and Drew were dealing with a spurious chief and represented to the United States that the Indians would not object to the grant to them of an exclusive right to fish in this highly prized area. Some fourteen canoes filled with Indians came to Mackinac to protest. They were angry that Biddle and Drew claimed they had an exclusive right to fish in this area because Nabanoi, the spurious chief, did not have the authority to confer such a right on anyone:

> [T]he Indians were fully aware that the traders were to blame, making the application and trusted that their Great Father would not allow this to take place. (Ex. P-23, 23A; Tr. 241; see also Ex. P-25, 25A, 27, 27A.)

A similar conflict arose in Whitefish Bay when Messrs. Ashmon and Abbott requested a permit to fish there in 1835. They too were refused such a permit. (Ex. P-37, 37A.) This incident explains why the fishing grounds at Whitefish Bay were mentioned explicitly and included within the land reserved there. (Tr. 245.)

Specific fishing grounds were not explicitly mentioned adjacent to the other Articles Second and Third reserves because there were no similar controversies with traders in these other locations. But the location of all these reserves reflected the Indians' choice or preference and their dependence on fishing. (Tr. 246.) Dr. Tanner stated:

> I think I remarked earlier that all of these reserved areas are adjacent to or have access to very well-recognized fishing grounds, areas that I have referred to this morning as being reported as good fishing grounds by Strang and Baraga and other people later on in the 19th century. (Tr. 246.)

The record discloses, therefore, that the United States was willing to give the Indians exclusive fishing rights in both locations where the Indians were aware that the white men were likely to fish competitively. The United States made no provision to secure the Indians' fishing rights in any other areas, even though it was aware that white men wanted the right to fish and it was represented by traders who were parties to the original conflicts over fishing rights. It is likely that this negotiation gave the Indians the impression, and was intended by the United States to give them the impression, that the United States did not seek the fishing rights of the Indians. The United States was apparently unconcerned about whether it acquired these rights from the Indians.*

[*In addition, it should be noted that the granting language of the treaty is quite limited: "The Ottawa and Chippewa nations of Indians cede to the United States all the tract of country within the following boundaries: . . . ." (Emphasis supplied.) Notably absent are the words such as "all their right, title, and interest." Cf. Treaty of August 3, 1795, with the Wyandots, Delawares, Shawanoes, Ottawas, Chippewas, Potawatimes (sic), Miamis, Eel River, Weea's, Kickapoos, Piankashaws, and Kaskaskias, 7 Stat. 49 (cede and relinquish forever, all their claims to the lands); Treaty of May 31, 1796 with the Seven Nations of Canada, 7 Stat. 55 (cede, release and quit claim . . . forever, all the claim, right or title . . .): Treaty of November 17, 1807, with the Ottaway, Chippeway, Wyandotte, and Pottawatamie (sic) Nations, 7 Stat. 105 (agree to cede, and forever quit claim . . . all right, title, and interest which said nations now have, or claim, or ever had, Treaty of September 8, 1823, with the Florida Tribes, 7 Stat. 224 (do cede and relinquish all claim or title which they may have . . .); Treaty of June 2, 1825, with the Great and Little Osage Tribes, 7 Stat. 240 (do cede and relinquish to the United States, all their right, title, interest, and claim, to lands . . .); Treaty of October 23, 1826, with the Miami Tribe, 7 Stat. 300 (cede to the United States all their claim to the land).

The United States knew how to put specific language limiting rights of hunting and fishing into an Indian treaty when it wished to secure such rights from the Indians. An example is found in the language of the Treaty with the Winnebago, signed September 15, 1832 (7 Stat. 370; Ex. P-187, Article XI):

> In order to prevent misapprehensions that might disturb peace and friendship between the parties to this treaty, it is expressly understood that no band or party of Winnebagoes shall reside, plant, fish, or hunt after the first of June next, on any portion of the country herein ceded to the United States. (Tr. 2238.)

[16] The willingness of the United States to give exclusive fishing rights in the areas prized by the Indians and the apparent lack of any concern about Indian fishing rights in other areas destroys any inference which might otherwise be derived from the fact that the area of concession included water area. It is most likely that, recognizing the Indians' dependence upon fishing, as noted above, the United States intended that the Indians rely upon their right to fish to provide for themselves while in Michigan.

Turning to Article Fourth, it provides for the payment of annuities to the Indians for a twenty-year period. It also provides for education, books, teachers and schoolhouses for the Indians for a like period. Money was provided to purchase tools, equipment, medicine, the services of a physician and tobacco. Of particular importance is the language in Article Fourth providing for ". . . one hundred barrels of salt, and five hundred fish barrels, annually, for twenty years." Dr. Tanner testified that the government provided barrels and salt so the Indians could participate in the commercial marketing of fish:

> The Indians are packing fish into barrels and salting them down, because they're transported in barrels. (Tr. 253.)

Article Fourth also provided $150,000 to the Indians, but only after they assented to the Senate's unilateral amendment limiting the land reserves to five years ". . . and no longer, unless the United States grant them permission to remain on said lands for a longer period." (Tr. 255.)

Article Fifth provided for the payment of the Indians' debts to traders. This, of course, ". . . is probably one of the principal interests the trading people have in the Treaty process." (Tr. 256.)

Article Sixth provided for payments to the half-breed relatives of the Ottawa and Chippewa. (Tr. 257-58.) The Indians had much concern for their half-breed relations and thought of them as part of their family. (Tr. 258.)

Article Seventh provided, *inter alia,* for blacksmith shops to be maintained for the Indians. This was of particular importance to them because the blacksmiths could make and repair metal goods used by the Indians to catch fish. These goods included metal hooks, ice cutters and other fishing implements. (Tr. 260.)

Article Eighth deals with the subject of removal and will be treated in a separate section of this opinion.

Article Ninth provided for land and monies to be given to certain individuals such as Leonard Slater, John Drew, Edward Biddle, John Holiday *(sic)* and Henry Levake, to mention a few. Many of these persons who were singled out for special gifts under the treaty were traders who escorted the Indians to Washington, D.C. and represented the Indians at the closed door sessions when the treaty articles were actually written. (Tr. 262.)

Article Tenth provided for the payment of monies to the Chiefs. This was a common practice in treaty negotiations. Further, the Indians, as a part of their culture and traditions, expected to exchange gifts after an important agreement like a treaty was negotiated. (Tr. 263.)

Article Eleventh provided for small annuities to two aged and infirm, but highly respected, old chiefs. (Tr. 263.)

In Article Twelfth the United States agreed to pay the expenses the Indians incurred traveling from their homes to Washington (and back) in order to participate in the treaty making process.

Article Thirteenth, an extremely important section of the treaty, provides:

> The Indians stipulate for the right of hunting on the lands ceded, with the other usual privileges of occupancy, until the land is required for settlement.

Dr. Tanner testified that "the usual privileges of occupancy can be interpreted to mean living in the way that Indian people have always been in the habit of living." (Tr. 264)

> I think that this particular type of a provision was of considerable importance to Indian people. It usually winds up a treaty and is given as kind of assurance to them that they can continue to live in the manner that they have been accustomed to, and have no fear that their life will be disrupted.

(Tr. 265.) Further, Dr. Tanner testified that the term "usual privileges of occupancy" includes the use of all natural resources for economic and ceremonial purposes and for travel. (Tr. 265.) It includes hunting, fishing, gathering berries, collecting grains, gathering rush for mats and the like. (Tr. 266.) Dr. Clifton's testimony corroborates Dr. Tanner's on the meaning of the term "usual privileges of occupancy." The Indians could ". . . make use of natural resources as they were accustomed to doing or had been doing." (Tr. 2278.)

Article Thirteenth was extremely important to the Indians for several reasons. (Tr. 274; see also Ex. P-44, 44A.) First, as previously stated, it was explained to the Indians to mean that their usual way of life would not change after the treaty was consummated:

> [Article Thirteenth] was to indicate and reassure Indian people that they could continue living the way they had been living.(Tr. 278.)

Second, the Indians were very reluctant to cede all of their land and water. Some wanted to convey only small parcels to the United States. However, the United States wanted an extensive cession, and got what it wanted by use of "any means." In a letter dated February 27, 1837, from Schoolcraft to his superior in Washington, the Indians' reluctance to enter into a large cession is discussed. (D. Ex. 32 and 32A.) The United States wanted to extinguish as much Indian title as possible. Treaty negotiations were time consuming and costly. The United States knew that the price they would pay for cessions in the future would be increasing over time. Article Thirteenth, therefore, was used to persuade the Indians to cede much of their Michigan land and waters on the theory that so long as the Indians were allowed to use all of the natural resources of the land and water, a large cession would not adversely affect them. (Tr. 270.)

Furthermore, Schoolcraft stated (State Ex. 32A) that not only did he explain that Article Thirteenth would allow the Indians to continue to use all of the land and water resources of the ceded area, but that since much of the ceded land was uninviting to agriculturalists, it would not be settled and the Indians could use the resources of this land *indefinitely.* Several months earlier, in July 1836, Schoolcraft wrote a cover letter to Lewis Cass over the Indians' assent to the unilateral Senate amendment limiting their land reserves to five years unless the United States allowed them to remain longer and said that the reasons the Indians agreed to this change was because of:

> . . . the practical operation of the provision contained in the 13th article of the treaty, *which seemed to them indefinitely the right of hunting on the lands ceded,* with the other usual privileges of occupancy until the land is required for settlement.(Ex. P-18A, p. 2; emphasis supplied.) See also Tr. 275.

Dr. Clifton testified concerning the Indians' understanding of the term "until the land is required for settlement" and how that concept might have been explained to them.*
> *[*Dr. Clifton has a background in the field of descriptive linguistics and is familiar with languages spoken by the Ottawa, Chippewa and Potawatomi.]*
He said:

I would emphasize that that specifies not a date, not a season of the year, but a condition which is coming. And it is coming—it came gradually, obviously, over the course of a long, a large number of years. And it is very ambiguous as to any idea by terminal point when that condition might end.

There will also be probably some land that is not occupied and not used and unsettled. (Tr. 2278-79.)

With regard to the use of the term "indefinitely," which Schoolcraft used to explain to the Indians how long their usual privileges of occupancy might last, Dr. Clifton testified:

> Now I don't know that there is any such phrasing as "indefinitely" in either of these dialects of the language that the people spoke. I doubt that there is anything like it, just as we would not anticipate to find much other correspondence between the vocabulary of English and the vocabulary of this language. The languages were constructed on very different principles, so I wouldn't think that the Chippewa—the interpreter would be able to reach for in his head and get an equivalent.... He might wind up saying something like "a very, very, very long time, many winters, or many, many seasons," or something to this effect, conveying the idea that it was a long period of time. (Tr. 2283.)

Even though Article Thirteenth reserved the right in the Indians to hunt, fish, gather fruits of the land and use all land and water resources, it also contains words of limitation—". . . until the land is required for settlement." Dr. Tanner testified this meant to the Indians that they could use all ceded land unless particular parcels were occupied by non-Indian settlers:

> Q: [By Mr. Greene] Well, now when might—assuming for the moment that the language of Article Thirteenth would have some impact on the Indians in terms of their right to continue to use certain lands, when do you suppose that impact would occur? How does this Article Thirteenth—how is it going to limit, if at all, the activities of the Indians?
>
> A: [By Dr. Tanner] Well, I think from taking the statements that we have, that are translations from the Indian people themselves, it would be until the lands were occupied, until there appeared to be some population pressure that would indicate a need for that land. And all in all, I would say that some significant population density would have to be achieved throughout the ceded area before it would become apparent to Indian people that their lands were needed or they were required for use by any other people.
>
> Indian people, as you know, are accommodating people, and if their life was not interfered with, they would probably not undertake to make an objection. I think that the only general statement that I could make, Mr. Greene, is the one that I have made, that there would have to be some apparent density population for the need to use the land before there was any requirement to take up the land. (Tr. 275-76.)

Dr. Clifton's testimony on this subject was similar to Dr. Tanner's. He stated:

> They would see—the Chippewa—I will say this on general terms—all of the Indians in the Great Lakes area saw land, and what was ever on the land, or streams, what was ever in the streams, that were not occupied and used by someone else, as open to their use.
>
> And this is a very ancient way of thinking, not easily and quickly changed by any such document as this. (Tr. 2285.)

Article Thirteenth was paraphrased in a variety of ways before the treaty was negotiated, always in the context of hunting or occupying the land:

"the right to hunt and live on the tract, until it is required," Henry Schoolcraft, September 23, 1835 (Ex. P-4l).

"a defined right of hunting on the lands sold," Henry Schoolcraft, November 3, 1835 (D. Ex. 12).

"a full right to hunt on the ceded lands, as long as they are unoccupied," William Johnston

(Ex. P-43), and John Clitz (Ex. P-44), both on November 17, 1835.

"the privilege of hunting upon the land, and of residing upon it, until it is surveyed and sold by the government," Agreement of the Ottawa and Chippewa chiefs to cede lands, December 29, 1835 (D. Ex. 290).

"the usual privileges of residing and hunting on the lands sold till they are wanted," Henry Schoolcraft, treaty minutes, March 15, 1836 (Ex. P-17).

After the treaty was signed, Henry Schoolcraft paraphrased and explained the provision in similar fashion: "the right to live on and occupy any portion of the lands until it is actually required for settlement," *Memoirs* . . . March 28, 1836 (D. Ex. 304, p. 534); "I employed the term 'settlement' in its ordinary meaning to denote the act or state of being settled," letter of February 27, 1837 (D. Ex. 32; Tr. 266). "While [the lands] remain the property of the United States," letter of February 27, 1837 (D. Ex. 33); "the conditional usufructuary right," Report for 1837 (Ex. P-62, p. 3).

The phrase "until the land is needed for settlement" is ambiguous as to the term of Indian occupation. It was explained to the Indians as indicating a very, very, very long time in the future. (Tr. 2278-84; D. Ex. 32.) Many of the Indians of the treaty region lacked any experience base with which to understand even the "ordinary meaning" of settlement invoked by Schoolcraft. (Tr. 2417.) In using this phrase and explaining it as they did, the treaty negotiators placed any understanding of the term of Indian occupancy beyond the comprehension of the Indians, whose sense of time was significantly different from that of white Europeans. The Indians lived in a "continuous present." The assurances given the Indians that settlement would not take place for a "very long time," an "indefinite time," and other phrases equally beyond the comprehension of the Indians, were successful in conveying an extended period of time to the extent that they placed the time of the ultimate devolution (if any) of the land, a condition sought by the United States, beyond the time frame within which the Indians could understand human affairs. Since they lived in a continuous present, any such time period related to events beyond their continuous present, which, to them, would never occur. I find this to be a fact. Accordingly, the Indians understood that they would go on hunting and fishing for as long as any Indians lived in Michigan. (Tr. 51-68, 535-7, 542-58, 2281-94, 2482-89.) According to the Indian understanding, Michigan Indians could hunt and fish "as long as the sun rose and the waters flowed."

The United States only intended to impose a time limitation upon Indian usufructuary rights with regard to Indian use of unreserved ceded land. The United States intended to provide for settlement, an occurrence which it always expressed as happening upon the land. Article Thirteenth was designed to regulate peaceably the potential conflict between the Indians and settlers in land use. (Tr. 269-70, 274.) In the minds and comprehension of the Indians, so long as any Indians resided in Michigan, their aboriginal fishing rights would be continuing and undiminished in vitality, whatever might happen to their use of unreserved land. (Tr. 276-78.)

The Indians were incapable of understanding sale or cession of lands as understood by white Americans. They understood the treaty as a gift exchange. They would secure benefits from the United States in return for some interests in land. From the Indians' only understanding of land use, stewardship, they conceived of their gift as some particular use of the products of land, for they could not conceive of giving everything on the land. Here it is not possible to determine what particular use or uses they thought were granted to the United

States because of the limited treaty minutes and the very general treaty language. In other treaties such general language hid the fact that the United States had asked the Indians for only their tops of pine trees, giving the Indians in that negotiation the impression that the oaks remained theirs. Here we do not know what the United States told the Indians they wanted. Upon giving of their gift the Indians would understand that the United States received the Indian's land to care for it. Such a view was expressed by the Chief Pabanmitabi of L'Arbre Croche when discussing the right of the United States to cut wood on Indian land under the terms of the Treaty of Greenville: "If any wood is cut upon our land hereafter, we should be paid for it, and we authorize you to take care of our land." (Ex. P-30)

In the 1836 treaty, the Ottawa and Chippewa understood that they could continue to use the land to the extent necessary to continue to live their former lives. The Indians were accustomed to accommodating settlers on their land, and the treaty obligation to accommodate them was seen as consistent with the Indians' continuing to live their lives of hunting and fishing as before. The Indians did not understand that they would have to accommodate in the exercise of their fishing right because of the concessions given them during the negotiation. (Tr. 51-58, 535-37, 542-44, 556-58, 2281-94, 2482-89.)

[17] The 1836 Treaty did not describe the Indians' reserved fishing right as a reservation of use upon a condition subsequent, nor did the Indians have any comprehension of such a legal estate. *United States v. Shoshone Tribe,* 304 U.S. 111, 116, 58 S.Ct. 794, 82 L.Ed. 1213 (1938); *Whitefoot v. United States,* 293 F.2d 658, 667, n. 15, 155 Ct.Cl. 127 (1961), *cert. denied,* 369 U.S. 818, 82 S.Ct. 629, 7 L.Ed.2d 784 (1962).

E. *THE "REMOVAL POLICY" AND THE 1836 TREATY.*

The concept of removal, causing the migration of Indians from eastern sections of the country to the territory west of the Mississippi, has been traced by historians to Thomas Jefferson, in approximately 1803. Based on previous commitments by the federal government to assist the original colonies to extinguish Indian title within their boundaries, Jefferson as President felt obligated to some affirmative action. His effort resulted in a draft proposal to amend the Constitution creating an Indian territory in the West and officially establishing removal as a national policy. The amendment never went beyond the draft stage and although removal did not become officially authorized until the passage of the Removal Act of 1830 (4 Stat. 411), it was an item for treaty negotiation where circumstances demanded. (Tr. 2120-24.) In addition to pressure from expanding white settlement, other stated rationalizations for removal were the need to separate Indians from the evil influences of white society and also for purposes of national security in case of war. (Tr. 2133-38.) Such policy reasons for removal varied according to the region of the country involved. Population pressures were an important reason, i.e., settlers coming into an uninhabited or sparsely inhabited area and beginning to farm the land. (Tr. 212X-29.) In the southern states, the Indian societies were powerful, adept at picking up white men's civilized ways and therefore constituted a threat to the whites living in the area who wished to exploit the Indians and their land. Removal was seized upon as the means to rid white settlements of these advanced Indian societies. (Tr. 2128-30.)

In the Northwest Territories, the fact that some of the Indians had previously allied themselves with the British meant that removal of these Indians from the borders would make the border with Canada more secure militarily for the United States. (Tr. 2132-34.)

Land speculation was also a factor in fueling both the removal of Indians and the subsequent population growth of a ceded area. One form of this speculation involved the United States buying land cheaply from the Indians, and then selling it at a substantially greater price to white settlers and speculators in order to finance treaty provisions, and to raise general funds. (Tr. 2134-36.) The true motive for the majority of whites was economic gain through exploitation of the Indian. (Tr. 2137-41.)

Although removal was to be a voluntary act on the part of the Indians, both before and after the Removal Act, there were instances of forced removal. Andrew Jackson, President from 1829 through 1837, made requests which were actually orders and was responsible for a forced removal involving the Cherokee and Creek. (Tr. 2138-43.) Jackson went so far as to defy a decision of the United States Supreme Court, *Worcester v. Georgia*, 31 U.S. (6 Pet.) 515, 8 L.Ed. 483 (1832). (Tr. 2151-52.) The Removal Act of 1830 specifically provided that removal was to be allowed for "such tribes or nations of Indians as may choose to exchange the lands where they now reside and remove there" ("there" being territory belonging to the United States west of the Mississippi River). (Emphasis supplied.) There was opposition to the passage of the Removal Act and by 1838 the removal pressure eased substantially. However, some removals did take place during the early 1840's. (Tr. 2153, 2372-73, 2449; D. Ex. 310). Not every treaty negotiated with eastern tribes in the 1830's obligated the tribe to remove; in fact, most of the treaties of that decade did not do so. Pressure for removal varied considerably depending upon a tribe's location. Generally, removal pressure was strongest in the southeast and weakest in northern Michigan and Wisconsin. (Tr. 227-28, 504-06, 2128-32, 2143, 2159-62, 2273-74.)

For analytic purposes the treaties of the 1830's may be classified in three broad categories, depending upon the degree to which they do or do not call for removal of the Indians involved:

(a) Land base reduction treaties. These treaties involve a cession of part of a tribe's land base, generally with retention of reservations in common of unlimited duration. The consideration for the cession is usually payable on or near the reservations. No mention is made of lands in the west or of removal. These treaties are not removal treaties. (Tr. 2162-81; Ex. P-178, 179, 180, 181.)

(b) Permissive removal treaties. These treaties generally follow the provisions of the Removal Act. (State Ex. 310.) They incorporate land base reduction features, but in addition provide for the possibility of the Indians removing west if they desire to do so. They are generally vague on the details of and the time for removal and on the location and extent of lands to be provided in the west. (Tr. 2182-99; Ex. P-182, 183, 184.)

(c) Obligatory removal treaties. These treaties use language obligating the tribes to remove, and generally involve a cession of all tribal lands east of the Mississippi. Often specifics are set forth regarding the details of the move, a deadline for removal, and the specific land in the west to which the tribe is to remove. Often payment of annuities and goods is to be made only in the west, as an inducement to removal. (Tr. 227-28, 504-06, 601-05, 2200-22, 2226-45; Ex. P-184, 185, 186, 187, 188, 189.)

With the aforestated removal concepts in mind, I turn to the situation in Michigan in 1836 and the treaty area in question. Pressure from settlers for acquisition of Indian land—an important factor which often resulted in obligatory removal treaties—was absent from all but the extreme southernmost portion of the treaty area, on the north bank of the Grand River. Even the rough geography of the treaty area was unknown at treaty time. Henry Schoolcraft did not believe in 1836 that settlers would enter the northern part of the treaty area for decades, if ever. (Tr. 209-10, 227-28, 274-75, 2273-74, 2382-94; Ex. P-125, 133; State Ex. 32, 63, 251, 311.) The 1836 treaty did coincide with pressures to make Michigan a state. Because of this, there was probably reason to acquire the ceded portions in order to make the prospects of statehood more attractive in terms of territory available for settlement, industry, etc. (Tr. 2265-66.)

There is no mention of removal in the letters to the treaty delegates, treaty minutes, the treaty instructions, or in any of the other correspondence before the treaty. The first mention of the possibility of removal is found in the treaty itself, in which the original version of Article Eighth provided:

> It is agreed, that as soon as the said Indians desire it, a deputation shall be sent to the west of the Mississippi, and to the country between Lake Superior and the Mississippi, and a suitable location shall be provided for them, among the Chippewas, if they desire it, and it can be purchased on reasonable terms, and if not, then in some portion of the country west of the Mississippi, which is at the disposal of the United States. * * * When the Indians wish it, the United States will remove them, at their expense....(Tr. 205-06, 219-22, 504-06; Ex. P-15.)

The Senate amended Article Eighth in the following material respects (amended language underlined):

> It is agreed, that as soon as the said Indians desire it, a deputation shall be sent *to the southwest of the Missouri River, there to select a suitable place for the final settlement of said Indians, which country, so selected and of reasonable extent, the United States will forever guaranty and secure to said Indians.* * * When the Indians wish it, the United States will remove them, at their expense...

The apparent purpose of the amendment was to eliminate the option of removal to the area among the Chippewa of northern Minnesota. (Tr. 205-06, 219-21; Ex. P-15; State Ex. 17, 304, pp. 538-39.) The Senate amendment was not introduced into the treaty for any substantive or policy reason, but, as Schoolcraft believed, to embarrass President Jackson. (Tr. 199-202, 538-39, 2267-72; D. Ex. 304.)

The Treaty of 1836 is a hybrid type of treaty, with characteristics of both a land base reduction treaty and a permissive removal treaty. At most it is a permissive removal treaty, because the provision for payment of annuities is to be in Michigan (indicating an intention to stay); the language of removal in Article Eighth—"as soon as the said Indians desire it," "[w]hen the Indians wish it"—is permissive, not obligatory; there is no preamble stating that because of population pressures the Indians must move out west (as is common in obligatory removal treaties); there is a cession of land with specific provisions for reservations of land for the Indians; the land reservations are held in common by the Indian tribes; there is no specific parcel of land set aside for the Indians out west; and there is no removal deadline contained in the Treaty. There is also a provision for the usage of the ceded land until some vague future time. (Tr. 203-06, 226-28, 370-71, 504-06, 509-11, 1740-44, 2245-67.)

After the Treaty of 1836 was signed, the Indians of the treaty area never had any serious intention of removing west of the Mississippi. It is inconceivable that, knowing that removal meant cruel travel hardships and leaving behind the most important single aspect of their life—fishing—the Indians would ever have agreed to remove. (Tr. 212, 831-32; Ex. P-94.)

In 1838 an exploring party under the direction of James Schoolcraft, Henry's brother, went west to examine lands on the Osage River in what is now Kansas. The Indians of the Upper Peninsula refused to participate in this exploring party. In refusing to send anyone on the exploring party, they stated we "are not aware of any obligation to go west of the Mississippi." (State Ex. 92.) The purported acceptance of lands in the west signed by the exploring party accepts the land "upon which we agree to remove in the event of our emigrating." (State Ex. 99; Tr. 218.) The exploring party was not representative of the leadership of the treaty area of the Lower Peninsula. (Tr. 2316; Ex. P-190.) Just before the return of the exploring party to their homes, the members signed a document purporting to accept the land in the west that they had selected as a place for the removal of those Indians of the treaty area who wished to do so. (Tr. 205-06, 212-18, 227-28, 2300-30; Ex. P-190; State Ex. 52, 60, 62, 63, 92, 93, 94, 97, 99, 100, 252, p. 341.) The court doubts the validity of the exploring party's acceptance: The delegation expressed displeasure with the land because it contained no sugar maple trees. (Tr. 1709; D. Ex. 92, 93.) The selection of a party to determine whether the lands to which they would remove would seem to be an important decision for the tribes, and they would have undoubtedly sent their chiefs if they were serious about removing. (Tr. 2322, 2495.) There was some discrepancy even between the list of the members of the party who went out to see the land, and the list of the persons who signed the document of assent accepting the lands out west. (Tr. 2318-19; Ex. P-190.) It appears that James Schoolcraft, who was in charge of the exploring party, forced the party to sign the acceptance of the lands before the Indian representatives had an opportunity to go back to their bands and report to them. (Tr. 2324.) It is probable that the Indians who went on the expedition went for ulterior motives; they wished to stall the United States on the subject of removal; the younger Indians loved to travel, and the members of the traveling party were given rewards for going, such as blankets and guns. (Tr. 2323, 2496.)

At a general council of Indians at Michilimackinac after the return of the exploring party, the Indians opposed removal but accepted the lands in the west for whomever "may personally agree to remove." (D. Ex. 62.)

Neither the federal government nor the Indians took any further steps toward removal. The removal of the Indians of the treaty area was tacitly abandoned soon after the return of the exploring party, and was officially abandoned in the Treaty of 1855. No Indian from the treaty area ever removed west of the Mississippi River. (Tr. 205-06, 227-28, 282-84, 289-91, 301-03, 509-11, 2158; Ex. P-65, 80, 89; D. Ex. 63, 251, p. 345, 352, p. 341.) Nor did the Indians change their lifestyle as a result of the Treaty. (Tr. 218, 620 21, 1450-52, 1697-99, 1710-13.)

In summary, although the 1836 treaty was negotiated during the Removal Period and was not in conflict with the provisions of the Removal Act of 1830, by its terms it was permissive as to removal from the area ceded. Since it was permissive and since removal from the treaty area never took place, the classification of the treaty as a removal treaty has no bearing or relevance to the issues here in question.

F. *1836 TO 1855.*

From the Indians' perspective, the period between the two treaties was marked by dissatisfaction with the government's implementation of the earlier treaty and confusion regarding the status of the Articles Second and Third land reserves. (Tr. 282.) The Indians of the treaty area were given tacit permission by the federal government to remain on the reservations beyond the five-year period—the reservations were withheld from sale and continued in existence until another provision was made in the Treaty of 1855. (Tr. 230-35, 282-84, 301-03; Ex. P-65, 89.) Nonetheless, the insertion of the Senate amendment regarding the longevity of the Articles Second and Third reserves created apprehension and uncertainty in the minds of Indians and non-Indians alike. (Tr. 284.) One way the Indians attempted to cope with this uncertainty was to buy land in fee. The missionaries encouraged these purchases and some Indians used annuity money from the 1836 treaty to buy land. (Tr. 285.)

In the Sault Ste. Marie area, there was a local problem related to the destruction of the important fishing site and encampment at the St. Mary's rapids caused by the construction of the canal and locks there. (Tr. 285.) Construction began in 1853 and displaced those Indians permanently encamped there. (Tr. 285; see also Ex. P-81, 81A.) The canal and locks were completed and opened to traffic in 1855, about one month before the Treaty of August 2, 1855 was negotiated. (Tr. 287.)

In 1853, Henry C. Gilbert, the Michigan Indian agent, wrote to his superior, George Manypenny, Commissioner of Indian Affairs (Ex. P-80, 80A), and stated that the Ottawa and Chippewa would never consent to removal and it would be difficult to forcibly remove them because they ". . . are divided into so many independent bands, and are scattered from one extremity of the state to the other." Gilbert's recommendation was to allow the Indians to remain in Michigan, set aside land reserves for their benefit and convey parcels to individuals in fee " . . . as they become sufficiently enlightened to be capable of taking charge of themselves." Gilbert also said that the residents of the state would not object to the Indians remaining there. (Tr. 291.) Shortly thereafter, in March 1854, Gilbert again wrote to his superior expressing his views on the policy the government should adopt to permanently benefit the Ottawa and Chippewa of Michigan. (Ex. P-82, 82A.) In that communication, Gilbert listed several claims the Indians had under the 1836 treaty. He advocated that certain tracts of land, far removed from the whites be set aside for the Indians and be subject to restraints on alienation which subsequently could be removed whenever it was deemed expedient.

The Indians' dissatisfaction with the implementation of the 1836 treaty is reflected in part by a message prepared by a delegation of Ottawa and Chippewa who visited Washington, D.C., in February 1856. (Ex. P-87, 87A.) At that same time, this delegation sent another letter to the Commissioner of Indian Affairs inquiring about certain promises of goods and services under the 1836 treaty and asking whether those promises had been carried out. (Ex. P-86, 86A.)

In May 1855, the Commissioner of Indian Affairs wrote to his superior, the Secretary of the Interior, and said:

> Firstly, as regards the Ottawas and Chippewas in the State of Michigan, that I am of the opinion that an officer or officers of this Department should be designated by the President to negotiate with the Indians with a view of adjusting all matters now in an unsettled condition, and making proper arrangements for their permanent residence in that state.

* * * * * *

> It was anticipated that after a few years, these Indians would remove southwest of the Mississippi.

Hence the provision of a home for them there, as per article 8 of the treaty and the Senate's amendment thereto; *but they were not limited by the treaty to any time within which they should remove to avail [sic] of the homes thus promised.*

They have never emigrated west, but have continued to hold the reservations described in the 2d and 3d articles of the treaty—which have accordingly been withheld from sale to accommodate the Indians.

Measures should now be taken, in my judgment, to secure permanent homes to the Ottawas and Chippewas, either on the reservations or on other lands in Michigan belonging to the Government, and at the same time, to substitute as far as practicable, for their claim to lands in common, titles in fee to individuals for separate tracts.

* * * * * *

It may also be considered of some value to the United States to have the Indians relinquish their right to a home west of the Mississippi, although in my judgment, it would not be unjust to deny them the benefit of that right, *as they have not heretofore, nor is it to be supposed they will hereafter, avail themselves of it.* The amount that should be allowed them for its relinquishment, ought not, in my opinion, to exceed the value of lands they might receive for homes in Michigan. (Emphasis supplied.) (Ex. P-89A, pp. 1-2; see also Tr. 301-03.)

In summary, then, the 1855 treaty was negotiated to address two principal issues: first, the provision of permanent homes for the Ottawa and Chippewa in Michigan; and second, the settlement and consolidation of monies and services owed to the Indians under previous treaties and in particular the Treaty of March 28, 1836. (Tr. 295-97.)

G. *MEANING OF THE TREATY OF JULY 31, 1855.*

Article 1 of the Treaty of July 31, 1855 (11 Stat. 621) designated certain land to be withdrawn from sale from which the Indians were to select homesites. (Tr. 304.) Tracts were withdrawn for particular bands and are depicted on [Ex. P-129C] a map and overlay prepared to illustrate Dr. Tanner's testimony. From these withdrawals, band members were to select 80 acres if they were the head of a household and 40 acres if single. (Tr. 306.) After the land was selected, it was not to be alienable for a period of at least ten years after which the restriction on alienation, in certain circumstances, could be removed. (Tr. 307.) The procedure set forth in Article 1, however, was rarely followed, and many Indians never received an allotment, notwithstanding the treaty provisions requiring the same. (Tr. 307.)

These promises proved to be as ethereal to the Indians as the promises which they replaced. The Indians relied upon them to their detriment as they had on the promises before.

The land reserves under the 1855 treaty correspond, for the most part, with the land reserves provided for under the 1836 treaty. (Tr. 312.) Dr. Tanner testified that the land reserved under the 1855 treaty redefined the 1836 land reserves. (Tr. 312.)

Article 2 provided for the delivery of certain goods and services to the Indians, including monies for education, agricultural and carpentry tools, cattle, household furniture and the like. The Indians were also to receive annuities (paid over a fourteen-year period), and the services of blacksmiths.

Article 3 of the treaty provided:

> ARTICLE 3. The Ottawa and Chippewa Indians hereby release and discharge the United States from all liability on account of former treaty stipulations, it being distinctly understood and agreed that the grants and payments hereinbefore provided for are in lieu and satisfaction of all claims, legal and equitable on the part of said Indians jointly and severally against the United States, for land, money or other thing guaranteed to said tribes or either of them by the stipulations of any former treaty or treaties; excepting, however, the right of fishing and encampment secured to the Chippewas of Sault Ste. Marie by the treaty of June 16, 1820.

(11 Stat. 624.) This release clause categorizes the Indians' claims into legal and equitable. The legal claims of the Indians pertained to certain goods, services and annuities promised to them under the 1836 treaty, but which were never delivered. (Tr. 319.) Equitable claims, by contrast, related to removal (Article Eighth of the Treaty of 1836) which was never implemented. (Tr. 320.)

Plaintiffs' Ex. P-19 and P-19a are the treaty minutes, which is a long and comprehensive document. In that document are examples of those claims the treaty commissioners considered to be legal, as opposed to equitable. Before considering those claims, the purpose of the treaty was made clear by Commissioner Manypenny early in the proceedings:

> *Com. Meanypeny* [sic]. There were two delegations of Ottawas and Chippewas at Washington last winter, each making nearly the same inquiries concerning the affairs of their people. They each had the impression that there was unsettled business under the older treaties running back as far as 1795 . . . . The examination I made led me to the conclusion that there was little foundation for many of the claims the delegates made, while they were at Washington. I directed the acting Commissioner, when I left Washington from which place I have been absent four or five weeks, to examine & if he found any default in the fulfillment of the old treaties by Government, to advise me of it. The fact in relation to your business, accords with the fair presumption, because it is a fair presumption, that when the Treaty of 1836 was made all questions, growing out of previous treaties, of an unsettled character, were adjusted. With this general remark I now say, that notwithstanding this fair presumption, if it shall appear that there is still any thing actually due to you under the old treaties, you may rely upon my efforts to obtain it for you.

(Ex. p-19A, pp. 10-11.)

Examples of legal claims the Indians had for promises made by the United States included the following: The Indians inquired about whether annuities promised under the 1836 treaty were paid. They wanted to know if the money for agricultural implements, school houses and books, medicines and vaccines, and annuities for half-breeds, has been paid. (Tr. 294-97, 318-21, 323-24; Ex. P-19, pp. 14, 17-22, 27-28, 52.)

Contrasting with these "legal" claims are those the treaty commissioners referred to as "equitable:"

> *As-sa-gon.* At the treaty of 36—in ceding lands there was a provision made for lands to Indians, who wished to remove West of the Mississippi. A year of two after a delegation of the tribes went West of that river & were told the land on which they stood was theirs. What is to be done with that land?

Heamlin Intpt. [undoubtedly Hamelin throughout] *Com. Meanypeny* [sic]. The Indians never having removed they hold not land West of the Mississippi. The question however, is of an equitable character & will be considered.

Heamlin Intpt.

Agt. Gilbert—explains that the treaty simply provides for a suitable home west of the Mississippi, if they desire to go there.

Heamlin Intpt.

As-sa-gon We next wish to call your attention to where the government, in the Treaty of 1836, provides that it will remove the Indians. We wish to claim the amount of the expense of removal, out-fit & one years subsistence.

Heamlin Intpt.

Com. Meanypeny [sic]. Those provisions relate to events that have not taken place & are consequently dependent upon contingencies that have never transpired. We may regard them equitably; but legally & strictly the Indians have no rights under them.

(Ex P-19A, pp 22-23.)

Com. Meanypeny [sic]. As I remarked to you yesterday you have no legal right to the lands West of Mississippi unless you remove. You rights, while you remain here are entirely equitable in their nature. Having determined that you will not remove it is now a question how you will settle your affairs here. It is vain to request money for those lands. We will not give it. I cannot listen to it.

(Ex. P-19A, p. 32.)

Com. Meanypeny [sic]...I do not understand that the Indians have any right under the treaty to commutation for the expense of removal, subsistence & outfit. That was in consideration of you removal. It was no part of the price of you land. I feel inclined, however, to be liberal with you in the adjustment of these equitable matters.

(Ex. P-19A, p. 47.)

Waw-be-geeg...You promised if you took me West of the Mississippi to give me lands, outfit and subsistence for a year. The land West of the Mississippi is better than the land here. You have kept a large amount of money in your pocket by not removing us. We wish you to give us what is equitable.

John Johnston, Intpt.

Com Meanypeny [sic]. I admire the ingenuity of Waw-be-geeg & I doubt not that this speech will impress our minds. I wish it understood though that the government is not *indebted* to the Ottawas and Chippewas for that removal and subsistence matter. It is time we saved some money by not removing you, but it was not yours but the government's money that we waved. *We have been ready to remove you. You thought it best to stay & you were right. We think we may say in view of the equities of the subject that we will allow some sum in commutation....*(Emphasis supplied.)

(Ex. P-19, p. 43.)

In summary, "equitable" claims that Indians had against the United States arose from Article Eighth (removal) of the 1836 treaty. (Tr. 323-34.) "Legal" claims of the Indians related to specific sums of money the United States had explicitly promised to pay under the 1836 treaty, but had not in fact been delivered to the Indians. The Indians were asking for an accounting from the United States. (Tr. 323.) They wanted to be certain the lengthy list of monies earmarked for particular purposes had in fact been expended as promised.

Dr. Tanner testified that a review of the 1855 treaty minutes (Ex. P-19, 19A), reveals no mention whatever of fishing or fishing rights. (Tr. 326.) She also testified Article 3 had no impact whatsoever on the fishing rights the Indians reserved under the earlier treaty of 1836. (Tr. 326.) Further, Dr. Tanner could discern nothing from the body of correspondence she reviewed or from any other source which would lead her to believe that Commissioners Gilbert and Manypenny thought that Article 3 of the 1855 treaty had any impact on Indian fishing. (Tr. 327.) The only mention of fishing in the treaty relates to the St. Mary's rapids;

however, at the time of the 1855 treaty, this important fishery had been destroyed due to the construction of the canal and docks [sic].

> A. [By Dr. Tanner] This [the 1855 treaty] is an accounting Treaty. They are trying to consolidate the debts of the Government to the Indian people, what Indian people are owed. They are interested in money and in getting permanent homes, and the Sault bands, of course, are interested in getting money for their   fishery that has been damaged, but there isn't any other discussion about fishing at all.
>
> Q. [By Mr. Greene] Is that a reference to the last portion of Article 3 of the 1855 Treaty?
>
> A. Yes, that is the only claim. The damage claim of the Sault bands....but that is the only item that is not handled by the terms of the July 31, 1855 Treaty. That is the only outstanding claim.
>
> Q. And is that the subject of another treaty?
>
> A. Yes, that is the subject of a separate Treaty on August—
>
> Q. When was that Treaty negotiated?
>
> A. On August 2nd.
>
> Q. So it was two days after the July 31st Treaty?
>
> A. Yes, two days later. It was a separate discussion.
>
> Q. And as to the claim there, that is for the fishery that had been destroyed at the Sault Rapids, is that it?
>
> A. Yes, that's it.
>
> Q. And how was it destroyed?
>
> A. By digging the canal....

(Tr. 325-27.) Neither the legal nor the equitable claims released by the third article of the treaty included the Indians' right to fish in the waters of the Great Lakes. (Tr. 294-97, 318-24; Ex P-19, pp. 2-5, 14, 20, 22-23, 27-28, 32, 47, 52; Ex. P-82, 87.) Only financial obligations were released. Apart from the issue of compensation for the diminishment of the fishery at the Sault rapids—itself a financial matter—the Treaty of 1855 had nothing whatever to do with fishing or the fishing rights of the Indians of the treaty area. There is nothing in the written records of the treaty councils or other accounts of discussions with the Indians to indicate that fishing rights were discussed at all, or that the Indians were told that their existing fishing activities would be in any way curtailed or restricted by the treaty. (Tr. 326-28; Ex. P-19.)*

*[*The financial claims released by Article 3 are well documented in the record. They are specifically enumerated a number of times. One key document is a letter from Henry Gilbert, the Indian Agent for Michigan, to the Commissioner of Indian Affairs, of March 6, 1954, in which he lists the claims of the Indians which should be settled in a new treaty (Ex. P-82 and 82A):*

The Indians of Michigan are principally of the Chippewas tribe. There ar also remaining small remnants of the Ottawas & Pottawatomies. Their business with the Government is mainly based upon the stipulation of the Treaty of Washington of March 28th, 1836. The Annuities due by this Treaty will expire with two more payments in 1855. The only remaining claims of the Indians under it upon the General Government will then be—

1. For amount withheld & invested in stocks, $1000 per annum for 20 years. See Art. 4.—$20,000 to which sum the accrued interest should be added.

2. For amount due the Indians for limiting their reservations by Senate Amendment to Art. 4—$200,000.

3. A reasonable commutation for lands west of the Mississippi to which they would have been entitled had they removed thither & in estimating this item the expenses of removal & subsistence, all which has been saved to the United States should be taken into account.

All other Treaty stipulations for the benefit of the Michigan Indians are permanent in their nature & under them small annuities have been paid for many years. They are as follows—

1. To the Ottawas under the provisions of the Treaties of 1795, 1807, 1818 & 1821: $1700.00

2. To the Chippewas of Saginaw & of Swan Creek & Black River, under the Treaties of 1795, 1807 & 1819: $2500.00

3. To the Pottawatomies under the Treaty of July 29, 1828: $1587.50

4. To the Pottawatomies of Huron [under the] Treaty of Nov. 17, 1807: $400.00

The Chippewas of Saginaw have also a claim upon the government under the Treaty of Detroit of Jan. 14, 1837 & which was modified & explained by the Treaty of Flint of Dec. 20, 1837 & the Treaty of Saginaw of Jan. 23, 1838 for the proceeds of the lands ceded by that Treaty whenever the same shall be sold.

There is also an annual appropriation under Art. 8 Treaty of 24th, Sept. 1819 of: $2000.00

I am of the opinion that all these claims of every description may be settled and compromised with the Indians, with great benefit to them & advantageously to the United States.

In valuing the various claims against the United States for purposes of arriving at a settlement figure, agent Gilbert, who was also a treaty commissioner, made the following calculation during the negotiations (Ex. P-19 and 19A, pp. 51-52):

Agent Gilbert: My Brothers I want to say a work to you. The Commissioner thinks that we can put this money matter into a shape that will enable you between now & Monday to arrive at a conclusion. I give you then the following amounts.

Reservations	*$200,000*
Annuity Retained	*26,000*
Inprt. Fund	*50,000*

In conceding the last amount as a basis for your deliberations, if the commissioner on his return to Washington finds the amount more or less, you will be paid accordingly. Our impression is that, that is what is due. You may further estimate the sum of $30,000 for equitable claims on the removal, outfit, & subsistence matter. You may further estimate the annuity of $1700 at $30.00 which seems to us its value. This makes in all $336,000. That is the amount the Commissioner is willing you should take as the basis of your calculations.

As a final example, the treaty commissioners explained the claims in their letter of transmittal of the treaty in the following terms (Ex. P-19 and 19A, pp. 4-5):

"In consideration therefore of the difference in the value of the western lands, and the home now secured to the Indians in Michigan and in the release and discharge of the United States from all claims or demands on account thereof, or on account of the claims for "articles and equipments to each person" and also in discharge and full satisfaction of the $200,000 stipulated to be paid them in lieu of the reservations by the Senate's amendment to the 4th Article of the treaty of 1836, and in like discharge of the sum which has accumulated from the investment of the $1,000 per annum, provided for by the 4th Article of the treaty aforesaid, and in discharge of the $1,700 permanent annuity due to the Ottawas and heretofore specifically alluded to; in fact, in lieu and satisfaction of all claims, legal or equitable, on the part of said Indians jointly and severally against the United States for land, money, or other things guaranteed to them by stipulations of any former treaty or treaties (excepting the rights of fishing and encampment secured to the Chippewas of Sault Ste. Marie by the treaty of June 16, 1820) the United States are to pay to them or expend for their benefit, the sum of $538,400 in manner following, viz.: . . .

Thus, even though on several occasions the legal and equitable claims released by Article 3 were carefully enumerated, there is not the slightest hint that the fishing right was included. Aside from the issue of compensation for the impairment of the reservation and fishery at the Sault rapids, dealt with separately in the Treaty of August 2, 1855 (11 Stat. 631)—which was itself a financial matter— the Treaty of 1855 had nothing whatever to do with the fishing rights of the Indians of the treaty area. There is nothing in the treaty minutes or other documents to indicate that fishing rights were discussed at all, or that the Indians were told that their existing fishing activities would be in any way curtailed or restricted by the treaty. (Tr. 326-28)

The treaty had no impact on any fishing rights the Indians might have had prior to the 1855 treaty.

It is probable that the Indians at these treaty negotiations did not understand such legal terms as "legal and equitable," "satisfaction of claims," and "release and discharge." (Tr. 1482-84, 1490-91.)

Article 5 of the 1855 treaty provides:

> ARTICLE 5. The tribal organization of said Ottawa and Chippewa Indians, except so far as may be necessary for the purpose of carrying into effect the provisions of this agreement, is hereby dissolved; and if at any time hereafter, further negotiations with the United States, in references to any matters contained herein, should become necessary, no general convention of the Indians shall be called; but such as reside in the vicinity of any usual place of payment, or those only who are immediately interested in the questions involved, may arrange all matters between themselves and United States, without the concurrence of other portions of their people, and as fully and conclusively, and with the same effect in every respect, as if all were represented. (11 Stat. 624.)

Article 5 must be understood in the context of the Treaty of 1836 and the culture or the Indians of the treaty area. The Treaty of 1836 was formally entered into by an entity called "the Ottawas and Chippewa nation of Indians." However, neither the Ottawa not the Chippewa was politically organized at the tribal level. The primary unit of political and economic organization was the band, a more localized entity frequently associated with a village. From both a cultural and a political perspective there never was such an entity as the Ottawa and Chippewa nation—it was put together by the federal government for the purpose of obtaining a cession in 1836. (Tr. 100-02, 772-76, 770-81.)

After the Treaty of 1836, however, this artificial entity had existence at least to the extent that there were problems regarding the implementation of the Treaty of 1836. The federal government in 1855 wished to put an end to the myriad financial problems which had arisen. A new treaty also was a good opportunity to put an end to the "Ottawa and Chippewa nation." The Indian problems of the era were of a localized and specific, rather than a broad and general nature, and dealing with these problems with the large artificial group was costly, time-consuming and unwieldy. By means of Article 5, the federal government was able in the future to deal with the tribes, bands or communities of the treaty area more cheaply, efficiently and effectively on matters of local concern. There was no change in the way in which they were dealt with by the federal Indian agents after the treaty, save one: they were never again convened or dealt with as one entity—not even to assent the the Senate amendments to the treaty. (Tr. 331-35, 779-81; Ex. P-19.)

The Indians of the treaty area also had strong reasons for wanting Article 5. Though they were closely related, the Ottawa and the Chippewa were never happy at being lumped together as one entity. Megis Ininne, an Ottawa chief from the Grand River, complained of the inclusion of the Chippewa in the Treaty of 1836 during the negotiation of that treaty. (Ex. P-17 and 17A, p. 9.) The same objection was raised in the negotiations in 1855, this time by Waw-be-geeg, a Chippewa chief from the Upper Peninsula:

> At the Treaty of 36, our fathers were in partnership with the Ottawas, but now the partnership is finished and we who come from the foot of Lake Superior wish to do our business for ourselves.

(Ex. P-19 and 19A, p. 33.) This concern was reported by Waw-be-geeg near the end of the negotiations and was met by Commissioner Manypenny, who explained the effect of Article 5 during this exchange.

> *Waw-be-geeg.****I told you when I first came that I wanted to be separated from the Ottawas and you have not answered me. We have sat here and heard you talk to the Ottawas—while you paid no attention to us.
>
> *Com. Meanypenny* [sic].***The very case you suggested is met in the treaty—you are separated as you desire. This treaty you and the Ottawas must sign together is because the old treaty of 36 was made in that way, but here we have followed your suggestion and provide . . . that no general council shall be called.

(Ex. P-19 and 19A, p. 69.) Thus, the Indians, like the federal government sought and obtained in Article 5 an end to the artificially constructed "Ottawa and Chippewa nation." (Tr. 331-35.)

H. *TRIBAL FISHING REGULATION.*

The Sault Ste. Marie Tribe of Chippewa Indians regulates the fishing of its members in the waters of the Great Lakes within the treaty area and requires its members who fish commercially to have a tribal fishing license and a treaty fishing identification card issued by the United States Department of the Interior pursuant to 25 C.F.R. part 256. The tribe enacts its own fishing rules and regulations subject to the review of the Secretary of the Interior, imposes and collects a license fee, imposes restrictions on time, manner and place of taking, and requires its fishermen to submit catch reports. (Tr. 1139-40; Ex. P-120, 165.)

The Bay Mills Indian Community regulates the fishing of its members in the waters of the Great Lakes within the treaty area and requires its members who fish commercially to have a tribal fishing license and a treaty fishing identification card issued by the United States Department of Interior pursuant to 25 C.F.R. part 256. The tribe has a conversation code and a conservation committee which includes ex-offficio members from the Michigan Department of Natural Resources and the United States Fish and Wildlife Service. The committee promulgates rules and regulations governing fishing. The tribe imposes and collects a license fee, imposes restriction on the time, manner and place of taking, and requires its fishermen to submit catch reports. (Tr. 1080-81; Ex. P-162,163.)

Members of the tribes which are parties to this action can trace their lineage to the Ottawa and Chippewa tribes which were beneficiaries of the Treaty of Ghent and whose leaders signed the Treaties of 1836 and 1855. (Tr. 1060-61, 1064, 1128,1179.)

V. Conclusions of Law

A. *PARTIES.*

[18] Ancestors and members of the plaintiff tribes have continuously exercised Indian fishing rights since the 1836 Treaty without abandonment. *Williams v. Chicago,* 242 U.S.

434, 37 S.Ct. 142, 61 L.Ed. 414 (1917). By organizing the tribes under the provisions of the Indian Reorganization Act, 25 U.S.C. § 471, *et seq.,* approving their constitutions, and issuing tribal treaty fishing identification cards to their members pursuant to 25 C.F.R. part 256, the Secretary or the Interior has recognized the plaintiff-intervenor tribes as the modern tribal successors to the Indians who were signatory to the Treaty of 1836. The Bay Mills Indian Community and the Sault Ste. Marie Tribe of Chippewa Indians are Indian tribes which are political successors in interest to the Indians who were signatory to the Treaty of March 28, 1836 (7 Stat. 491). *United States v. John,* 437 U.S. 634, 98 S.Ct. 2541, 57 L.Ed.2d 489 (1978); *United States v. Jackson,* 280 U.S. 183, 50 S.Ct. 143, 74 L.Ed. 361 (1930); *United States v. Sandoval,* 231 U.S. 28, 34 S.Ct. 1, 58 L.Ed. 107 (1913); *United States v. Holliday,* 70 U.S. (3 Wall.) 407, 18 L.Ed. 182 (1866); *United States v. Washington,* 520 F.2d 676 (9th Cir. 1975); *United States v. Wright,* 53 F.2d 300 (4th Cir. 1931).

B. *CANONS OF TREATY CONSTRUCTION.*

[19] Certain axioms of treaty construction must be applied when interpreting Indian treaties to determine the extent of the rights reserved thereunder. First, the courts have held that treaties with Indians must be interpreted as the Indians would have understood them. This rule is first set forth in *Worcester v. Georgia,* 31 U.S. (6 Pet.) 515, 581, 8 L.Ed. 483 (1832) (concurring opinion of Justice McLean).*

> *[*"The most celebrated opinion written by Justice John McLean of Ohio during his thirty-one years on the Supreme Court was his dissent in* Dred Scott v. Sanford. *{60 U.S. (19 How.) 393, 15 L.Ed. 691} His biographer states that McLean's dissent was perhaps the most important of all of the opinions in the case because it 'expressed the northern consensus on the slavery question and was eventually written into the Constitution by the Civil war and the fourteenth amendment.'"* History of the Sixth Circuit, a Bicentennial Project, *at 51. (Cites omitted.)*

> The language used in treaties with the Indians should never be construed to their prejudice. If words be made use of, which are susceptible of more extended meaning than their plain import, as connected with the tenor of the treaty, they should be considered as used only in the latter sense .... How the words of the treaty were understood by this unlettered people, rather than their critical meaning, should form the rule of construction.

Some of the reasons for this rule of construction are expressed in *Jones v. Meehan,* 175 U.S. 1, 10-11, 20 S.Ct. 1, 5, 44 L.Ed. 49 (1899):

> In construing any treaty between the United States and an Indian tribe, it must always... be borne in mind that the negotiations for the treaty are conducted, on the part of the United States, an enlightened and powerful nation, by representatives skilled in diplomacy, masters of a written language, understanding the modes and forms of creating the various technical estates known to their law, and assisted by an interpreter employed by themselves; that the treaty is drawn up by them and in their own language; that the Indians, on the other hand, are a weak and dependent people, who have no written language and are wholly unfamiliar with all the forms of legal expression, and whose only knowledge of the terms in which the treaty is framed is that imparted to them by the interpreter employed by the United States; and that the treaty must therefore be construed, not according to the technical meaning of its words to learned lawyers, but in the sense in which they would naturally be understood by the Indians.

Accord, Choctaw Nation v. Oklahoma, 397 U.S. 620, 90 S.Ct. 1328, 25 L.Ed.2d 615 (1970); *Choctaw Nation v. United States,* 318 U.S. 423, 63 S.Ct. 672, 87 L.Ed. 877 (1943); *Tulee v. Washington,* 315 U.S. 681, 62 S.Ct. 862, 86 L.Ed. 1115 (1942); *Starr v. Long Jim,* 227 U.S. 613, 33 S.Ct. 358, 57 L.Ed. 670 (1913).

And in another treaty case the Court stated:

> In treaties made with them the United States seeks no advantage for itself; friendly and dependent Indians are likely to accept without discriminating scrutiny the terms proposed. They are not to be interpreted narrowly, as sometimes may be writings expressed in words of art employed by conveyances, but are to be construed in the sense in which naturally the Indians would understand them.

United States v. Shoshone Tribe, 304 U.S. 111, 116, 58 S.Ct. 794, 797, 8 L.Ed. 1213 (1938).

The Court of Claims has also addressed this issue:

> The treaty was dictated by white conquerors of a subjugated race. It is inconceivable that there was the kind of arms-length bargaining as to terms which would have made relevant as ascertainment of the Indian intention [sic]. Naturally the Indians wanted the unattainable—to be left alone. It is doubtful that the untrained Indian mind understood the ambiguities of Article III even though the white representatives went to some pains to explain the provision. A great and unbridgeable void existed between the language and culture of the two races. When one considers that the meaning of Article III was sufficiently in doubt as to require the interpretative services of the Supreme Court and several lesser courts in subsequent years, one can readily forgive the Indians for any lack of perspicacity or, indeed clairvoyance.

Whitefoot v. United States, 293 F.2d 658, 667, fn. 15, 155 Ct.Cl. 127 (1961), *cert. denied,* 369 U.S. 818, 82 S.Ct. 629, 7 L.Ed.2d 784 (1962).

In the context of Indian fishing rights, the Supreme Court long ago rejected contentions that Indians obtained no greater rights by virtue of a treaty than non-Indian citizens:

> This [that the Indians acquired no rights but those they would have without a treaty] is certainly an impotent outcome to negotiations and a convention which seemed to promise more, and give the word of the nation for more. And we have said we will construe a treaty with the Indians as "that unlettered people" understood it, and "as justice and reason demand, in all cases where power is exerted by the strong over those to whom they owe care and protection," and counterpoise the inequality "by the superior justice which looks only to the substance of the right, without regard to technical rules." . . . How the treaty in question was understood may be gathered from the circumstances.

United States v. Winans, supra 198 U.S. at 380-81, 25 S.Ct. at 644 (citations omitted). See also the United States Court of Appeals' decision in *United States v. Washington,* 384 F.Supp. 312 (1974), aff'd, 520 F.2d 676 (9th Cir. 1975), cert. denied, 423 U.S. 1086, 96 S.Ct. 877, 47 L.Ed.2d 97 (1976), wherein the court stated: "In treating treaty Indian fishermen no differently from other citizens of the state, the state has rendered the treaty guarantees nugatory."

In holding that the State of Washington could not exact a fishing license fee from Indians fishing outside their reservation because of the special off-reservation fishing rights secured to them by treaty, the Supreme Court followed a similar approach. It stated:

> From the report set out in the record before us of the proceedings in the long council at which the treaty agreement was reached, *we are impressed by the strong desire the Indians had to retain the right to hunt and fish in accordance with the immemorial customs of their tribes. It is our responsibility to see that the terms of the treaty are carried out, so far as possible, in accordance with the meaning they were understood to have by the tribal representatives at the council and in a spirit which generously recognizes the full obligation of this nation to protect the interests of a dependent people.*

Tulee v. Washington, 315 U.S. 681, 684-85, 62 S.Ct. 862, 864, 86 L.Ed. 1115 (1942) (citations omitted). (Emphasis supplied.)

[20] A second principle of Indian treaty construction is that doubtful expressions are to be resolved in favor of the Indian parties. See, e.g., *McClanahan v. Arizona Tax Com'n,* 411 U.S. 164, 174, 93 S.Ct. 1257, 36 L.Ed.2d 129 (1973); *Carpenter v. Shaw,* 280 U.S. 363, 367, 50 S.Ct. 121, 74 L.Ed. 478 (1930).

The rule of treaty interpretation that requires unclear phrases in treaties with Indians to be resolved in their favor was well stated in an important Indian water rights case:

> By a rule of interpretation of agreements and treaties with the Indians, ambiguities occurring will be resolved from the standpoint of the Indians. And the rule should certainly be applied to determine between two inferences, one of which would support the purpose of the agreement and the other impair or defeat it. On account of their relations to the government, it cannot be supposed that the Indians were alert to exclude by formal words every inference which might militate against or defeat the declared purpose of themselves and the government, even of [sic] it could be supposed that they had the intelligence to foresee the "double sense" which might some time be urged against them.

Winters v. United States, 207 U.S. 564, 576-77, 28 S.Ct. 207, 211-212, 52 L.Ed. 340 (1908). Followed in *Arizona v. California,* 373 U.S. 546, 83 S.Ct. 1468, 10 L.Ed.2d 542 (1963). *Accord, Alaska Pacific Fisheries v. United States,* 248 U.S. 78, 89, 39 S.Ct. 40, 63 L.Ed. 138 (1918); *Moore v. United States,* 157 F.2nd 760, 762 (9th Cir. 1946), cert. denied, 330 U.S. 827, 67 S.Ct. 867, 91 L.Ed. 1277 (1947); *Standing Rock Sioux Tribe v. United States,* 182 Ct.Cl. 813 (1968).

[21] In this case, if there is any question about the meaning of any of the treaty phrases, the interpretation must be that which is most favorable to the Indians. Thus, the meaning does not depend upon today's conditions, Indian policies of the past, or what is best to effect an accommodation between non-Indians and Indians. Rather, courts are charged with the responsibility of interpreting those phrases most favorably to Indians.

[22] Finally, the courts have prescribed that treaties should be construed liberally in favor of the Indians. The United States Supreme Court said in *Choctaw Nation of Indians v. United States, supra,* 318 U.S. at 431-32, 63 S.Ct. at 678:

> Of course treaties are construed more liberally than private agreements, and to ascertain their meaning we may look beyond the written words to the history of the treaty, the negotiations, and the practical construction adopted by the parties. . . . Especially is this true in interpreting treaties and

agreements with the Indians; they are to be construed, so far as possible, in the sense in which the Indians understood them, and "in a spirit which generously recognizes the full obligation of this nation to protect the interests of a dependent people." (Citations omitted.)

In *Antoine v. Washington,* 420 U.S. 194, 95 S.Ct. 944, 954, 43 L.Ed.2d 129 (1975), Justice Douglas concurring, recalled the still-operative language of *Choate v. Trapp,* 224 U.S. 665, 32 S.Ct. 565, 56 L.Ed. 941 (1912) as expressing the general rule of construction governing contracts or agreements with Indians:

> The construction, instead of being strict, is liberal; doubtful expressions, instead of being resolved in favor of the United States, are to be resolved in favor of a weak and defenseless people, who are wards of the nation, and dependent wholly upon its protection and good faith. This rule of construction has been recognized, without exception, for more than a hundred years. . . .

Accord, Tulee v. Washington, 315 U.S. 681, 62 S.Ct. 862, 86 L.Ed. 1115 (1942); *United States v. Shoshone Tribe,* 304 U.S. 111, 58 S.Ct. 794, 82 L.Ed. 1213 (1938).

[23] To adjust for the circumstances under which treaties were negotiated with Indians and to compensate for the advantage of the non-Indian parties in those negotiations, the canons of treaty construction set forth above were developed by the United States Supreme Court and other courts called upon to interpret Indian treaties. Only the clearest language depriving Indians of the rights which they had prior to the treaties will limit their rights today. *Menominee Tribe v. United States,* 391 U.S. 404, 413, 88 S.Ct. 1705, 20 L.Ed.2d 697 (1968). Therefore, a full understanding of Indian fishing as it existed at the time of the treaties is required to discover the meaning of the treaty in this case and the full extent of the fishing rights which were reserved by the treaty language in question.

If construction of the Treaties in this light results in a meaning which seems to deprive today's non-Indians of privileges which they thought were theirs, it only points up the great injustice which has been done to treaty Indians during the many years they have been deprived of their full rights for the sake of others without rights.*

> [*See *Settler v. Lameer,* 507 F.2d 231 (9th Cir. 1974); *United States v. Ahtanum Irrigation District,* 236 F.2d 321, 327 (9th Cir. 1956), *cert. denied,* 352 U.S. 988, 77 S.Ct. 386, 1 L.Ed.2d 367 (1957), *reh. denied,* 338 F.2d 307 (9th Cir. 1964), *cert. denied,* 381 U.S. 924, 85 S.Ct. 1558, 14 L.Ed.2d 683 (1965).]

[24] The rules of treaty construction which dictate such a result are the product of the circumstances in which the treaties were negotiated:

> The Indian Nations did not seek out the United States and agree upon an exchange of lands in an arm's-length transaction. Rather, treaties were imposed upon them and they had no choice but to consent.

Choctaw Nation v. Oklahoma, supra 397 U.S. at 630-31, 90 S.Ct. at 1334.

[25] Several of the factors relied upon by courts in applying the canons of construction to treaties exist in the present case. Virtually none of the Indian participants to the treaty spoke English. All affixed an "X" mark in place of their signature. The Indians had to rely on interpreters for an explanation of concepts, most of which were foreign to their culture. Dr. Clifton testified about the lack of correspondence between English and the Ottawa and Chippewa languages. Only general concepts were discussed, not the precise meaning of par-

ticular words. Under these circumstances, to interpret particular words in the treaty so as to defeat or diminish a reserved right would be flatly contrary to these canons of construction.

[26] It is also noteworthy that the Indians did not draft the treaty provisions. Rather, that was done out of their presence and behind closed doors by the treaty commissioners and the traders who escorted the Indians to Washington. It would be unconscionable, as the state has urged from time to time, to construe words in the treaty against the Indians when the facts establish that the Indians were not responsible for their selection.

The record is also clear regarding Schoolcraft's and the traders' conflicts of interest *vis-a-vis* the Indians. The traders were anxious that a treaty be negotiated in order that the Indians' debts to them be paid. Altogether the traders received over $220,000 as a result of the treaty. Five of the traders who escorted the Indians to Washington and wrote the treaty out of their presence—John Holiday, John Hulbert, Robert Stuart, Rix Robinson and Henry Levake—received in the aggregate of $57,000. (Tr. 1633; D.Ex. 312.) Members of Schoolcraft's family—James Schoolcraft, William Johnston, Susan Johnston, George Johnston and the estate of John Johnston—received approximately $53,000 in payment for debts owed them by the Indians. Further, there is evidence that Schoolcraft knew about the existence of these debts before the treaty was negotiated. (Tr. 1652.)

In addition to the payments to traders, Article Ninth provided for payments to certain individuals in lieu of individual reservations. Those persons included Rix Robinson, John Holiday, Mary Holiday, William Lasley, Henry Levake and others. (Tr. 1643.) These persons received almost $50,000 under this article of the treaty.

Before their arrival in Washington and afterward, the trader-escorts engaged in liquor trade with the Indians, and other of the principals had provided liquor to the Indians. It is probable that Schoolcraft relied upon them to provide liquor at the time of the treaty signing.

Combining these factors and considering the conflicts that Schoolcraft and many traders had, there can be little doubt but that the canons of treaty construction should be adhered to rigorously in this case.

This court adopts the meaning of the 1836 treaty consistent with the canons of construction. Under the 1836 treaty of cession, the Indians granted a large tract of land and water area to the United States. At the same time they reserved the right to fish in the ceded waters of the Great Lakes.

Because of the documented evidence demonstrating that the Indians were absolutely dependent upon fishing for subsistence and their livelihood, and reading the treaty as the Indians must have understood it, they would not have relinquished their right to fish in the ceded waters of the Great Lakes. Since the treaty does not contain language granting away the prior right to fish, that right remains with the Indians and was confirmed by the 1836 treaty.

[27] The language contained in Article Thirteenth of the Treaty of 1836, by its own terms could not have limited the Indians' right to fish in the waters of the Great Lakes because these large bodies of water could not possibly be settled by homes, barns and tilled fields. While the Indians might have been willing to give up their right to hunt on various parcels of land as that land became occupied with settlers, the vital right to fish in the Great Lakes was something that the Indians understood would not be taken from them and, indeed, there was no need to do so. The western movement of non-Indian settlers could be accommodated without requiring the Indians to relinquish their aboriginal and treaty rights to fish. While the

United States has the power to abrogate treaties by subsequent treaty or statute, it must do so expressly and emphatically. No such abrogation of the reserved treaty right to fish can be found.

C. RESERVED FISHING RIGHTS.

[28] Guiding this court is a key concept essential to a proper interpretation of the treaty. This concept is deeply rooted in federal Indian law and was very recently reaffirmed by the Supreme Court in *United States v. Wheeler*, 435 U.S. 313, 98 S.Ct. 1079, 55 L.Ed.2nd 303 (1978). In *United States v. Winans*, 198 U.S. 371 25 S.Ct. 662, 49 L.Ed. 1089 (1905), the United States sought to enjoin non-Indians from obstructing certain Indians from exercising their treaty rights to fish in the Columbia River. The Indians under their treaty reserved the right to fish at their usual and accustomed sites.

However, in order to reach those sites it was necessary to cross land which, subsequent to the treaty, was acquired by private individuals. The Court stated:

> . . . the treaty was not a grant of rights to the Indians, but a grant of rights from them,—a reservation of those not granted. And the form of the instrument and its language was adapted to that purpose. Reservations were not of particular parcels of land, and could not be expressed in deeds, as dealings between private individuals. The reservations were in large areas of territory, and negotiations were with the tribe. They reserved rights, however, to every individual Indian, as though named therein. They imposed a servitude upon every piece of land as though described therein.

198 U.S. at 381, 25 S.Ct. at 664. (emphasis supplied.) See also *Seufert Bros. Co. v. United States*, 249 U.S. 194, 39 S.Ct. 203, 63 L.Ed. 555 (1919), which affirmed *Winans, supra*. The conceptual framework, then, for interpreting the treaty is that the grant or cession in the treaty is not made from the United States to the Indians. Rather, the Indians were the grantors of a vast area they owned aboriginally and the United States was the grantee. The grant from the Indians must be narrowly construed, especially in light of the wardship relationship existing between the Indian grantors and the grantee United States.

[29] In addition to providing a conceptual framework for interpreting the treaty, *Winans* also teaches that reservations in treaties are not limited to land. Although the term "reservation" is commonly thought to pertain to land, other valuable rights not relinquished when Indians convey their aboriginal title are also reservations. The Indians can, and have, reserved rights to cross private land to reach traditional fishing sites as in *Winans, supra, and Seufert, supra*. In *Winters v. United States*, 207 U.S. 564, 28 S.Ct. 207, 52 L.Ed. 340 (1908), the Indians reserved or retained water sufficient to irrigate their land reserve. The agreement creating the Fort Belknap Reservation out of a much larger tract occupied by the Indians was silent regarding rights to water from the Milk River. Both the area of cession and the smaller land reserve within it were arid and of little use without water:

> And this, it is further contended, the Indians knew [that the lands were arid], and yet made no reservation of the waters. We realize that there is a conflict of implications, but that which makes for the retention of the waters is of greater force than that which makes for their cession. The Indians had command of the lands and the waters—command of all their beneficial use, whether kept for hunting, "and grazing roving herds of stock," or turned to agriculture and the arts of civilization. Did

they give up all this? Did they reduce the area of their occupation and give up the waters which made it valuable or adequate?

Winters v. United States, supra at 576, 28 S.Ct. at 211. See also *Cappaert v. United States,* 426 U.S. 128, 96 S.Ct. 2062, 48 L.Ed.2d 523 (1976); and *Arizona v. California,* 373 U.S. 546, 83 S.Ct. 1468, 10 L.Ed.2d 542, *reh. denied,* 375 U.S. 892, 84 S.Ct. 144, 11 L.Ed.2d 122 (1963).

During the last term of the Supreme Court, *United States v. Wheeler, supra,* was decided. There the Court was faced with the issue of whether a tribe had authority to criminally prosecute an Indian despite the lack of a congressional act authorizing such prosecution. The Supreme Court, reaffirming the *Winans* concept,*

[*This Court has referred to treaties made with the Indians as "not a grant of rights to the Indians, but a grant of rights from them—a reservation of those not granted." United States v. Winans, 198 U.S. 371, 381, 25 S.Ct. 662. 49 L.Ed. 1089.]

stated:

> That the Navajo Tribe's power to punish offenses against tribal law committed by its members is an aspect of its retained sovereignty is further supported by the absence of any federal grant of such power. If Navajo self-government were merely the exercise of delegated federal sovereignty, such a delegation should logically appear somewhere. But no provision in the relevant treaties or statutes confers the right of self-government in general, or the power to punish crimes in particular, upon the Tribe.

United States v. Wheeler, supra 435 U.S. at 315, 98 S.Ct. at 1088. Thus, modernly the *Winans* doctrine is "alive and well" and applies not only to reserved rights to land, but to reserved rights to fish, reserved rights to water and reserved or retained rights of sovereignty, i. e., the right to tribal self-government. Equally important is that reserved rights, as in *Winters,* arise by *implication.* And those notions are buttressed by the canons of treaty interpretation requiring a narrow construction of the grant made by the Indians.

[30, 31] The Indians' claim to reserved fishing rights here depends upon their having possessed such rights at the time of the cession. The legal predicate to this holding is a holding that they possessed aboriginal rights in the area of cession. European nations coming to the New World claimed title to lands which they discovered and conquered. See, *Tee-Hit-Ton Indians v. United States,* 348 U.S. 272, 75 S.Ct. 313, 99 L.Ed. 314 (1955), *Johnson v. M'Intosh,* 21 U.S. (8 Wheat) 543, 5 L.Ed. 681 (1823). Yet, the European nations generally, and Great Britain in particular, recognized an Indian right to occupy and use the lands claimed by these nations because of the Indians' aboriginal possession of the land. This right, a right of Indians to occupy land until the right is expressly extinguished by the claiming nation, was recognized by the United States in the Nineteenth century and is still recognized today. *Oneida Indian Nation v. County of Oneida,* 414 U.S. 661, 94 S.Ct. 772, 39 L.Ed.2d 73 (1974); *United States v. Santa Fe Pacific R. Co.,* 314 U.S. 339, 62 S.Ct. 248, 86 L.Ed. 260 (1941); *Worcester v. Georgia,* 6 Pet. 515, 8 L.Ed. 483 (1832); *Johnson v. M'Intosh,* 8 Wheat 543, 5 L.Ed. 681 (1823). Termination of this right is a political question. *Northwestern Bands of Shoshone Indians v. United States,* 324 U.S. 335, 339, 65 S.Ct. 690, 89 L.Ed 985 (1945). The Indians' right of occupancy, his "Indian title" is "as sacred as the fee simple of the whites." *Mitchel v. United States,* 9 Pet. 711, 746, 9 L.Ed. 283 (1835).

The Confederated Congress recognized Indian aboriginal rights when it passed the Northwest Ordinance . These were then reaffirmed in the Treaty of Ghent. During the War of 1812 with the British, certain members of the Chippewa tribes fought in the War on the side of the British. The British suffered a series of defeats during the war, but Britain was determined not to permit this to affect her Indian allies.*

> [*The British record with regard to treatment of the American Indians is remarkably better than that of the United States. For an Indian expression of this viewpoint, see the speech of O-Ge-Maw-Ke-to, n. 3, supra.]

Britain recognized Indian aboriginal rights during her occupation of the New World. She was resolved not to submit the Indians under her care to American sovereignty without treaty assurances that their rights would be absolutely respected. As noted by Senator Henry Clay and discussed above, Britain insisted that the Indians' rights not be interrupted, that this matter be included in the treaty ending the War of 1812, and made this demand a *sine qua non* to the conclusion of a peace treaty with the Americans. The Treaty of Ghent guarantees the Indians all the possessions, rights, and privileges which were recognized before the war.

[32] As is clear from the history of these Indians in Michigan, the Chippewas and Ottawas actually, exclusively and continuously used and occupied the ceded areas for the "long time" required to establish aboriginal possession. Although Chippewas predominated in the Upper Peninsula and the Ottawas predominated in the southern areas of the ceded lands, these peoples inhabited the region in joint and amicable possession. *Strong v. United States,* 518 F.2d 556, 207 Ct.Cl. 254 (1975); *United States v. Pueblo of San Ildefonso,* 513 F.2d 1383, 206 Ct.Cl. 649 (1976); *Turtle Mountain Band of Chippewa, Inc. v. United States,* 490 F.2d 935, 203 Ct.CI. 426 (1974); *Sac and Fox Tribe v. United States,* 315 F.2d 896, 903, n. 11, 161 Ct.CI. 189, 202 n. 11 (1963). These facts were implicitly and explicitly recognized by the United States when it negotiated the 1836 treaty.

As Dr. Tanner testified, the Indians' aboriginal occupation included not only a large land area but a significant portion of the Great Lakes. Accordingly, the cession is described as "all that tract of country . . . to the boundary line *in Lake Huron* between the United States and the British province of Upper Canada . . ." Further into Article First, the ceded area is described as:

> ". . . to a point in Lake Superior . . . thence south to the mouth of said [Chocolate] river . . . thence, in a direct line, *through the ship channel into Green bay* . . . thence south to a point *in Lake Michigan* . . . [and] comprehending all the lands and *islands* within these limits . . . . [Emphasis supplied.]*

> [*In Choctaw Nation v. Oklahoma, *397 U.S. 620, 623, 90 S.Ct. 1328, 1334, 25 L.Ed.2d 615, reh. denied, 398 U.S. 945, 90 S.Ct. 1834, 26 L.Ed.2d 285 (1970), the Supreme Court was required to interpret certain treaties to determine whether a reservation included the streambed of the Arkansas River. The Court concluded that the language ". . . thence down the main channel of the Arkansas River" was purposefully included and ruled that the tribe did have title to the bed of the river. If the United States had wanted to exclude the streambed it could have described the cession by reference to the north side or bank of the Arkansas River.]

The important decision of the Michigan Supreme Court in *People v. LeBlanc,* 399 Mich. 31, 248 N.W.2d 199 (1976) reached precisely the same conclusion regarding Article First:

Moreover, the area described in Article First, that being the territory ceded by the Ottawas and the Chippewas to the United States, extends well into the Great Lakes. For example, the ceded area is bounded in part by a line traveling from the mouth of the Thunder-bay river, "thence northeast to the boundary line in Lake Huron . . . thence northwestwardly, . . . through the straits, and river St. Mary's, to a point in Lake Superior north of the mouth of Gitchy Seebing, or Chocolate River...

People v. LeBlanc, 248 N.W.2d at 206 (emphasis in original, footnote omitted).

In exchange for this large cession of land and water the Indians received certain monetary payments and other goods and services from the United States. Within the area of cession the Indians reserved certain land parcels and rights under the treaty. In particular, they reserved nine land areas on the Upper Peninsula and five areas on the Lower Peninsula. The issue in question here is whether the Indians also possessed a right to fish in the waters ceded which they did not grant to the United States but reserved for themselves.

[33] The right to fish is one of the aboriginal usufructuary rights included within the totality of use and occupancy rights which Indian tribes might possess. *Menominee Tribe v. United States,* 391 U.S. 404, 88 S.Ct. 1705, 20 L.Ed.2d 697 (1968); *Kimball v. Callahan,* 493 F.2d 564 (9th Cir. 1974); *People v. LeBlanc, supra; State v. Tinno,* 94 Idaho 759, 497 P.2d 1386 (1972).

[34] The factual predicate giving rise to the reservation or retention of the right to fish in the Great Lakes is a showing of the Indians' dependence upon that resource. The evidence relating to Indians' use of the fishery resource, as related above, is overwhelming.

Dr. Tanner testified about the life cycle of the Indians during treaty times which included two major fishing seasons, spring and fall, as well as ice fishing in the winter. Dr. Cleland placed the treaty Indians' use of the resource into a historic and prehistoric context. All Indians of the Upper Great Lakes, including the Ottawa and Chippewa, were fishing peoples. The settlement patterns of native peoples of the Upper Great Lakes, including the treaty Indians in the case at bar, were strongly influenced by available resources, especially fish. It is no mere coincidence that the Articles Second and Third land reserves are all located on the Great Lakes and all adjacent to important fishing grounds. It is also noteworthy that most major archaeological sites in the Upper Great Lakes are near or within Articles Second and Third land reserves. In order to reach a conclusion that the Indians were not dependent upon this valuable fishery resource, the court would have to ignore hundreds of years of recorded testimony and thousands of years of prehistoric information.

That the treaty Indians were commercial, as well as subsistence, fishermen is also well documented and beyond dispute. The Indians caught fish and traded them for goods available to them from the European market. They were employed by the American Fur Co. to catch fish. Indians operated their own commercial outfits and sold their catch to the American Fur Co. as well. Years after the treaty, Smith and Snell (Ex. P-4) reported that most of the fishermen they surveyed were of Indian heritage. Right down to today a significant proportion of commercial fishermen on the Great Lakes included within the area of cession are of Indian heritage.

The Michigan Supreme Court decision in *People v. LeBlanc, supra,* also supports plaintiffs' contentions regarding the commercial dimension of the Indian fishery:

> The record below [which was much less detailed than the record here] clearly indicates that fishing was central to the Chippewa way of life at the time the Treaty of 1836 was negotiated.

* * * * * *

> Clearly, too, Chippewa fishing had a commercial dimension. In fact, Article Fourth of the Treaty of 1836 provided for the delivery of 10,000 fish barrels and 2,000 barrels of salt to the Indians over a twenty year period to be used in the fishing business.

People v. LeBlanc, 248 N.W.2d at 204 (footnote omitted).

The State would have this court find that the Indian fishery had no commercial aspect because, in effect, they did not own and operate the American Fur Co. But even the State's own witness testified that the Indians did not have the capital or the business experience to start such a venture. (Tr. 1770.) Besides, the American Fur Co. was "one of the most successful economic companies in the early American history, one of the prime examples of big business at this early period." (Tr. 1770.) This type of business activity simply has no analogue in the society of the Ottawa and Chippewa. If the standard the tribes are required to meet is that they too controlled a business like the American Fur Co.—the General Motors of the Great Lakes—then plaintiffs have failed. (See Tr. 1884.) However, there is no such burden on the Indians. Plaintiffs have shown that treaty Indians relied upon the resource for subsistence purposes and that their fishery had a substantial commercial dimension as well. From the beginning of the commercial market, as we understand and use that term today, the Indians were participants. Obviously they could not participate in a European-type market economy until there was one.

[35] On the basis of the findings of fact above, which concluded that the Ottawa and Chippewa Indians of northern Michigan have relied upon the catching of fish in the Great Lakes for subsistence and for commerce for centuries, and that such a reliance has been the one most important single aspect of their lives from a time at least one hundred years before any contact with Europeans right up until the time of the signing of the Treaty of 1836, this court rules as a matter of law that the Indians who are plaintiffs in this action held an aboriginal and treaty right under the Treaty of Ghent to catch fish in the Great Lakes at the time of the 1836 Treaty. *United States v. Santa Fe Pacific R. Co.,* 314 U.S. 339, 62 S.Ct. 248, 86 L.Ed. 260 (1941).

[36] Under *Winans, supra,* Indians retain whatever rights they possess which are not relinquished by treaty or taken by Congress. Rights are reserved by implication if they are not expressly relinquished and a contrary conclusion is inconsistent with the use of the resource by the Indians at the time of the treaty. *United States v. Wheeler,* 435 U.S. 313, 98 S.Ct. 1079, 55 L.Ed.2d 303 (1978); *Cappaert v. United States,* 426 U.S. 128, 96 S.Ct. 2062, 48 L.Ed.2d 523 (1976); *Arizona v. California,* 373 U.S. 546, 83 S.Ct. 1468, 10 L.Ed.2d 542 (1963); *Winters v. United States,* 207 U.S. 564, 28 S.Ct. 207, 52 L.Ed. 340 (1908); *United States v. Winans,* supra.

[37] On the basis of the following facts: (l) the Treaty of 1836 contains no language expressly relinquishing the aboriginal right of the treaty Indians to fish in the ceded waters; (2) at the time of the 1836 treaty subsistence and commercial fishing was essential to the livelihood of these Indians and for them to have relinquished fishing rights would have been tantamount to agreeing to a systematic annihilation of their culture, and perhaps of their very existence; (3) both parties to the negotiation were aware that the Indians had no way of sustaining themselves in Michigan except by fishing, and (4) the Indians did not understand the

treaty to limit their right to fish, it is clear that by the Treaty of 1836 the Indians impliedly reserved a right to fish commercially and for subsistence in the ceded waters of the Great Lakes. *Winters v. United States,* 207 U.S. 564, 28 S.Ct. 207, 52 L.Ed. 340 (1908); *United States v. Winans,* 198 U.S. 371, 381, 25 S.Ct. 662, 49 L.Ed. 1089 (1905). This holding is required by the above findings of fact and conclusions of law and by the rules of construction set forth in the beginning of this opinion. Further, however, in view of the dismal history which generally surrounds the dealings of the United States with these first inhabitants of this land, and the history of this specific treaty negotiation, punctuated by numerous instances of underhanded and perfidious dealings with these trusting and gentle people, simple justice requires that this court begin to put an end to the unfairness which has plagued the Indians in their dealings with the white man from their first contact with him, and restore to the Indian that which was by nature his, and now by right also. The holding does not go so far as to void the treaty because of lack of consent. See, *e.g, Lone Wolf v. Hitchcock,* 187 U.S. 553, 23 S.Ct. 216, 47 L.Ed. 299 (1903), where the Court held that it could not consider the validity of an agreement allegedly obtained by fraudulent misrepresentation because the question of the validity of the agreement belonged to Congress. The language of the treaty does grant territory to the United States. *DeCoteau v. District County Court,* 420 U.S. 425, 95 S.Ct. 1082, 43 L.Ed.2d 300 *(1975); United States v. Choctaw Nation,* 175 U.S. 494, 531, 21 S.Ct. 149, 45 L.Ed. 291 (1903). Were it not for *Lone Wolf, supra,* and *DeCoteau, supra,* which proscribe invoking the canon that legal ambiguities are to be resolved to the benefit of the Indians to the extent of disregarding clear expressions of tribal and Congressional intent, this court, would, on the record before it, identify this as an invalid treaty because it was the product of fraud, duress, conflicts of interest, coercion, and was very likely produced by the alcohol of liquor peddlers who sought to keep the Indians from knowing what they were doing.

D. *ARTICLE THIRTEENTH AS PROTECTION OF THE RIGHT.*

As the court ruled in *People v. LeBlanc, supra,* the language of Article Thirteenth embraced the right to fish even though fishing is nowhere specifically mentioned in the language of the treaty article:

> Given the central position of fishing, both subsistence and commercial, in the Chippewa culture during the time period of the Treaty of 1836, there can be little doubt that the Indian stipulation in Article Thirteenth "for the right of hunting on the lands ceded, with the other usual privileges of occupancy" was understood by the Chippewas to include the right to fish.

People v. LeBlanc, supra, 248 N.W.2d at 205.

The construction of the treaty language is consistent with numerous state and federal decisions. In *Menominee Tribe of Indians v. United States,* 391 U.S. 404, 405-6, 88 S.Ct. 1705, 1707, 20 L.Ed.2d 697 (1968), the Supreme Court held that the Treaty of Wolf River which created a home for the Indians "... to be held as Indian lands are held ..." included the right to hunt and fish:

> Nothing was said in the 1854 treaty about hunting and fishing rights. Yet we agree with the Court of Claims that the language "to be held as Indian lands are held" includes the right to fish and to hunt. The record shows that the lands covered by the Wolf River Treaty of 1854 were selected pre-

cisely because they had an abundance of game. See *Menominee Tribe v. United States,* 95 Ct.Cl. 232, 240-241 (1941). The essence of the Treaty of Wolf River was that the Indians were authorized to maintain on the new lands ceded to them as a reservation their way of life which included hunting and fishing.

391 U.S. at 406, 88 S.Ct. at 1707 (footnotes omitted). See also *Kimball v. Callahan,* 493 F.2d 564 (9th Cir. 1974), *cert. denied,* 419 U.S. 1019, 95 S.Ct. 491, 42 L.Ed.2d 292 (1974), and *State v. Tinno,* 94 Idaho 759, 497 P.2d 1386 (1972).

Both Drs. Tanner and Clifton testified regarding the Indians' understanding of Article Thirteenth and said that the term "usual privileges of occupancy" included the use of all of the ceded area including the Great Lakes fishery. The phrase of Article Thirteenth which purports to limit the right—"until the land is required for settlement"—was discussed above in the findings of fact. It is ambiguous as to any definite period of Indian occupancy. Since it was understood by the Indians not to effect their aboriginal and treaty rights to fish, but to leave them with the right to fish, "as long as the sun rose and the waters flow," it cannot operate to terminate these fishing rights. It was only intended by the United States to limit Indian use of particular plots of land.

The Supreme Court of Michigan came to an analogous conclusion in *People v. LeBlanc, supra,* when it stated:

> Undoubtedly this clause ["until the land is required for settlement"] was intended to protect the right of non-Indians to settle in the ceded area without interference from Chippewas claiming "the usual privileges of occupancy," and has limited the rights of the Chippewas to hunt. However, the ceded water areas of the Great Lakes have obviously not been required for settlement, and therefore the fishing rights reserved by the Chippewas in these areas have not been terminated.

People v. LeBlanc, supra, 248 N.W.2d at 207. The Michigan Supreme Court relied upon the fact that any other conclusion would contort the English language.

[38] I expressly adopt this holding as an additional ground for the conclusion that the limiting clause of Article Thirteenth does not impose a temporal limitation upon Indian aboriginal and treaty fishing rights in the Great Lakes.

In summary, the wellspring of the reserved right to fish in the ceded waters of the Great Lakes rests on its implied reservation from the grant of land from the Indians to the United States and also on Article Thirteenth. The right is implied because it was never explicitly ceded away by the Indians; thus, they retained it. The reason it was not granted was because the Indians were too heavily dependent upon fish as a food source and for their livelihood to ever relinquish this right.

[39] It must be remembered that one of the principal purposes behind the 1836 treaty was to pave the way for anticipated population growth caused by the westward and northward movement of settlers. Clearly this could be accomplished without the Indians surrendering their pre-existing rights to fish in the Great Lakes.

In addition to the Indians' implied reservation of this aboriginal right protected by the 1836 Treaty and their right under the Treaty of Ghent, the express language of Article Thirteenth protects the Indians' right to fish in the ceded waters of the Great Lakes.

E. *SCOPE OF THE PRESENT INDIAN FISHING RIGHTS.*

[40] The scope of the Indian right to fish at the present time is defined by the character of Indian fishing at the time of the treaty. Accordingly, the retained aboriginal right is not limited to any geographical area within the ceded area. Evidence has revealed that the Indians of 1836 fished extensively over the entire ceded area. They had the means to cover the entire ceded area and went where the fish were to be found. Therefore, the right cannot be limited in any artificial manner to imaginary and unrealistic boundaries within the area of cession. *Choctow Nation of Indians v. United States,* 318 U.S. 423, 431-32, 63 S.Ct. 672, 87 L.Ed. 877 (1943).

[41] Similarly, the means used to fish were not restricted by the Treaty of 1836 nor by the Indians in any other agreement with the United States. The Indians' right to fish, like the aboriginal use of the fishery on which it is based, is not a static right. The reserved fishing right is not affected by the passage of time or changing conditions. The right is not limited as to species of fish, origin of fish, the purpose of use or the time or manner of taking. The right may be exercised utilizing improvements in fishing techniques, methods and gear. It may expand with the commercial market which it serves, and supply the species of fish which that market demands, whatever the origin of the fish. *Peterson v. Christensen,* 455 F.Supp. 1095 (E.D.Wis.1978); *United States v. Washington,* 384 F.Supp. 312 (W.D.Wash.1974); *State v. Gurnoe,* 53 Wis.2d 390, 192 N.W.2d 892 (1972).

F. *THE REMOVAL ACT.*

The State endeavored to show that the Treaty of 1836 obligated the Indians to remove from Michigan to lands west of the Mississippi and that consequently the Indians were not concerned to preserve their aboriginal rights. Testimony was adduced through the State's witness, Dr. Mason, to the effect that removal was tantamount to an accomplished fact and that all persons associated with the treaty, including the Indians, knew that removal would take place at the time the treaty was negotiated.

The State's position in this matter ignores the history of the Michigan Indians, the Removal Act, and the language of the treaty here in question.

[42] First and foremost it must be remembered that removal of the Ottawa and Chippewa never occurred. Indeed, descendant Indians and successor tribal groups to those signing the 1836 treaty have remained in Michigan to this date and are party plaintiffs in this litigation. So long as the Indians remain in the area of the cession, they may continue to exercise their reserved aboriginal and treaty rights to fish in the Great Lakes.

[43,44] The Removal Act of 1830 does not mandate that the President negotiate treaties requiring removal. It is permissive in nature. Congress did nothing to lessen the obligation of the Executive toward the Indians.*

[*4 *Stat. 411.* American Heritage Pictorial History of the Presidents, *Vol. 1, p. 224 (1968).*]

The principal authorization of the Act is to make it lawful for the President to offer Indians who chose to exchange their homelands, lands west of the Mississippi belonging to the United States. The Act did nothing to relieve the United States of prior treaty obligations toward any Indian tribes. Section 7 of the Act declares: "Provided, That nothing in this act contained shall be construed as authorizing or directing the violation of any existing treaty between the United States and any of the Indian tribes."

When the removals took place under this Act, it was at the "request" of President Jackson. It was at Jackson's behest that Cass and Schoolcraft sought to have the Indians of Northern Michigan removed. They were not successful, however. The language of the 1836 treaty does not mandate removal of the Indians. It stated that ". . . as soon as the said Indians desire it . . ." and later in the Article ". . . When the Indians wish it, the United States will remove them . . . ." To argue that this language mandates removal is patently absurd. Similarly, many of the treaties negotiated during the 1830's did not mandate removal.

Government officials and the United States Senate knew how to select language mandating removal when they desired.*

*[*The language of two removal treaties introduced into evidence clearly establishes this point. The 1833 Treaty with the Chippewa (Ex. P-188) includes the following language:*

And it is further agreed that as fast as the said Indians shall be prepared to emigrate, they shall be removed at the expense of the United States, and shall receive subsistence while upon the journey, and for one year after their arrival at their new home. It being understood, that the said Indians are to remove from all that part of the land now ceded, which is within the State of Illinois, immediately on the ratification of this treaty, but to be permitted to retain possession of the country north of the boundary line of the said state, for the term of three years, without molestation or interruption and under the protection of the laws of the United States.

The 1832 Treaty with the Winnebago (Ex. P-87) provided in pertinent part:

The exchange of the two tracts of country to take place on or before the first day of June next: that is to say, on or before that day, all the Winnebagoes now residing within the country ceded to them, as above, shall leave the said country, when, and not before, they shall be allowed to enter upon the country granted by the United States, in exchange.

Later in that same treaty, Article XI provided:

Article XI: In order to prevent misapprehensions that might disturb peace and friendship between the parties to this treaty, it is expressly understood that no band or party of Winnebagoes shall reside, plant, fish, or hunt after the first day of June next, on any portion of the country herein ceded to the United States.]

Comparing the language of the 1832 Treaty with the Winnebago and the 1833 Treaty with the Chippewa to the language employed in Article Eighth in the Treaty of 1836, the conclusion is inescapable—the Treaty of 1836 did not require, obligate, or mandate removal of the Indians to lands west of the Mississippi.

None of the critical correspondence between government officials leading to the 1836 treaty mentions the word "removal." The treaty instructions to Schoolcraft from Lewis Cass dated March 11, 1836 (Ex. P-53, 53A) did not mention the word "removal." The treaty minutes (Ex. P-17, 17A) are devoid of that word as well. The first time the term "removal" appears is in the treaty itself, and then only in the context of permissiveness.

Dr. Tanner testified regarding the Indians' objections to removal. The Indians in the Upper Peninsula did not even regard removal to be a threat. They refused to send delegates to travel with James Schoolcraft to view the land west of the Mississippi. Those Indians who went were largely from the Lower Peninsula and did not represent the Indians throughout the area of cession. With the exception of one person, none of the Indians were designated as first, second or third class chiefs in the list attached to the Treaty of 1836. (See Ex. P-190). Those Indians who went on the James Schoolcraft exploring party did not agree to remove, assuming *arguendo* they were clothed with authority to represent all Indians throughout the ceded territory. They agreed to accept the land they visited, but only if any Indians personally chose to remove. (State Ex. P-62, 99.)

Straining these facts to their limit and beyond would not demonstrate that the parties to the treaty knew that removal was an accomplished fact at the time the treaty was negotiated.

At best the facts demonstrated that the treaty commissioners were planning for future contingencies. If settlement of the state occurred at the pace anticipated, which it did not, and if Indians requested removal, which they did not, it was possible that removal might occur at some time in the future. There was not even a time certain at which removal was to occur.

The fact that the Indians stayed in Michigan expresses their intentions more eloquently than any other fact which has been presented to the court. The Indians did not remove. Because the Indians stayed in Michigan and it has been previously determined that they retained their aboriginal rights and Treaty of Ghent rights to fish in the Great Lakes, they retain the right to fish in the waters of the Great Lakes today.

G. *THE FISHING RIGHTS RESERVED BY THE TREATY OF 1836 WERE NOT RELINQUISHED BY THE TREATY OF 1855.*

1. *A Treaty Right May Be Abrogated or Extinguished Only by the Most Explicit and Unequivocal Act of Congress.*

[45, 46] Through the interweaving of thousands of statutes, treaties and court decisions, a complex relationship has developed interrelating the respective powers of Indian tribes, the federal government and the states. From the founding of this nation to the present, however, certain principles governing those relationships have held firm. One such principle is that Indian tribes retain all powers of self-government, sovereignty and aboriginal rights not explicitly taken from them by Congress. *McClanahan v. Arizona Tax Com'n, supra; Williams v. Lee,* 358 U.S. 217, 79 S.Ct. 269, 3 L.Ed.2d 251 (1959); *United States v. U.S. Fidelity & Guaranty Co.,* 309 U.S. 506, 60 S.Ct. 653, 84 L.Ed. 894 (1940); *Ex parte Crow Dog,* 109 U.S. 556, 3 S.Ct. 396, 27 L.Ed. 1030 (1883). Another principle is that the federal government, acting primarily through Congress, has plenary authority over Indians and Indian tribes. *Warren Trading Post v. Arizona Tax Com'n,* 380 U.S. 685, 85 S.Ct. 1242, 14 L.Ed.2d 165 (1965); *Williams v. Lee, supra; United States v. Nice,* 241 U.S. 591, 36 S.Ct. 696, 60 L.Ed. 1192 (1916); *United States v. Rickert,* 188 U.S. 432, 23 S.Ct. 478, 47 L.Ed. 532 (1903); *United States v. Kagama,* 118 U.S. 375, 6 S.Ct. 1109, 30 L.Ed. 228 (1886).

[47-49] These two principles—plenary federal authority over Indians and retention of tribal powers—interface in the doctrine surrounding abrogation of existing treaty rights. While Congress has the plenary authority to abrogate the fishing rights reserved by the Treaty of 1836, it must do so expressly and unequivocally. The intention to abrogate or modify a treaty provision will not be lightly imputed to Congress. *Menominee Tribe v. United States, supra; Pigeon River Improvement Slide & Boom Co. v. Cox, Ltd.,* 291 U.S. 138, 54 S.Ct. 361, 78 L.Ed. 695 (1934); *United States v. White,* 508 F.2d 453 (8th Cir. 1974); *Kimball v. Callahan, supra.* Congressional acts purporting to abrogate or modify treaty rights are subject to the same canons of construction as are Indian treaties.

An important case applying the express abrogation doctrine to hunting and fishing rights is *Menominee Tribe v. United States, supra.* In that case the Supreme Court was faced with the issue of whether the tribe's hunting and fishing rights, which were reserved by the Treaty of Wolf River, had been abrogated by a later congressional act terminating the reservation. Under the (Menominee Indian Termination Act of 1954, 68 Stat. 250, 28 U.S.C. §§ 891-902), the reservation was taken out of federal ownership, and federal supervision over the tribe and its members ended. Because the language of the termination act did not explicitly mention the extinguishment of hunting and fishing rights, the Supreme Court held that those treaty rights survived termination. Thus, tribal members were free to hunt and fish, pursuant to their treaty, even though the United States no longer considered them to be its wards. See also, *Kimball v. Callahan, supra.*

Defendants have argued that the Treaty of 1855 abrogated the Indians' reserved fishing rights. This contention has centered in Articles 3 and 5 of the Treaty. Neither of those articles had any effect whatever on the reserved fishing rights.

2. *Article 3 of the Treaty of 1855.*

[50] As the record amply demonstrates, the "liabilities" and "legal and equitable claims" released by Article 3 were *financial—*and *only financial—matters,* and did not include the reserved fishing right. Given those facts, it is clear that the Michigan Supreme Court was correct when it held that the fishing rights secured by the Treaty of 1836 were not released or abrogated in Article 3 of the Treaty of 1855. *People v. LeBlanc, supra.* As that Court said:

> While it is conceivable that the United States intended "claims . . . for other things" in the Treaty of 1855 to refer to fishing rights reserved by the Chippewas in the Treaty of 1836, such seems highly unlikely given the complete absence of any discussion of the termination of such rights in the treaty negotiations. In any case, it is clear that the Chippewas and the Ottawas would not have understood Article Three of the Treaty of 1855 to terminate hunting and fishing rights reserved in the Treaty of 1836 given the absence of any mention of such prospect.

* * * * * *

> Given, then, the rules of construction mandating that a treaty should be interpreted as the Indians understood it, and that the language of the treaty should not be read to the prejudice of the Indians, we will not strain the language of Article Three of the Treaty of 1855 to mean that reserved fishing rights pursuant to the Treaty of 1836 were terminated.
>
> Our conclusion is buttressed by the directive of the United States Supreme Court that "the intention to abrogate or modify a treaty is not to be lightly imputed."

Menominee Tribe v. United States, supra, 391 U.S. 404, 413, 88 S.Ct. 1705, 1711, 20 L.Ed.2d 697. 248 N.W2d at 211-12.

This interpretation of Article 3 is also supported by the decision of the Court of Claims in *Ottawa and Chippewa Indians v. United States,* 42 Ct.Cl. 240 (1907). There, the Indians sued the United States to recover $19,000 plus accrued interest which represented the $1,000 per year mandated by the 1836 treaty to be invested in stock of the Treasury Department. The United States set the money aside each year beginning in 1836 and ending in 1855 when it "covered" the money into the Treasury.

The government in that litigation contended that Article III of the 1855 treaty operated to release the United States from the Indians' claim to the $19,000 plus accrued interest. The Court of Claims disagreed because the treaty released the United States from delivering various goods, services or annuities in the future. Thus, as to the consideration flowing from the United States to the Indians which had been promised under old treaties but not yet delivered, Article III operated as a release. However, the $1,000 annuity appropriated by Congress and in fact set aside was not released by Article III because it was not an *executory promise* of the United States. Rather, it was an *executed promise*, a promise already performed by the United States and, therefore, not released by Article III of the 1855 treaty.

[51] The Court of Claims' analysis is consistent with plaintiffs' contention herein and with the Michigan Supreme Court's decision in *LeBlanc*. A reserved "right" is not a "legal or equitable claim or liability." Article 3 operated to release the United States from those promises previously made to the Indians, but not fulfilled, for goods, services and monies; it did not release the United States from promises made and in fact performed. *Ottawa and Chippewa v. United States, supra.* The fishing "right" originated in and remains to this day with the Indians; the right did not originate with and was not given to the Indians by the United States. The United States could not release a right it did not own. It was the Indians alone who had the power to release their fishing rights and this they have never done.

As we have seen, the Treaty of 1855 constituted a formal abandonment by the federal government of any effort to remove the Indians of the treaty area from Michigan. (See, e.g., Ex. P-89 and 89A.) One of its avowed purposes was to provide the Indians with permanent homes in Michigan. It would have been wholly illogical to allow the Indians to stay in Michigan but prohibit them from engaging in their fishing practices in the Great Lakes. Such a prohibition would have left the Indians destitute and deprived them of a traditional activity vital to their subsistence and commercial pursuits.

Since the reserved right to fish in the ceded waters is not a "liability on account of former treaty stipulations" or a "legal or equitable claim" within the meaning of Article 3 of the Treaty of 1855, as set forth above, the Indians did not cede, surrender or relinquish their fishing right by Article 3. *People v. LeBlanc, supra,* 248 N.W.2d at 211-12. See also, *Ottawa and Chippewa Indians v. United States,* 42 Ct.Cl. 240 (1907). The right to fish was not even discussed in the treaty negotiations. The restriction of Indian rights proposed by the State will not be implied from such general treaty language. *Menominee Tribe v. United States,* 391 U.S. 404, 88 S.Ct. 1705 (1968). Article 3 had nothing whatever to do with fishing rights and no impact whatever upon them.

3. *Article 5 of the Treaty of 1855.*

[52] It is clear that Article 5 has no effect either upon fishing rights secured by the Treaty of 1836 or the modern political successors to the treaty Indians—Bay Mills and the Sault Tribe.

Article 5 of the Treaty of 1855 was inserted in that treaty for the convenience of the United States in its future dealings with the Indian bands.

This clause was intended to accomplish two goals: to relieve the United States of the burden of convening general councils in the event local matters required attention in the future, and to satisfy the Ottawa and Chippewa's desire to be treated separately. Article 5 had no impact on the governmental structure of the bands. There was no change in the way in which the Indian agents dealt with them after the treaty, except that they were never convened again as one group. (Tr. 331-35.)

Like Article 3, Article 5 has nothing whatever to do with reserved fishing rights. Although this issue was not raised in the *LeBlanc* litigation, the Michigan Supreme Court's reasoning concerning Article 3 is dispositive. The Court refused to construe the release clause as an abrogation of reserved rights because there was no discussion of fishing rights during the treaty negotiations, because the Indians would not have understood Article 3 to terminate hunting and fishing rights and because construing the language as an abrogation would be wholly contrary to the canons of treaty construction.

This same reasoning applies to Article 5. But the meaning of Article 5 can be easily discerned from the four corners of the treaty. There are no ambiguities to be resolved in favor of the Indians. The United States wanted to handle disputes arising as a result of the 1855 treaty on a localized basis and sought to avoid the need for calling a general convention of the Indians to resolve future problems, and the Indians of the treaty area wished to be treated with locally, and not as an artificial "Ottawa and Chippewa nation." This—and only this—is what Article 5 accomplishes.

Article 5 also has no effect upon the plaintiff-intervenor tribes, Bay Mills and the Sault Tribe. Both tribes are modern political successors in interest to the Indians who were party to the Treaty of 1836. Both are recognized by the United States as currently functioning Indian tribes maintaining tribal governments. Both tribes have reservations held in trust for them by the federal government—reservations which are within the boundaries of the reservations retained in the Treaty of 1836. Each tribe is organized pursuant to Section 16 of the Indian Reorganization Act, 25 U.S.C. . 476, and operates under a constitution and by-laws adopted pursuant to that section. The membership criteria embodied in the constitutions of both tribes require that tribal members be Indians of the treaty area. (Tr. 1059-62, 1127-29; Ex. P-119, 120.)

[53-55] The federal government, through the Department of the Interior, has recognized and confirmed that Bay Mills and the Sault Tribe are political successors in interest to the Indians of the treaty area. The Department is holding reservations in trust for the tribes, approving tribal constitutions and issuing treaty fishing identification cards to tribal members pursuant to 25 C.F.R. Part 256. The proclamation of a reservation and the approval of a tribal constitution are acts of recognition and acknowledgment of a federal relationship. *United States v. John*, 437 U.S. 634, 98 S.Ct. 2541, 57 L.Ed.2d 489, 500 (1978). Courts will not disturb what Congress or the executive have done in terms of organizing or recognizing the political authority of Indian tribes. *United States v. Sandoval*, 231 U.S. 28, 34 S.Ct. 1, 58 L.Ed. 107 (1913); *United States v. Holliday*, 70 U.S. (3 Wall.) 407, 18 L.Ed. 182 (1867); *United States v. Washington, supra*. As the agency charged with the administration of laws affecting Indians, actions and interpretations of the Department of the Interior are entitled to "great weight." *United States v. Jackson*, 280 U.S. 183, 50 S.Ct. 143, 74 L.Ed. 361 (1930).

[56, 57] Even if the federal relationship with Indian tribes or bands is not continuous, this does not destroy federal rights or bar the recognition of present tribal groups as political successors in interest. *United States v. John, supra*. Even if the Treaty of 1855 were the only source of the tribe's federal relationship, the treaty provision would not end aboriginal federal rights or prevent recognition of a modern tribal group as a political successor in interest. *United States v. John, supra*. See also, *United States v. Wright*, 53 F.2d 300 (4th Cir. 1931), *cert. denied*, 285 U.S. 539, 52 S.Ct. 312, 76 L.Ed. 932 (1931).

H. *WHETHER A RESERVATION EXISTS IN WHITEFISH BAY IS NOT BEFORE THE COURT IN THIS PHASE OF THE TRIAL.*

Phase One of the trial in this case was limited to questions about fishing rights. The question of whether a reservation continues to exist in Whitefish Bay has implications for whether the Bay Mills tribe has exclusive fishing rights in that area of Lake Superior, but this question goes beyond whether the Indians retained aboriginal and Treaty of Ghent fishing rights in the Treaty of 1836 which were not abrogated by the 1855 treaty. Accordingly, at the present time I decline to consider the evidence presented on this issue and do not rule on the questions of law involved.

I. *THE STATE OF MICHIGAN CANNOT REGULATE INDIAN TREATY FISHING IN ACCORDANCE WITH EXISTING PRINCIPLES OF INDIAN LAW.*

1. *The State's Power to Affect Treaty Rights Fishermen is Preempted by the Supremacy Clause.*

[58-60] A fundamental principle of federal constitutional law is that a state may not enact or enforce any statute or regulation in conflict with treaties between the United States and Indian tribes. The Supremacy Clause of the United States Constitution (Article VI, clause 2) states just that:

> This Constitution, and the Laws of the United States which shall be made in Pursuance thereof; and all Treaties made, or which shall be made, under the Authority of the United States, shall be the supreme Law of the land; and the Judges in every State shall be bound thereby, any Thing in the Constitution or Laws of any State to the Contrary notwithstanding.

The Supremacy Clause is applicable to international treaties and Indian treaties alike. See *United States v. 43 Gallons of Whiskey,* 108 U.S. 491, 2 S.Ct. 906, 27 L.Ed. 803 (1883); *United States v. 43 Gallons of Whiskey [U.S. v. Lariviere],* 3 Otto 188, 93 U.S. 188, 23 L.Ed.2d 846 (1876); *Worcester v. Georgia, supra.* It is equally well established that a matter generally within the exclusive power of a state, such as fish and game management, is preempted by the federal government when a federal purpose, as evidenced by a treaty or statute, is dominant and would otherwise be frustrated. See *Douglas v. Seacoast Products, Inc.,* 431 U.S. 265, 97 S.Ct. 1740, 52 L.Ed.2d 304 (1977). The Ninth Circuit in *United States v. Washington, supra,* at 684, cogently summarized these principles in a treaty fishing rights case:

> By virtue of its police power, the state has initial authority to regulate the taking of fish and game. *Geer v. Connecticut,* 161 U.S. 519, 16 S.Ct. 600, 40 L.Ed. 793 (1896). The federal government, however, may totally displace state regulation in this area .... The Federal government may also preempt state control over fish and game by executing a valid treaty and legislating pursuant to it. *Missouri v Holland,* 252 U.S. 416, 432, 40 S.Ct. 382, 64 L.Ed. 641 (1920). Furthermore, such a treaty may preempt state law even without implementing legislation; a treaty guaranteeing certain rights to the subjects of a signatory nation is self-executing and supersedes state law. *Asakura v. City of Seattle,* 265 U.S. 332, 341, 44 S.Ct. 515, 68 L.Ed. 1041 (1924). Consequently, the state may enact and enforce no statute or regulation in conflict with treaties in force between the United States and Indian nations.

To paraphrase the Ninth Circuit's analysis, the issue in this case is not whether the federal government has the power to preempt Michigan fishing laws and regulations (since it clearly does), but whether the federal government has done so by entering into the treaties of 1836 and 1855 and by their subsequent implementation. See, *e.g, Menominee Tribe v. United*

States, supra; Puyallup Tribe v. Dept. of Game (Puyallup I), 391 U.S. 392, 88 S.Ct. 1725, 20 L.Ed.2d 689 (1968); *Tulee v. Washington, supra; United States v. Winans, supra; Worcester v. Georgia, supra; Kimball v, Callahan, supra; Skokomish Indian Tribe v. France*, 320 F.2d 205 (9th Cir. 1963), cert. denied, 376 U.S. 943, 84 S.Ct. 797, 11 L.Ed.2d 767 (1964); *Maison v. Confederated Tribe of the Umatilla Indian Reservation*, 314 F.2d 169 (9th Cir. 1963).

[61] Although generally state law is often applicable to Indians outside a reservation, there can be no application where it would "impair a right granted or reserved by federal law." *Mescalero Apache Tribe v. Jones* 411 U.S. 145, 148 (1973). A treaty guaranteeing a right to fish distinct from that enjoyed by other citizens is such an express federal law. *United States v. Washington, supra*, 520 F.2d at 684. As is clear in this case, the Michigan Indians had both aboriginal rights and rights guaranteed by the Treaty of Ghent when they signed the 1836 Treaty. They retain these rights. Other citizens of Michigan possess only a privilege to fish. That they possess a mere privilege is recognized by Michigan law. M.C.L.A. 308.1 (Supp. 1978). The Treaty of March 28, 1836 (7 Stat. 491) guarantees a right to fish which is distinct from the privilege to fish enjoyed by other citizens of the State of Michigan *United States v. Winans*, 198 U.S. 371, 380-81, 25 S.Ct. 662, 49 L.Ed. 1089 (1905); *United States v. Washington*, 384 F.Supp. 312 (1974).

[62] The point of the preemption doctrine, simply stated, is that state regulation in an area where the federal purpose is dominant and state regulation would be at cross purposes with federal objectives is violative of the Supremacy Clause and must fail even where Congress has not explicitly proscribed the reach of state law. The principle is especially important where federal purposes are expressed not by mere legislation but by a solemn exercise of the treaty power and where the exercise concerns Indians, a subject manifestly within the ambit of federal powers.*

[*See* McClanahan v. Arizona Tax Com'n, supra *at 172*. *See also* Byran v. Itasca County, *426 U.S. 373, 96 S.Ct. 2102, 48 L.Ed.2d 710 (1976), where the Supreme Court construed a federal statute authorizing states, under certain circumstances, to assume civil and criminal jurisdiction over reservation Indians so as not to include state or local taxing authority to affect Indian lands or Indian income derived from activities within reservations.*]

[63] It is well established that the usual right of a state to manage game within its boundaries*

[*Geer v. Connecticut, 161 U.S. 519, 16 S.Ct. 600, 40 L.Ed. 793 (1896)*].

is not infringed by a federal treaty and regulations under it concerning taking game within the state, because the sovereign power of the state must yield to paramount federal power.*

[*Cf. New Mexico State Game Com'n v. Udall, *410 F.2d 1197 (10th Cir. 1969)*, cert. denied sub nom., New Mexico State Game Com'n v. Hickel, *396 U.S. 961, 90 S.Ct. 429, 24 L.Ed.2d 426 (1969)*; Lacoste v. Department of Conservation, *263 U.S. 545, 549, 44 S.Ct. 186, 68 L.Ed. 437 (1923)*; Hunt v. United States, *278 U.S. 96, 100, 49 S.Ct. 38, 73 L.Ed. 200 (1928)*.]

Missouri v. Holland, 252 U.S. 416, 40 S.Ct. 382, 64 L.Ed. 641 (1920). In *Holland*, the court rejected a challenge by the state to federal enforcement of certain game regulations promulgated in furtherance of the Migratory Bird Treaty on the ground that it would be an unconstitutional interference with the state's sovereign power. While recognizing that the subject matter—game regulation—is generally a state prerogative, the court found that "a treaty may override its power," 252 U.S. at 434, 40 S.Ct. at 384, because "[H]ere a national interest of very nearly the first magnitude is involved. It can be protected only by national action in concert with that of another power." 252 U.S. at 435, 40 S.Ct. at 384.

The circumstances in this case bear out the tremendous national importance placed upon the treaties at the time the United States sought to negotiate them. Legal authorities support the proposition that it continues to be in the national interest to observe and enforce treaty obligations owed to Indians. Fulfilling these obligations to Indians is no less lofty a national priority than the protection of migratory birds.

The line of cases dealing with treaty fishing rights secured by the "Stevens treaties" of the Northwest, such as *Puyallup Tribe v. Washington (Puyallup I),* 391 U.S. 392, 88 S.Ct. 1725, 20 L.Ed.2d 689 (1968) and its progeny, which have allowed a sharply limited power in the state to regulate the exercise of off reservation treaty fishing rights, must be distinguished from the present case.

In *Puyallup Tribe of Indians v. Washington,* 391 U.S. 892, 88 S.Ct. 1725, 20 L.Ed.2d 689 (1968) (Puyallup I), and *Washington v. Puyallup Tribe,* 414 U.S. 44, 94 S.Ct 830, 38 L.Ed.2d 254 (1973) *(Puyallup II),* the United States Supreme court ruled that because of the language contained in the Indian treaty with the Puyallup Indians, the state had a right to regulate Indian fishing for purposes of conservation of the fishing resources, provided that those regulations did not discriminate against the Indians.

However, there appears to be some inconsistency within the Court's two opinions on the right to regulate treaty rights. In *Puyallup I,* the Court seemed to be making a distinction between the treaty right to fish in certain places, and the right to fish in a particular manner. It appears that the Court saw the first right—the right to fish in accustomed places—as being a Treaty right, and the second as a right which was held in common with the rest of the citizens of the State, and therefore subject to the ordinary state police power, i.e., regulation for conservation purposes. The second right was not seen as being a treaty right.

For example, in *Puyallup I,* the Court states: "the right to fish 'at all usual and accustomed' places may, of course, not be qualified by the State ..." 391 U.S. at 398, 88 S.Ct. at 1728. Thus even though the Indians may hold this right in common with the non-Indian citizens of the state (e.g., Indians and non-Indians may fish side-by-side at the same spot), since this is an express Treaty right, it may not be regulated by the State.

However, it appears that the Court in *Puyallup I* saw the manner of fishing as being outside the rights conferred by the treaty:

> [T]he manner in which the fishing may be done and its purpose, whether or not commercial, are not mentioned in the Treaty. We would have quite a different case if the Treaty had preserved the right to fish at the "usual and accustomed" manner. But the Treaty is silent as to the mode or modes of fishing that are guaranteed.

391 U.S. at 898, 88 S.Ct. at 1728. Again, later in the Opinion, where it was speaking of a similar case which it had advanced in support of this distinction, the court states:

> In other words, the "right" to fish outside the reservation was a treaty "right" that could not be qualified or conditioned by the State. But the "time and manner of fishing necessary for the conservation of fish," not being defined or established by the treaty, were within the reach of state power.
>
> The overriding police power of the State, expressed in nondiscriminatory measures for conserving fish resources, is preserved.

391 U.S. at 399, 88 S.Ct. at 1729.

The Court in *Puyallup I* appears to be saying that the treaty *right* is the *right* to fish at accustomed places, and being a treaty right, it is not subject to regulation by the State. The right to fish in a certain manner is not a treaty right, however, and thus is subject to the usual police powers of the State.

In *Puyallup II,* however, the Court appears to shift ground. First, it states that the manner of fishing is now also a treaty right: "Our prior decision recognized that net fishing by these Indians for commercial purposes was covered by the Treaty." 414 U.S. at 48, 94 S.Ct. at 333. However, there is no language in *Puyallup I* which indicates that Indian commercial fishing was protected by the Treaty. In fact, the language in *Puyallup I* indicates that the Court recognized that Indian commercial fishing existed at the time of the signing of the Treaty, but the Court nevertheless went on to draw its place-manner distinction: "But the manner in which the fishing may be done and its purpose, whether or not commercial, are not mentioned in the Treaty." 391 U.S. at 398, 88 S.Ct. at 1728.

It appears that instead of acknowledging that its definition of the Indian treaty fishing rights was too narrow in *Puyallup I* though, the Court let that decision stand while implicitly modifying it in *Puyallup II.*

A second major shift in *Puyallup II* from the opinion in *Puyallup I* is that the Court indicates that the Treaty rights may now be restricted by the State police power:

> Rights can be controlled by the need to conserve a species; . . . the police power of the State is adequate to prevent the steelhead from following the fate of the passenger pigeon; and the Treaty does not give the Indians a federal right to pursue the last living steelhead until it enters their nets.

414 U.S. at 49, 94 S.Ct. at 334. Thus the Court changed the legal framework of the situation. It went from a treaty right to fish a certain location, totally free from state regulation, plus an ordinary right to fish in a certain manner, subject of course to the state police power, to a scenario where all aspects of Indian fishing are now treaty-granted rights, but that the state has an undefined right to regulate this treaty right to "conserve a species."

In *United States v. Washington,* 384 F.Supp. 312 (W.D.Wash.1974), Judge Boldt noted that dicta followed by the United States Supreme Court in cases approving state police power regulation of Washington Indians' treaty right fishing is not sound in legal logic or principle. Before *Puyallup I* was decided, 391 U.S. 392, 88 S.Ct. 1725, 20 L.Ed.2d 689 (1968), there were no cases which provided judicial analysis or citation of a non-dictum decision supporting police power state regulation of the exercise of Indian off-reservation treaty fishing. 384 F.Supp. at 336. See, *Tulee v. Washington,* 315 U.S. 681, 62 S.Ct. 862, 86 L.Ed. 1115 (1942); *Lacoste v. Department of Conservation,* 263 U.S. 545, 44 S.Ct. 186, 68 L.Ed. 437 (1924); *Patsone v. Pennsylvania,* 232 U.S. 138, 34 S.Ct. 281, 58 L.Ed. 539 (1913); *United States v. Winans,* 198 U.S. 371, 25 S.Ct. 662, 49 L.Ed. 1089 (1905); *Ward v. Race Horse,* 163 U.S. 504, 16 S.Ct. 1076, 41 L.Ed. 244 (1896); *Geer v. Connecticut,* 161 U.S. 519, 16 S.Ct. 600, 40 L.Ed. 793 (1896). *Kennedy v. Becker,* 241 U.S. 556, 36 S.Ct. 705, 60 L.Ed. 1166 (1919), involved a treaty which contained a fishing clause "fully satisfied by considering it a reservation of a *privilege* of fishing...." At 563, 36 S.Ct. at 707-708. (Emphasis supplied.) The conveyance there was not to the United States; the lands passed directly into private ownership, the Indians retaining a right against the grantees and all who might become owners of the lands. Here the Indians assert, and this court has held that they retained an aboriginal right to fish, confirmed and reaffirmed by treaty, when they conveyed their lands to the United States. There can be no contention that this right was a mere privilege. The Indians did not submit to the sovereignty of the State when they made their conveyance, nor did they retain rights only relative to a private owner.

The district court in *United States v. Washington,* 384 F.Supp. 312 (1974), also commented on the lack of supporting authority in the Supreme Court's decisions:

> [T]hat the exercise of such [an Indian fishing] right may be limited in any way by the police power of a state, without having previously received authority to do so from Congress, seems to be diametrically opposed to relevant treaty law and personal civil rights decisions, particularly those of recent years.
>
> In the *Puyallup II* decision, . . . it was stated (414 U.S. p. 2, 94 S.Ct. p. 332): "The sole question tendered in the present cases concerns the regulations of the Department of Game concerning steel head trout."
>
> Other than by recital or quotations from *Puyallup-I* and State Supreme Court decisions, in *Puyallup-II* there was no discussion of or ruling upon the basis of state police power to regulate off reservation treaty right fishing unless it be derived from the next to the last paragraph in the opinion of Justice Douglas (pp. 5-6, 94 S.Ct. p. 333): "We do not imply that these fishing rights persist down to the very last steel head in the river. Rights can be controlled by the need to conserve a species; and the time may come when the life of a steel head is so precarious in a particular stream that all fishing should be banned until the species regains assurance of survival. The police power of the State is adequate to prevent the steel head from following the fate of the passenger pigeon; and the Treaty does not give the Indians a federal right to pursue the last living steel head until it enters their nets."
>
> Whatever the above quoted statement may have added to or taken from the right to exercise the off reservation treaty fishing rights of the plaintiff tribes, to the present time there never has been either legal analysis or citation of a non-dictum authority in any decision of the Supreme Court of the Land in support of its decisions holding that state police power may be employed to limit or modify the exercise of rights guaranteed by national treaties which the federal Constitution mandates must be considered and applied as "the supreme Law of the Land."

384 F.Supp. at 337-38.

The district court also questioned whether or not Congress was the only one permitted under the Constitution to restrict treaty fishing rights:

> It also appears that the United States Supreme Court has exercised a prerogative specifically reserved by and to Congress in the treaties. Congress has never exercised its prerogative to either limit or abolish Indian treaty right fishing. In recent years it declined to do the latter by three times failing to enact proposed legislation for the termination of Indian treaty fishing rights. It may be that the refusal or failure of Congress to exercise a specific prerogative, by enactment of legislation, would legally justify judicial exercise of that particular prerogative. If so, it has never been stated or indicated in any United States Supreme Court decision as the basis or source of authority for the federal judicial decisions authorizing state regulation of off reservation treaty fishing rights.
>
> [16] Since Congress has the power to qualify or revoke any treaty or any provision thereof, unquestionable federal authority is available to provide federal regulation, or to authorize state regulation, for the protection of fishery resources against any threatened or actual harm that might arise

> from off reservation treaty right fishing by tribal members limited only by tribal regulation. In these circumstances it is unfortunate, to say the least, that state police power regulation of off reservation fishing should be authorized or invoked on a legal basis never specifically stated or explained.

Id. at 338-39 (footnotes omitted.)

However, because it was construing the same Indian treaty language which the Supreme Court had before it in the *Puyallup* cases, the district court in *United States v. Washington, supra,* was constrained to follow the Supreme Court decisions. Id. at 339.

This court believes that the older Supreme Court decisions holding that federal treaty rights cannot be restricted by the states are the better reasoned cases. Were it construing the *Puyallup* treaty, however, it would also find itself bound to follow the Supreme Court's interpretations of that treaty.

This court is not construing the Treaty found in *Puyallup,* though. In that treaty, the operative language read:

> The right of taking fish, at all usual and accustomed grounds and stations, is further secured to said Indians, in common with all citizens of the territory, and of erecting temporary houses for the purpose of curing,....

The United States secured the right of non-Indians to fish alongside the Indians. The Indians' right of taking fish in that Treaty is explicitly shared with the citizens of the state, and it is this aspect which may have led the Supreme Court to conclude that the state police power is applicable to both parties.

[64] This language is not contained in the Treaty of 1836. The Indians' aboriginal rights and Treaty of Ghent rights to fish in the Great Lakes is not shared with non-Indians through treaty provision. Consequently, this court holds that the State of Michigan does not have any right to regulate Ottawa and Chippewa Indian fishing on the Great Lakes in exercise of their rights, because the Treaty of 1836 and the Treaty of Ghent do not permit state regulation of these Indian fishing rights.

2. *THE STATE'S POWER TO AFFECT TREATY RIGHT FISHERMEN IS PREEMPTED BY FEDERAL AND TRIBAL REGULATION.*

[65] In this case state regulation has been preempted not only by virtue of the treaties, but by virtue of federal regulation and Indian self regulation as well.

In 1967, the Secretary of the Interior took steps to implement the exercise of treaty rights to fish when he enacted 25 C.F.R. Part 256. These regulations are detailed and explicit and provide a means by which off-reservation fishing rights may be regulated in order to meet conservation goals. This provision gives full deference to tribal rights as opposed to state regulation, for it takes into account state regulations only insofar as they govern "persons not fishing under treaty rights." A state may itself initiate the regulatory procedure via a request from its governor. The State of Michigan has thus far ignored this federally-sanctioned approach to the very type of regulation which it purports so ardently to desire. The Secretary is presently operating under these regulations since he has issued tribal identification cards to treaty right fishermen which are signed by both tribal and federal officials. Here again, the federal government, acting in cooperation with the tribes, occupies the field of regulating treaty right fishermen, thereby preempting state regulation over these same persons.

Part 256 of 25 C.F.R. is the very sort of pervasive federal regulation which was found to preempt state jurisdiction in *Warren Trading Post v. Arizona Tax Com'n,* 380 U.S. 685, 85 S.Ct. 1242, 14 L.Ed.2d 165 (1965). In that case the United States Supreme Court held that the federal government had promulgated such a pervasive system of regulation of retail trading on Indian reservations that no room was left for any state regulation. On its way to this conclusion the court said: "[F]rom the very first days of our Government, the Federal Government had been permitting the Indians largely to govern themselves, free from state interference." 380 U.S. at 686-87, 85 S. Ct. at 1243. The federal regulation found in 25 C.F.R. Part 256 is hardly less pervasive than that found in *Warren Trading Post.* Moreover, unlike the regulation of retail trading on Indian reservations, here the federal government has specifically provided a means by which a state may participate, should it so desire. It is clear, therefore, that the federal government has preempted state regulation of off-reservation Indian fishing rights secured by treaty. Unfortunately, the state consistently refuses to accept the principle that treaty tribe fishermen enjoy unique rights derived from federal law and, therefore, are not subject to the rules and regulations governing citizens who do not enjoy such rights. The State maintains simplistically that a disparity of treatment between Indian fishermen and citizens fishing as a matter of privilege under state law would constitute unlawful discrimination prohibited by the Fourteenth Amendment. If the state were correct, however, Indian fishermen would derive nothing from their treaty. Indeed, it would be as if there were no treaty at all.

[66] The Supreme Court rejected the State's discrimination contention long ago, reiterated it recently in *Morton v. Mancari,* 417 U. S. 535, 94 S.Ct. 2474, 41 L.Ed.2d 290 (1974). The issue there concerned the constitutionality of a federal law affording job preference within the Bureau of Indian Affairs to Native American applicants. The Court said:

> Literally every piece of legislation dealing with Indian tribes and reservations, and certainly all legislation dealing with the BIA, single out for special treatment a constituency of tribal Indians living on or near reservations. If these laws, derived from historical relationships and explicitly designed to help only Indians, were deemed invidious racial discrimination, an entire Title of the United States Code (25 USC) would be effectively erased and the solemn commitment of the Government toward the Indians would be jeopardized.

417 U.S. at 552, 94 S.Ct. 2483-2484. Clearly then there are no constitutional impediments to treating Indian fishermen differently than other state citizens. To the contrary, the Supremacy Clause mandates different treatment because Indian fishermen derive their rights (not privileges) under federal law.

Relying upon a similar claim of denial of equal protection, fishermen licensed by the State of Michigan would on the basis of their payment of an annual $5.25 fee, assert a right to preempt the Indian fishing right proclaimed here, a right acquired over a period of 12,000 years. From the evidence received by this court, during the entire period for which the Indians alone exploited the Great Lakes, there was no diminution of the fishery, no need to replenish it by artificial means nor any anxiety to stock it with unnatural species. These are the conditions which the fee is intended to address. The licensed fishermen would obliterate the Indians' record, appropriate their rights and conquer them anew by paying yearly dues of five dollars, so long as they are interested in participating in despoiling the Indians. Under the proposed theory, so long as someone is interested in paying the fee, the Indians' right to fish is accordingly limited.

A comparison might be made to bring this theory into relief. By the treaty of cession, the state received deposits of oil and natural gas. Under the system by which these resources are administered, the average household in this state pays many hundreds of dollars a year to acquire an allotment of these resources. Yet, no one appears to be so bold as to assert that by virtue of his payment he alone, or he in conjunction with others, acquires a right to exploit the resource, a right which is superior to the rights of utility companies and the state acquired by purchase or cession. The state admittedly owns the resource. It is peculiar, then, to hear of a supposed interest in the fish which arises by paying a minimal fee and which forecloses the rights of the prior owner of the right to exploit the resource, an owner who acquired his interest not by virtue of purchase or cession, but by "the Laws of Nature and of Nature's God."

Sportsmen and non-Indian commercial fishermen cannot raise the issue of equal protection without showing entitlement founded upon use and occupancy similar to that of the Indians. But the white man is a late comer to the Great Lakes fisheries when it is considered in the light of centuries. Payment of an annual fee is not a sufficient predicate to permit an abridgment of the Indians' right to fish. This case is not an equal protection case under the Fourteenth Amendment or the Declaration of Independence; it is an Indian treaty case, supplemented with a full panoply of aboriginal rights acquired and preserved over the centuries and existing in full to the present

[67, 68] The fishing right reserved by the Indians in 1836 and at issue in this case is the communal property of the tribes which signed the treaty and their modern political successors; it does not belong to individual tribal members. *United States v. Washington,* 520 F.2d 676 (9th Cir 1975); *Settler v. Lameer,* 507 F.2d 231 (9th Cir 1974); *United States v. Three Winchester 30-30's,* 504 F.2d 1288 (7th Cir. 1974); *Whitefoot v. United States,* 293 F.2d 658, 155 Ct.Cl. 127 (1961); *Montana Power Co. v. Rochester,* 127 F.2d 189 (9th Cir. 1942). The right is presently exercised by the plaintiff tribes under extensive tribal regulation which pre-empts state regulation.

Both Bay Mills and the Sault Tribe have adopted constitutions and by laws under the Indian Reorganization Act of 1934. (Tr. 1060, 1127; Ex. P-119, 120.) Both constitutions authorize the tribes to regulate and protect resources under their control. Further, both constitutions authorize the tribes to regulate the internal relations of their members. Pursuant to the constitutions and by-laws, the tribes have developed conservation codes and fishing regulations. (Tr. 1080, 1139; Ex. P-162, 163, 165.) Pursuant to this constitutional and ordinance authority, the treaty fishing activities of the Indians in the area ceded by the Treaty of 1836 are comprehensively regulated and enforced.

[69] Federal law provides that Indian tribes retain the inherent sovereign right to regulate and enforce the internal affairs of their members, including hunting and fishing rights. *United States v. Wheeler, supra; McClanahan v. Arizona Tax Com'n, supra* 411 U.S. at 173, 93 S.Ct. 1257; *United States v. Mazurie,* 419 U.S. 544, 95 S.Ct. 710, 42 L.Ed.2d 706 (1975); *Byran v. Itasca County, supra* 426 U.S. at 388, 96 S.Ct. 2102; *Williams v. Lee, supra* 358 U.S. at 221-22, 79 S.Ct. 269; *Menominee Tribe v. United States, supra* 391 U.S. at 409-10, 88 S.Ct. 1705; *United States v. Washington, supra* at 520 F.2d 686; *Settler v. Lameer, supra* at

237; and *Quechan Tribe of Indians v. Rowe,* 531 F.2d 408, 411 (9th Cir. 1976).

In *United States v. Wheeler,* supra, the United States Supreme Court stated:

> The powers of Indian tribes are, in general *"inherent powers of a limited sovereignty which has never been extinguished."* F. Cohen, *Handbook of Federal Indian Law* 122 (1941) (emphasis in original). Before the coming of the Europeans, the tribes were self-governing sovereign political communities. See *McClanahan v. Arizona Tax Comm'n,* 411 U.S. 164, 172, 93 S.Ct. 1257, 36 L.Ed.2d 129. Like all sovereign bodies, they then had the inherent power to prescribe laws for their members and to punish infractions of those laws.
>
> Indian tribes are, of course, no longer "possessed of the full attributes of sovereignty." *United States v. Kagama, supra,* [118 U.S. 375] at 381, 6 S.Ct. 1109, 30 L.Ed. 228. Their incorporation within the territory of the United States, and their acceptance of its protection, necessarily divested them of some aspects of the sovereignty which they had previously exercised. By specific treaty provision they yielded up other sovereign powers; by statute, in the exercise of its plenary control, Congress has removed still others.
>
> But our cases recognize that the Indian tribes have not given up their full sovereignty. We have recently said that *"Indian tribes are unique aggregations possessing attributes of sovereignty over both their members and their territory .... [They] are a good deal more than 'private, voluntary organizations.'"* *United States v. Mazurie,* 419 U.S. 544, 577, 95 S.Ct. 710, 42 L.Ed.2d 706; see also *Turner v. United States,* 248 U.S. 354, 355, 39 S.Ct. 109, 63 L.Ed. 291; *Cherokee Nation v. Georgia, supra,* [5 Pet. 1] at 16-17, 8 L.Ed. 25. The sovereignty that the Indian tribes retain is of a unique and limited character. It exists only at the sufferance of Congress and is subject to complete defeasance. But until Congress acts, the tribes retain their existing sovereign powers. *In sum, Indian tribes still possess those aspects of sovereignty not withdrawn by treaty or statute, or by implication as a necessary result of their dependent status.*

435 U.S. at 322, 323, 98 S.Ct. at 1086, 55 L.Ed.2d at 312-13 (emphasis supplied) (footnote omitted). Similarly, in *Williams v. Lee,* the Supreme Court observed:

> Implicit in these treaty terms as it was in the treaties with the Cherokees involved in *Worcester v. Georgia,* was the understanding that *internal affairs* of the Indians remained exclusively within the jurisdiction *of whatever tribal government existed.*

358 U.S. 221-22, 79 S.Ct. 271 (emphasis supplied).

The Ninth Circuit Court of Appeals in *Settler v. Lameer, supra,* dealt expressly and in detail with the question of tribal control over fishing rights which under the tribe's treaty allowed members to travel great distances from their reservation to fish in common with citizens of the State of Washington. The Ninth Circuit agreed with the Indians that included within their treaty right to fish was tribal authority to control and regulate its members fishing off its land reservation.

> This conclusion is supported by the nature of the fishing rights. As set forth in *Whitefoot, supra,* 293 F.2d at 663, the fishing rights reserved in the Treaty of 1855 are communal rights of the Tribe even though the individual members benefit from those rights. *The determination of when and how the rights may be exercised is an "internal affair" of the Tribe. As the district court correctly pointed out, "One of the last remnants of sovereignty retained by the Yakima Indian Tribe is the power to regulate their internal and social relations."*

507 F.2d at 237 (emphasis supplied).

Subsequently, the Ninth Circuit in *United States v. Washington, supra,* confirmed the authority of Indian tribes to control the internal relations of their members, including the exercise of treaty fishing rights:

> Preservation of fishery resources is of vital importance to Indians as well as to other citizens. *At the same time, regulatory interference by the state with treaty fishing is obnoxious to the treaty tribes.* These tribes have the power to regulate their own members and to arrest violators of their regulations apprehended on their reservations or at usual and accustomed fishing sites. *Settler v. Lameer,* 507 F.2d 231 (9th Cir., 1974).

520 F.2d at 686 (emphasis supplied).

In so holding that Indian tribes have the power to regulate the treaty fishing activities of their members and to enforce those regulations through arrest and seizure of equipment, the Ninth Circuit determined that the right to fish retained by the Indians in the Treaty with the Yakima (12 Stat. 951) was understood by them to include the power to control the exercise of that right through tribal regulation of members:

> We conclude that by the Treaty of 1855 the Yakima Indian Nation retained regulatory and enforcement powers with respect to tribal fishing at all "usual and accustomed places" off the reservation. No act of Congress, including the Washington Enabling Act, 25 Stat. 676 (1889), has qualified these reserved powers. The powers therefore continue to exist.

Settler v. Lameer, supra, 507 F.2d at 239.

The court was also concerned with the effect upon the fishery resource if tribal self-regulation did not exist:

> The Yakima Nation may be in a better position than the state of Washington to regulate off-reservation fishing. The Tribe possesses the knowledge of its individual members and their fishing sites, and only the Tribe has the authority to revoke a Tribal member's fishing privileges.

Id. at 240, n. 21.

> In view of the strict limitation on the power of the state to regulate Indian off-reservation fishing, there would be no effective regulation and enforcement of a broad range of fishing activities if enforcement powers are denied to the Tribe.

Id. at 239, n. 18.

The right of the Bay Mills Indian Community and the Sault Ste. Marie Tribe of Chippewa Indians to regulate the off-reservation treaty fishing activities of their members was not given up when the Indians signed the Treaty of 1836. As cited *supra,* the law of treaty construction is clear that rights not expressly relinquished in the treaty are retained by the Indians. The tribes have asserted their right to regulate by promulgating fishing regulations and enforcing them.

The right of the treaty tribes herein to regulate tribal members fishing in the area ceded by the Treaty of 1836 is no less than the rights of Indians elsewhere. The courts have been careful to preserve treaty rights even when the lands ceded were later privately owned, so long as the interests of private landowners are not ignored. For example, in *Kimball v. Callahan, supra,* the court held that the Klamaths may exercise:

> ... treaty hunting, trapping and fishing rights free of state fish and game regulations on lands constituting their ancestral Klamath Indian Reservation, including that land now constituting United States National Forest land and that privately-owned land on which hunting, trapping or fishing is permitted.

493 F.2d at 569-70. And in *Leech Lake Band of Chippewa Indians v. Herbst,* 334 F.Supp. 1001 (D.Minn.1971), the court found that the Indians have the "right to hunt and fish and gather wild rice on public lands and public waters of the Leech Lake Reservation free of Minnesota game and fish laws." Similarly, in *State v. Tinno, supra,* Chief Justice McQuade, concurring, specially said:

> ...the fishing right was reserved by treaty to protect a source of tribal subsistence and to preserve an integral part of the native American culture. These purposes may be given meaningful effect in 1972, when many fishing streams have been dammed, depleted or polluted, only if the treaty is interpreted liberally to extend to any unoccupied federal land where fishing opportunities remain.

497 P.2d at 1395.

[70] Both Bay Mills' and the Sault Tribe's treaty rights include the power to regulate their members so long as they are fishing under tribal regulation and in the area ceded by the Treaty of 1836. Both tribes presently exercise that power and regulate the fishing activities of their members. This regulation preempts any state authority to regulate the fishing activity of the tribal members.

[71] Under the Supremacy Clause of the United States Constitution, state regulation of Indian fishing rights secured by the treaties here in question, and implemented by Federal and tribal regulations, is preempted. Any regulation must be by Congress or Congressional authorization. Any different understanding of the Supremacy Clause, that part of the Constitution which governs the relationship between the states and the federal government and makes our system of interrelated state and federal governments possible, must come from the Supreme Court. That Court presently has before it several cases growing out of *United States v. Washington, supra.* These cases could revise the present understanding of the Supremacy Clause as related to Indian treaties. Under the law as it presently stands, only Congress has the power to regulate Indian treaty right fishing in the areas of the Great Lakes covered by the treaties before this court.

J. *THE SUBMERGED LANDS ACT DID NOT, AS A MATTER OF LAW, REPEAL BY IMPLICATION THE INDIANS' TREATY FISHING RIGHTS.*

[72] Amicus MUCC argued that Congress *sub silentio* abrogated the Indians' treaty fishing right by the passage of the Submerged Lands Act, 43 U.S.C. § 1301 *et seq.* This Act was not intended to, nor did it have, such an effect.

The Submerged Lands Act does not expressly deal with Indian fishing rights. Any abrogation of Indian fishing rights would be by implication. The intention to abrogate or modify a treaty is not to be lightly imputed to the Congress. *Menominee Tribe v. United States,* 391 U.S. 404, 88 S.Ct. 1705, 20 L.Ed.2d 697 (1968).

The impetus behind the Submerged Lands Act seems to have been several Supreme Court cases holding that off-shore oil belonged to the federal government rather than to the individual states. *United States v. Texas,* 339 U.S. 707, 70 S.Ct. 918, 94 L.Ed. 1221 (1950); *United States v. Louisiana,* 339 U.S. 699, 70 S.Ct. 914, 94 L.Ed. 1216 (1950); *United States v. California,* 332 U.S. 19, 67 S.Ct. 1658, 91 L.Ed. 1889 (1947). The Act restored the rights to the submerged land and its resources to the individual states.

The specific language of the Submerged Lands Act gives title to and ownership of "the submerged lands," and the "Natural resources within such lands and waters," and "the right and power to manage, administer, lease, develop, and use the said land and natural resources" to the states. At one time legal opinion had held that the states held title over this off-shore land and resources, but the Supreme Court held otherwise in *United States v. California, supra.* Thus, this legislation "recognized, confirmed, established and vested in and assigned to the respective states" the rights to the submerged lands. In essence the Act said that the federal government recognized the states' interests if they had such interests, and gave the states those interests if they in fact had none under prior law.

The definition of natural resources contained in the Submerged Land Act includes fish. 43 U.S.C. § 1301(e). However, natural resources such as oil and minerals were the main target of the legislation. Biological resources were included in the definition by Congressmen who were worried that traditional state regulation of the ocean shrimp, lobster, and clam industries, etc., would be adversely affected unless these items were also included within the definition. Legislative history reveals that the inclusion of fish in the definition of "resource" is strictly a secondary consideration of the Act. 2 U.S. Code Congressional and Administrative News, (1953) at 1385.

A recent Supreme Court case, *Douglas v. Seacoast Products, Inc.,* 431 U.S. 265, 97 S.Ct 1740, 52 L.Ed.2d 304 (1977), re-established important principles while considering this act. Before the Court in that case were laws enacted by the State of Virginia governing the commercial taking of fish within its waters. Those laws required that persons seeking licenses be citizens; that corporations seeking licenses be owned 75 percent by citizens; and placed certain restrictions on non-residents. Seacoast claimed the state laws did not limit its right to fish commercially in Virginia waters because it was a licensed United States flag ship pursuant to federal law and that under the Supremacy Clause of the Constitution, Virginia's prohibition against its fishing in state waters could not stand.

The Court first looked to federal law to determine the rights granted to Seacoast. It ruled that Seacoast had a federal license to carry on a fishing business in Virginia waters. Because state law conflicted with federal statutes, the former could not prevail under the Supremacy Clause.

The state argued that the Submerged Lands Act required a different result. The court conceded that the state has the right to manage lands beneath navigable waterways and has title to those lands, but nonetheless ruled against the state:

> But when Congress made this grant [ownership of the lakebeds] pursuant to the Property Clause
> of the Constitution, it expressly retained for the United States "all constitutional powers of regula-
> tion and control" over these lands and waters for purposes of commerce . . . Since the grant of the
> fisheries license is made pursuant to the Commerce power, the Submerged Lands Act did not alter

its pre-emptive effect. Certainly Congress did not repeal by implication, in the broad language of the Submerged Lands Act, the Licensing Act requirement of equal treatment for federal licenses.

Douglas v. Seacoast Products, Inc., supra at 284, 97 S.Ct. at 1751 (citations omitted). This case is significant for several reasons. First, it reaffirms the obvious—the Supremacy Clause as a matter of constitutional obligation requires the state to refrain from interfering with a federal right. Second, it reaffirms the well-established notion that abrogations by implication are not favored. In *Seacoast, supra,* the court refused to rule that the 1953 Submerged Lands Act repealed by implication the 1792 Licensing Act.

[73] The present case involves a federal right established by treaty. Under the Supremacy Clause the state may not interfere with such a federal right. Section 1313(b) of the Submerged Lands Act speaks of lands or interests held therein for the benefit of Indians and excludes these lands from the operation of the Act.

> [There is excepted from this grant:] (b) such lands beneath navigable waters held, or any interest in which is held by the United States for the benefit of any tribe, band, or group of Indians or for individual Indians;

MUCC assumes that fishing rights are not interests in land and argues that the exclusion of the rights mentioned by 1313(b) is an inclusion of all other rights within the operation of the Act. Granting this assumption, the argument is not persuasive. This section merely reflects the principle concern of the Act—title to submerged land and the oil and other resources it contains. The Act was intended to restore submerged, off-shore land and its resources to the states, thereby effectively reversing *United States v. California,* 332 U.S. 19, 67 S.Ct. 1658, 91 L.Ed. 1889 (1947). Neither the language of the Act nor its purposes are in conflict with the Indians' retention of fishing rights. The state may own the resources of these lands, even the fish, but this does not necessarily abrogate the Indians' right to fish. *Seacoast Products* makes clear that a federal license to fish does not interfere with the state's rights.

[74] However, it does not appear necessary to grant the assumption. If not, the Indian rights asserted here are within the terms of the exclusion. Indian title to lands has never been a fee; it has always been a right to use and occupy lands claimed by the United States. This interest in land gives the tribes holding it the right to fish, hunt, gather fruits and cross the land. It is analogous to a profit a prendre or an easement. *Winans v. United States, [sic] supra.* The Indians reserved such an interest in land by the Treaty of 1836. If this is so, then this interest is excluded from the conveyance of the Submerged Lands Act by the terms of that Act.

If this court had any hesitation in determining whether the Submerged Lands Act abrogated the Indians' fishing right, it would be overcome by the fact that an even stricter standard than was used in *Seacoast* must be applied to legislation purporting to abrogate Indian treaty fishing rights. See *Morton v. Mancari,* 417 U.S. 535, 94 S.Ct. 2474, 41 L.Ed.2d 290 (1974); *Menominee Tribe v. United States,* 391 U.S. 404, 88 S.Ct. 1705, 20 L.Ed.2d 697 (1968); *Squire v. Capoeman,* 351 U.S. 1, 76 S.Ct. 611, 100 L.Ed. 883 (1956); *Pigeon River Improv. Slid & B Co. v. Cox,* 291 U.S. 138, 54 S.Ct. 361, 78 L.Ed. 695 (1934); *Kimball v. Callahan,* 493 F.2d 564 (9th Cir. 1974), *cert. denied,* 419 U.S. 1019, 95 S.Ct. 491, 42 L.Ed.2d 292 (1974). In *Menominee Tribe, supra,* the statute which assertedly abrogated the treaty fishing right dealt specifically and drastically with the tribe by abolishing the federal existence of the very entity which held the fishing right. Nevertheless, the Court held that individual Indians continued to possess the right to hunt and fish on their ancestoral lands. The repeal by implication was not made out, even where the legislation directly affected the particular tribe in question. The Submerged Lands Act only remotely relates to the subject of Indian fishing rights and does not approach the standard which must be met to establish abrogation of an Indian treaty right. As in *Morton v. Mancari,* 417 U.S. 535, 94 S.Ct. 2474, 41 L.Ed.2d 290 (1974), where the issue was whether the Civil Rights Act amendment of 1972 prohibiting discrimination in the federal government implicitly abrogated an earlier federal statute giving hiring preference to Indian applicants for employment in the Bureau of Indian Affairs, the later statute was "designed to deal with an entirely different...problem [from the Act argued to be repealed]. Any perceived conflict is thus more apparent than real." 417 U.S. at 550, 94 S.Ct. at 2482.

Epilogue

Justice is a virtue which cannot be exercised apart from love of neighbor. Love is, indeed "superior" to justice. At the same time love of neighbor proves itself in the form of justice. If justice is weakened, love itself is jeopardized. No man can profess to adhere to the greatest of all commandments—Love thy neighbor—if he should visit violence upon fellow men who would exercise centuries-old fishing rights which have been recently confirmed, little more than 150 years ago, and again 130 years ago, by most solemn promise of our nation.

Declaratory Judgment and Decree

This judgment and decree are based upon the Findings of Fact, Conclusions of Law and Opinion of the Court entered in this case, all of which by this reference are hereby made a part hereof as though set forth herein. No language herein shall be interpreted as superseding the Opinion of the Court, which shall control if in any respect it appears to be in conflict with any Finding herein.

It is hereby ORDERED, ADJUDGED AND DECREED that the right of the Plaintiff tribes to fish in the waters of the Great Lakes and connecting waters ceded by the Treaty of 1836, 7 Stat. 491, is as follows:

(1) Each of the Plaintiff tribes, the Bay Mills Indian Community and the Sault Ste. Marie Tribe of Chippewa Indians, is a present-day tribal entity which, with respect to the matters which are the subject of this litigation, is a political successor in interest to the Indians who

were party to the Treaty of Ghent and the Treaty of 1836. Their members can trace their ancestry to the Indians who were beneficiaries of the Treaty of Ghent of 1814, 8 Stat. 218, and the Treaty of 1836. Members of these tribes and their predecessor bands and the individual ancestors of their members have fished the ceded waters of the Great Lakes under claim of aboriginal right, Treaty of Ghent and Treaty of 1836 right from ancient times until the present.

(2) The Indians who comprised the Ottawa and Chippewa bands which were signatories to the 1836 treaty occupied the ceded territory of Michigan for centuries. They lived off the fruits of the land, continuing the dependence of Upper Great Lakes Indians upon the Great Lakes fishery dating back several thousand years. The culture, subsistence and livelihood of these Indians centered around and depended upon the Great Lakes fishery. In the spring the Indians would gather in large fishing villages of around 200 persons, where they would remain until the onset of winter. These villages were on the shores of the Upper Great Lakes in locations with convenient access to productive fishing grounds. Fish comprised up to sixty-five percent of the usable meat in the Indians' diets at these times. In winter the villages would break up into small family groups which would disperse inland to hunt. Various species of fish were taken depending upon the season and the method of fishing. Fishing took place throughout the ceded area, wherever the fish were to be found.

(3) The Indians' participation in the fishery of the ceded area evolved over time. The fishery was transformed when nets and gill nets became available at about the time of the birth of Christ. When the European market economy arrived, the Indians quickly adapted their fishing skills to serve it. Especially after the decline of the fur trade, fishing was the principal means of making a living and participating in trade with the non-Indians. Long before the Treaty of 1836 commercial fishing took place throughout the treaty area, including the Whitefish Bay area, the Sault Rapids, the Michilimackinac area, and various other places in the Northern lower peninsula and lower Lake Superior. Indian participation in and dependence upon commercial and subsistence fishing continued throughout the 19th century, and remains important today.

(4) By virtue of their joint and amicable occupation of the land and water area ceded by the Treaty of 1836, the Ottawa and Chippewa Indians of Michigan possessed aboriginal rights to occupy and use this area. By virtue of their use of the fishery of the Great Lakes and their connecting waters, the Ottawa and Chippewa bands, signatory to the Treaty of 1836, possessed an aboriginal right to fish in those waters for subsistence and commercial purposes. The United States and Britain recognized their sovereignty over these lands was limited by the Indians' aboriginal right to use and occupy these lands. The United States expressed this in the Northwest Ordinance and acknowledged an obligation not to take Indian lands or property without the Indians' consent. The consent was to be accepted by the United States with the utmost good faith, justice and humility. The right of the Ottawa and Chippewa Indians to fish in the Great Lakes and connecting waters, along with their right to occupy and use the area generally, was expressly guaranteed to them by the United States in the 1814 Treaty of Ghent. At the time of the Treaty of 1836, they possessed both aboriginal and treaty-guaranteed rights to fish for subsistence and commercial purposes in the waters of the Great Lakes and connecting waters.

(5) The United States was aware, when it negotiated the Treaty of 1836, that the Indians of the treaty area depended upon subsistence and commercial fishing for their existence and

livelihood. The United States intended that the Michigan Indians be able to fish in order to maintain their livelihood and way of life then and in the future. By the treaty the Indians ceded certain rights to the United States, and reserved all rights not ceded. The Indians ceded to the United States a tract of country including areas of the Great Lakes belonging to them, described in the treaty. They excepted from this cession and reserved for themselves certain land reservations. The United States did not negotiate for, nor did it obtain, the Indians' right to fish off reservation in the ceded area. The Indians implicitly reserved and retained their right to fish. This right is confirmed by the Treaty. The right is further protected by Article Thirteenth of the Treaty, which stipulates for the "usual privileges of occupancy."

(6) The Indians understood that they would have to accommodate the exercise of their right to hunt on the ceded lands to the rights of settlers on the ceded land. They understood that they could continue to use the land to the extent necessary to continue to live their lives as before. By the terms of the treaty, specifically the retention of exclusive rights to fish in each of the areas where whitemen had previously sought fishing rights, they were led to believe—consistent with the intention of the United States—that they would not have to accommodate with settlers in the exercise of their fishing rights.

(7) The Indians understood the limiting language of Article Thirteenth —"Until the land is required for settlement"—to mean that Indians could continue to exercise their fishing right for as long as Indians lived in Michigan. The phrase is ambiguous as to the term of possible occupancy and can only be enforced as it was understood by the Indians. The United States inserted the clause into the Treaty only because it wanted to insure settlers access to particular plots of land. The limitation was not intended to affect Indian fishing. It is not possible to "settle" the Great Lakes and their connecting waters.

(8) The Indians assented to the Senate Amendment to Articles Second and Third because of the assurance that they could use their ceded territory indefinitely or so long as Indians lived in Michigan. The United States subsequently granted the Indians permission to remain on their reservations beyond the five year limitation. The land reservations remained in existence until new land reservations were provided for in the Treaty of 1855.

(9) The Removal Act of 1830 did not mandate that the Executive secure removal of Indians to lands west of the Mississippi. Nor did it authorize violation of prior Indian treaties. It merely made United States lands available for effecting Indian removal. It left the choice of whether to remove to the Indian tribes.

(10) The 1836 Treaty was not a removal treaty. It merely provides for possible removal. Treaty commissioners were providing for a future contingency, in the event the Indians chose to remove, a contingency which was actually inconceivable to the Michigan Indians. The commissioners were not attempting to ensure that removal would take place at some particular time. Neither the United States nor the Indians understood the treaty to be a removal treaty. The Indians clearly understood that they were under no obligation to remove. They denied any obligation to investigate proposed lands west of the Mississippi, and, when the time came for an exploring party to visit these lands, they only sent representatives who lacked authority to accept the lands for the tribes. The purported acceptance of the lands by these representatives was only for those "who might personally chose to remove."

(11) The Senate amendment to Article Eighth of the Treaty merely eliminated the option of removal to an area in Minnesota which might have been considered by the Michigan Indians. It was another amendment introduced by Senator Hugh White to embarrass [Jackson].

(12) Neither the federal government nor the Indians took any steps toward removal after the return of the exploring party from the Osage River area. Any attempt to effect the removal of the Michigan Indians was tacitly abandoned soon after the party returned and was officially abandoned in the Treaty of 1855. No Indian of the treaty area ever removed west of the Mississippi River.

(13) The Treaty of 1855 (11 Stat. 621) was negotiated to provide permanent homes for the Ottawa and Chippewa in Michigan and to settle and consolidate monies and services owed to the Indians under previous treaties and in particular the Treaty of March 28, 1836. Article Three of the treaty released legal and equitable claims of the Indians against the United States. These claims were financial. The Indians' right to fish was not a legal or equitable liability of the United States nor was it even discussed during the negotiations. Article Three operated to release the United States from promises previously made to the Indians, but not fulfilled. The United States could not be released from a right originating in the Indians which it never owned and could never give. The clause has no impact on the fishing right the Indians possessed before the treaty.

(14) Article Five of the Treaty of 1855 ended an artificial construction—the Ottawa and Chippewa Nation—which the United States had created in order to obtain the cession of 1836. It did not result in any change in the way in which the Indians of the treaty area functioned politically or in the way in which they were dealt with by the federal Indian agents, save one: they were never again convened or dealt with as one entity, not even to assent to the Senate amendments to the treaty. To the Indians the article meant only that they would not be considered a single entity. The termination of this entity, not the termination of the Ottawa and Chippewa tribes or bands, was all that was accomplished by this Article.

(15) Nothing in the Treaties of July 31 and August 2, 1855, 11 Stat. 621, et seq. abrogated, alienated, surrendered, granted away, extinguished or otherwise diminished the fishing right affirmed by the Treaty of Ghent and reserved by the Treaty of 1836.

(16) The fishing right reserved by the Indians in 1836 and at issue in this case is the communal property of the bands which signed the treaty. Their modern political successors, plaintiffs in this action, presently hold the right. It does not belong to individual tribal members who exercise it, although the rights were reserved for every individual Indian, as though named in the treaty. It is exercised by members of the plaintiff tribes under extensive tribal regulation. Both Bay Mills and the Sault Tribe retain the power to regulate their internal affairs and have adopted constitutions and by laws under the Indian Reorganization Act of 1934. Both constitutions authorize the tribes to regulate and protect resources under their control. Further, both constitutions authorize the tribes to regulate the internal relations of their members. Pursuant to the constitutions and by-laws, the tribes have developed conservation codes and fishing regulations. Pursuant to this constitutional and ordinance authority, the treaty fishing activities of the Indians of the plaintiff tribes are comprehensively regulated and enforced.

(17) The mere passage of time has not eroded, and cannot erode the rights guaranteed by solemn treaties that both sides pledged on their honor to uphold. The Indians have a right to fish today wherever fish are to be found within the area of cession—as they had at the time of cession—a right established by aboriginal right and confirmed by the Treaty of Ghent, and the Treaty of 1836. The right is not a static right today any more than it was during treaty times. The right is not limited as to the species of fish, origin of fish, the purpose of use or

the time or manner of taking. It may be exercised utilizing improvements in fishing techniques, methods and gear.

[75] (18) Because the right of the Plaintiff tribes to fish in ceded waters of the Great Lakes is protected by treaties of the Ottawa and Chippewa Indians with the United States, that right is preserved and protected under the supreme law of the land, does not depend on State law, is distinct from the rights and privileges held by non-Indians and may not be qualified by any action of the state or its agents nor regulated by the state or its agents except as authorized by Congress. Congress has not authorized the state or its agents to regulate the exercise of the treaty fishing rights of the Indians of Michigan. To the extent that any laws or regulations of Michigan are inconsistent with the treaty rights of the Michigan Indians, such laws and regulations are void *ab initio* and of no force and effect as to the plaintiff tribes and their members.

[76] (19) The State has always lacked authority to arrest and prosecute Indians for violation of its statutes governing fishing, and lacks authority to maintain records of such arrests and prosecutions. It is the duty of the state to expunge such records, cease such enforcement and to provide such relief, including payment of damages and expenses, as may be necessary to make the affected Indians whole.

(20) The Secretary of the Interior has taken steps to implement the exercise of treaty rights to fish under 25 C.F.R. 256. This pervasive federal regulation provides a federally-sanctioned approach for state involvement in treaty-right fishing regulation and preempts independent state regulation.

(21) Regulation of treaty-right fishing by the plaintiff tribes preempts any state authority to regulate the fishing activity of the tribal members. The state lacks authority to enforce its police power regulations against members of the plaintiff tribes.

(22) The Submerged Lands Act does not repeal by implication the Indians' treaty fishing rights.

(23) It is the responsibility of all citizens to see that the treaty protected rights of the plaintiff tribes are carried out, so far as possible, in accordance with the meaning they were understood to have by the tribal representatives at the councils, and in a spirit which generously recognizes the full obligation of this nation to protect the interests of a dependent people.

(24) All findings of Fact and Conclusions of Law pertinent to the nature, scope, and effect of the fishing rights of the treaty Indians are specifically incorporated by reference herein.

(25) The court retains jurisdiction of this case for the life of this decree to take evidence, to make rulings and to issue such orders as may be just and proper upon the facts of law, and in the implementation of this decree.

(26) Plaintiffs' application for an injunction will be considered and determined upon hearing thereof at the earliest practicable date following entry of this judgment and decree.

NOTES

1: The Tribes of the Northern Lakes

1. The quotation is approximate and from Birge's memory, as is its date (in the early 1950s, not long before Osogwin's death). Birge came north to Hessel as a summer visitor from shortly after his birth (1907) and moved onto his Point Brulee property, where he still lives, full-time in 1933. He became a friend to the Indian community, learned enough Indian "to get by on," and was accepted into its fellowship from a very early time in his life from which experience he is well accepted locally as an expert in Indian matters and, still, a friend of the tribes. The quotation is used with his permission. In the Indian tongue *Osogwin* means "yellow feather."
2. Peterson, *Hunter's Heritage,* 5.
3. Ibid. Peterson gives the date as 1622. I prefer the earlier date, following Butterfield, *History of Brulé's Discoveries and Explorations: 1610-1626,* and Newton, *The Story of Sault Ste. Marie and Chippewa County,* 39-42. See also my *The Les Cheneaux Chronicles,* 29-37.
4. Ted Williams, *Don't Blame the Indians,* 32.
5. Ibid., 32-33.
6. See Justice Williams's opinion in *People v. LeBlanc* (248 N.W. 2nd 199 [1976]), II.— RESERVED FISHING RIGHTS UNDER THE TREATY OF 1836, A. *Article Thirteenth of the Treaty of 1836,* [1], [2], {pp 203-4}; also, Judge Fox in *United States v. State of Michigan* (471 F. Supp. 192 [1979]), V. —CONCLUSIONS OF LAW, B. Canons of Treaty Construction, [19], [20], [21], [22], {pp. 249-52}.
7. Pittman, *The Les Cheneaux Chronicles,* 127.
8. Ted Williams, *Don't Blame the Indians,* 35. See also Hinsdale, *Primitive Man in Michigan* 39-40, and Cornell et al., *People of the Three Fires,* "Introduction: The Prehistoric Roots of Michigan Indians," iii-iv.
9. Peterson, *Hunter's Heritage,* 3.

10. See Parkman, *France and England in North America,* 2 vols.; in vol. 1, *Pioneers of France in the New World* and *The Jesuits in North America in the Seventeenth Century;* and Butterfield, *History of Brulé's Discoveries.* Many of the standard historical texts treat Brulé's winter of captivity among the Iroquois and Champlain's expedition into Iroquois territory and unsuccessful siege of such a walled installation.

11. See Pittman, *The Les Cheneaux Chronicles,* 46-47; also Parkman, *France and England in North America,* vol. 1: *The Jesuits in North America in the Seventeenth Century.*

12. Peterson, *Hunter's Heritage,* 3.

13. See Thwaites, ed., *The Jesuit Relations and Allied Documents;* Parkman, *France and England in North America,* vol. 1; most subsequent standard histories touch on the subject. See also Warren, *History of the Ojibway People* and Kinietz, *The Indians of the Western Great Lakes.*

14. See Pittman, *The Les Cheneaux Chronicles,* 23-27.

15. "The Ojibway," in Cornell et al., *People of the Three Fires,* 76-77. Cornell cites medical historian Frederick F. Cartwright, *Disease and History.* Cartwright's observations together with Cornell's add to an interesting concurrence of Indian oral tradition with ongoing ethnohistorical and archeological research that, in other instances, such as that of the eastern migration from Asia of the tribal ancestors, Cornell wishes to obviate. Without adequate explanation, discussion, or demonstration of proof he simply prefers the Indian tradition of a separate creation on grounds that a cultural group must be allowed the benefit of its beliefs—in defiance of the other fields of ethnological research and despite his own brief comments on the Paleo-Indians of the Great Lakes region (c. 12,000-8,000 B.C.) in his "Introduction" to the book cited here.

16. Warren, *History of the Ojibway People,* 82-84; 180-82.

2: Contact with the French

1. See Pittman, *The Les Cheneaux Chronicles,* 28-33.

2. For a fuller discussion of the French feudalism as opposed to the British colonial model, see my *The Les Cheneaux Chronicles,* 95-97. It is important to remember that the colonials on the American East Coast were but transplanted freeborn English with their own rights and freedoms guaranteed by charter. They were among the first Europeans operating under an essentially new set of rules and moving toward a "modern" nonrestrictive economic and political organization. The Bourbon dynasty in France, however , clung stubbornly to the medieval feudal model. Church at all times informed the state (at times even running it) and royal power was absolute. This was the context of the French closed fur-trading corporation on the St. Lawrence.

3. Peterson, *Hunter's Heritage,* 2. See also Hinsdale, *Primitive Man in Michigan,* pass.

4. Ibid., 93.

5. For more information on the fish see McClane, *Standard Fishing Encyclopedia* and Bates, Jr., *Fishing.*

6. Pittman, *The Les Cheneaux Chronicles,* 128-30.

3: The British Administration

1. Pittman, *The Les Cheneaux Chronicles,* 89-126.
2. Ibid., 89-91. See also Wells, *The Outline of History,* 385ff.; Dunbar, *Michigan,* 114ff.
3. Farmer, *History of Detroit and Wayne County and Early Michigan,* 233-34; see also *The Les Cheneaux Chronicles,* 91-93.
4. For all of which, and also what immediately follows, see Farmer, *History of Detroit and Wayne County and Early Michigan,* 234-35; Dunbar, *Michigan,* also discusses the subject, as does Bald, *Michigan in Four Centuries.* See also *The Les Cheneaux Chronicles,* 92-93.
5. Dunbar, *Michigan,* 116-17.
6. For a coherent discussion of this subject see Bald, *Michigan in Four Centuries,* 66-67.
7. Dunbar, *Michigan,* 123.
8. Pittman, *The Les Cheneaux Chronicles,* 95-97.
9. See Bert Klopfer, "Pontiac's Conspiracy," in Fuller, ed., *Historic Michigan,* esp. 118-20; also Dunbar, *Michigan,* 122-25; Bald, *Michigan in Four Centuries,* 66-71; Farmer, *History of Detroit and Wayne County and Early Michigan,* 235-41.
10. *Travels and Adventures of Alexander Henry,* ed. James Bain (Boston, 1901); also cited by Dunbar, *Michigan,* 126-27; Bald, *Michigan in Four Centuries,* 70ff. The fullest account is in Farmer, *History of Detroit and Wayne County and Early Michigan ,* 235-41.
11. Quoted by Dunbar, *Michigan,* without documentation, 104.
12. Pittman, *The Les Cheneaux Chronicles,* 82. See Dunbar, *Michigan,* 58-60.
13. Dunbar, *Michigan,* 84ff.
14. Ibid, 108.
15. Pittman, *The Les Cheneaux Chronicles,* 87.
16. Dunbar, *Michigan,* 130.
17. Bald, *Michigan in Four Centuries,* 76-77.
18. Dunbar, *Michigan,* 131-34.
19. Ibid., 131.
20. Pittman, *The Les Cheneaux Chronicles,* 106-7.
21. Dunbar, *Michigan,* 134.
22. Ibid., 137. They thus created the Louisiana "Cajuns."
23. Johnson, *The Michigan Fur Trade,* 76.
24. Bald, *Michigan in Four Centuries,* 79.
25. Johnson, *The Michigan Fur Trade,* 78.
26. The fullest account of the English-Indian military activity during this period is in Farmer, *History of Detroit and Wayne County and Early Michigan,* 242-62.
27. Dunbar, *Michigan,* 140-41.
28. *History of Detroit and Wayne County and Early Michigan,* 243.
29. For all of which, see Dunbar, *Michigan,* 141- 42.

30. See Newton, *Mackinac Island and Sault Ste. Marie,* 111. The 1781 Indian deed is on display in the commissary of Fort Mackinac to this date, in which the Chippewa chiefs "acknowledge to have received on His Majesties' behalf the sum of five thousand pounds Sterling being the adequate and compleat value of the Island of Michilimackinac."

4: Articles of Peace: Paris (1783)

1. Farmer, *History of Detroit and Wayne County and Early Michigan,* 247.
2. Ibid.; also 247-48. That is an almost unbelievable sum of money for the time.
3. *A Diplomatic History of the American People,* 6th ed. (New York, 1958), 51; cited by Dunbar, *Michigan,* 148.
4. For a good account of which see Ashley, *Islands of the Manitou,* 74-81. See also Dunbar, *Michigan,* 148.
5. Probably the best account of British behavior during this postwar period is in Farmer, *History of Detroit and Wayne County and Early Michigan,* 264-69.
6. Ibid., 267.

5: The Northwest Ordinance (1787)

1. Dunbar, *Michigan,* 158. Both Connecticut and Massachusetts claimed strips across the Lower Peninsula of Michigan south of Saginaw Bay; Virginia claimed this and all the rest of the Northwest as far as the Mississippi River.
2. Ibid., 163-64.
3. See Bald, *Michigan in Four Centuries,* 87; Dunbar, *Michigan,* 161-63; also Lewis, *State and Local Government in Michigan,* 127-30.
4. The Ohio Company in fact pushed its deal through and in 1788 founded the first American settlement in the Old Northwest—Marietta, Ohio (after Queen Marie Antoinette of France, ironically enough in the year before the French Revolution broke out). See Dunbar, *Michigan,* 164.
5. Ibid., 165.
6. Webster's first edition (1828) so defines *compact* as a term in American government and law, citing the Constitution as an example. See Webster, *An American Dictionary.* See also Taylor, Jr., ed., *The Northwest Ordinance 1787,* 56.
7. Bald, *Michigan in Four Centuries,* 88.
8. Ibid., 89.
9. "The Ottawa," in Cornell et al., *People of the Three Fires,* 19-20.
10. Dunbar, *Michigan,* 169.

6: The Treaty of Greenville (1795)

1. Bald, *Michigan in Four Centuries.* Lieutenant Governor Simcoe detained President Washington's peace commissioners at Detroit until British agents had induced the Indians to ignore all American proposals.
2. Dunbar, *Michigan,* 170-71. Indian historian George Cornell acknowledges the formal tribal role as mercenaries as early as the French and Indian War; he does less well with Fallen Timbers and the Greenville treaty. See "The Ojibway," in Cornell et al., *People of the Three Fires,* 92-94.
3. Dunbar, *Michigan,* 171-72.

7: The Treaty of Detroit (1807)

1. Alpheus Felch, "Michigan Indians of the Historic Period," in Fuller, ed., *Historic Michigan* 49-50. This treaty is usually called the Treaty of Detroit, but often the Treaty of Brownstown.
2. It is important to remember that all treaties of cession were federal treaties that recognized the Indian tribes as coequal foreign powers with all rights and dignities implied therein. They thus could be negotiated *only* by duly appointed federal officials, most often specifically named for the occasion. Then only could the United States government legally deed the ceded lands to the appropriate states or territories for development.
3. In the part of the Old Northwest that would become the state of Michigan, only the major treaties duly commissioned by the federal government were ever considered legally binding.
4. Dunbar, *Michigan,* 202-3.
5. Ibid., 201-2.
6. Farmer, *History of Detroit and Wayne County and Early Michigan,* 272.
7. Ibid., 272-73. Stroud was a coarse, woolen cloth manufactured for the Indian trade.
8. For all of which, see Bald, *Michigan in Four Centuries,* 116-17.
9. Ibid., 118.
10. Dunbar, *Michigan,* 207-8; also Ashley, *Islands of the Manitou,* 27-28. Ashley treats events in the north during the 1812 war quite fully.
11. Ashley, *Islands of the Manitou,* 28; also Dunbar, *Michigan,* 208. There are other good accounts of the incident, notably Newton, *Mackinac Island and Sault Ste. Marie,* 112-13.
12. Dunbar, *Michigan,* 206ff; Bald, *Michigan in Four Centuries,* 119ff. The fullest discussion is in Farmer, *History of Detroit and Wayne County and Early Michigan,* 247ff.
13. Bald, *Michigan in Four Centuries,* 129.
14. See, for instance, Dunbar, *Michigan,* 216-17; Bald, *Michigan in Four Centuries,* 132-38; Farmer, *History of Detroit and Wayne County and Early Michigan,* 283.
15. Ashley, *Islands of the Manitou,* 28.
16. Dunbar, *Michigan,* 220.
17. A full account of the naval engagement is in Ashley, *Islands of the Manitou,* 31-34.

8: The Treaty of Ghent (1814)

1. For all of which, see Bald, *Michigan in Four Centuries,* 141-42.
2. Ashley, *Islands of the Manitou,* 36-40. Dickson had his case reviewed in London and was vindicated.
3. Ibid., 47.
4. Ibid., 40-59, contains a decent account of this period in the north.
5. Johnson, *The Michigan Fur Trade,* 123.
6. Ashley, *Islands of the Manitou,* 50 (slightly edited).
7. Dunbar, *Michigan,* 226-27.
8. Ibid., 228.
9. Bald, *Michigan in Four Centuries,* 144.
10. Dunbar, *Michigan,* 241-42.

9: Treaty of Saginaw (1819)

1. Dunbar, *Michigan,* 236.
2. Bald, *Michigan in Four Centuries,* 149.
3. Felch, in Fuller, ed., *Historic Michigan,* 50-51, n. 26 ; Dunbar, *Michigan,* 236-38; Bald, *Michigan in Four Centuries,* 146. Dunbar gives a full account of the negotiations at Saginaw.
4. At Saginaw, in fact, when the $3,000 in silver was placed on the table, half of it was quickly claimed as debt by the trader Louis Campau.
5. See Morse, *A Report to the Secretary of War of the United States.*

10:Treaty at the Sault (1820)

1. For an account of the trip see Schoolcraft, *Narrative Journal of Travels;* also Dunbar, *Michigan,* 243-44; Bald, *Michigan in Four Centuries,* 147-48; Newton, *The Story of Sault Ste. Marie,* 115-16.
2. The source was discovered twelve years later (1832) by an expedition led by Schoolcraft.
3. Schoolcraft's *Algic Researches* (1839) provided the rough material in the form of legend and tale that Longfellow worked into *The Song of Hiawatha.* See also Bremer, *Indian Agent and Wilderness Scholar.*
4. Jamison, "The Survey of the Public Lands in Michigan," 197-98; also Lewis, *State and Local Government,* 4.
5. Brown, "William Austin Burt," 268. See also Cannon, "The Life and Times of William A. Burt, of Mt. Vernon, Michigan," 120.
6. Dunbar, *Michigan,* 274-75.

7. Ibid., 307, and variously throughout. An extremely full account of the Lucas County fracus is in Farmer, *History of Detroit and Wayne County and Early Michigan,* 299-303.
8. Dunbar, *Michigan,* 313-14.
9. Ibid., 312-16.

11: Treaty of Washington (1836)

1. Schoolcraft, *Personal Memoirs,* 524.
2. Ibid.; see also Bremer, *Indian Agent and Wilderness Scholar,* for a good account of the same period.
3. For all of which, see Felch, in Fuller, ed., *Historic Michigan,* 51-58; and esp. Grover, *A Brief Early History of Les Cheneaux,* 53-58. Grover is particularly thorough in discussing the 1836 treaty.
4. Grover, *A Brief Early History of Les Cheneaux,* 56.
5. See, for instance, Blackbird, *History of the Ottawa and Chippewa Indians,* 51-52.
6. Pittman, *The Les Cheneaux Chronicles,* 314-18.
7. Schoolcraft, *Thirty Years among the Indian Tribes,* 541, 543.
8. See "The William H. S. Hearding Story," in Pittman, *The Les Cheneaux Chronicles,* 234.
9. Bremer, *Indian Agent and Wilderness Scholar,* 165-74.

12: Treaties at Detroit (1855)

1. See Felch, in Fuller, ed. *Historic Michigan,* 54-59; Grover, *A Brief Early History of Les Cheneaux,* 58-62; Blackbird, *History of the Ottawa and Chippewa Indians,* 62-65
2. Grover, *A Brief Early History of Les Cheneaux,* 59-60.

13: Into the Twentieth Century

1. East, "Indian Netting," 81. The Jondreau case is stated as precedent in *People v. LeBlanc,* [16].
2. East, "Indian Netting," 81.
3. Ted Williams, *Don't Blame the Indians,* 35.
4. The treaty is found in Kappler, *Indian Affairs,* vol. 2 , p. 732. The 1820 treaty is in the same volume, 187ff.
5. Farmer, *History of Detroit and Wayne County and Early Michigan,* 16.

6. Bremer, *Indian Agent and Wilderness Scholar,* 157. Also, notes from an interview with Dr. Eugene T. Peterson, retired director of the Mackinac Island State Park Commission, April 17, 1989; and McKee, ed., *Mackinac,* 13.
7. Armour and Widder, *At the Crossroads,* 133.

BIBLIOGRAPHY

Allen, Barbara, and William Lynwood Montell. *From Memory to History: Using Oral Sources in Local Historical Research.* Nashville, Tenn.: The American Association for State and Local History, 1981.

Allen, Lenox. *Across the Fields of Yesterday.* n.p.: Ernest Walker Press, 1976.

Altrocchi, Julia Cooley. *Wolves against the Moon.* 1940. Reprint. Grand Rapids: Black Letter Press, 1979.

Armour, David A., and Keith R. Widder. *At the Crossroads: Michilimackinac during the American Revolution.* Mackinac Island, Mich.: Mackinac Island State Park Commission, 1978.

Ashley, Katherine Belden. *Islands of the Manitou.* Coral Gables, Fla.: Crystal Bay Publishers, 1978.

Atanoqken, Inaqtik (Raven Legendbard), Johan G. R. Baner, and John I. Bellaire. *Kitch-iti-ki-pi (Namesakes): The Ojibway and Chippaway Indian Legends.* Ironwood, Mich.: privately printed, 1933.

Bald, F. Clever. *Michigan in Four Centuries.* 1954. Rev. and enl. ed. New York: Harper & Row, 1961.

Barsh, Russel. *Understanding Indian Treaties as Law.* Olympia, Wash.: Office of Public Instruction, n.d.

Bates, Joseph D., Jr. *Fishing: An Encyclopedic Guide to Tackle and Tactics for Fresh and Salt Water.* New York: E. P. Dutton & Company, 1973.

Blackbird, A. J. (Chief Mack-E-Te-Be-Nessy). *History of the Ottawa and Chippewa Indians of Michigan; A Grammar of Their Language, and Personal and Family History of the Author.* 1887. Reprint. Petoskey, Mich.: Little Traverse Regional Historical Society, Inc., n.d.

Boeri, David. *People of the Ice Whale.* New York: E. P. Dutton, 1983.

Bremer, Richard G. *Indian Agent and Wilderness Scholar: The Life of Henry Rowe Schoolcraft.* Mount Pleasant, Mich.: Clarke Historical Library, Central Michigan University, 1987.

Brown, Alan S. "William Austin Burt: Michigan's Master Surveyor," *Papers of the Michigan Academy of Science, Arts, and Letters* 47 (1962): 263-74.

Burt, William Austin. "Autobiography." *Collections of the Michigan Pioneer and Historical Society* 28 (1900): 646-47.

———, and John Mullett. *Field Notes for T41N-R2E, T41N-R1E, T41N-R1W, T42N-R1E, T42N-R1W.* Unpublished notebook (copy).

Butterfield, Consul Willshire. *History of Brulé's Discoveries and Explorations: 1610-1626.* 1898. Reprint. Grand Rapids: Black Letter Press, 1974.

———. *History of the Discovery of the Northwest by Jean Nicloet in 1634 with a Sketch of His Life.* Cincinnati: Robert Clark & Co., 1881.

Cannon, Scott. "The Life and Times of William A. Burt, of Mt. Vernon, Michigan." *Collections of the Michigan Pioneer and Historical Society* 5 (1884): 115-23.

Cartright, Frederick F. *Disease and History.* New York: Thomas Y. Cromwell Co., 1972.

Charlevoix, Rev. P. F. X. de, S.J. *History and General Description of New France.* Translated and edited by Dr. John Gilmary Shea. 6 vols. New York: Francis P. Harper, 1900.

Chippewa-Ottawa Treaty Fishery Management Authority Rules and Regulations Governing Tribal Commercial and Subsistence Fishing Activities in the 1836 Treaty Ceded Waters of Lake Superior, Lake Huron, and Lake Michigan. Sault Ste Marie, Mich.: Chippewa-Ottawa Treaty Fishery Management Authority, 1987.

Cohen, Felix. *Handbook of Federal Indian Law.* Albuquerque: University of New Mexico Press, 1942.

Coles, Edward. *History of the Ordinance of 1787.* Philadelphia: The Historical Society of Pennsylvania, 1856.

Cook, Darius B. *Six Months among Indians, Wolves and Other Wild Animals, in the Winter of 1839 and 1840.* 1889. Reprint. Au Train, Mich.: Avery Color Studios, 1983.

Cornell, George L., James A. Clifton, and James M. McClurken. *People of the Three Fires: The Ottawa, Potawatomi, and Ojibway of Michigan.* Grand Rapids: The Michigan Indian Press, Grand Rapids Inter-Tribal Council, 1986.

Danziger, Edmund Jefferson, Jr. *The Chippewas of Lake Superior.* Norman: University of Oklahoma Press, 1978.

Deloria, Vine, Jr. *Custer Died for Your Sins: An Indian Manifesto.* New York: Macmillan, 1969.

Downes, Randolph C. *Council Fires on the Upper Ohio: A Narrative of Indian Affairs in the Upper Ohio Valley until 1795.* Pittsburgh: University of Pittsburgh Press, 1940.

Dunbar, Willis Frederick. *Michigan: A History of the Wolverine State.* Grand Rapids: William B. Eerdmans Publishing Co., 1965.

East, Ben. "Indian Netting." *Outdoor Life* (March 1980): 80-84.

Ellis, William Donohue. *Land of the Inland Seas: The Historic and Beautiful Great Lakes Country.* Palo Alto, Calif.: American West Publishing Co., 1974.

Ewert, Charles. *No Man's Brother: The Story of Etienne Brulé.* New York: Avon Books, 1984.

Farmer, Silas. *History of Detroit and Wayne County and Early Michigan.* 1890. Reprint. Detroit: Gale Research Co., 1969.

Fasquelle, Ethel Rowan. *When Michigan Was Young: The Story of Its Beginnings, Early Legends, and Folklore.* 1950. Reprint. Au Train, Mich.: Avery Color Studios, 1981.

Ford, R. Clyde. *A Tale of the Mackinaw Fur Trade: Sandy MacDonald's Man.* 1929. Reprint. Au Train, Mich.: Avery Color Studios, 1985.

Fuller, George N., ed. *Historic Michigan: Land of the Great Lakes.* n.p.: National Historical Association, Inc., 1924.

Fuller, Iola. *The Loon Feather.* 1940 Reprint. New York: Harcourt Brace Jovanovich, 1984.

Getches, David H., Daniel M. Rosenfelt, and Charles R. Wilkinson. *Federal Indian Law: Cases and Materials.* St. Paul, Minn.: West Publishing Co., 1979.

Gringhuis, Dirk. *Lore of the Great Turtle: Indian Legends of Mackinac Retold.* Mackinac Island, Mich.: Mackinac Island State Park Commission, 1970.

Grover, Frank R. *A Brief Early History of Les Cheneaux Islands: Some New Chapters of Mackinac History.* Evanston, Ill.: Bowman Publishing Co., 1911.

Hatcher, Harlan, Erich A. Walter, and Orin W. Kaye, Jr. *A Pictorial History of the Great Lakes.* New York: Crown Publishers, 1963.

Havighurst, Walter, ed. *The Great Lakes Reader.* 1966. Reprint. New York: Collier Books, 1978.

————. *Three Flags at the Straits.* Englewood Cliffs, N. J.: Prentice-Hall, Inc., 1966.

Hickerson, Harold. *The Chippewa and Their Neighbors: A Study in Ethnohistory.* New York: Holt, Rinehart and Winston, 1970.

————. "Chippewa of the Upper Great Lakes: A Study in Sociopolitical Change." In Eleanor Burke Leacock and Nancy Oestreich Lurie, eds., *North American Indians in Historical Perspective.* New York: Random House, 1971.

Hinsdale, W. B. *Primitive Man in Michigan.* 1925. Reprint. Au Train, Mich.: Avery Color Studios, 1983.

Horsman, Reginald. *Expansion and American Indian Policy, 1783-1812.* East Lansing: Michigan State University Press, 1967.

————. *The Frontier in the Formative Years, 1783-1815.* New York: Holt, Rinehart, and Winston, 1970.

Hubbard, Gurdon Saltonstall. *Autobiography.* 1911. Reprint. Grand Rapids: Black Letter Press, 1981.

Hubbs, Carl L., and Carl F. Lagler. *Fishes of the Great Lakes Region.* 1941. Reprint. Ann Arbor: University of Michigan Press, 1983.

Hunt, George T. *The Wars of the Iroquois: A Study of Intertribal Trade Relations.* Madison: University of Wisconsin Press, 1940.

Irwin, R. Stephen, M.D. *The Providers: Hunting and Fishing Methods of the North American Natives.* Surrey, B. C.: Hancock House Publishers, Ltd., 1984.

Jamison, Knox. "The Survey of the Public Lands in Michigan." *Michigan History* 42 (1958): 197-214.

Johnson, Ida Amanda. *The Michigan Fur Trade.* 1919. Reprint. Grand Rapids: Black Letter Press, 1971.

Jones, Dorothy V. *License for Empire: Colonialism by Treaty in Early America.* Chicago: University of Chicago Press, 1982.

Kane, Grace Franks. *Myths and Legends of the Mackinacs and the Lake Region.* 1897. Reprint. Grand Rapids: Black Letter Press, 1976.

Kappler, Charles J. *Indian Affairs: Laws and Treaties, 1778-1883.* Vol. 2, *Treaties.* 2d ed. United States Government Printing Office, 1904. Reprint. New York: Interland Publishing Company, 1972.

Karpinski, Louis C. *Bibliography of the Printed Maps of Michigan: 1804-1880.* Lansing: Michigan Historical Commission, 1931.

Kinietz, W. Vernon. *The Indians of the Western Great Lakes: 1615-1760.* 1940. Reprint. Ann Arbor: University of Michigan Press, 1965.

Knoblock, C. G. *Above Below.* Norwood, Mass.: The Plimpton Press, 1952.

Landin, Ed. *A Great Lakes Fisherman.* Au Train, Mich.: Avery Color Studios, 1983 (for The Isle Royale Natural History Association).

Lawrence, Verna. Texts of several speeches, untitled, undated, provided by Mrs. Lawrence of Sault Ste. Marie, Mich..

Lewis, Ferris E. *State and Local Government in Michigan.* 1960. Reprint. Hillsdale, Mich.: Hillsdale Educational Publishers, Inc., 1974.

Lowman, Bill. *220 Million Custers.* Anacortes, Wash.: Anacortes Printing and Publishing, 1978.

Martin, Calvin. *Keepers of the Game: Indian-Animal Relationships and the Fur Trade.* Berkeley: University of California Press, 1978.

Mason, Philip P., ed. *Schoolcraft's Expedition to Lake Itasca: The Discovery of the Source of the Mississippi.* East Lansing: Michigan State University Press, 1958.

McKee, Russell, ed. *Mackinac: The Gathering Place.* Lansing: Michigan Natural Resources Magazine, 1981.

McLane, A. J. *McLane's Standard Fishing Encyclopedia and International Angling Guide.* New York: Holt, Rinehart and Winston, 1965.

McNickle, D'Arcy. *Native American Tribalism.* New York: Oxford University Press, 1973.

Michigan: A Guide to the Wolverine State. Compiled by workers of the Writers' Program of the Work Projects Administration in the State of Michigan. New York: Oxford University Press, 1941.

Morison, Samuel Eliot. *The Oxford History of the American People.* New York: Oxford University Press, 1965.

Morse, Jedidiah. A *Report to the Secretary of War of the United States, Comprising a Narrative of a Tour Performed in the Summer of 1820, under a Commission from the President of the United States, for the Purpose of Ascertaining, for the Use of the Government, the Actual State of the Indian Tribes in Our Country.* Washington, D.C.: Davis & Force, 1822 (various other publishers and places of publication in the same year).

Nesbit, Robert C. *Wisconsin: A History.* Madison: University of Wisconsin Press, 1973.

Newton, Stanley. *Mackinac Island and Sault Ste. Marie.* 1909. Reprint. Grand Rapids: Black Letter Press, 1976.

————. *The Story of Sault Ste. Marie and Chippewa County.* 1923. Reprint. Grand Rapids: Black Letter Press, 1975.

Nicholas, Edward. *The Chaplain's Lady: Life and Love at Fort Mackinac.* Mackinac Island, Mich.: Mackinac Island State Park Commission, 1987.

Onuf, Peter S. *Statehood and Union: A History of the Northwest Ordinance.* Bloomington: Indiana University Press, 1987.

Osborn, Hon. Chase S., and Stellanova Osborn, comps. *"Hiawatha" with Its Original Indian Legends.* Lancaster, Pa.: The Jaques Cattell Press, 1944.

————. *Schoolcraft: Longfellow: Hiawatha.* Lancaster, Pa.: The Jaques Cattell Press, 1942.

Parkman, *Francis. France and England in North America. 2 vols. (7 vols. in 2).* Vol. 1: *Pioneers of France in the New World, The Jesuits in North America in the Seventeenth Century, La Salle and the Discovery of the Great West, The Old Regime in Canada;* vol. 2: *Count Frontenac and the New France under Louis XIV, A Half-Century of Conflict, Montcalm and Wolf.* New York: The Library of America, 1983.

Pathways to the Old Northwest: An Observance of the Bicentennial of the Northwest Ordinance. Indianapolis: Indiana Historical Society, 1988.

Pekkanen, John. "The Land: Who Owns America?: Part I." *Town and Country* 137 (1983): 175-86; "Part II," 137 (1983): 89-96.

Peters, Richard, ed. *The Public Statutes at Large of the United States of America,* Vol. 7. Boston: Charles C. Little and James Brown, 1848.

Peterson, Eugene T. *Conservation of Michigan's Natural Resources.* Lansing: Michigan Historical Commission; John M. Munson Michigan History Fund, Pamphlet No. 3, 1960.

————. *France at Mackinac: A Pictorial Record of French Life and Culture 1715-1760.* Mackinac Island, Mich.: Mackinac Island State Park Commission, n.d..

————. *Hunter's Heritage: A History of Hunting in Michigan.* Lansing: Michigan United Conservation Clubs, 1979.

————. *Mackinac Island: Its History in Pictures.* Mackinac Island, Mich.: Mackinac Island State Park Commission, 1973.

Pittman, Philip McM. *The Les Cheneaux Chronicles: Anatomy of a Community.* Cedarville, Mich.: Les Cheneaux Ventures, 1984.

————. *Ripples from the Breezes: A Les Cheneaux Anthology.* Cedarville, Mich.: Les Cheneaux Ventures, 1988.

Powell, J. W. *Seventh Annual Report of the Bureau of Ethnology to the Secretary of the Smithsonian Institution, 1885-'86.* Washington, D.C.: Government Printing Office, 1891.

Prucha, Francis Paul. *American Indian Policy in the Formative Years: The Indian Trade and Intercourse Acts, 1790-1834.* Cambridge: Harvard University Press, 1962.

Quaife, Milo M., ed. *The John Askin Papers: 1747-1820,* 2 vols. Detroit: The Detroit Library Commission, 1928.

Questions and Answers on Treaty Rights. Seattle: National Coalition to Support Indian Treaties, n.d.

Ratigan, William. *Soo Canal!* Grand Rapids: William B. Eerdmans Publishing Co., 1955.

————. *Young Mister Big: The Story of Charles Thompson Harvey.* Grand Rapids: William B. Eerdmans Publishing Co., 1955.

Reimann, Lewis C. *When Pine Was King.* 1952. Reprint. Au Train, Mich.: Avery Color Studios, 1981.

Repplier, Agnes. *Pere Marquette: Priest, Pioneer, and Adventurer.* New York: Doubleday, 1929.

Riordan, John J. *The Dark Peninsula.* Au Train, Mich.: Avery Color Studios, 1976.

Royce, Charles, ed. *Indian Land Cessions in the United States.* Eighteenth Annual Report of the Bureau of American Ethnology, 1896-97, part 2. Washington, D.C.: U. S. Government Printing Office, 1899.

Schoolcraft, Henry Rowe. *History of the Indian Tribes of the United States.* Philadelphia: J. P. Lippincott & Co., 1857. Reprint. Historical American Indian Press, n.d.

————. *The Myth of Hiawatha, and Other Oral Legends, Mythologic and Allegoric, of the American Indians.* 1856. Reprint. New York: Kraus Reprint Co., 1971.

————. *Narrative Journal of Travels through the Northwestern Regions of the United States . . . in the year 1820.* Edited by Mentor L. Williams. East Lansing: Michigan State College Press, 1953.

————. *Personal Memoirs of a Residence of Thirty Years with the Indian Tribes on the American Frontiers.* Philadelphia: Lippincott, Grambo & Co., 1851.

Sommers, Lawrence M., ed. *Atlas of Michigan.* Michigan State University Press, 1977.

Stebbins, Catherine L. *Here I Shall Finish My Voyage!* Omena, Mich.: Solle's Press, 1960.

Taylor, Robert M., Jr., ed. *The Northwest Ordinance 1787: A Bicentennial Handbook.* Indianapolis: Indiana Historical Society, 1887.

Thwaites, Reuben Gold, ed. *The Jesuit Relations and Allied Documents: Travels and Explorations of the Jesuit Missionaries in New France, 1610-1791.* 72 vols. Cleveland: Burrows Brothers, 1896-1901.

Tindall, George Brown. *America: A Narrative History.* 2 vols. New York: W. W. Norton & Co., 1984.

Utley, Henry M., and Byron M. Cutcheon. *Michigan as a Province, Territory, and State.* 4 vols. New York: Americana Press, for the Publishing Society of Michigan, 1906.

Van Fleet, Rev. J. A. *Old and New Mackinac.* 1874. Reprint. Grand Rapids: "The Lever" Book and Job Office, 1880.

————. *Summer Resorts of the Mackinaw Region and Adjacent Localities.* 1882. Reprint. Grand Rapids: Black Letter Press, 1970.

Vogel, Virgil J. *Indian Names in Michigan.* Ann Arbor: University of Michigan Press, 1986.

Wakefield, Larry. "Drummond Island." *Chronicle: The Quarterly Magazine of the Historical Society of Michigan* 21, no. 4 (1986): 2-7.

Warren, William W. *History of the Ojibway People.* 1885. Reprint. St. Paul: Minnesota Historical Society Press, 1984.

Webster, Noah. *An American Dictionary of the English Language.* 1828. Facsimile reprint San Francisco: Foundation for American Christian Education, 1967.

Wells, H. G. *The Outline of History.* New York: The Macmillan Company, 1921.

Widder, Keith R. *Reveille till Taps: Soldier Life at Fort Mackinac 1780-1895.* Mackinac Island, Mich.: Mackinac Island State Park Commission, 1972.

Williams, C. Herb, and Walt Neubrech. *Indian Treaties: American Nightmare.* Seattle: Outdoor Empire Publishing Co., 1976.

Williams, Frederick D., ed. *The Northwest Ordinance: Essays on Its Formulation, Provisions, and Legacy.* East Lansing: Michigan State University Press, 1989.

Williams, Ted. *Don't Blame the Indians: Native Americans and the Mechanized Destruction of Fish and Wildlife.* South Hamilton, Mass.: GSJ Press, 1986.

Wood, Edwin O. *Historic Mackinac.* 2 vols. New York: The Macmillan Co., 1918.

Wright, J. Leitch, Jr. *Britain and the American Frontier, 1783-1815.* Athens: University of Georgia Press, 1975.

INDEX

The Northwest Territory

The Northwest Territory with Major Tribes

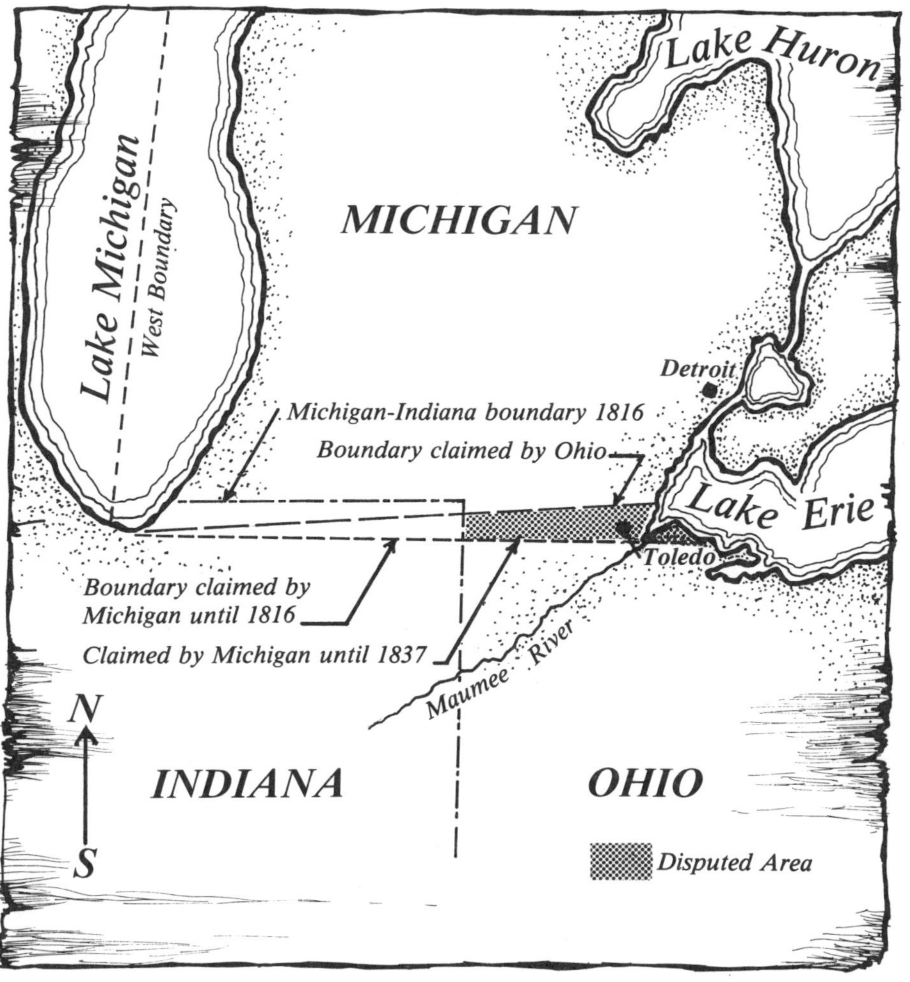

The Ohio Border Dispute 1817–1837

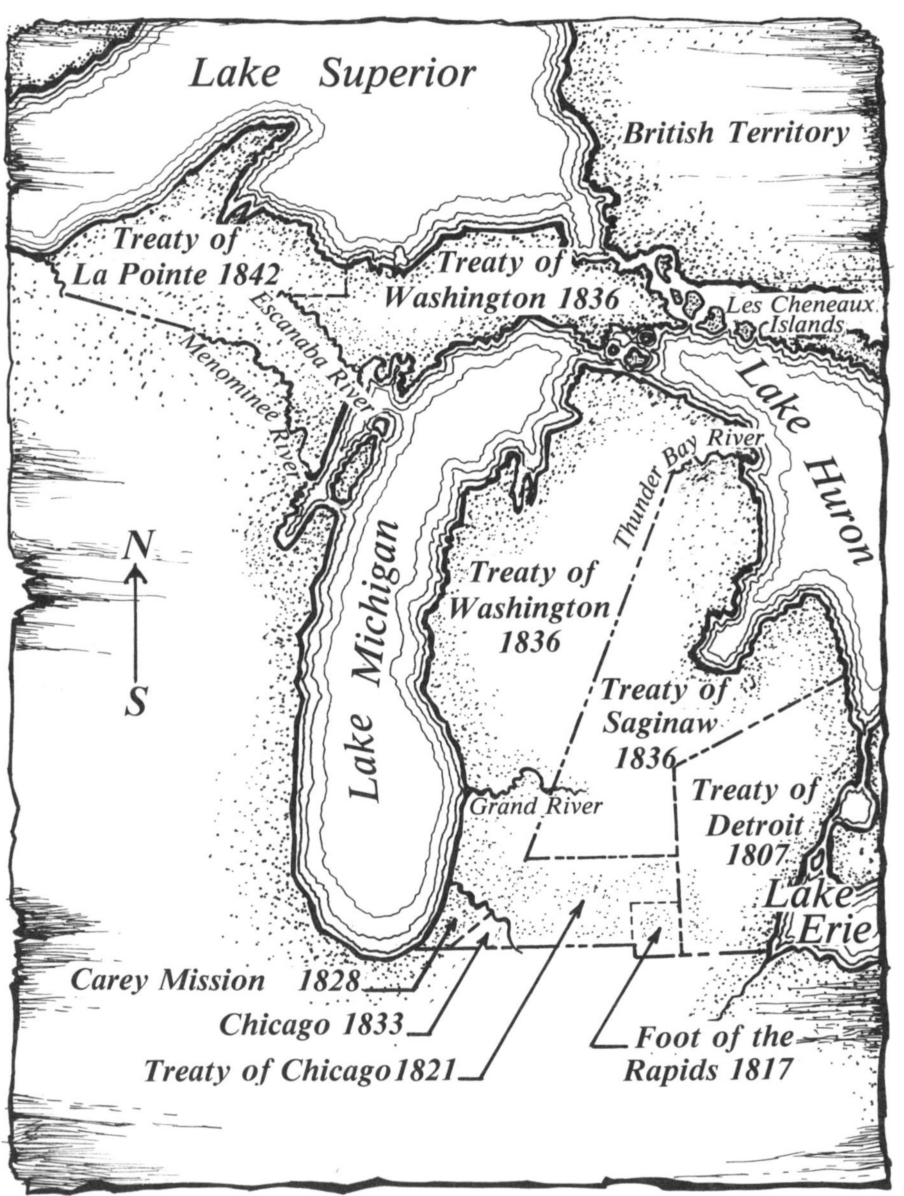

Michigan Indian Treaties 1807–1842